ANALYZING CAPITAL EXPENDITURES
Private and public perspectives

Analyzing Capital Expenditures

Private and public perspectives

G. David Quirin
Faculty of Management Studies
University of Toronto

John C. Wiginton
School of Business
Queen's University (Kingston)

1981

RICHARD D. IRWIN, INC.   Homewood, Illinois   60430
IRWIN-DORSEY LIMITED   Georgetown, Ontario   L7G 4B3

ISBN 0-256-00460-9
Library of Congress Catalog Card No. 80–84718

Printed in the United States of America

1 2 3 4 5 6 7 8 9 0 MP 8 7 6 5 4 3 2 1

Preface

This book was originally intended to be a revised edition of an earlier text, *The Capital Expenditure Decision,* published in 1967. The original volume provided a systematic and thorough treatment of the theory of capital expenditure management for students and for managers faced with problems in this area. This aim remains for the current volume. As the work progressed, however, it became clearer to us that to deal satisfactorily with developments in contemporary financial theory, the unprecedented (in North America) inflation of prices, and the increasing involvement of governments and public-sector agencies in capital-expenditure decision making, both directly and indirectly, we would need to write virtually a new book. Therefore, we have done so in large measure. Readers familiar with the earlier book may recognize some portions whose relevance has been unaffected by the changes we noted. In recognition of the extent of the new material, a new title was also chosen.

The motives for writing this book at this time are very similar to those behind the original text. Treatment of capital-expenditure analysis in standard textbooks on financial management has improved, but it is still necessarily brief. The journal literature is extensive and perhaps even more scattered than before because of the emergence of new journals. It is primarily oriented toward research issues of positive theory and its testing and thus remains relatively inaccessible, if not irrelevant, to would-be users whose interests lie in application. In spite of the many advances, there still remain a number of gaps and unresolved conflicts. By virtue of our integrative treatment, we have again sought to fill some of the former and to suggest tentative, practical solutions for the latter.

The present text has a framework based on contemporary financial theory which we have found useful in knitting together the various threads which we have included. Chapter 1 establishes the need to consider capital-expenditure decisions explicitly. Based on the economic theory of consumer behavior, it provides us with a single overall criterion to be satisfied in reaching such decisions, at least under certain simplifying assumptions. Chapter 2 looks at the capital-budgeting process in organizations and introduces the important notion of strategic versus routine capital expenditures. Many of the complications debated at length in the literature simply do not apply to the latter class of decisions, and since they may constitute the larger proportion of decisions, practical approaches may be much simpler than otherwise.

Chapter 3 establishes that preferred evaluation procedures for decision making must satisfy the criterion presented in Chapter 1. The various procedures used or proposed are described and themselves evaluated against that standard. The preferred procedures involve measuring cash inflows and outflows (benefits and costs) to be weighed using a cost of capital (required rate of return) through a discounting process. Chapter 4 looks at correct measurement of benefits and costs in the private-sector context, while Chapters 5 and 6 describe correct determination of the required rate of return. Chapter 7 notes that we have avoided explicitly discussing risk as it affects capital-expenditure decisions. For routine decisions, the procedures described to this point are adequate since risk considerations have been incorporated implicitly. The main topic of the chapter, however, is the issue of capital rationing as it affects capital-expenditure decisions.

Chapters 8 and 9 are the public-sector analog of the discussions of measuring required rate of return and benefits and costs in the private sector. We show that many commonly held notions do not meet our efficiency criterion when suitably generalized. The case for private-sector failure and/or increased public-sector involvement is not as compelling as some might wish to argue.

Increasing rates of inflation throughout the 1970s have made consistent analysis of capital expenditures more difficult since it is necessary to know whether the data include (implicit) allowances for inflation and adjust accordingly to a consistent basis. Chapter 10 examines two alternative approaches to this problem, that is, dealing entirely with nominal or real dollar magnitudes.

When we consider strategic capital expenditures that may materially alter the risk profile of an enterprise, we need some method of making appropriate allowances. The main contribution of contemporary financial theory has been to provide us with one approach which may serve this purpose. The basis and procedures for making such allowances and some discussion of when it may be necessary, along with some caveats regarding remaining problems, are presented in Chapters 11 and 12.

Market structure and competitor response faced by the firm may have a major impact on the outcome of capital-expenditure decisions. Yet, much socially oriented legislation makes consideration of such issues a delicate matter, as we describe in Chapter 13. Since public policy may also aspire to affect the amount, timing, and direction of capital expenditures, these issues are examined briefly, but critically, in Chapter 14.

Many colleagues and practitioners have commented upon and cited the earlier book, and we are indebted to them for their constructive criticisms. It is obvious, too, that we are indebted as well to the many researchers and practitioners who have advanced our understanding of capital-expenditure analysis both in principle and in practice. We have attempted to provide suitable citations without turning the text into an exegesis of the literature. We here issue a blanket acknowledgement to those whose work has contributed substantially to the field but have not been cited specifically because of our selective strategy.

We wish to thank our respective secretaries, Mary Brubacher and Rose Marie Baird, for their help in typing the mathematical equations and tables. The bulk of the text was typed and extensively edited using the IVI (Eleven-Text) Word Processing program implemented on a DEC PDP11V03 computer in the School of Business at Queen's University. Our special thanks go to Michael Levison and Robert Stevens, Department of Computing and Information Science at Queen's, who developed this program, as well as to the School of Business for providing the equipment. We have not attempted a benefit-cost analysis for this particular capital expenditure—to us the benefits have been very great indeed.

G. David Quirin
John C. Wiginton

Contents

ANALYZING CAPITAL EXPENDITURES
Private and public perspectives

An introduction to capital-expenditure management

1

1.1 Capital expenditures and capital-expenditure decisions

Capital expenditures are usually thought of as expenditures made to acquire fixed assets, such as plant and equipment. For some statistical and accounting purposes, they are indeed so defined. Decisions to undertake such expenditures are viewed as the special problems of business firms and those government agencies which undertake public works expenditures. While such a definition of capital expenditures may be useful for accounting and statistical purposes, since it captures by far the greater part of such expenditures made in the business and government sectors, it gives us an unduly restrictive view of the decision-making process. It focuses on the physical choices, that is, the acquisition of bricks, mortar, or machines, and not on the underlying economic choices, which involve the outlay of cash or current spending power in exchange for anticipated, but usually uncertain, future benefits. It is the nature of this exchange which renders capital expenditures distinctive and which necessitates the adoption of a particular decision-making framework.

So defined, capital-expenditure decisions are made by virtually all types of economic decision-making units, from the utility company deciding to build a nuclear power plant to the primitive tribesman taking a couple of hours off from hunting with a spear to fashion a bow and arrow. Sometimes the objects acquired are physical, as they are in the examples cited, but often they are not. Research and development expenditures undertaken in the hope of developing a new product are capital expenditures, as are those incurred in sending Johnny to college. So is the time expended in writing this book. They share, with the nuclear power plant and the archer's equipment, the characteristic features which distinguish capital expenditures from current operating or consumption expenditures, namely, that they are made in anticipation of deferred and uncertain payoffs. Sometimes the payoffs are in cash, as they are in the case of the power plant or the research and development program, but other times they are in kind, as they are in the case of the archery equipment. And sometimes they may be partly in cash and partly in kind, as in the case of Johnny's college education.

So defined, the capital-expenditure concept is rather all-embracing. In principle at least, the purchase of a ticket to next week's baseball game or a chicken to put in the freezer until next Sunday's dinner are capital expenditures. In business firms, where the accounting process is highly formalized, such transactions may indeed be charged to asset accounts and labeled "prepaid expenses" and "inventories" respectively. The capital-expenditure characteristics of expenditures which create assets that are turned over quickly are often ignored, because the time lag between the expenditure and the receipt of benefits is short enough to be overlooked. Business firms, households, and other spending units need working capital to be invested in such assets, and while working-capital investment decisions may benefit from analytical study using some of the tools of capital-expenditure analysis, they are usually considered separately.

Because of the lack of formal accounting, certain capital expenditures by households are treated, for statistical purposes at least, as consumption expenditures. Those so treated include expenditures on consumer durables, such as washing machines, automobiles, and yachts, and a host of expenditures on what economists call "human capital" ranging from Johnny's education to face-lifts and silicone injections for an aging movie star. This approach may be justified from a national income accounting point of view, where the focus is on aggregate behavior and the process of averaging across households provides some stability to the aggregates. However, most of these outlays involve all of the attributes of capital expenditures and should be analyzed as such. It is, however, convenient to ignore the capital-expenditure characteristics of inexpensive durables, such as pots, pans, and alarm clocks. The reason for doing so is that the cost of making elaborate calculations in support of the decision exceeds the potential saving from the refinement of the decision-making process. It does not take a great deal of financial acumen to determine that a $5.95 alarm clock is more economical than a telephone wake-up service at $4.75 per month. Similarly, in many business firms, expenditures involving less than a certain dollar amount are usually charged to expense as a matter of routine, simply because it does not pay to quibble over what the expenditure is.

The accounting treatment of certain kinds of expenditures has been noted. However, accounting treatment may not be a reliable guide. While accountants' concern for matching revenue against expenses will usually lead them to capitalize the bulk of capital expenditures, their concern for conservatism may well dictate the expensing of others. Thus advertising expenditures are usually expensed, even if they are directed at producing long-term benefits for the company. So, in most instances, are research and development expenditures and many other expenditures on intangibles that may produce significant future benefits. Accounting treatment, in many instances, will be determined by what taxation authorities will tolerate in the direction of reducing the tax bill and by the nature of the assets acquired. From the manager's point of view, these are secondary. The timing of the stream of benefits should determine whether an expenditure should be considered as a capital expenditure or not.

If accounting classifications are nonexistent in the typical household and unreliable in business firms, they are irrelevant in many government bodies and in other nonprofit organizations, such as universities. Many have accounting systems which simply list expenditures and receipts. Where separate capital budgets are operated, the selection of items for inclusion is usually quite arbitrary.

The decision maker in the capital-expenditure context must determine whether the benefits of a particular expenditure under consideration justify making the expenditures and which expenditures out of the possible infinity of available alternatives should be considered and chosen. These basic dimensions of the problem are independent of the economic sector in which the decision maker is located. In the following chapters, we shall examine capital expenditures in the context of these basic similarities, although the complicating features affecting different types of decisions made by different types of decision-making units will also be examined in some detail. As noted earlier, working-capital expenditures, that is, those in inventories, accounts receivable, and similar items, are seldom analyzed in the full capital-expenditure framework. Including such asset decisions would require extending the scope of our analysis beyond the limits we have set for this work.

1.2 Why are capital-expenditure decisions so important?

At this point, the impatient reader may well wonder why capital expenditures deserve to be treated differently than consumption expenditures, operating expenses, or routine purchases of any kind. After all, as has been noted by some observers, they only involve money, and in some instances smaller amounts than routine expenditures on operations. Ought not all expenditures, or at least all expenditures of equivalent magnitude, deserve equal consideration and care? This is indeed a tempting suggestion, and while we are by no means advocating careless expenditure of current operating funds, there are several practical reasons why rationality in capital spending should be given greater emphasis.

First of all, capital expenditures are inherently future-oriented in a way that current consumption expenditures or investments in working capital are not. This week's consumption patterns may be altered next week, and investments in inventory will turn themselves into accounts receivable and then into cash within a few months in the normal operation of the financial cycle. Funds invested in more permanent types of capital do not turn over nearly so quickly. As a result, their consequences have to be endured for a much longer period of time.

Second, in many cases, capital expenditures are virtually irreversible, either because the asset acquired (for example, an individual's professional education) is inherently nontransferable, or because secondhand markets are such that the asset can be disposed of, if at all, only at an enormous sacrifice in price. The only alternative, once the asset is acquired, is to scrap it, recognize the loss, and start over (if there is anything left to start over with).

Because of these two features, capital expenditures involve the choice of and commitment to a given production technology that involves not only the capital inputs, but inputs of cooperating factors and intermediate products. Because these can only be slightly modified, the commitment goes far beyond the initial capital sum and involves virtually the entire stream of future operating expenses. Choosing a Mercedes-Benz instead of a Honda does not simply involve a different initial outlay; it also involves a whole series of subsequent outlays for fuel, repair bills, and insurance premiums.

Consequently, many capital expenditures acquire a strategic character that is almost wholly absent from routine operating expenditures. The extent of the strategic component is partly a matter of relative size and is likely to be less significant in the case of a typewriter than a turret-lathe and less in the acquisition of a service station site than a refinery. But all, save the very smallest, incorporate a strategic element.

For a household, the strategic element is probably most pronounced in the purchase of a home. This purchase often determines where the family will shop, what school the children will attend, what church they will go to, and what recreational activities will be open to them. In short, it determines a lifestyle, or, perhaps more correctly, it is a choice which must be made as an integral part of a choice of lifestyle. Smaller-scale capital expenditures—for example, purchase of a car, a boat, a swimming pool, or a summer cottage—have perhaps fewer strategic consequences but are not free of lifestyle implications which may be of some importance (such as choosing the right brand).

Similarly, in a business firm, decisions to build plants of particular types, with particular facilities, in particular locations involve commitments to a product line, to given geographic markets, and to the local labor pools. Once these are committed, the remaining options become almost marginal in character.

If anything, capital-expenditure decisions made by governments have even larger potential strategic impacts. Decisions to build harbors and highways, to dam rivers for water supply, hydroelectric power, or flood control determine the fates of entire communities and even regions, not just in terms of the level of economic activity, but in terms of the range of options open to, and the kind of lives led by, individuals within the regions. Even a decision to buy a particular kind of airplane may not only have consequences in terms of its effectiveness, but consequences in terms of employment levels in Toronto, Montreal, Santa Monica, and Seattle.

Because of their strategic character, capital expenditures warrant particular attention. In many corporate financial control systems, concern for the fundamentally strategic character of capital expenditures manifests itself in differential discretionary limits assigned to subordinate managers, which provide tighter limits on capital expenditures than on routine expense items. The folklore of almost any corporation will usually contain pages about how the branch manager in some location, suitably exempt from physical scrutiny by head-office officials for months on end, outsmarted the controller's department and obtained a piece of equipment turned down through regular channels by buying it in pieces, as spare parts charged to sundry expense accounts, and assembling it within the plant at only twice the cost of outright purchase. These are exceptions that prove the rule works, clumsily perhaps, depending on the quality of internal audit procedures. The same principle is involved in systems which assign increasing discretionary limits on capital expenditures to successively higher managerial levels, reserving major plant commitments to the board or executive committee level.

From a social perspective, capital expenditures are important for additional reasons. They are an indispensible factor in economic growth. Such growth historically has involved both *capital-widening* expenditures, required to complement added population at the existing capital-labor ratio, and *capital-deepening* expenditures, which raise the prevailing capital-labor ratio. While these features have been important, capital expenditures have been the vehicle through which new technologies have made their appearance. New technology has made a greater contribution to the growth process than that made by mere additions to the capital stock, but such new technologies are typically embodied in new equipment or in replacements for old.

While there has been a degree of rebellion against the growth ethic in recent years, population growth for at least another 30 years is built into the existing age structure of the population, despite declines in the net reproduction rate. Effects of increasing energy costs aside, whatever the merits of the "no-growth" case, cessation of economic growth prior to stabilization of the population would imply falling per capita real incomes and have catastrophic political and social effects in most countries. Should the day come when capital expenditures need to be restricted on environmental or other grounds, it will become that much more important that they are efficiently chosen within the new constraints.

1.3 Why do capital-expenditure decisions pose a problem?

While capital-expenditure decisions are important, equally important decisions are made daily without the benefit of any particular theory about how they should be made. Many decisions can be made rationally with no decision criterion other than the general requirement that the most advantageous alternative be chosen and that the benefits be worth the costs incurred.

While the same rule underlies the making of rational decisions with respect to capital expenditures, it is not so easy to apply in practice. In the first place, the desired benefits will be received in the future. The future, in the real world, is never known with certainty, although it may be convenient for theorists and decision makers to assume for some purposes that it is.

Second, even if they were certain and capable of exact description, the benefits may frequently be difficult to measure in quantitative terms that bear comparison with the associated costs. This aspect of the problem of incommensurability is most pronounced in the case of the decisions which must be made by governments and households. Should the family get a new car, or go on a vacation in Europe? How do the benefits to be derived from 100 sophisticated missiles compare with those of a comparable expenditure on developing new energy sources? On medicare? They are perhaps more obvious in industry, where monetary profit as the ultimate objective is more or less taken for granted. But should a mining company in a remote northern community spend $250,000 on an addition to the local hospital or on a new hockey arena, given that either will make the community more attractive, improve employee morale, and reduce labor turnover?

Measurement requires some kind of common unit in which both benefits and costs may be expressed. The most natural unit for most purposes is the *monetary unit of account*. Most costs are already expressed in such units, and many benefits can easily be expressed in monetary units also. But many are not, and consistent use of the monetary measure requires that all benefits and costs be estimated in dollars-and-cents terms, if only in terms of such limited statements as "We believe the benefits of the proposed hockey arena are worth at least $300,000 to the company." Where social values are involved, monetary measures are considered highly objectionable by some. It has been asserted that an economist is someone who knows the price of everything and the value of nothing. Certain values are often asserted to be beyond price or, by implication, infinitely valuable in monetary terms. However appealing such sentiments may be, they are apt to be self-defeating. It is all very well to insist on the absolute priority of some environmental values, for example, when the cost difference between project A, which causes some environmental harm, and project B, which does not, is $10,000. But do they deserve absolute priority if the cost difference is $1 million or $100 million?[1] At some point, someone, either because of his lesser concern for environmental issues or because of competitive constraints on his behavior, is going to accept the cheaper project, and the environmental damage will occur. Either that, or the capital expenditure will be foregone entirely, with the attendant loss in economic growth. Failure to attach monetary values to environmental damage leaves decision makers with no guide as to those environmental values which are really critical and those which would merely be nice to preserve. While monetary values for many benefits and costs are produced by the marketplace, as a by-product of its normal operations, a number of benefits and costs, like the environmental damage in our example, do not get valued in the marketplace. In the normal workings of competitive markets, these are assigned an implicit value of zero (in some cases because of a failure to assign property rights). While the results are frequently less than satisfactory, they are not demonstrably worse than would be achieved by assigning infinite values to all of them. General improvement in performance in these areas requires the development of realistic, defensible, finite estimates of benefits and costs and the construction of an institutional framework in which they are regularly incorporated into the decision-making process. This matter is discussed in greater detail in Chapter 9.

Another by-product of dissatisfaction with the use of monetary values has been the development of so-called social indicators. Effects on social indicators could, in principle, provide an alternative to measurement of benefits and costs at least in the public sector. Social indicators provide scales which measure the impact of various factors on the quality of life. Unfortunately, there is no agreement on precisely what factors should be measured, nor on how the trade-offs between the various scales are to be handled. Ultimately, this will require a weighting of the factors and their aggregation into a single scale, which poses more than just technical problems. While the approach has some intriguing possibilities, it is probably premature to consider its use in any decision-making framework for capital expenditures at this time.[2]

Difficulties in providing monetary estimates of benefits and costs are not the only aspect of the incommensurability problem. Benefits received this year are not the same as benefits of equivalent dollar value to be received ten years from now, next year, or even next month. The difference to a starving man is obvious. For the rest of us, the difference is less obvious, but nonetheless real. It stems from two sources. One is the instability in the value of the monetary unit, resulting from inflation, which has become an increasingly serious problem in recent years. The other would remain even if next year's dollar would buy precisely the same basket of goods as this year's. But next year's dollar can only buy next year's goods, while this year's allows us to buy this year's, next year's, or a variety of combinations of the two. It is thus worth more, if only because it provides us with a wider range of consumption alternatives.

Uncertainty, measurement problems, and the problem of comparing amounts spent and received at different points in time are the three basic factors which create difficulties and complexities for the decision maker faced with capital-expenditure decisions. Theorists and practitioners have wrestled with these problems for years in an attempt to understand them and to formulate rational decision rules. While none of them is fully understood, except perhaps at the most abstract level, considerable success has been attained in resolving the third problem and, more recently, in coping with the problem of uncertainty. However, a chain is only as strong as its weakest link, so the usefulness of the solutions depends significantly on how well the measurement problem is handled in specific cases. Where such estimates are vague and unreliable, little can be gained by using elaborate techniques in other parts of the procedure.

The usefulness of a decision-making technique does not depend on its ability to generate perfect solutions. All that is needed is that the solutions be better than those generated by other methods or that they can be used by less expensive personnel to produce solutions of equivalent value. Over the past two decades, certain features of the decision-making models have become accepted practice in well-managed organizations and have displaced more intuitive methods of decision making. Other features remain less common, and some are as yet relatively new. They are advanced in the belief that they too will meet the pragmatic test described earlier.

1.4 Consumer choice in an intertemporal context

As our examples in Section 1.1 suggest, the capital-expenditure decision is closely related to and occasionally synonymous with a consumer's decision to save. Further, in the aggregate, savings must equal capital expenditures. Individuals save or forego current consumption in order to accumulate wealth as a means of spreading consumption over future time periods. This choice may be examined using a wealth-allocation model, which is, of course, a particular application of the general theory of consumer choice in microeconomic theory.[3]

We need first to consider the opportunities and preferences of individuals to study how time preferences are developed and expressed. From this, we will find that the rate of interest can be interpreted, from the consumer's point of view, as the price paid for postponing consumption, or as expressed by the classical economists, for waiting. Consequently, the rate of interest will be found to enter into computations for capital-expenditure decisions in a manner which adjusts the magnitudes for their time of occurrence, one of the major problems described in Section 1.3. As we will show in Chapter 3, an extensive superstructure of normative decision rules has been erected on this narrow base. Many capital expenditures are not made by the individual who does the saving. We must show how to apply these decision rules when these decisions are being made on his behalf by the managers of corporations of which he is a stockholder, or by the bureaucrats in the various government agencies to which he pays taxes directly or indirectly.

We begin by assuming that an individual's preferences can be described by preference functions, such as those used in the general theory of consumer choice.[4] In this context, however, the objects of choice are not particular commodities out of the current budget (apples and oranges, today), but rather dated consumption claims. This simplifies the analysis and allows us to examine the problem of achieving an optimal balance among consumption claims of differing dates (which is what the benefit streams from our capital expenditures make available). The objective of the individual is to specify and obtain a preferred time pattern of consumption, illustrated for the single-period case in Figure 1–1. Here the curves U_1, U_2, U_3, represent the consumer's tastes with respect to combinations of present consumption (c_0) and future consumption (c_1). The slope of these indifference curves at a

Figure 1–1
Indifference curves for patterns of total consumption

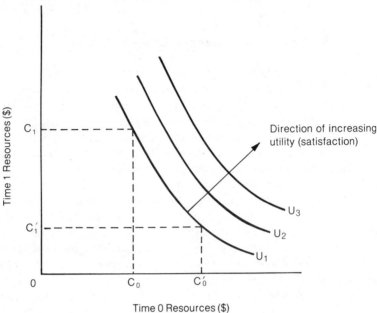

given point is the marginal rate of substitution between present and future consumption, often referred to as the *marginal rate of time preference*. In general, the consumer should have such a preference mapping over his whole lifetime (for $t = 0, 1, \ldots, T$, conceptually, where T is the end of his life, and final-period consumption is defined to include bequests). We assume that these time-preference functions satisfy the usual axioms of consumer choice and also that rational behavior will lead the individual to seek to maximize utility as represented by the time-preference functions, where it is understood that higher indifference curves, such as U_3, are preferred to lower curves, such as U_2 and U_1, in an ordinal sense.

The resources that individual consumers can draw upon for consumption include income plus initial wealth endowments. Income consists of wages, salaries, or other payments received on income account in period t and will be denoted y_t. Wealth consists of stocks of real durable goods, plus certain financial assets carried over from previous periods. The individual may either consume their services directly (in the case of durable goods) or may dispose of them (by renting or selling) and use the proceeds to acquire other consumption goods. We defer explicit consideration of durable goods, even though they are the main concern of this book, until Section 1.5 while we develop some basic concepts involving financial assets. For now, we assume that any required additions to the household's stock of durables may be rented on a period-by-period basis. Thus we ignore for the moment any initial wealth holdings and concentrate on period income.

Individual consumers usually have current income and generally anticipate further income in future time periods. We assume perfect certainty in the sense that this future income is known exactly at any time. The problem with such future income, even though it is known with certainty, is that it cannot be used for current consumption unless the individual can arrange to transfer some of this future income to another person in exchange for resources he may use immediately for current consumption. Given that some individuals may seek to consume parts of their future income now, it should not be surprising if suitable institutional arrangements arise, where they are permitted to do so. These are referred to as *capital markets,* and we assume the existence of such markets where exchanges of claims against current and future incomes can be made. Further, we assume them to be *perfect* in the economist's sense. Perfect capital markets are characterized by the availability of complete and costless information to everyone, large numbers of participants so that actions of no one individual is large enough to affect prices, and by an absence of transactions costs or taxes. Whether such markets exist in the real world is not at issue here. The purpose of such restrictive assumptions is to begin our analysis under idealized conditions to generate hypotheses predicting the behavior of individuals, and consequently, what prices we may expect to observe in the capital market. Such predictions can, at best, approximate reality, but they may be close enough to be useful for particular purposes. We will see that this is sometimes the case, but not always, and one of our basic problems is to recognize the difference.

One of the main reasons for using the concept of a perfect capital market is that it implies that in equilibrium only one price may prevail in the market. In capital markets, the commodities being bought and sold are sums of money to be delivered at various future points in time. In the single-period case, we will assume that p is the single, current (spot) price at time 0 (now) for delivery of \$1 at time 1 (the future). Furthermore, we will assume that the individual may use this market to buy claims against others' income or to sell claims against his own. While we use the concept of a price for buying or selling a claim against future income to stress the similarity between capital markets and markets for other commodities, it will be convenient to express this rate of exchange between present and future sums in a different, and perhaps more familiar, manner.

Suppose we have P dollars currently and wish to determine what sum of dollars S we will have in the future (at time 1) if we purchase a contract for the future delivery of dollars at the current market price p. The future or terminal amount may be written:

$$S = P(1/p) \qquad (1.4.1)$$

Now let us define the difference between S and P as dP, so that we may write the ratio of S to P, which is equal to $1/p$, as:

$$\frac{S}{P} = \frac{P + dP}{P} = 1 + \frac{dP}{P} \qquad (1.4.2)$$

The term dP/P is the *rate of growth* of the initial amount invested and will be denoted as r, the spot *rate of interest* between the present and future points in time. Just as there is only one value of p in a perfect market, there will only be one value for r. The term $(1 + r)$ is often referred to as the *compound amount factor*. We can also write equation 1.4.1 as the inverse operation and obtain:

$$P = Sp = S/(1 + r) \qquad (1.4.3)$$

which tells us the market value at time 0 of S dollars to be delivered at time 1. The amount P is called the *present value* of the future sum S, and the term $1/(1 + r) = p$ the *present value factor* at the rate of interest r.

Consider now an individual who has an income stream, fixed and unalterable, of y_0, y_1 now and at time 1, respectively, as shown in Figure 1–2. What is the present value of this stream? It will clearly be the sum of current income y_0, plus the present value for future delivery of the amount y_1 or $(1 + r)$, or:

$$\text{Present value of income stream} = y_0 + \frac{y_1}{(1 + r)} \qquad (1.4.4)$$

We will call this sum *current wealth,* denoted w_0, also shown in Figure 1–2 as the intercept on the time 0 axis of the straight line passing through the point (y_0, y_1). By elementary analytical geometry, the slope of this line must be $-(1 + r)$ from equation 1.4.4. Now, since any point along the line in Figure 1–2 has the same intercept on the time 0 axis, each must have the same present value. In particular, w_1, where all income occurs at time 1, and none currently, is equivalent in present value terms to any other combination of incomes along the line. This line will be referred to as the individual's *income (budget) constraint.*

Figure 1–2
Individual's income constraint

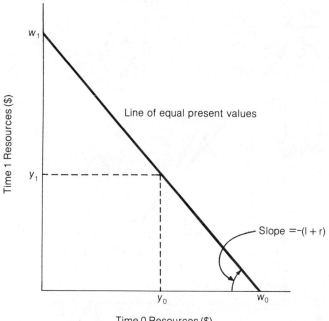

The consumer's problem now becomes that of choosing consumption levels now and at time 1 so as to maximize utility, subject to the income (wealth) constraint. This problem can be represented by combining Figures 1–1 and 1–2 as shown in Figure 1–3. In general, the optimum consumption combination choice (c_0^*, c_1^*) will not correspond to the consumer's income stream (y_0, y_1), and thus the consumer will either borrow (sell a claim against his future income) or lend (purchase a claim against some other person's future income) through the capital markets in order to achieve the utility-maximizing, income-constrained choice of consumption levels. In our particular example, the consumer will borrow $c_0^* - y_0$ currently, and repay $y_1 - c_1^* = (c_0^* - y_0)(1 + r)$ at time 1. This latter expression must hold because the income constraint represents a set of points of equal present values.

The individual might have an initial wealth endowment as well as a periodic income stream. If the initial wealth is held in the form of previously acquired claims against the future income of others, these can be

Figure 1–3
Preferred allocation of consumption standards

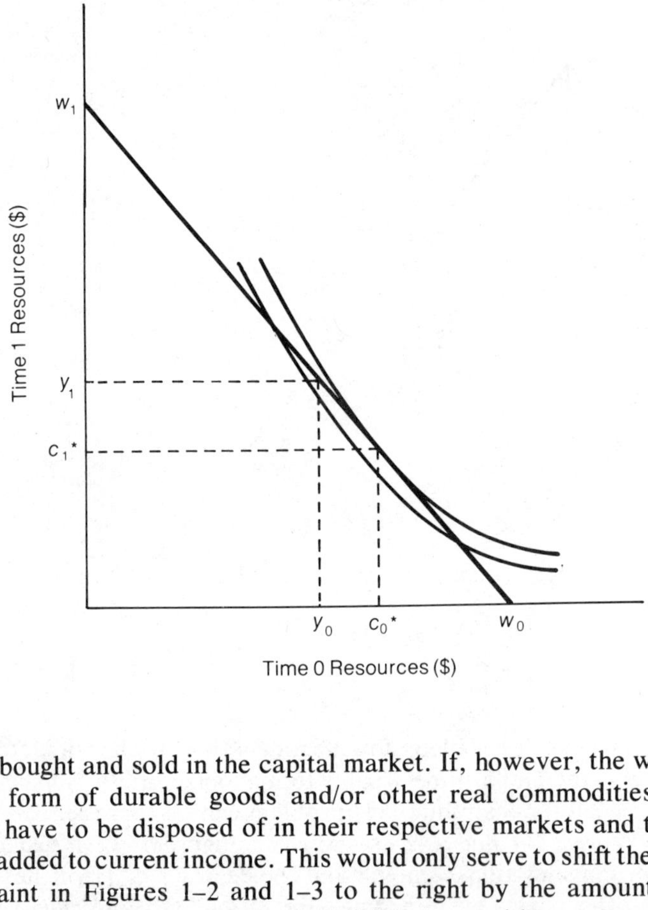

Time 1 Resources ($)

Time 0 Resources ($)

freely bought and sold in the capital market. If, however, the wealth is in the form of durable goods and/or other real commodities, these would have to be disposed of in their respective markets and the proceeds added to current income. This would only serve to shift the budget constraint in Figures 1–2 and 1–3 to the right by the amount of the proceeds of disposition. Thus, the individual's wealth, expressed as the present value of the periodic income stream plus the current market value of other initial endowments, is the only constraint on the choice of consumption patterns over time and conveniently summarizes the budget constraint.

In the present context, it is irrelevant whether these other markets are assumed to be perfect or not. With respect to durable goods, however, certain transactions may not be costlessly reversible. The existence or lack of such markets for durable goods was described earlier as one of the reasons why care is needed in making capital expenditures to acquire such goods.

The extension of our analysis to several periods is straightforward.

For the n-period case, we may write the present value of the individual's income stream $y_0, y_1, \ldots, y_n$ as:

$$w_0 = y_0 + \frac{y_1}{(1 + r_1)} + \frac{y_2}{(1 + r_1)(1 + r_2)}$$

$$+ \cdots + \frac{y_n}{(1 + r_1)(1 + r_2) \ldots (1 + r_n)} \quad (1.4.5a)$$

or,

$$w_0 = y_0 + \sum_{t=1}^{n} \frac{y_t}{\prod_{j=1}^{t} (1 + r_j)} \quad (1.4.5b)$$

In general, any two income streams with the same present value are *equivalent* in the sense that they each provide the same consumption alternatives to the individual. This is a consequence of our assumption of perfect capital markets which implies that the individual can borrow or lend freely at the market rates of interest to transform one stream into another. This also explains why we may refer to present value as wealth because two individuals with the same wealth will have the same consumption opportunities even though they may have different preferences. The power of this apparently simple concept which permits us to convert a stream (flow) of income into an analytically equivalent market value (stock) of wealth cannot be overstated.

While the equivalence of different income streams having equivalent present values is dependent on the assumption of perfect capital markets, it is frequently employed in more general contexts without regard to whether capital markets are perfect or not. Individuals in economies with smoothly functioning capital markets are better off because they can borrow or lend freely to adjust their income streams to attain a higher level of satisfaction than they could attain if prevented from borrowing or lending. As this applies to all individuals, social welfare is also enhanced by the existence of efficient and effective capital markets. Thus, capital markets perform a vital economic function. Without such markets, individuals would be forced to consume according to their income patterns, which for some may be very irregular indeed, for example, professional athletes. In such circumstances, individuals might prefer some other activity offering a smoother income pattern, even if their aggregate income is less. This would make some worse off individually and none better off. Economic welfare would be lessened. Such a choice is wasteful and inefficient. Smoothly functioning capital markets make it possible to separate consumption-level decisions from income patterns.[5]

Economic theory has made considerable progress in resolving the problem of comparing sums received at different points in time at least in principle. It has done so by making restrictive assumptions about the nature of markets in which claims to such sums may be exchanged and also by assuming away the problems posed by risk and uncertainty, on the one hand, and the difficulties of measuring benefits, on the other hand. We should not belittle the magnitude of this accomplishment, as it only appears trivial because we are accustomed to it. The intellectual problems posed managed to baffle most of the world's greatest minds for centuries, as a casual examination of the rather depressing literature on usury from Aristotle to some of the later scholastic philosophers indicates only too well.

1.5 Introducing durable goods and productive opportunities

In our discussion in the previous section, we explicitly abstracted from the existence of durable goods and productive investment opportunities in order that we might focus on the function of the capital markets in permitting individuals with given income streams to reallocate their consumption patterns. These elements are now introduced in order to consider how income streams may themselves be determined. Let us allow individuals (who will also be called entrepreneurs) to engage in commodity production and storage as a means of carrying wealth forward from one period to another, in addition to the purchase of claims (securities). These individuals may be viewed as owner managers of proprietary *firms*. The next section of this chapter examines how these decisions are affected if production is carried on by a firm of the joint stock, corporate variety having many owners and employing professional managers. The extension of the wealth-allocation model is straightforward if the owner of the firm is also the manager. When we have a multiowner firm in which much of the decision-making power has been delegated to managers, serious problems are often encountered in defining a suitable criterion for decision making since we can no longer assume the simple utility-maximization criterion used heretofore. While this problem is difficult in dealing with firms in the private sector of the economy, some of the concepts already used can be extended to deal with this issue. However, when we turn to considering similar problems in the public sector, the solution to our dilemma is much less clear and still fraught with considerable controversy, even in principle.

To illustrate our arguments, we again consider only a single-period world. While many opportunities for carrying over resources appear superficially different, they are fundamentally the same, even in this simple context. Such diverse activities as storing a real commodity, such as soybeans currently for sale or consumption in the future; the purchase of a durable good, such as a house, which the individual may either rent or live in to consume its services, then subsequently dispose of by resale; the ownership of some productive opportunity, such as a farm or manufacturing operation, which the individual may exploit as a means of transforming labor services and raw materials purchased now into finished products for sale or consumption in the future, are all the same in principle. That being so, we will use a variation on the last example as our prototype for further analysis.

Regardless of which opportunity is considered, it can be represented by a transformation or implicit production function $T(K_0, K_1) = 0$, where K_0 represents the (dollar value) of the initial resources, and thus the consumption possibilities, provided currently by the particular opportunity, and correspondingly for K_1, if the resources are liquidated and converted into consumption goods. We will assume that, in general, the function $T(.)$ has the form shown in Figure 1–4, where K_0 represents the current market value of initial resources. The meaning of this transformation function may be understood by considering the point x which represents the strategy of selling K_0' of initial resources

Figure 1–4
Productive opportunities

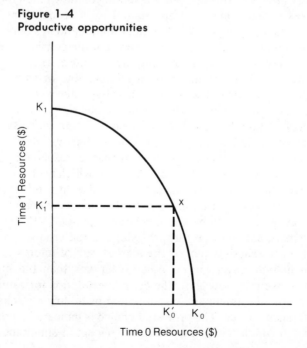

immediately, and investing $K_0 - K_0'$ in the productive opportunity currently. The net value of the yield on this investment at time 1, after deducting the cost of input factors, is K_1'. Note that as drawn here, the marginal rate of transformation of K_0 into K_1 (the slope of the function $T(.)$) falls steadily as we move from K_0 to K_1. This is the same thing as saying that the marginal yield, or marginal rate of return on investment, declines steadily as the level of investment increases.

The shape and position of the transformation function $T(.)$ embody a number of implicit assumptions about previously derived decisions with respect to the technology of production, sale of the outputs, and about the policies which the individual follows in making his price and output decisions, all of which are more appropriate subject matter for a text on production theory than for one on capital expenditures. We assume these have been made, resulting in the (concave) transformation function we represented. (We will return to this problem again in Chapter 3 where we relate certain decision criteria to the concept of the long-run costs of the firm, which our transformation function implies.)

We next consider what the opportunity set for the individual will look like when we allow *both* production *and* capital market opportunities together, as shown in Figure 1–5. If the individual immediately liquidates his productive resources K_0, the combinations of consumption c_0 and c_1 that can be obtained, depending on how much the individual chooses to lend, may be represented by a straight line of slope $-(1 + r)$ passing through K_0. If the individual liquidates only a portion of his productive resources, we may represent the consumption combination that may be obtained by using the capital market to reallocate the resource combination again by a straight line of slope $-(1 + r)$ passing through x, for example. This line has intercept on the time 0 axis which exceeds the initial resources and clearly dominates the previous policy of liquidating the initial resources entirely. By repeated application of this reasoning, we are able to discover that the investment policy which dominates all others is that represented by the point y, where the straight line with slope $-(1 + r)$, which we have called the present value line, is exactly tangent to the efficient production opportunity set. The important implication of this tangency condition is that we may say that the dominant investment policy is that policy for which the marginal rate of return (the slope of the production opportunity set at y) is exactly equal to the market rate of interest.

For an individual having no other resources than the productive opportunity, we may now show the complete solution for simultaneous choice of both investment and consumption by adding his consumption time-preference curves. The preferred choice is indicated by the point z in Figure 1–6 which represents the following set of simultaneous deci-

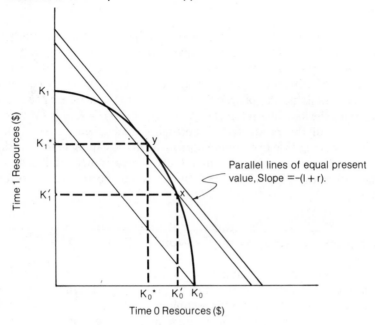

Figure 1–5
Productive and capital market opportunities

Time 1 Resources ($)

K_1

K_1^*

K_1'

Parallel lines of equal present
value, Slope $= -(1 + r)$.

y

x

K_0^* K_0' K_0

Time 0 Resources ($)

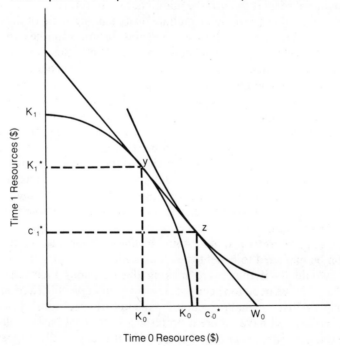

Figure 1–6
Joint equilibrium of production and consumption sections

Time 1 Resources ($)

K_1

K_1^*

c_1^*

y

z

K_0^* K_0 c_0^* W_0

Time 0 Resources ($)

sions: (a) immediately liquidate and withdraw K_0^* of the currently held K_0 of productive resources; (b) invest the remaining $K_0 - K_0^*$ in the productive process now to yield proceeds of K_1^* at time 1; (c) consume c_0^* now, borrowing $c_0^* - K_0'$ dollars to finance the gap between desired consumption and the proceeds of step (a); (d) consume c_1^* at time 1, repaying the loan plus interest $(c_0^* - K_0')(1 + r) = K_1^* - c_1^*$ from the proceeds of the productive opportunity established in step (b). By virtue of being able to combine borrowing in the capital market with the productive opportunity, this individual is clearly better off than if he had either the productive opportunity or the borrowing opportunity alone.

1.6 Corporations and the market-value criterion

As indicated at the beginning of Section 1.5, we assumed that the individual had some opportunities to carry forward resources from one point in time to another by investing in productive assets. We further assumed that such opportunities arose in the context of a business firm of which the individual was the sole owner-manager. We were then able to conclude that the utility-maximizing decision involved investing some initial resources until the marginal rate of return was equal to the market rate of interest, and simultaneously lending some of the balance of the initial resource, or borrowing against future resources, to achieve the preferred time pattern of consumption. While this is a valid statement of the optimal decision principle for the unincorporated business sector of the economy, in fact the corporate sector represents by far the larger amount of total resources invested. This compels us to extend our decision principle to deal with two issues which are implied by the organization in corporate form: (a) corporations have many owners, and there is no reason to assume that their consumption time-preference functions are the same; and (b) the stockholders (owners) of the corporation do not make the day-to-day operating decisions of the firm, but rather they elect a board of directors who, on behalf of the owners, hire professional managers, and then effectively delegate decision-making power to these managers.

Now, it seems to us that it should be unexceptionable that the corporation be managed to benefit the stockholders in exactly the same way they would do if they were making the decisions themselves. This implies that we need to specify a clear and unequivocal criterion for the managers' use in making capital-expenditure decisions. But, if the stockholders all have different preferences, on what basis shall we derive this criterion? Section 1.7 shows that it is essentially impossible to aggregate preferences across individuals directly in any meaningful way. This would appear to leave us in rather a hopeless position. But do not despair. Once again the economic theory of the functioning of capital markets provides the necessary guidance and leads directly to the very important *market-value criterion.*

We now assume the existence of organized capital markets where ownership shares of the corporation (claims against the corporation's future income, and implicitly against some of its resources or assets) can be freely bought or sold. Given these assumptions, a criterion can be developed for management, which is both objective and operational and which has the following desirable properties: (*a*) it does not involve the owners' or stockholders' preferences directly; but, (*b*) it leads to exactly the same decisions the owners would make if they were themselves managing the firm!

This apparently amazing feat requires only that we reconsider the results already found in Section 1.5. We recall that the overall optimum set of decisions regarding consumption, lending, borrowing, and investment was characterized by the simultaneous satisfaction of two tangency conditions (see Figure 1–6): (*a*) between the production opportunity transformation curve and the capital market opportunity line; and at the same time (*b*) between the capital market opportunity line and the individual's consumption time-preference (indifference) curve.

This first condition can be satisfied without needing to know anything about the individual's (subjective) preferences which enter the second condition. On the presumption that the professional manager is technically competent and possesses (objective) knowledge of the firm's technology, then the manager may solve the production optimization problem, subject to the assumed universally available information regarding the ruling rate of interest in the capital market.

The next step in our argument is the one toward which we have been building and is key to understanding and appreciating much of the rest of this book. Recall that we have interpreted the capital-market opportunity lines as present value, or market-value lines, because current market value is necessarily equal to present value under our assumption of perfect capital markets. Thus, when we instruct the manager to satisfy the first of the two conditions for the optimum, this is equivalent to telling him that he must maximize the current market value of the withdrawals which the current owners will be able to make from the firm, or alternatively, telling him that he must maximize the wealth of the current owners. This criterion is referred to as the *market-value rule,* or wealth-maximizing criterion. The market-value rule provides a utility-maximizing surrogate for the managers of the corporation regardless of the number of individual stockholders—whatever their preferences or other opportunities. Their aggregate wealth is increased from the initial amount contributed to its maximum possible value. The managers of the corporation can leave the rest of the individual optimizing solution to the individual stockholders.

The individual stockholders themselves meet the second condition for the optimum through their own transactions in the (perfect) capital market. Recall that an individual's current wealth is sufficient to describe all consumption opportunities over time. In perfect capital markets, any set of consumption choices with a given market value can be exchanged for any other set with the same market value. In particular, this implies that any set of consumption possibilities that a stockholder can derive from the firm against which he holds a claim can be converted uniquely and unambiguously to a (present) wealth equivalent by calculating the present value using the rate of interest prevailing in the capital market. Thus, if any given management decision increases the stockholders' current wealth, the stockholders are unequivocally better off.

The market-value criterion is actually more general than would be apparent from our having developed it in a single-period context. Regardless of the number periods under consideration, the critical assumptions in our argument are that (a) more wealth is always preferred to less and (b) perfect capital markets exist which permit us to take the results of all relevant management actions expressed as a sequence of consumption possibilities for the owners in all time periods, both current and future, into the common measure of current wealth.

The market-value rule implies a *separation principle* which operates to separate management decisions from specific knowledge of stockholders' preferences. This is not unique to this application, but it is merely another example of the general principle of using markets and market prices to decentralize decisions. We wish also to point out briefly the relationship between our concept of managerial decision rules which maximize the market value of stockholders' equity (a stock concept) with the concept of (long-run) profit maximization in the standard theory of the firm (a flow concept). These stock and flow concepts are not in conflict if they are properly interpreted. In ordinary static price theory, the (long-run) profits to be maximized are those in every time period for the apparently unlimited life of the firm, and if all of them are increased, the value of the firm to its owners has been unequivocally increased. We will also subsequently use this notion when we deal with methods of handling problems of long-run cost minimization. The two criteria are *not* equivalent when alternative decisions increase profits in some periods and reduce them in others. In such circumstances, the correct choice must be based on the market-value criterion. The simple flow (profit) criterion is not adequate when the timing of returns is the key difference between alternatives. Failure to recognize this can lead to unnecessary confusion and possibly incorrect decisions.

Finally, while the market-value criterion requires managers to be concerned with stockholders' preferences, managers are not computers and will have their own preferences which may conflict with those of the stockholders. How can we ensure that the market-value rule will be followed? While it is beyond the scope of this book, the *economic theory of agency* is one way in which this problem can be approached.[6]

1.7 Rationality in public expenditures

Specifying suitable goals for governments is somewhat more difficult since claims against the benefit streams which their investments are alleged to generate are not traded in capital markets and probably could not be in many cases even in principle. Thus, the market-value rule invoked earlier is of no help. This has provided an opportunity to advance a variety of proposed rules, but many of the traditional criteria which have been advanced can be shown to be either meaningless or self-contradictory. For example, Bentham's slogan "The greatest good for the greatest number" is of little use in choosing between two projects—one of which will yield benefits yielding $1,000 to each of 1,000 citizens and the other of which will yield benefits of $100 each to 9,000 citizens. There have been many subtle and sophisticated attempts to solve problems of this kind, but these have invariably run into snags.[7]

Several difficult problems, partly interrelated, must be resolved in some fashion if public-sector capital expenditures are to be made on economically rational grounds. Some of these problems are theoretical and have profound and ill-understood philosophical implications. The others are merely operational, but no more tractable on that score.

The most fundamental difficulty is the problem of defining a social welfare function, comparable in interpretation and usage to the individual utility function used in our basic analysis. It is on this bed of thorns that most of the recent discussion by economic theorists has been impaled. While the problem is simple, obtaining a fully satisfactory solution is difficult. A social welfare function seeks to measure social benefits and costs. However, in the strictest sense, it is meaningless to speak of social benefits and costs. Benefits are enjoyed by individuals, and costs must, in the end, also be borne by individuals. The net social gain or loss resulting from any project which creates benefits and imposes costs within the social group is *not* simply the sum of individuals' satisfaction created and destroyed by the project. Such satisfactions are personal and psychological and can neither be compared nor added in any meaningful sense. We can specify necessary conditions for maximum welfare: these are comprehended in the general notion of Pareto optimality. But we cannot choose between conflicting Pareto optima without comparing and adding or otherwise combining the utilities attained by individuals.

To be fair, we admit that economists have long recognized these problems and have proposed several alternative ways of dealing with the combination of individual preference functions into some form of aggregate. Given the democratic premise of our society, we might be tempted to recommend a "vote" and choose that alternative preferred by the majority. This notion has been studied by Arrow, who has managed to show that even if the individuals' preferences each satisfy all the necessary axioms of choice, majority rule still breaks down in situations which are not highly contrived as counterexamples.[8] Suppose that we have three individuals in our society, and there are three possible, but mutually exclusive, public projects from which one (at most) is to be selected. The citizens are asked to rank these projects in order of preference. After duly consulting their own preference functions, they provide the following sets of orderings:

Citizen	1st Choice	2d Choice	3d Choice
A	1	2	3
B	2	3	1
C	3	1	2

Now consider a choice between projects 1 and 2. Project 1 would be selected because it is ranked higher than 2 by both A and C. Next, compare the winner, project 1, against project 3. Now we see that project 3 would be chosen because it is preferred by both B and C. Finally, just to be sure we have done our analysis correctly, we compare project 3 with project 2. Now we come up with the result that project 2 should be selected by exactly the same line of reasoning, because it is preferred by A and B. In this example, the use of majority rule gives a completely circular outcome. On the other hand, if we did not reconsider an alternative after it had once been rejected, the choice would be capricious and arbitrary, because the final outcome would depend on the order in which the alternatives were examined.

Unfortunately, this result is not just an isolated pathological case. What has been demonstrated quite thoroughly and convincingly elsewhere is that even if we impose certain minimal standards of a priori sensible behavior for any aggregation rule we may wish to propose, there exists *no* sensible nondictatorial aggregation rule that can guarantee that we will not encounter the kind of intransitivity of choice which our example has illustrated.[9] Or, to put the matter bluntly, there is no way of directly combining the preference or utility functions of individual citizens into a single global preference function which meets all the axioms of choice and which could be used as an unambiguous criterion for making decisions in the best interests of society.

The economists' perplexity over the problem of making interpersonal comparisons of utility must seem amusing to the practical politician, who has been making them for years. He knows, in his reflective moments, that he has made a few mistakes, but his success in politics has rested on his ability to make just such comparisons and make use of them in a manner satisfactory to his constituents. In fact, we can only gaze with wonder and admiration at the intricacy of some of the apparent interpersonal comparisons regularly made by political leaders. This suggests that the sort of rationality used by politicians is not the same as that which economists have defined and which has been adopted for our analysis. At the very least, one of the major factors which enters into political decisions is *power* and its distribution in society,[10] something which economic theory has never sought to explain. In that sense, it is presumptuous for economists to be critical of the decisions made by politicians on the basis of their own narrowly defined notion of what constitutes rational behavior. At the same time, it is well within the sphere of their professional competence to make statements regarding the distribution of economic costs and benefits attendant upon any particular decision. They may even advocate a particular alternative, providing that they at least recognize the limitations to their competence, and providing they are honest enough with themselves and others to admit when they have stepped outside of the boundaries of their own specialty. At that point, their recommendations are merely opinions which may be no more or less informed than that of any other well-informed citizens, and they cannot be permitted to pretend otherwise.

Since this book is aimed at the practical administrator, we propose to skirt the problem of the criterion rather than solve it. We will merely act as if some sort of social welfare function existed and show how the tools developed for dealing with private-sector decisions may be applied in the public sector by examining relevant benefits and costs, abstracting from distributional considerations. This problem aside, some formidable difficulties still remain in evaluating public expenditures. Assuming we know how to add up the benefits and costs imposed on different individuals, we are still faced with the problem of measuring them and determining their incidence. This problem is bad enough in the business firm, but it is magnified in the public sector because the benefits and costs are frequently intangible. Market prices may also be an inappropriate guide even for the tangible ones in certain cases where external economies or diseconomies are involved or where otherwise unemployed resources are being used for the project. While this problem is practical, it is nevertheless serious. It is also complicated by the natural propensity of the proponents of a project which will benefit them or their constituents (and these are often the only ones who give it detailed scrutiny) to magnify real benefits and create imaginary ones to the limits of decency, and sometimes beyond, while sweeping aside consideration of as many of the costs as possible.

The public-sector expenditure decision is a twofold problem, just as in the private sector. The spending authority is (or should be) concerned first of all with allocating its budget efficiently regardless of the size of the budget. The second half of the problem is knowing when to stop, that is, determining what the size of the budget ought to be. This problem is not too serious for the private-sector decision maker, for market forces will operate in such a way as to keep him from straying very far, but there is no such constraint on the public decision maker, except for rather infrequent elections which focus on a broad range of issues. Thus the public-sector decision maker can call upon the taxing power of the state or the money-printing power of the central bank. Taken in isolation, since human wants are insatiable, bureaucrats can always make a case for any particular expenditure and thus convince the politicians that they should "go to the well." Temptations to do this are very strong, as the growing public-sector budgets of the 1970s attested. The problem is that many of these expenditures were often less productive than the private-sector capital expenditures they displaced. There is, in principle, a way of determining an appropriate balance between private- and public-sector expenditures based on market criteria which will be discussed in Chapter 8. However, because it is based on market evidence, it will be rejected as irrelevant by many who regard markets as unplanned, chaotic manifestations of institutionalized greed. Rejection on these grounds would be unfortunate. Greed exists. It was neither created by nor confined to market institutions. It has even been known to occur among statesmen. Markets have shown themselves to be a uniquely effective device for harnessing greed and turning its exercise to public advantage. Some of the alleged defects of the market, for example, that it is unduly responsive to the demands of the affluent rather than the needs of the poor, are not valid criticisms of markets at all, but of the income distributions in the society in which they operate.

1.8 Needed: A systematic approach to capital-expenditure management

While our primary focus is on the decision problems involved in the administration of capital spending, there is more to its administration than just decision making. Successful use of capital, whether by a business firm, a household, or a government, requires generating and analyzing proposed projects, deciding which projects to carry out, and executing the projects selected. In any going concern, control must be exercised over the entire process.

The importance of generating proposals ought to be self-evident. Even if a perfect solution to the decision-making problem existed, which is not the case at the present time, its application to the ill-assorted lot of generally deficient proposals will not lead to the efficient utilization of capital resources. While many possible uses for funds just appear (particularly in government), little doubt exists that the relative lack of success of many firms is due to a failure to generate enough profitable outlets for funds. The institutionalization of research and development activity is the result of efforts to systematize the generation of investment opportunities rather than waiting for them to happen along. There is an economic limit to this process, which itself is subject to the same analysis as the projects it generates. It costs money—sometimes rather large sums—to generate and consider projects. Our understanding of the process of innovation is rudimentary, and the economics of information (of which this is viewed as a part) remains quite undeveloped. While there is room for much improvement in this area, it is beyond the scope of the present work.

It has been argued that, because of these deficiencies, the emphasis on evaluation and decision-making procedures in the literature on capital-expenditure management has been misplaced, and most of it has little relevance to practical decision makers, whether business executives, bureaucrats, or politicians.[11] There is a germ of truth in this position, but it should not become an excuse for sloppy or inappropriate evaluation procedures. The generation of many investment proposals means, inevitably, the generation of much effort for their evaluation. Evaluation procedures can be made relatively routine in many instances, and it is not demonstrably more expensive to evaluate projects correctly than to evaluate them incorrectly. The only cost is the added cost (if any) of getting the evaluation system right in the first place or of replacing a bad system with a good one. For a firm adding to its assets by as little as $50,000 per year, an improvement of 2 percent in the average return on investment after taxes could justify spending over $78,000 on overhauling the firm's capital-budgeting system if the firm's required rate of return is 12 percent. For a firm spending $1 million yearly, the corresponding amount is $1.5 million. If you do not understand how these figures were derived, then it would be worth your while to read the rest of this book.

In Chapter 2, we turn to some rather more practical issues of the sort we have just raised. In particular, we make a distinction between strategic and routine capital expenditures, which is not adequately recognized. The systematization referred to earlier applies to the routine decisions, but strategic decisions require more attention be paid to the associated organizational and administrative problems.

Chapter 3 details the various criteria for measuring and comparing the desirability of alternative capital expenditures and evaluates them in the context of the theory developed in this chapter. As we indicated in Section 1.7, all capital-expenditure decisions, whether in the public or private spheres, imply attendant benefits and costs to be evaluated using the criteria of Chapter 3. Regardless of whether the most appropriate criterion is selected, the exercise is fruitless unless the benefits and costs are correctly measured. The problem presents its own challenges which are examined for the private sector in Chapter 4 and for the public sector in Chapter 9.

Under the assumptions of perfect certainty and perfect capital markets of Chapter 1, only one prevailing rate of interest is found in the capital market, and this will be the *risk-free rate of interest*. However, many of the criteria of Chapter 3 use the *required rate of return* to the firm for the evaluation process, which implicitly incorporates an allowance for risk and uncertainty. Since we deal with methods of explaining theoretically and measuring empirically the *risk premium* in detail later, in Chapter 3 we use the term *modified certainty* to refer euphemistically to risk-adjusted rate of return without being explicit about how these risk adjustments ought to be made. Chapters 5 and 6 examine some of the traditional issues involved in measuring required rate of return (cost of capital) in the private sector and certain problems of financing policy and the impact of departures from our perfect capital market assumptions. Chapter 8 considers the corresponding issues for the public sector. With the introduction of capital-market imperfections, their impact on decisions using the modified certainty approach is examined more fully in Chapter 7. Chapter 4 ignored any problems in capital-expenditures decision making which arise under inflationary conditions, and so this issue of considerable current interest is examined in Chapter 10.

Contemporary financial theory has made considerable gains in explicitly incorporating risk and uncertainty into the analysis of investment and financing decisions. Chapters 11 and 12 provide enough of this theory to show how much or how little our market-value criterion is affected, both in principle and in practice.

One of the strategic capital expenditures made by a significant number of firms has been to form conglomerates by acquiring other firms or to merge with other corporations. Such decisions are examined theoretically in Chapter 13. Finally, Chapter 14 examines how capital expenditures affect the process of economic growth.

Notes

[1] Taken at face value, the decision by the U.S. Supreme Court in June 1978 to prohibit the Tennessee Valley Authority from completing the Tellico Dam across the Little Tennessee River would seem to be a case where infinite value has been placed on preventing the extinction of 10,000 tiny fish, the snail darter, unique to those waters.

[2] See, for example, R. A. Bauer, ed., *Social Indicators* (Cambridge, Mass.: M.I.T. Press, 1966).

[3] As in, for example, G. S. Becker, *Economic Theory* (New York: Alfred A. Knopf, (1971); M. Friedman, *Price Theory: A Provisional Text,* rev. ed. (Chicago: Aldine, 1962); or G. J. Stigler, *The Theory of Price,* 3d. ed. (New York: Macmillan, 1966). For its application in an intemporal context, see I. Fisher, *The Theory of Interest* (New York: Macmillan, 1930).

[4] Some confusion has resulted from the conflicting ways of denoting time in the development of financial theory. This arises because time does not enter into static microeconomic theory in any essential way. However, it is essential in the analysis of the financial problem which seeks to build on this theory. Microeconomic theory envisions all economic decisions for a period of time, whose duration is unspecified and irrelevant to that theory, as taking place at the beginning of that period, so that it has become conventional to refer to that point in time as a period. Normal usage would convey the notion of a duration of time this way, but we use the economic convention, denoting passage of time by a succession of periods.

[5] E. F. Fama and M. H. Miller, *The Theory of Finance* (New York: Holt, Rinehart & Winston, 1972), p. 28.

[6] D. G. Heckerman, "Motivating Managers to Make Investment Decisions," *Journal of Financial Economics* 2 (1975), pp. 273–92.

[7] K. J. Arrow, *Social Choice and Individual Values,* 2d ed. (New Haven: Yale University Press, 1963); W. J. Baumol, *Welfare Economics and the Theory of the State* (Cambridge, Mass.: Harvard University Press, 1952); I. M. D. Little, *A Critique of Welfare Economics,* 2d. ed. (London: Oxford University Press, 1957); J. Rothenberg, *The Measurement of Social Welfare* (Englewood Cliffs, N.J.: Prentice-Hall, 1961); R. G. Lipsey and R. K. Lancaster, "The General Theory of Second Best," *Review of Economic Studies* 24 (1) (1956–57), pp. 11–32.

[8] Arrow, *Social Choice,* pp. 46–60.

[9] Arrow, *Social Choice,* p. 60 and 75–86; and K. J. Arrow, *The Limits of Organization* (New York: W. W. Norton, 1974).

[10] See, for example, J. S. Coleman, *Power and the Structure of Society* (New York: W. W. Norton, 1974).

[11] W. W. Haynes and M. B. Solomon, Jr., "A Misplaced Emphasis in Capital Budgeting," *Quarterly Review of Economics and Business* (February 1962), pp. 39–46.

Problems

1. Considering personal education as an investment project, can you identify (*a*) the benefits and (*b*) the costs which you would use in an analysis to determine its economic desirability? Which of these can be measured in monetary terms? What difficulties arise in attempting to measure them?

2. What is the present value of the following future payments, assuming annual compounding?

Amount due	Due in	Interest rate
100	1 year	6%
350	3	4
200	2	5
600	4	8
1,000	50	20
1,000	100	3

3. *a.* Distinguish between the following projects as (*i*) capital widening, (*ii*) capital deepening.
   (1) Construction of a new restaurant by a chain.
   (2) Installation of automatic dishwashers in one of its restaurants.
   (3) Construction of a parking garage adjacent to one of its restaurants.
   (4) Acquisition of a frozen-foods processor by the restaurant chain.
   b. Should this classification make any difference in the selection process? Why?

4. For the case where an individual ends up lending in the capital market, demonstrate graphically that, given perfect and complete capital markets, the production decision is governed solely by an objective market criterion (represented by attained wealth) without regard to the individual's subjective consumption time-preference which enter into their consumption decisions.

5. The aggregation of individuals' borrowing and lending decisions determines the supply of and demand for loanable funds in the capital market and hence the equilibrium rate of interest. Suppose some exogenous shift in preferences occurred decreasing the equilibrium rate of interest. Analyze graphically the effect of this change on (*a*) the utility of borrowers and

lenders, (*b*) the present wealth position of borrowers and lenders, and (*c*) the amount of investment in real, productive assets.

6. Consider the following statement: "The interest rate cannot be less than the rate of return from storage (of a commodity) net of storage costs (including any spoilage allowance)." Is this statement true or false? Why?

7. Examine a recent legislative enactment (national or local) involving the raising of funds by a specific tax and their expenditure. Can you identify the implicit weights used by the legislature in evaluating the contributions to and from the particular groups affected? Are these weights consistent with other enactments of the same legislature?

The capital-expenditure decision process

2.1 Introduction

The capital-expenditure process in any economic unit involves several distinct steps. Proposals to spend money must be generated, alternatives must be weighed against one another, decisions must be made to carry out specific projects, and action must be taken on these decisions. These steps, which we will refer to as project generation, project evaluation, project selection, and project execution, are necessary in any organization which makes capital expenditures. Executive action which is directed at control of the capital-expenditure process must concern itself with each of these and will usually find it necessary to add additional steps to keep the process under control.[1] Thus it may impose budgetary controls on the execution of projects to see that authorized expenditure limits are not exceeded without review. Where appropriate, it may establish a system of "postaudit," that is, following up the results of completed projects, either within the organization's regular accounting system or in addition to it, to provide a continuing check on the effectiveness of the decision-making process.

The extent to which the process needs to be formalized and systematic procedures established depends on the size of the organization, on the number of projects which must be considered, and on their complexity and diversity. What's good for General Motors may not be good for the corner store. While even the latter may face occasional decisions calling for careful evaluation along the line to be discussed here, it must be remembered that increasing sophistication costs money and that the cost of the decision-making process should not be increased beyond the savings likely to result from the superior decision.[2]

In most organizations, ultimate control over the magnitude of the capital-spending program and the major components within it is reserved for the highest levels of management. There are two reasons for this. First, financing of the organization must normally be carried out centrally, since capital expenditures affect the extent to which financing must be obtained, and their aggregate amount must be reconciled with the organization's financial plan and must be controlled centrally to

35

keep within that plan. Second, even minor capital expenditures carry with them a commitment in terms of future operating expenses that may ultimately involve amounts several times as great as the capital expenditures themselves. Buying a furnace involves a commitment to a succession of fuel bills and to a particular fuel. The extent to which managers at subordinate levels are permitted to commit the enterprise to such ongoing expenditures must be controlled, usually by limiting the size of capital expenditures they may authorize. As major capital expenditures involve major commitments and may effectively delineate the firm's product line and geographic market opportunities, they assume a strategic character which makes them candidates for decision at the highest management levels.[3]

2.2 Project Generation

It is normally not too difficult to obtain a set of proposals for spending money. The trick, however, is to obtain the *right* set of proposals. The decision to establish a firm is in nearly all cases a decision to undertake certain capital expenditures. Based on their studies of the market for the proposed product, the promoters will examine alternative plans for meeting the demand and will select using capital-budgeting criteria the alternative which appears to be the most economic. The investment proposal originates within the entrepreneurial group, although they may call on technical specialists for advice.

Once the firm has been established as a going concern, investment proposals may be generated at several levels within it. These will normally fall into one of the following classifications:

1. *a.* Proposals to add new products to the product line.
   b. Proposals to expand capacity in existing product lines.
2. Proposals designed to reduce costs in the output of existing products without altering the scale of operations.

In the literature on capital theory, decisions of type 1 involve the choice of scale and lead to so-called capital widening, while decisions of type 2 involve the choice of technique and lead to capital deepening. The distinction is for the most part of theoretical rather than practical importance, and in practice many proposals include elements of both. However, to the extent that new products may imply entry into new markets, they may also imply different business risk characteristics. As we will discuss in Chapters 11 and 12, this may require modifications to evaluation procedures. Either type of proposal may originate at any level within the firm from the board of directors down to the production line worker, and it is probable that a large proportion of proposals originate in a rather haphazard fashion. New products are suggested by the salesforce or by plant foremen who see a way of utilizing idle capacity, while improvements in techniques may result from suggestions coming from the factory floor. Few managements seek to discourage new ideas, and the ubiquitous suggestion box may sometimes yield something more valuable than discarded gum wrappers.

However, because of the eventual obsolescence of most products and management's desire for sustained growth in the firm, many firms have found that it pays to be more systematic in the search for new investment opportunities. A firm which does not generate enough investment proposals to keep its funds fully employed is not going to grow but is going to decline and vanish sooner or later. A firm which merely generates this volume is unlikely to do much better. The healthy firm is one in which there is a continual flow of profitable investment proposals, and one in which the problem of choice between proposals is serious.

The search for opportunities of type 2 is most frequently systematized by continuous review of production operations, either as part of the responsibility of line managers or by separate work study or industrial engineering groups in staff positions, or both. These same sources are likely to be involved along with marketing management in proposals to increase the scale of operations.

In the early industrial revolution and well into the 20th century, ideas for new products tended most frequently to originate with inventors, who either started new enterprises with the aid of promoters or took their ideas to existing firms.[4] One of the outstanding features of the continual evolution of capitalism has been the assimilation of the process of invention into the firm itself and its subsequent systematization. This has lead to a continuous search for new and better products to supplement or supplant those currently being produced. One of the results which is the favorite target of social critics has been the phenomenon of *planned obsolescence*. While there may be aspects of this which deserve criticism, it should be remembered that if the firm itself did not plan to make its own products obsolete, its competitors would, so that we would probably get to the same place but more slowly, with more turnover in the business population, dislocation in the labor force, losses to investors, and disruption of communities. The wastes resulting from planned obsolescence within the firm are easily seen and noted, while the wastes that would have resulted from its alternatives did not occur and are easily ignored. The other alternative is to forbid change entirely, which is not feasible in a free society.

This institutionalization of the inventive process has come about through the growth in science and technology as formal academic disciplines and the establishment of engineering departments and research departments in business firms. The firm which wants to stay healthy must organize itself in this fashion if it is to continue to innovate and grow.

Research and development spending is, of course, itself a form of capital expenditure which must find its justification in the new investment opportunities it creates. It is a high risk form of spending since, particularly at the research end of the spectrum, it is difficult if not impossible to forecast results or ultimate costs. In many firms, the research budget offers an interesting current example of justification by faith alone, and its amount is determined by looking at how much the company can afford to risk, with one eye over the shoulder to what expenditures are being made by competitors.[5]

In government, there is never a shortage of proposals to spend money, although the shortage of really productive outlets appears to be even worse than it is in the private sector. In North America, traditional political beliefs concerning the government's role in the economy tend to inhibit its activity as an innovator. In spite of this, its scope has been continuously growing. Within the boundaries it has set for itself, however, two possible approaches can be found to the allocation of funds. Roads can either be built where the political pressures are too great to resist or as part of a coherently planned highway system. While there have been undoubted improvements in the way governments approach problems of this type, there is still a great deal of room for improvement. Government activity has grown without any systematic search for investment opportunities, with few standards for evaluation, and without the discipline of the marketplace. As a result, large sums have been invested in the pet projects of pressure groups, the rates of return on which by any rational system of evaluation are exceedingly low, if not negative. Other projects also within the political responsibility of government, but which could yield very high social rates of return, have been neglected. While lack of standards for evaluation must bear part of the blame, a large part must be attributed to the passive, haphazard nature of government's search for investment opportunities.

Government has a need to adopt and adapt the practices of industry in this regard. This must embrace the search for all types of socially profitable investments, whether of the cost-reducing, scale-increasing, or new-product variety, within its defined sphere of activity. The systematic search for cost-reducing projects has been routine in industry for well over half a century, but the systematic search for efficiency within the public sector has only begun to assume significant proportions within the last decade. Many government activities have resisted analysis, as have groups with vested interests in particular aspects of government inefficiency. There has been improvement, but not enough.

Another dimension of the problem has been the frequent subordination of long-term public welfare considerations to the understandable objective of getting reelected. While the democratic process may discriminate against the more blatant examples of waste, it is far from clear that it can lead to budgets which maximize social welfare.[6]

The need for efficiency in public spending is even more pressing for the developing countries. Many of these envisage a greater economic role for government, which, whatever its possible philosophical merits, offers greater opportunities for waste if the whole expenditure process is not brought under control. A level of waste which might be tolerable in a more affluent society can destroy the prospects of a society where capital for development of both the public and private sectors is scarce.

2.3 Project evaluation

The basic steps in project evaluation are the estimation of benefits and costs and the conversion of such estimates into measures of desirability. The basic difference between the evaluation process within the firm and within government is in the estimation of benefits and costs; the measures of desirability are formally identical. Strictly speaking, the firm need only concern itself with the private benefits and costs accruing to the firm, which are usually expressed in the values of the marketplace. Government, on the other hand, must identify and measure social benefits and costs which are frequently not measurable from market data and must further identify the incidence of such benefits and costs on particular groups in society, then apply appropriate weights to the different interests involved before the estimates can be converted into measures of desirability.

It has sometimes been argued that it is a fundamental social responsibility of business firms to take account of social benefits and costs in their operations.[7] While the firm is certainly at liberty to do so if it wishes, its suitability as an institution for this social role is questionable. This is particularly true in those cases where there are large discrepancies between private and social costs, on the one hand, and benefits, on the other. If the firm is operating in a highly competitive industry and competitive factor markets, the attempt to provide for social costs (for example, smoke or industrial diseases) is a royal road to competitive ruin, unless competitors do likewise. Ignoring them may be the key to success. But it is essential for the state to intervene in such instances to make private costs equal to social costs for all firms if the socially irresponsible are not to drive the socially responsible out of the industry. This principle has been recognized, at least in part, since the first factory acts in England in the early 19th century.

Even if the firm has sufficient market power to assess the full social cost of its operations against the consumers of its product, the desirability of its doing so is open to question. Such a decision involves a value judgment to the effect that compensation should be paid, and another to the effect that customers should be assessed to pay for it. Such decisions are clearly political in nature, and corporate managements do not have any express mandate from the electorate to make them. To the extent that the state does not intervene in the exercise of such judgments, there is an implicit delegation of authority, but this is hardly enough. Such responsibility is unsought, and its exercise calls for judgments of a type qualitatively different from normal managerial decisions. If society wishes to equalize social and private costs and to redistribute real income, then it should do so systematically, through political processes, rather than expect corporate management to fill the power vacuum.

At the same time, failure of the firm to consider possibly significant elements of social costs imposed on outsiders through its choice of projects may be harmful in that it invites unilateral intervention by the state, without any particular regard for competitive factors. If we imagine a continuum along which projects may be arrayed from purely economic (private benefits and costs) to purely political (social benefits and costs), many of the critical, strategic projects of the firm will be found to lie, not at the purely economic end, but at various distances toward the opposite end. If the problems of project evaluation were purely economic, the measures of desirability discussed in Chapter 3 would be sufficient. To the extent that projects are not purely economic, they involve an element of what may be called *political* risk, and we claim no special qualifications or expertise at prescribing ways of dealing with this particular form of risk.[8]

As a concrete example, consider the following case. Company A has substantial control over the price of its product, through the possession of market power, and is faced with a strong union under a closed shop union agreement. The product is of minor importance in the economy. The rest of the economy and the labor market are perfectly competitive or nearly so.

Suppose further that pension costs may be considered as part of the long-run social cost of labor. In the competitive sector of the economy, labor sells for a price dominated by short-run conditions, that is, containing no element of pension. Nor can employers in the competitive sector offer pensions unilaterally because their competitors will not. If A grants its unionized employees a pension, its management is behaving in a socially responsible manner. To the extent that the pension costs are met through higher prices, real income is transferred to its employees from its customers, most of whom do not have pensions. To the extent that pension costs are met out of profits, real income is transferred away from its stockholders, who may not have pensions either. The equity of such an arrangement is at least open to question, although we will not pursue the matter further here.

There are few cases in which benefits and costs are known precisely beforehand, so their estimation inevitably involves forecasting.[9] Because the future is uncertain, such estimates differ widely from the ultimate results. This has at least two implications for evaluation.

Outcomes are a priori random variables. Single-value estimates may represent the expected value of the probability distribution of outcomes or may be systematically biased. In either case, the relative dispersion of outcomes and the consequent risks associated with different projects usually differ, and this should be taken into account in the decision process. We will examine various ways of doing this in Chapters 11 and 12. The important point to be noted here is that some analysis of possible alternative outcomes, a form of *sensitivity analysis,* must be an integral part of the evaluation process. In other words, we ask how robust our decision may be with respect to changing circumstances.

The other implication is that evaluation ought to be done by an impartial group with no axe to grind. Operating departments are prone to want the latest in equipment for reasons having little to do with productivity, and this may consciously or unconsciously affect their estimates of the potential benefits to be derived from it. Good salesmen are by nature or by training optimistic and may not be the best source to estimate the marketability of a new product. All projects ought to be scrutinized carefully by a staff group which has no vested interest in their adoption, and the evaluation should be subject to review to ensure that objectivity remains their basic concern and is not replaced with mere conservatism.

Evaluation also involves converting measures of benefits and costs into measures of desirability. Once desirability measures are established, such conversion is a routine clerical operation or can be easily programmed on a computer. Care should be taken, however, that the desirability measures chosen do not unconsciously discriminate in favor of certain types of projects rather than others which may be more productive but unusual in some respect. While many of the criteria proposed may give similar results on most types of projects examined by the company, they may seriously misevaluate the unusual project. Criteria chosen should be as general in application as possible.

2.4 Project selection

As indicated, responsibility for the results of capital expenditures rests with top management. Top management may delegate authority to approve certain types of capital expenditures, while limiting the amount, controlling the criteria used in selection, and holding the lower levels accountable for the results.

In a healthy organization, actual selection among projects which have been proposed must be done by responsible line executives. Much of the evaluation of projects will ordinarily be done by staff specialists, and the calculation of measures of desirability is essentially clerical in nature. While a great deal of screening must be done at the evaluation stage, care should be taken to ensure that the function of line management is not reduced to one of rubber stamping capital budgets prepared in all their essentials by the staff group. A sufficiently large number of proposals should survive the evaluation process to ensure that the real decisions are being made at the appropriate level in the organization and to ensure that no unusual but worthwhile proposals are eliminated. Judgment must be exercised ultimately by those responsible and will remain, inevitably, as a factor modifying the specialists' evaluation. Proposals passed to management for the ultimate selection should be presented with sufficient detail and supporting data to enable the estimates of the evaluation group to be checked and modified where necessary. When the final selection has been made, funds are appropriated and the budget system takes over.

2.5 The budgetary system

The funds appropriated for capital expenditures make up the capital budget, which is usually administered by the controllership function through the accounting department of the organization. While appropriation of funds normally constitutes approval in principle for the expenditures, control must continue to be exercised to ensure that funds are spent as intended. Before they sign contracts, those responsible for the execution of projects will be required to apply through the controller for formal authority to spend the funds. After comparing the proposed expenditures with the budget, the controller will authorize the expenditures. Then, as invoices appear, they will be charged against the budget. Monthly budget reports will indicate the status of all projects, that is, total appropriated outstanding authorizations and actual expenditures made. Most systems will permit individual appropriations to be exceeded by some small margin to allow for errors in estimating, the balance to be transferred from other projects. Major overruns will ordinarily require supplementary appropriations from the approving authority, while minor ones will usually require explanation. There are, of course, endless variations of the basic system in actual use, but there is no point in pursuing the accounting technicalities here.

Besides the control of expenditures, the accounting department will be responsible for preparing the data for budget reviews, separating the costs and revenues associated with particular projects for several years after their completion in order to provide a check on the operation of the evaluation and selection process. Without this feedback relationship, estimates can diverge further and further from reality without anyone being the wiser.

The budgetary process in most governmental bodies is deficient in several respects. There is control over expenditures but seldom any follow-up. Costs are not traced to projects, and capital and operating expenditures are frequently scrambled together in ways that not only preclude rational decision making, but which waste disproportionate amounts of legislators' time in the examination of trivia which happen to be identifiable.

New techniques which hold promise in terms of improving public-sector budgeting practice have been developed in recent years. The first of these is *program budgeting* which classifies expenditure decisions so as to focus decision-makers' attention on the functional purpose of the expenditures rather than on the objects on which funds are being expended.[10] A further development is *zero-base budgeting,* in which all proposed expenditures on a given program, and not simply the proposed increase, must be justified anew for each budgetary period.[11]

2.6 Capital-budgeting criteria and project design

All levels of management should understand the budgeting system and the criteria by which proposals are selected. Communication should embrace not only the criteria but also the approximate standards required for acceptable projects. Nowhere is this more important than in the engineering design of new projects. Good engineering practice seeks optimal *economic* solutions for technical problems and considers economic data in addition to technical data. Design personnel require an understanding of the standards used for selection if they are to do their job effectively. In particular, when a required-rate-of-return criterion is used for deciding between alternative projects on the basis of their prospective rates of return, it is essential that the rate assumed for design purposes be the appropriate required rate of return if design engineers are not to be working at cross-purposes with the rest of the organization. The most economical plant, designed on the assumption that the required rate of return is 10 percent, is not likely to be the most economical plant for a firm whose required rate of return is actually 25 percent. The techniques selected will be too capital intensive, and/or the scale too large. This failure of communication, if carried far enough, can lead to the design of projects which are never acceptable. Alternative designs based on varying assumptions about the required rate of return could be prepared, but the designing of plants is expensive.

The need to know the appropriate required rate of return for design purposes well in advance of the actual proposal of projects is one of the basic reasons for using the estimated required rate of return rather than some rule which determines the effective rate by considering the availability of funds on some arbitrary basis. It is also a practical objection to the suggestion that estimation of the required rate of return is not necessary since both the required return and the optimum budget may be simultaneously determined using an investment decision model.[12] While the theoretical case for this position is excellent because of the *separation principle* described in Chapter 1, it cannot be applied in practice unless investment analysis can be broadened to incorporate project design as well.

2.7 Strategic and routine capital expenditures

Some decentralization of the capital-expenditure decision-making process is almost a necessity in large organizations. The object of any such decentralization is usually twofold. It serves to free top management from trivial detail, permitting them to concentrate their attention on more important matters. At the same time, subordinate managers gain autonomy and experience in making decisions for which they are accountable. The critical issue in establishing a decentralized budgetary system is to determine which decisions are to be delegated to subordinate managers, subject only to scrutiny as to total amounts, and which are to be retained at the top.

Magnitude of the proposed expenditure is frequently chosen as the criterion determining if a proposed expenditure can be approved by local management or whether it must be passed up the line for decision at a higher level. The major virtue of the size criterion (and it is a significant one) is its simplicity. At least in principle, a more suitable basis for making the distinction is in terms of the *strategic* implications of projects and the extent to which they expose the organization to further commitments or changes in *risk* exposure. Thus, new product investments, even if relatively minor in amount, can result in a company being in on the ground floor of a major new market or being excluded. Participation may involve further major investments in the relatively near future. Such investments clearly have more far-reaching implications than the replacement of production or distribution facilities for an existing and profitable product line. They are, therefore, the ones on which top management attention should be focused. Many systems attempt to accomplish this by combining size criteria with strategic considerations. In such systems, for example, lower-level managers may have lower discretionary limits for new product investments than for facilities replacement, and even greater discretion with respect to cost-reducing expenditures.

2.8   Budget review and follow-up calculations

The information feedback provided by reviewing project results has been mentioned as a necessary part of the control structure.[13] Obtaining the required information may require some modification of existing information systems in the business firm and more elaborate gathering of statistics in a government body.

In the business firm, the only change normally necessary will be to keep direct cost and sales records on a sufficiently detailed basis to enable the identification of those revenues or costs associated with a particular project.[14] It will ordinarily suffice to compare actual cash outlays and expenditures with those forecast; there is no need to get unduly elaborate. Additional identification of data inputs will normally be required along with some additional reports. What should normally be provided is an attempt to integrate data for this purpose into an all-purpose cost accounting information system. Fully distributed costs may be useful for many purposes, but the essence of project evaluation is the consideration of what are essentially direct costs, on a cash basis rather than on an accrual basis, so that fully distributed costs are of little use in checking evaluation estimates. The eventual outcome of a project will only be one of the outcomes that was considered in the initial evaluation. Even if a probability distribution of outcomes was explicitly considered, only one can emerge. Serious difficulties often develop in attempting to evaluate the performance of the valuation group insofar as its estimates of probabilities is concerned on the basis of accounting data. This problem has yet to be resolved.

There will always be some subjective elements in the review. Insofar as the selection of a project means the rejection of alternatives, there will not be any actual figures for the alternatives. It will ordinarily suffice if the projected cash flows of the adopted alternative turn out to be reasonably consistent with the results.

In government bodies, benefit-cost studies on completed projects are fraught with many difficulties similar to those involved in preparing the initial projections. Many of the benefits and costs will be external and will not appear in the government's accounts; others will be nonmonetary in nature and difficult to measure in monetary terms. Still other benefits and costs may have been overlooked. While we must, because of the nature of the data and the projects, be willing to make allowances for uncertainty, no excuse can be made for failure to attempt an objective appraisal of results, even if the project was undertaken by the opposing party.

2.9 Organizational and administrative problems in managing strategic capital expenditures

Certain capital expenditures have strategic consequences in that they involve commitments to locations, to product lines, to technologies, and to cost structures that may extend well into the future. Because of these, they may be felt to deserve particularly careful scrutiny. What is frequently less obvious is the extent to which the company has been committed, or at least partially so, to making the strategic expenditures. Initially they are a gleam in someone's eye. That individual or someone else undertakes a preliminary investigation and is convinced of the merits of the project. If the preliminary investigation is unfavorable, the project is apt to die right there, because the cost of going to the next stage in the analysis is often substantial. If it is favorable, the project has probably gained one or more enthusiastic supporters, well placed in the organization, who may keep pushing for the project, even in the face of unfavorable subsequent evaluations, until it eventually finds its way into the capital budget. If second-stage evaluations are unfavorable, new ones may be ordered, possibly with some modifications, until a favorable evaluation is generated. Intervention of chief executive officers in the evaluation process to ensure that the numbers come out right is not exactly unknown: it is sufficiently frequent that most individuals with a few years' experience in project evaluation can provide concrete examples.

As a consequence, the projects may well have been studied and restudied, but they are often accepted into the budget and undertaken with less objective evaluation than that which is routinely applied to the purchase of a screwcutting lathe. Oil company X purchased an independent refinery with an obsolescent plant in city Y, where its national head office in country Z was located some 15 years ago. Almost immediately, it began laying plans eventually to build a larger ultramodern facility in the area in order to be properly represented. By the time the construction began, estimated unit cost of the facility was three times those of its competitors, the regional market was glutted with unsalable products from the competitors' existing refineries with no sign of a respite, and several politicians were proposing to turn refining into a public utility. Construction went ahead anyway, because by the time the ultimate decision had to be made, the organization was so committed to going ahead that a "no-go" decision was unthinkable.

In many organizations, this is compounded by the fact that individuals and projects make their way up the corporate ladder at the same time. Bower[15] cites several examples in which almost identical small groups of individuals who did preliminary investigations and submitted proposals supervised engineering design work and the elaboration of divisional submissions in support of a project, and were promoted into head office decision-making roles just in time to speed their pet projects on the road to completion.

On the basis of our own experience, we believe the problem is at least as great as Bower has suggested. We recognize that it can make a mockery of an otherwise healthy decision-making system. We have no particular remedies to offer other than the customary injunction that evaluation should be kept on an independent basis. Where organizational commitment is too strong, outside consultants may be useful. Unfortunately, even they may be of doubtful value; a competent management can often select consultants so as to get the desired conclusion. However, the problem may not be as bad as we have painted it. The commitment, enthusiasm, and drive which carry a marginal project into the capital budget may well be all that is needed to make it a success.

Notes

[1] As described, for example, by J. B. Weaver, "Organizing and Maintaining a Capital Expenditure Program," *The Engineering Economist* 20, no. 1 (Fall 1974), pp. 1–35.

[2] W. J. Baumol and R. E. Quandt, "Rules of Thumb and Optimally Imperfect Decisions," *American Economic Review* 54 (March 1964), pp. 23–46.

[3] W. H. Newman, "Basic Objectives which Shape the Character of a Company," *Journal of Business* 26 (October 1953), pp. 211–33.

[4] J. Jewkes, D. Sawers, and R. Stillerman, *The Sources of Invention* (London: Macmillan and Company, 1958).

[5] The research and development process has been most effectively analyzed by F. M. Scherer, *Industrial Market Structure and Economic Performance* (Chicago: Rand McNally, 1971), chap. 15.

[6] For discussion of this issue, see A. Downs, *An Economic Theory of Democracy* (New York: Harper & Bros., 1957); J. M. Buchanan and G. Tulloch, *The Calculus of Consent* (Ann Arbor: University of Michigan Press, 1962); and M. Olsen, *The Logic of Collective Action* (Cambridge: Harvard University Press, 1965).

[7] Many firms do this. J. M. Fremgren, "Capital Budgeting Practices: A Survey," *Management Accounting* (May 1973), pp. 19–25, reports one of the leading "nonfinancial considerations" to be "social concern or enhanced community relations."

[8] J. S. Coleman, *Power and the Structure of Society* (New York: W. W. Norton, 1974).

[9] L. J. Gitman and J. R. Forrester, Jr., "A Survey of Capital Budgeting Techniques Used by Major U.S. Firms," *Financial Management* (Fall 1977), p. 68, report that a large proportion of executives studied indicated "project definition and cash flow estimation" as both the "most difficult" and "most critical" stage in capital-expenditure management. J. C. T. Mao, "Survey of Capital Budgeting: Theory and Practice," *Journal of Finance* 25 (May 1970), p. 359, suggests that since accurate cash flow estimates are crucial to evaluating business investments, theorists can contribute more by developing concepts and techniques to assist executives in making more reliable cash flow forecast (than presumably concerning themselves with other issues). It is not clear that financial theorists have much to offer in that regard, although others may.

[10] As described in, for example, D. Novick, ed., *Program Budgeting* (Washington, D.C.: U.S. Government Printing Office, 1965), and *The Analysis and Evaluation of Public Expenditures: The PPB System,* vol. 1, Joint Economic Committee, 91st Congress, 1st Session (Washington, D.C.: U.S. Government Printing Office, 1969).

[11] Extensive discussion is given in P. A. Pyhrr, *Zero-Base Budgeting* (New York: Wiley, 1973). An earlier, condensed discussion may be found in P. A. Pyhrr, "Zero-Base Budgeting," *Harvard Business Review* (November–December 1970), pp. 111–21.

[12] M. J. Gordon, *The Investment, Financing, and Valuation of the Corporation* (Homewood, Ill.: Richard D. Irwin, 1962), p. 219.

[13] See also J. S. Schnell and R. S. Nicolosi, "Capital Expenditure Feedback: Project Reappraisal," *The Engineering Economist* 19, no. 4 (Summer 1974), pp. 253–61.

[14] G. A. Welsch, *Budgeting: Profit Planning and Control,* 4th ed. (Englewood Cliffs, N.J.: Prentice-Hall, 1976), pp. 355–80.

[15] J. L. Bower, *Managing the Resource Allocation Process* (Boston: Division of Research, Graduate School of Business Administration, Harvard University, 1970).

Problems

1. Which of the following groups do you think would be the most suitable to assume responsibility for evaluating proposed capital expenditures in a medium-sized firm? Why?

   a. The accounting department.

   b. The engineering department.

   c. A special group reporting to the sales manager.

    d.   The purchasing department.

    e.   Someone else.

2. *a.*   Reclassify the projects listed in problem 3 of Chapter 1 as to whether they are (*i*) routine, or (*ii*) strategic.

    b.   Does this classification affect your previous answer to part (*b*) of that problem?

3. Construct flow charts showing the steps in the capital expenditure process in (*a*) the federal government, (*b*) a system you would regard as ideal. Ignore the actual evaluation procedure and decision criteria, but focus your attention on identifying the location of responsibility for various steps in the overall process, the structure of controls, and the information feedbacks in the system. Compare the two.

The evaluation process: criteria for measuring desirability

3

3.1 Basic requirements

A systematic review of the literature on capital-expenditure decisions will reveal a bewildering variety of suggested criteria on which to base them. Terborgh, in a review of the literature to 1948, found several dozen proposed rules for equipment replacement decisions alone, most of which he stated "are theoretical orphans" which "border on superstition."[1] If the whole literature on capital-expenditure decisions (including that dealing with government decisions) were surveyed, many more could be added to this list, although it is questionable whether more light would be shed on the problem in the process.

Our discussion of criteria will be confined to the most widely used and will attempt to produce some order out of chaos. Except as indicated, our theoretical discussion will continue to be based on the assumptions of perfect certainty and perfect capital markets introduced in Chapter 1. In particular, we will derive some techniques for project evaluation from the market-value rule and use these as a standard of comparison for evaluating alternative criteria. Part of the conflict among the different criteria arises out of the possible multiplicity of goals which are apparently being sought. A major part of the confusion is due to attempts to deal with risk and uncertainty without introducing them explicitly into the analysis. This is especially true in connection with the continued use of the payback criterion in Section 3.8. In addition to our earlier assumptions regarding the decision environment, we will assume for purposes of this chapter that the goal to be sought is either long-run maximum profit (maximum wealth for current stockholders) in the case of the firm, or efficiency in the use of capital (in the case of society as a whole), as discussed in Chapter 1.

While the market-value rule, wealth-maximizing optimum investment decision found in Chapter 1 is correct under our assumptions, it is not yet quite in the form that can be given to managers for choosing among capital-investment opportunities. There are several remaining difficulties: first, the criterion implicitly deals with the whole capital budget, not with particular projects; and second, we derived the criterion in the single-period context, whereas capital assets have lives extending far into the future. This latter would not be a problem if there existed markets for these real capital assets (similar to the capital markets for claims against income) that are also perfect in the economists' sense. We implicitly assumed the existence of such markets in Chapter 1 when we spoke of converting our resources into money or consumption goods either now, and especially in the future. With such markets, the multi-period problem can be shown to be nothing more than a repeating sequence of similar single-period problems.[2] For each such single period decision, we would find the optimum using the information on productive opportunities and prevailing market rates of interest relevant to that period, then by extension of our earlier argument, use the market rates to discount all of the single-period present values back to the current time. Note, however, that the market rates of interest need not be the same in all future periods, as they will depend on economic conditions then prevailing. We now explicitly assume that the market rates of interest will be equal for all future periods so that we may refer to the rate of interest, or *discount rate*.

On this argument, in the multi-period context, the *strategic* capital-budgeting decision requires the firm to consider *all possible present and future* productive investment opportunities and select from that set those which maximize present value (stockholders' wealth), as calculated earlier. The options selected for each period give us the *budget* for that particular period. While there is a large conputational problem implied by this solution under our assumptions of perfect certainty, we note that management needs only to solve this problem once. After the solution has been found and the optimum set of budgets specified, management need not concern itself with investment policy again. Under conditions of uncertainty, however, we may only have rather ill-defined notions of what productive investment opportunities may arise in future periods. If the market for real capital assets were perfect, we would need only to find the optimum budget one period at a time in order to satisfy the wealth-maximizing objective, because we can always costlessly sell our existing assets for their full economic (present market) value, then redirect our resources for the following period. In such markets, our current decisions do not preclude us from making any future alternative decisions. In practice, however, current decisions frequently close off future alternatives because the perfect markets for real capital assets we have been imagining are not available. It is still appropriate to give weight to future opportunities by including them in the analysis of the current budget as contingent opportunities in the definition of projects described in Section 3.3.

In considering capital-expenditure decisions, in which time must enter as an explicit feature of the calculation, maximization of profits will be taken to mean maximization of the *present value* of (long-run) profits, according to the wealth-maximizing, market-value rule. Present value is used to provide a common yardstick, enabling us to resolve conflicts which might arise between present and future profits in the operational definition of the long run. In the next section of this chapter, we will define exactly what measures the manager should use to represent suitably the benefits and costs which produce the relevant profit in the private sector context.

Any criterion must provide at the least a means of distinguishing between acceptable and unacceptable projects. It must also solve the problem of choosing techniques; if there are two acceptable ways of doing something, it must choose between them. This is also known as the problem of choosing among *mutually exclusive alternatives*. For several reasons, which we later show to result from departures from our perfect capital-market assumptions, we would also like our criterion to provide us with a ranking of projects in order of their desirability. In some respects, it may seem simpler to provide a ranking than a clear-cut yes or no. On the other hand, alternative criteria which produce identical accept-reject decisions may not produce identical rankings, so we must tread warily and understand the reasons for this inconsistency, and how to resolve it, if we are to use the appropriate criterion in particular circumstances.

In reaching decisions, any suitable criterion must respect the following two principles:

1. The "bigger-the-better" principle: Other things being equal, bigger benefits are preferable to smaller benefits.
2. The "bird-in-the-hand" principle: Other things being equal, early benefits are preferred to later benefits (the market-value rule implies these contribute more to current wealth).

As the other things which must be held equal for each of these principles includes variables on which the other depends, and as other things are seldom equal in any event, these principles themselves can hardly be used as criteria. And yet some means must be found of taking account of both in a single yardstick.

Finally, our preferred criterion must be one which is applicable to any conceivable investment project. As long as the investments being considered are fairly similar in terms of size, life, and the time shape of the benefits streams, many of the proposed criteria will do a tolerable ranking job, if that is to be the criterion for choice. When something of a different nature comes along, they may fail signally to give it an appropriate ranking among the conventional alternatives. Present-value measures, however, never fail to distinguish between acceptable and unacceptable alternatives in the circumstances we have assumed.

3.2 Cash-flow concept of profit

We have spoken repeatedly of the wealth-maximizing, market-value rule which managers must use for capital-expenditure decisions, but we have only vaguely alluded to certain benefits and costs which somehow produce long-run profits which satisfy this rule. For the private sector at least, we may identify these benefits and costs as cash inflows and outflows associated with a project, using a cash-flow model[3] of the market valuation of the common stock held by stockholders and assumed to be traded in a perfect capital market. The standard economic theory of the firm has been based on a concept of long-run profit maximization where profit has been somewhat loosely defined as the difference between revenue received from goods produced and sold during some period, and the payments made to productive factors embodied in that product. This concept of profit is difficult to relate to our wealth-maximizing objective, and thus to apply meaningfully to capital-expenditure decisions. If, however, we define profit in cash-flow terms, then by means of a cash-flow theory of stock valuation, we may provide the necessary link between profit and wealth maximization.

The cash-flow concept of profit has three desirable properties: (*a*) it can be used in decision making within the firm, since profit maximization in cash-flow terms is in the stockholders' interest; (*b*) the profit of the firm in cash-flow terms coincides with the stockholders' income in each time period; and, (*c*) past profit can be measured from market values, so that it is an objective measure of performance.[4]

The cash flow discussed here is the net cash flow between the firm and its stockholders. When the firm pays a cash dividend or repurchases stock, this is a positive cash flow. Conversely, a negative cash flow occurs when the current stockholders contribute more cash to the firm than they are receiving from the firm, such as exercising rights or warrants or a new stock subscription. The associated theory of stock valuation is based on several assumptions, many of which are already familiar to us. These are (*a*) the cash receipts and cash payments of the firm have been projected for each time period forever; (*b*) there are no transaction costs in buying or selling the firm's shares; (*c*) there are either no taxes, or at least no differential tax rates, on income or capital gains so that stockholders are indifferent between them. The *cash-flow theory of valuation* then says that the current total market value of all the outstanding stock is the present value of the future net cash flows as defined. Note that this theory implies that stockholders do not care whether the firm repurchases stock or pays cash dividends, since either one is a cash flow from the firm to the stockholders, or even whether the stockholder sells a suitable fraction of his shares to someone else other than the firm for cash at the current market price. He receives the same amount of cash each way, so each has the identical impact on his current wealth position, from this point of view. Therefore, the stockholder is indifferent to holding or selling out his shares under our current assumptions of certainty and perfect capital markets because all productive opportunities must yield the same market (risk-free) rate of return to be adopted. Otherwise he can always lend his cash at the same return. Under other assumptions, he might not be quite so sanguine about disposing of the particular shares he currently holds.

The apparent emphasis of this theory on dividend payments should not be misconstrued to imply that this is the same as a *dividend-valuation model* and thus to imply that dividend *policy* is important in determining the value of shares. This is not the case and under our assumptions cannot be the case (see Chapter 6). If the firm decides to undertake an investment project, it is irrelevant whether the firm retains cash and reduces cash dividends or pays cash dividends to the current stockholders and then finances the new project by selling these same stockholders new stock. The important point in the context of deciding to accept or reject a project is that, if the present value of the net cash flows from the project is positive, then the wealth of the stockholders would be increased by that amount according to the valuation model, and the project should be accepted. Again, whether earnings are retained (cash dividends withheld), or new stock issued to current stockholders to finance the project is irrelevant to the decision.

The definition of net cash flow in any period in the development of this theory is that it is the difference between cash received by the firm from purchasers of its products, or the proceeds of borrowing arrangements made with banks or bondholders, and the cash used by the firm to pay for goods and services employed in making its products, or to pay interest, retire debt, or perhaps to *lend* (purchase marketable securities, or hold accounts receivable). The cash proceeds from sales and the cash payments for productive services are directly related to the projects representing the firm's productive opportunities. Since the other cash flows are related to financing arrangements and thus irrelevant to the investment decision, we will define the relevant *benefits* to be the cash inflows from sales and *costs* to be the cash outflows to pay for productive inputs. We will, however, *net* the payments for labor and commodity inputs against the receipts to get *net benefits* and treat cash outlays for capital goods separately, as that is our main focus. In essence, the question we address is *whether the former inflows justify the latter outflows?*

3.3 Definition of projects

In spite of the dearth of suitably perfect markets for real capital assets, we will restrict ourselves for the time being at least to considering how best to determine the *current capital budget*. This budget will consist of all productive investment opportunities to be undertaken in the current period. The problem is to choose that set of opportunities which both defines the efficient productive opportunity set, and also selects the optimum, wealth-maximizing point in that set. We need to devise an efficient, operational method of determining this optimal budget by suitably defining and then choosing its constituent projects.[5]

For our purposes, it is useful to distinguish between two types of productive investment opportunities: those which are *economically independent* of one another and those which are *economically dependent* in some way. By *economic* dependence, we mean that the costs or benefits of one project (and thus the cash flows in the private sector) are affected by the acceptance or rejection of another project, although not necessarily the converse. Such dependencies would include *externalities,* where some benefits are conferred and/or some costs are imposed, which is particularly important in the public sector; *contingent* projects, where one is available only if the other is also accepted; and, *mutually exclusive* projects, where the adoption of one project necessarily precludes the adoption of the other (this latter case is most frequently encountered in the choice-of-techniques problem).[6]

The importance of being able to define an economically independent project is that the only decision which the manager then needs to make is whether to accept or reject this project. That is, independent projects may be evaluated independently, and the subsequent combination of correctly chosen projects clearly and efficiently defines the optimum, current capital budget. This being so, we must take care to define projects that are independent to ensure that our procedure is both efficient and correct. A *project* will be made up of a set of productive opportunities to meet the following conditions: (*a*) each opportunity included within a project will be economically independent of all other opportunities excluded from that project; (*b*) whether an opportunity included in a project is, in fact, accepted is *conditional* on the project itself being accepted, thus a project is rejected only if all the opportunities within it are rejected, and conversely, acceptance of an opportunity implies that its associated project has been accepted; (*c*) every opportunity *must* be included in some project, even if it stands alone; and (*d*) no opportunity can belong to more than one project.[7]

Although it may seem wrongheaded at first glance, the most efficient situation would be where all opportunities are independent projects. It is more efficient, however, to approach investment analysis by breaking opportunities into the maximum number of projects. This procedure is efficient because we thereby maximize the number of independent decisions that can be made and minimize the number of combinations of alternatives that must be considered.[8] This also implies that, where possible, each project should be further divided into as many *conditionally independent* subprojects as can be defined. This means defining sets of opportunities whose benefits and costs are economically independent of other opportunities within the overall project but will only be implemented if the whole project is undertaken. A certain amount of judgment is required in applying this definition of independence, as it is unlikely that it is the case that any two projects are absolutely independent. At best, it may be an approximation, but one that must be exploited to minimize costs of evaluating projects.

We earlier remarked that one special form of dependence among opportunities occurs when they are mutually exclusive. We now emphasize that *any* form of dependence *must* be cast as a representative set of mutually exclusive alternatives for evaluation, where each alternative is a suitably designed combination of opportunities. In particular, we note that the concept of economic independence means *total* independence for all future time, otherwise a special form of contingent relationship exists. In that case, the combination being evaluated would consist of the current and future projects together, not just the current project, to ensure an optimal current budget. From this set, the best alternative will be chosen to represent the project, and the project will then be accepted or rejected on the basis of that alternative. Finally, we observe that this procedure of defining opportunities, constructing the maximum number of independent projects, and then evaluating will be the most efficient regardless of which criterion is used for evaluation.

3.4 Net present value

Given the development presented in Chapter 1 and to this point in this chapter, we follow the somewhat unusual strategy of presenting the net present value criterion first. We do this in order to demonstrate that it meets our two standards and is implied by the market-value rule. The net present value criterion may be used both for choice among alternatives within projects and also for selection of projects to be included in the capital budget. Under our assumptions, it is always an appropriate method of analysis and thus will serve as a standard for comparison with other criteria which will be presented subsequently.

Net present value is simply the difference between the present value of benefits (cash inflows) and the present value of costs (cash outflows). If we define Q_t to be benefits to be received in period t, and, correspondingly, C_t to be costs, we may represent net present value (NPV) algebraically as:

$$\text{NPV} = \sum_{t=0}^{n} Q_t(1 + r)^{-t} - \sum_{t=0}^{n} C_t(1 + r)^{-t} \qquad (3.4.1)$$

where r is the required (market) rate of return, and n is the number of periods in the life of the project. Alternatively, if we define a *normal* project as having a single large outflow at the beginning, say C_0, and net inflows (possibly negative) $Q_1, \ldots, Q_n$, we may write equation 3.4.1 more simply as:

$$\text{NPV} = \sum_{t=1}^{n} Q_t(1 + r)^{-t} - C_0 \qquad (3.4.2)$$

Expressed either way, any project for which net present value is positive should be accepted into the current capital budget. Under our assumptions, the positive net present value measures the increase in the value of the shares of the firm which would occur once the capital market learned of the acceptance of the project. Stockholders could either dispose of their stock immediately or wait for the cash flow to be realized. Either way, the net present value is the increase in present consumption or wealth available to the stockholders.

It may be clearer if we relate this net present value concept to our earlier theoretical model and the figures used to express it. In Figure 3–1, the market lines, such as K_0K_1, are lines of constant present value $[K_0 = K_1/(1 + r)]$ as noted earlier. The net present value of any selection of investments can be found by simple geometry. Assume that the firm was originally at the point K_0 so that all resources could be converted to cash flow in the first period. It could, however, choose to invest some of these funds in the productive opportunities shown by the frontier. The net present value of any point on the productive opportunity frontier may be found by drawing through that point a line of slope $-(1 + r)$, say through point x, and dropping a perpendicular through x to the horizontal axis at point x'. That segment of the horizontal axis lying between x' and the intercept K_0' of the market line

Figure 3–1
Net present value criterion

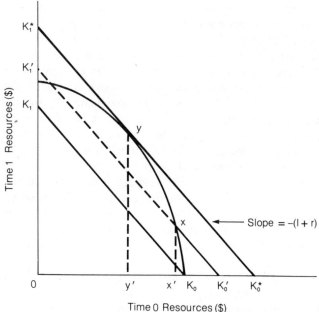

Time 0 Resources ($)

through x with the horizontal axis measures the *gross* present value from accepting the projects which constitutes the capital budget represented by x. The net present value of this capital budget is found by subtracting the present value of the required investment outlay, $x'K_0$ from the segment $x'K_0'$.

The length of the net present value segment can be enlarged by continuing to move up along the productive opportunity frontier from point x to point y, where the length of the net present value line segment $K_0K_0^*$ is maximum. However, going beyond point y would begin to reduce the length of the net present value segment. Thus the point y which represents the optimal capital budget can be attained by accepting all projects whose net present values are positive and rejecting all those projects whose net present values are negative. Projects with zero net present value are a matter of indifference.

The net present value criterion satisfies our two principles set out at the beginning of this chapter. It looks at all the benefits to be gained from the project and uses them to compare the magnitudes. It also weighs benefits to be expected earlier more heavily by virtue of the discounting implied by the market-line evaluation.

Some practical difficulties are associated with the use of the net present value rule which our simple analysis has abstracted away. Coping with some of these difficulties will occupy us at some length in subsequent parts of this book. First, real world capital markets are not always as perfect as we have assumed. If, however, we cannot assume that capital markets are reasonably perfect for practical purposes, virtually all finance theory is of questionable validity and value. Worse still, we have nothing of a general nature to use in its place. While some progress is being made in incorporating certain specific sorts of departures from these assumptions into the framework (for example, divergence between borrowing and lending rates), the resulting models become complex. Second, in the real world we must cope also with uncertainty, in this context with respect to the cash flows which we anticipate from projects, and with respect also to the future projects which may be available to us. We present one modification to the net present value criterion, the notion of *modified certainty,* later in this chapter and subsequently undertake an extensive analysis of the impact of uncertainty on the market-valuation model in Chapters 11 and 12.

To summarize, we have only shown that the net present value criterion will produce correct accept-reject decision for projects, and thus an optimal capital budget, under our assumptions of perfect capital markets and perfect certainty. Granting that, we will, however, find that no other criterion is as reliable, even under these restrictive conditions.

3.5 Terminal value

A present value figure can be turned into a terminal value at the planning horizon n periods hence simply by multiplying the present value by $(1 + r)^n$. Thus, accepting all projects with a positive net present value is equivalent to accepting all projects with a positive net terminal value. If nothing is gained by the change in focal date for the evaluation, why would we even mention it as an alternative? Recall, however, that we mentioned the possibility that in a multi-period context, the market required rate of return might be different in each period, but that we would assume it to be the same. When the rates are different, it is sometimes easier and more correct to compound ahead using explicit assumptions regarding future interest rates than to discount back.[9] We will also find certain other conditions where this criterion has been recommended to deal with special problems, such as the problem of reinvestment rate assumptions discussed later.

3.6   Internal rate of return

The internal rate of return is another widely used measure of investment worth that takes the interest factor into account. It is also known as the *marginal efficiency of capital*,[10] or the *rate of return over cost*,[11] and by a number of other names.

By definition, the rate of return is the rate of discount which will equate the present value of the net benefits with the cost of the project. As such, it makes no reference to any economic values outside of the benefits and costs associated with the project, thus it is termed *internal*. The internal rate of return may be found by solving the following equation for r:

$$\sum_{t=0}^{n} Q_t^{(1+r)^{-t}} = \sum_{t=0}^{n} C_t(1 + r)^{-t} \qquad (3.6.1)$$

where r is the (internal) rate of return, and the other quantities have the meanings previously ascribed to them. In the following discussion, we shall denote the present value of benefits as V:

$$V = \sum_{t=0}^{n} Q_t^{(1+r)^{-t}} \qquad (3.6.2)$$

and that of costs as C:

$$C = \sum_{t=0}^{n} C_t^{(1+r)^{-t}} \qquad (3.6.3)$$

The decision rule for the internal rate of return is to accept any project whose internal rate of return is equal to or greater than the market required rate of return and to reject those projects whose internal rate of return is less than the required rate of return. The calculations required to find r are more complex than those for net present value. Indeed, we may have to calculate a whole series of net present values before we have found the rate we are seeking. To find the value of r, we are required effectively to solve a polynomial in r, and in most instances, one of high degree corresponding to the number of periods for which we have cash inflows. Manually, this can only be solved by trial and error. The approach is to pick an estimated rate,[12] calculate the present values, then sum to find $V - C$. If $V - C$ is positive, a higher rate must be tried; if it is negative, a lower rate must be used. If $V - C = 0$, the initial guess was fortunate and the rate has been found. Otherwise, the procedure is continued until a rate is found for which $V - C = 0$ or, in practice since not all values for r are tabulated, two rates are found for which, respectively, $V - C$ is positive but small and

$V - C$ is negative but small. The correct value is then found by interpolation to some desired accuracy. Since finding the roots of polynomials is a standard problem in numerical analysis, the necessary calculations can be easily and efficiently performed using a digital computer (or even using some hand calculators).

It can be shown why the internal-rate-of-return criterion will lead to the same optimal capital budget as the net present value criterion when used for accept-reject decisions. As before, in Figure 3–2 the market

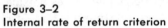

Figure 3–2
Internal rate of return criterion

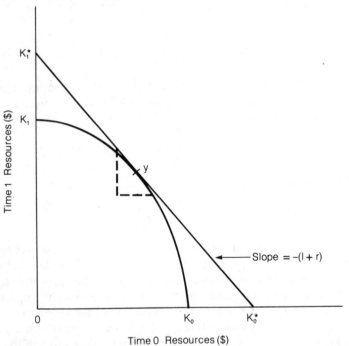

Time 0 Resources ($)

rate of return can be represented by a line with slope $-(1 + r)$ and the productive opportunities of the firm by the frontier K_0K_1. For the simple single-period case illustrated here, the internal rate of return is that rate which, when used as a discount rate, equates the value of sacrifices now with the present value of gains later. Assuming that projects are infinitely divisible, the slope of the opportunity curve at any point measures the incremental return from the marginal project at that point. To find the optimal capital budget, the firm can be imagined to start at point K_0 and to accept all projects whose internal rate of return is greater than or equal to the required market rate of return. This is equivalent to moving along the frontier until the point y is reached, which is the optimal capital budget as before. The projects selected will be the same as those suggested by the net present value criterion. Thus, for accept-reject decisions, both criteria give the same results.

Example 3.6.1: A project costs $10,000 and promises cash flow of $5,000, $4,000, $3,000, and $2,000 over a four-year life.

Required: Find the internal rate of return.

Calculations: Using the rate of 40 percent as an initial trial value, calculate the present value of the income stream.[13]

Year	Cash flow		Discount factor 40 percent		Present value
1	$ 5,000	×	0.714	=	$3,570
2	4,000	×	0.510	=	2,040
3	3,000	×	0.364	=	1,092
4	2,000	×	0.260	=	520
Sums	$14,000				$7,222

$$V - C = \$7,222 - \$10,000 = -\$2,778$$

Since the $V - C$ calculation indicates that this rate is far too high, we then try 20 percent, then 18 percent, and 16 percent, with the following results:

Year	Q_t	20 Percent		18 Percent		16 Percent	
1	$5,000	0.833	$4,165	0.847	$4,235	0.862	$ 4,310
2	4,000	0.694	2,776	0.718	2,872	0.743	2,972
3	3,000	0.579	1,737	0.609	1,827	0.641	1,923
4	2,000	0.482	964	0.516	1,032	0.552	1,104
			$9,642		$9,966		$10,309
$V - C$			-358		-34		309

The rate which makes $V - C = 0$ lies somewhere between 16 and 18 percent. By interpolation, it is:

$$16 + \left(\frac{309}{343} \times 2\right) = 17.8 \text{ percent approximately.}$$

That this is the rate of return on the outstanding balance can be shown by deducting this return from the cash flows in each year, using the balance of the cash flow to reduce the amount outstanding each year:

Year	Cash in	17.8 percent return on balance	Reduce investment	Balance at year end
0	$ 0	$ 0	$ 0	$10,000.00
1	5,000	1,780.00	3,220.00	6,780.00
2	4,000	1,206.84	2,793.16	3,986.84
3	3,000	709.66	2,290.34	1,696.50
4	2,000	301.97	1,698.03	(1.53)

The $1.53 overrecovery results from the rounding of the initial return estimate and/or the use of straight-line interpolation.

Note that the internal rate of return satisfies both of our fundamental principles and makes satisfactory accept-reject decisions. It can also be used to choose between mutually exclusive alternatives, providing we use it to find the internal rate of return on the *incremental investment* required for the more expensive or capital-intensive technique. This is a very important qualification. By way of illustration, we present the following example.

Example 3.6.2: Alternative A costs $1,000 and produces receipts of $500 per year for three years. Alternative B costs $1,200 and produces receipts of $600 per year for three years.

Required: What is the incremental return on the extra investment in alternative B?

Calculations: Alternative B can be viewed as being comprised of two contingent alternatives, A′, identical to the actual project A, plus B − A′, for which the income stream is the difference between that of alternatives B and A. We then calculate the internal rate of return on this second project B − A′.

Year	B	A′	B − A′
0	$(1,200)	$(1,000)	$(200)
1	600	500	100
2	600	500	100
3	600	500	100

This rate of return is found to be 23.7 percent. Choosing alternative B over A would be sensible providing that the required rate of return is less than 23.7 percent and that alternative A is already acceptable as a project on its own merits.

Computationally, finding an internal rate of return is more difficult than using the net present value criterion, if only because it involves repeated application of the same calculation which need only be done once, given the required rate of return. Nevertheless, this is a lot of heavy artillery which may not be readily available or necessary.

Conceptually, the notion of internal rate of return ought to be simple enough, for it is identical to that of the yield on a bond and is even referred to as *yield* by some writers. Apparently, this is one reason for defining and discussing it because it is familiar to many people who deal with financial markets. While it will usually provide accept-reject decisions identical to those of net present value for projects to be included in the overall capital budget, it tends to break down when used for choosing among the mutually exclusive alternatives being examined within a project. One reason for this is that the correct way of making such comparisons using this criterion must be to compare benefits and costs on an *incremental* basis. This may lead to a situation where the internal rate of return is not uniquely defined (see Section 3.16). While attempts have been made to force all alternatives to fit into the same mold one way or another, the Procrustean properties of these attempts, together with their questionable economic interpretations, force us into a fairly complete examination of some hidden assumptions (see Section 3.14).

An added advantage often cited in support of the internal rate of return is that it is alleged to provide a ranking of projects which is independent of any assumptions regarding the required rate of return. As we will see, this is only apparently true and is of questionable benefit in any case.

3.7 Urgency or necessity

These are superficially appealing criteria, particularly in the public sector where they are frequently given a moral overtone by indignant refusal to compromise human values for mere dollars and cents. Yet, either as a criterion is usually a semantic cover for the lack of any criterion at all. Satisfying unlimited human wants requires the use of resources which are limited in amount even in an affluent society, so that using them in one way necessarily implies that they cannot be used in another. Objection to the prices sometimes attached to human values may be quite appropriate on moral or philosophical grounds, but objection to the use of prices attached to scarce resources is an invitation to a needless sacrifice of the human welfare (which allegedly motivates the objection in the first instance) by wasting those resources through inappropriate uses. Acceptance of projects on the grounds of necessity or urgency means that they are accepted on the basis of nothing more substantial than the persuasiveness of their proponents. The only valid measure of urgency in a firm which seeks to maximize profits is the contribution of the project to that goal. In the public sector, a project is not needed unless it benefits the community by an appropriate margin over what it costs the community. If a project does not contribute appropriately to the attainment of the goals of the organization, then it is a figment of the imagination to describe it as either urgent or necessary.

Merely to insist that these characteristics are derivative rather than intrinsic is not to deny their existence or importance if properly understood. Under certain circumstances of genuine emergency, necessity or urgency may provide suitable and sufficient justification. Insistence on involved calculations may be a pedantic quibble, but more often this will lead to significant wastes in situations where complete production stoppages will persist until a minor tool is replaced or repaired, for example. Line managers should, and frequently do, have the authority to make emergency expenditures in such situations, subject to subsequent review to control abuse. Otherwise, if there were not suitable controls, pet projects which would not gain approval through normal procedures are apt to be slipped in under the guise of an alleged emergency. Again, the distinction between routine and strategic decisions is useful for determining when to delegate authority to make emergency decisions. Urgency is related to the problem of optimal timing, which is discussed in Chapter 4.

3.8 Payback

Pride of place in any discussion of investment criteria is frequently accorded to payback, not because of its merits, but because of its wide usage. Its advocates frequently stress its hardheadedness and claim that it is particularly easy to understand. Superficially this is so, but on deeper examination, it may be questioned whether it provides a reliable index of profitability. In spite of the many criticisms which have been made of this criterion, it continues to be very durable. Along with the problems of its continued use, some of the reasons for this phoenixlike quality are discussed in this section.

Payback is simply a measure of the time required for the cash income from a project to return the initial investment. The basic ranking depends on the length of the payback period, projects having quicker paybacks being preferred. The method can be extended to the analysis of the problem of choosing between more or less capital-intensive techniques by calculating the payback (out of the difference in cash flow between the two projects) on the additional investment required for the more expensive of two conflicting and mutually exclusive projects, as shown in Table 3–1. If the payback period on the incremental invest-

Table 3–1
Application of payback analysis to technique problem

	Project A	Project B	Incremental
Initial cost	$5,000	$7,000	$2,000
Cash flow year:			
1	2,000	2,500	500
2	2,000	2,500	500
3	2,000	2,500	500
4	2,000	2,500	500
Payback	2.5 years	2.8 years	4.0 years

ment for the more expensive project exceeds the minimum standard required, then the more expensive alternative should not be adopted. In the example shown in Table 3–1, if the required payback standard is three years or less, project A should be adopted rather than project B, for although project B itself meets the standard, the part of it representing the increase in investment over A does not.

Is payback a suitable criterion for evaluating projects? It is difficult to give an entirely unequivocal answer, for it does have certain advantages, especially with regard to routine decisions. In the first place, it is easy to calculate. All that is needed are estimates of the cash flows for the first few years, the ability to subtract these successively from the initial investment, and then to calculate the fractional remainder. Its apparent simplicity also accounts for its widespread popularity. But the answer to our question must unfortunately be, in general, no. It ignores the bigger-the-better principle completely in that it does not take any account of cash flows after the investment has been recovered. While it gives some attention to timing, it does not adequately satisfy the bird-in-hand principle because it gives all receipts prior to recovery a weight of one and all subsequent receipts a weight of zero. The pairs of projects shown in Table 3–2 (*AB, XY*) would be ranked equally by the payback criterion. Are they really equally desirable?

Table 3–2
Ambiguity of the payback criterion

	A	B	X	Y
Initial cost	$5,000	$5,000	$6,000	$6,000
Cash flow year:				
1	2,500	2,500	3,000	1,000
2	2,600	2,600	2,000	2,000
3	0	2,800	1,000	3,000
4	0	3,000	500	500
5	0	3,200	0	0

There are cases where all projects have long lives, substantially in excess of the payback period, and where income streams are equal from year to year. In such cases, the payback is a good approximation to the internal-rate-of-return criterion discussed in Section 3.6. However, we seek a criterion usable with any conceivable project type, for short-lived projects as well as long, for highly irregular cash flows as well as regular ones, and if such projects may have to be considered, payback is not an adequate criterion.

Some administrative difficulty arises because of the need to determine a cutoff point. This is not too serious a problem, however, as the reciprocal of the required rate of return may be used as a maximum acceptable payback period, for example, if the required rate of return is 25 percent, payback must be less than four years.

All is not quite so straightforward, however. While recognizing the desirability of using lifetime earnings estimates and giving due weight to each year, many investments are made where the income from the investment is highly uncertain and its life expectancy even more so. Under such circumstances, payback may become important not so much as a measure of profitability, but as a means of establishing an upper bound on the acceptable amount of risk exposure. Where we might appraise the near future with some confidence, but are quite unsure about longer-term prospects, a short payback period may provide some protection against loss, investment being undertaken as a sporting proposition in the hope that some of the projects will last long enough to make the whole operation profitable. In such circumstances, any attempt to maximize profits is really a gamble and not a procedure we can recommend with any confidence.

One extended discussion of the payback criterion provides an interesting set of conjectures regarding why it is so ubiquitous in spite of the criticisms leveled against it.[14] While many writers on the subject of capital-expenditure decisions espouse some of the alternative criteria we discuss, the challenging question is raised as to whether the problem which managers are attempting to solve by the use of payback is not adequately handled by any of the measures discussed here. As we will see somewhat later, the response to this challenge requires us explicitly to examine the impact of uncertainty on our decision criteria, and so we will reserve judgment on it for the time being. The challenge requires us to consider (a) payback not as a criterion as here, but rather as a constraint, (b) to think about the liquidity of capital assets versus the liquidity requirements of the firm, arising at least in part from considerations of the firm's capital structure and the probability of not meeting current obligations from current cash flows, and (c) to consider the relationship between payback and the resolution of uncertainty. We clearly need to develop our analysis further before we are able to properly appreciate the implications of all these various, alleged functions of payback. At this point, however, we repeat that given our basic assumptions of perfect certainty and perfect capital markets, we may interpret the reciprocal of the payback period as an indirect measure of return.[15] For a project of infinite life with a uniform stream of receipts, the reciprocal of the payback period is the discounted cash flow rate of return (internal rate of return). It is a good approximation to this rate for a long-lived project.[16]

3.9 Accounting rates of return

This general heading is used to describe a number of similar approaches which use accounting records or pro forma statements to measure profitability as an annual percentage of the capital employed.[17] Much heat, but little light, has been generated by a discussion of whether these are true rates of return.[18] Our answer to that in brief is that they are, if that is how you want to define the true rate of return, but whether it in any way resembles the economic, market rate of return or is particularly useful as a criterion for investment decision making, is another story.

Version 1, which is the most elaborate and the most thoroughly consistent, takes average income, as measured by a series of pro forma income statements, as a percentage of the average investment, that is, average book value after deducting depreciation. Table 3–3 indicates such calculations for a project costing $5,000 with a scrap value of $1,000 and annual incomes as shown.

Version 2 uses original cost rather than average book value as the denominator, that is, $1,250/$5,000 \times $100 = 25$ percent. This is a little

Table 3–3
Accounting rate of return: version 1

	Year 1	Year 2	Year 3	Year 4	Average
Cash income	$1,500	$2,000	$2,500	$3,000	$2,250
Depreciation	1,000	1,000	1,000	1,000	1,000
Net income	500	1,000	1,500	2,000	1,250
Book value:					
January 1	5,000	4,000	3,000	2,000	
December 31	4,000	3,000	2,000	1,000	
Average	4,500	3,500	2,500	1,500	3,000

$$\text{Rate of Return } \frac{\$1,250}{\$3,000} \times 100 = 41.7\%$$

less consistent in that income is averaged but investment is not. As an approximation to the internal rate of return, this frequently gives a closer result than using average investment.

How well do these function as criteria? The calculations are not more difficult than those for payback, except that they must be extended to cover the project's entire life. The notion of a rate of return is easy to grasp for all but the most obtuse managers. And, after all, in our earlier discussion in Chapter 1 on finding the optimum point on the efficient productive opportunity curve we did speak of finding the tangency with the capital market opportunity line where the slope is the market rate of return. That is all quite correct, so far as it goes, but the rate of return needed for that condition is the internal rate of return as shown in Figure 3–2, and not some other arbitrary definition which resembles it.

These criteria can be extended to the analysis of the choice of technique problem by an approach similar to that used in Table 3–4. There is little difficulty in relating them to measures of the required rate of return for purposes of determining a cutoff point, for they are both expressed as a percentage (although this does not necessarily imply that the percentages are comparable in terms of their economic meaning). Version 1 is probably more consistent with conventional measures of cost, at least of debt capital.

As far as the two basic principles are concerned, these criteria are compatible with the bigger-the-better principle but not with the bird-in-the-hand principle, for equal weight is given to profits earned in the first and last years. Related to this problem is the fact that the calculated year-by-year rates of return vary from year to year in version 1, even if income is perfectly stable, which is annoying to some and dis-

Table 3–4
Accounting rate of return: versions 3 and 4

	Version 3 (first year)	Version 4 (first full year)
Cash income	$1,500	$2,000
Depreciation	1,000	1,000
Net income	500	1,000
Book value:		
January 31	5,000	4,000
December 31	4,000	3,000
Average	4,500	3,500
Rate of return:		
a. On lifetime average investment	$\frac{500}{3,000} \times 100 = 16.7\%$	$\frac{1,000}{3,000} \times 100 = 33.3\%$
b. On average investment in year studied	$\frac{500}{4,500} \times 100 = 11.1\%$	$\frac{1,000}{3,500} \times 100 = 28.5\%$
c. On initial cost	$\frac{500}{\$5,000} \times 100 = 10.0\%$	$\frac{1,000}{\$5,000} \times 100 = 20\%$

concerting to many. As a result, they resolve the choice between *A* and *B* in Table 3–2, but not that between *X* and *Y*.

A second type of accounting measure is the single-year rate of return. This, as the name implies, is a measure of profit in a single year, which may be the first year (version 3), the first full year (version 4), or some other equally elusive standard. It may be applied either against average investment over the life of the project, against average investment in the year selected for study, or simply against initial cost. Table 3–4 shows the calculations for these six variants for the project analyzed in Table 3–3, assuming year one is the first year and year two is the first full year.

The widely varying results point to the desirability of ensuring uniformity of practice if an accounting measure is to be employed. These versions ignore all years except the one studied, so contravene both our basic principles. Their dangers when applied to projects having anything except a stable income should be too obvious to require elaboration. Needless to say, they resolve the ambiguities of Table 3–2, but not necessarily in a desirable fashion.

3.10 Benefit-cost ratios: undiscounted

A benefit-cost ratio is, as the name implies, simply a ratio between the sum of benefits measured in some manner and the costs of the project.

In the undiscounted version, the benefits are taken at face value, while in the discounted versions, to be discussed in the next section, calculations are complicated by a discount factor.

There are two versions of the undiscounted benefit-cost ratio. In the *gross version,* benefits are calculated without deducting depreciation, then added and the sum divided by the investment cost. In the *net version,* depreciation is deducted in computing the benefits. We have not explicitly discussed what to do with depreciation in connection with the other criteria since this is included in our discussion of measuring costs and benefits in Chapter 4.

In symbols, if Q_t is the cash flow in period t, D_t the depreciation in period t, and C the cost of the asset, the following formulas may be used to calculate benefit-cost ratios (BCR):

$$\text{BCR (undiscounted, gross)} = \Sigma Q_t/C \qquad (3.10.1)$$

$$\text{BCR (undiscounted, net)} = \Sigma(Q_t - D_t)/C \qquad (3.10.2)$$

The equation used is a matter of indifference since both give identical rankings. In fact, the net ratio equals the gross ratio minus 1.0. As the gross ratio is slightly easier to calculate, this relationship makes it simpler to arrive at the net ratio.[19]

These are easy to calculate, and it is easy to understand what they purport to measure. They are compatible with the bigger-the-better principle, since all income is taken into account, but not with the bird-in-hand principle, since early receipts are given identical weights to those late in the project's life.

3.11   Benefit-cost ratios: discounted

A discounted benefit-cost ratio is a somewhat more sophisticated tool. It is the ratio of the present value of the future benefits, at a specified rate of discount, to the present value of the present and future investment outlays and other costs, discounted at the same rate. It may be gross or net, net simply being gross minus one.

Algebraically, the gross discounted benefit-cost ratio is:

$$\text{BCR (discounted, gross)} = \Sigma Q_t(1 + r)^{-t} \Big/ \sum_t C_t(1 + r)^{-t} \qquad (3.11.1)$$

where Q_t represents the net cash inflow during a period t when the net flow is positive, C_t represents the net cash outflow during a period when the net flow is negative,[20] and r is the required rate of return per period, expressed as a (decimal) fraction.

A variation on this criterion has been called the *profitability index*.[21] In this definition, no distinction is made between Q_t and C_t, that is, Q_t may be positive or negative. The profitability index is defined algebraically as:

$$\text{Profitability index} = \sum_t Q_t(1 + r)^{-t}/C_0 \qquad (3.11.2)$$

The definition given in equation 3.11.1 is sometimes referred to as an *aggregate* form, whereas that of equation 3.11.2 is called *net*. The net index is proposed to differentiate the initial cash outlay for the current capital budget from subsequent cash outlays on the grounds that the initial cash outlay is discretionary while the rest are not. The initial cash outlay is discretionary in the sense that we may choose to commit capital funds to the project in our current capital budget or to use them elsewhere. Once the decision is made to go ahead with the project, subsequent cash outlays are already decided. We can, of course, decide to abandon a project at any time, which changes this commitment. Barring that decision, it is argued that since the aggregate index does not differentiate between initial and subsequent outlays, the net measure is a more rational choice.[22]

In either form, the discounted benefit-cost ratio takes account of all income, whenever received, and to this extent complies with the bigger-the-better principle. The discounting also effectively gives more weight to earlier receipts than to late, so it also satisfies the bird-in-hand principle.

Since net present value and internal rate of return also satisfy these principles, we might expect that somehow they are all related. We note that whereas net present value was defined in equation 3.4.1 as the *difference* between the discounted benefits and costs, the discounted benefit-cost ratio has been defined in equation 3.11.1 as their *ratio*. We may infer then that, since we may accept any project whose net present value is greater than zero, then a discounted benefit-cost ratio (profitability index) greater than 1.0 also defines an acceptable project. Apparently the same calculations are needed for both the net present value and discounted benefit-cost ratio criteria, so that they are essentially the same measure. Why then have they both been proposed? It is alleged that the discounted benefit-cost ratio is more suitable under conditions of *absolute capital rationing*, as we explore further in Sections 3.13 and 3.14.

Calculations of the discounted benefit-cost ratio are relatively simple, as the following examples show:

Example 3.11.1:

Required: To calculate the benefit-cost ratio, at a discount rate of 10 percent, of a project costing $10,000 and yielding annual returns of $4,000, $5,000, and $6,000 in the three years of its useful life.

Calculations:

Year	Annual benefits		Discount factor (Appendix A)		Present value
1	$ 4,000	×	0.909	=	$ 3,636
2	5,000	×	0.826	=	4,130
3	6,000	×	0.751	=	4,506
Sums	$15,000				$12,272

$$\text{Benefit-cost ratio (gross)} = \frac{\$12,272}{10,000} = 1.23$$

$$\text{(net)} = 0.23$$

Example 3.11.2

Required: To calculate the benefit-cost ratio at 10 percent for a project costing $10,000 and yielding annual returns of $1,000 per year for 20 years.

Calculations: Because the annual payments are uniform, it is possible to use the formula for the present value of an annuity. From Appendix B, the present value of an annuity of $1.00 per year for 20 years at 10 percent is $8.514. The present value of the benefits in this case is simply $1,000 × 8.514 or $8,514 and the gross benefit-cost ratio is 0.85.

Example 3.11.3

Required: To calculate the benefit-cost ratio for a project costing $10,000 and yielding annual benefits of $2,500, $2,000, and $1,500 for the first three years of its life and of $1,000 for the next seven.

Calculations: This is a hybrid case consisting of three unequal payments followed by an annuity lasting for seven years. While it is possible to use the technique indicated in Example 3.11.1 for the entire problem, the calculation can be simplified by treating the first three years in this manner, and the last seven as a deferred annuity. The present value of an annuity of $1 for 10 years at 10 percent is, from Appendix B, $6.145 while the present value of a three-year annuity is $2.487. The value of a seven-year annuity beginning in the fourth year is simply the difference or $3.658. The complete calculations follow:

Year	Annual benefits		Discount factor		Present value
1	$ 2,500	×	0.909	=	$2,273
2	2,000	×	0.826	=	1,652
3	1,500	×	0.751	=	1,127
4– 10	1,000	×	3.658	=	3,658
Sums	$13,000				$8,710

Benefit-cost ratio (gross) = 0.87
(net) = (negative)

3.12 Equivalent annual costs and benefits (uniform annual series)

A formula quite widely used in engineering economic studies converts capital costs, including an interest component, into an equivalent annual payment which is then compared with average annual savings or profits to evaluate the desirability of alternative projects.[23] This is a variant of the benefit-cost ratio approach, as the following discussion will indicate. Finding the equivalent annual payment is simply equivalent to finding the size of the annual annuity which has a present value equal to the cost of the asset (ignoring salvage value).

Example 3.12.1:

Required: Find the annual cost and benefits at a 10 percent discount rate of a project costing $10,000 and yielding $1,000 per year over a 20-year period.

Calculations: Since the flow of benefits is uniform, the annual benefit is simply $1,000. To find the annual costs, we must find the size of an annuity which has a present value of $10,000. The 20-year annuity factor, from Appendix B, is 8.514, and the annual cost is found by dividing $10,000 by 8.514. The resulting annual cost is $1,175. If the annual benefits are then divided by the annual costs, the resulting benefit-cost ratio is ($1,000/1,175) = 0.85. On referring back to Example 3.11.2, we note that the present problem is identical with the one discussed there. Therefore, the result is necessarily the same.

Where annual benefits are equal, it is a matter of indifference whether the annual benefits-annual costs approach or the conventional discounted benefit-cost ratio is used. Where annual payments are irregular (as they would be even in this case if there were any scrap value), the use of the annual benefits-annual costs approach requires that benefits be converted into an equivalent annual stream. To do this requires first of all that the irregular benefits be discounted to find their total present value, and, as a second step, that an equivalent annual income be calculated in the same manner used to calculate equivalent annual cost.

In these more complex circumstances, the relationship to NPV as well as discounted benefit-cost ratio is more apparent. The resulting values are frequently called *uniform annual series* (UAS), which converts an arbitrary flow into an equivalent series of equal annual flows instead of a lump sum as in net present value. For this purpose, we first discount the irregular flows to find their present value (PV), then define this as equivalent to the discounted value of a uniform annual series over the time horizon (n periods):

$$PV = UAS \left[\sum_{t=1}^{n} (1 + r)^{-t} \right] \tag{3.12.1}$$

where r is the required rate of return. On rearranging, we find:

$$UAS = PV \left\{ \frac{1}{\Sigma(1 + r)^{-t}} \right\} \tag{3.12.2}$$

The quantity in braces is the *capital recovery factor* and is frequently tabulated in engineering economy texts.

The flows being discounted may be benefits, costs, or net. But in the latter form, since it is really net present value carried one step further, why would anyone bother? If the net flows are cash flows in the case of the firm, for example, then we can think of the uniform annual series as the average annual economic profit from undertaking a project. Economic profit is accounting profit less the required return to stockholders for the use of capital. Since we know that the capital recovery factor is always greater than zero, whenever net present value is greater than zero, uniform annual series will likewise be greater than zero. As a criterion, we would accept any project whose uniform annual series is greater than zero. We will later show that when choosing among mutually exclusive alternatives, other things equal, the alternative with the higher net present value is preferred. Correspondingly, choosing alternatives with highest uniform annual series leads to long-run profit maximization in the aggregate. By a similar argument, looking only at the costs of alternatives (and implicitly assuming equal benefits), choosing the lowest uniform annual series of costs will lead to long-run cost minimization. As a consequence, costs are perhaps more useful in making the preliminary evaluations of alternative technological options before formal project design takes place than in the capital-budgeting process, narrowly defined.

3.13 Relationships between net present value and internal rate of return

The fact that both net present value and internal rate of return satisfy both our bigger-the-better and bird-in-hand conditions suggests that the two concepts are, if not mathematical twins, at least cousins.[24] And so they are. Bringing the required rate of return into consideration for a moment, the market-value maximizing rule for net present value may be stated as:

> Accept all projects for which the net present value is greater than zero, using the required (market) rate of return as the discount rate.

The equivalent rule for the internal rate of return criterion is:

> Accept all projects for which the internal rate of return is greater than the required rate of return.

The marginal investment to which we are indifferent will, in either case, be that for which the internal rate of return equals the required rate of return or the net present value equals zero.

Figure 3–3 combines both of these criteria, shown separately in Figure 3–1 and 3–2, into a single graph. Point y is still the optimal budget where net present value is maximized (using the required rate of return for discounting), and the internal rate of return is equal to the (market) required rate of return. Consider starting now at time 0 with no productive investments, but an initial wealth endowment, so that we are at point K_0 on the productive opportunities frontier, and assume that all opportunities are infinitely divisible. As we begin to move along the opportunities frontier, taking the line of slope $-(1 + r)$ through the point x as an example, we note that the distance $x'K_0$ increases, while the distance K_0K_0' increases relatively less, implying that the net present value increases at a decreasing rate. Note also that the point slope of the opportunities frontier at x is the internal rate of return, and that it

Figure 3–3
Relationship between net present value and internal rate of return

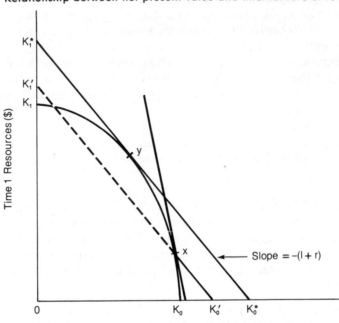

Time 1 Resources ($)

K_1^*

K_1'

K_1

y

x

Slope $= -(1 + r)$

0 K_0 K_0' K_0^*

Time 0 Resources ($)

decreases as we move away from K_0 towards y. This implies that if we rank projects in the order of decreasing values of either net present value (or discounted benefit-cost ratio), or internal rate of return, that we will get the same rankings. This result may seem contrary to much of the discussion and controversy in the financial literature which suggests possibly conflicting rankings. Our result here arises because of our assumptions, but most especially because the analysis shown in the figure is valid only for the single-period context. When conflicts in rankings among the alternative criteria do arise, it is due to the fact that we are evaluating (nonuniform) flows of benefits over many periods and are likely to get different results because of the fact that discounting of the flows uses possibly widely differing rates under the differing criteria, a problem we discuss in Section 3.14.

3.14 Practical resolution of some theoretical problems

The relationship between net present value and internal rate of return may be examined further by considering net present value as a function of the discount rate. This function may be plotted on a graph, and we will follow the convention of depicting net present value along the vertical axis and the discount rate along the horizontal axis. The resulting graph is referred to as a *present value profile* and is portrayed in the following example.

Example 3.14.1:

Required: Construct a present value profile for the data given in Example 3.6.1.

Calculations: We have present values for four discount rates in the example. For a zero discount rate, net present value is simply the sum of expected receipts minus the cost of the asset. Adding a couple of intermediate values, we have the following, which are plotted in Figure 3–4.

r	$V - C$
0	
0.05	$4,000
0.10	2,626
0.16	1,468
0.18	309
0.20	−34
0.40	−358
	−2,778

The typical profitable investment, that is, one which involves an initial outflow of funds followed by inflows which more than repay the initial investment, has a present value profile that looks something like that shown in Figure 3–4, in that it has a positive intercept on the vertical axis and slopes downward monotonically to the right (we are not concerned with the portion to the left of the vertical axis).

However, this shape is all that different projects have in common, and it is quite possible to have situations such as that depicted in Figure 3–5 where the present value profiles of two (mutually exclusive) proposals cross. This is how contradictory rankings arise. If A and B both cost the same amount, and the benefit-cost ratios are calculated at a discount rate r_1, B will be ranked ahead of A. At a rate of r_2, or at any rate in excess of r^*, A will be ranked ahead of B, as it will by the internal rate of return criterion since its internal rate, r_4 is higher than B's internal rate, r_3. This contradiction may arise whenever there is a difference in profiles of the benefits streams over time.

If we are interested only in accept-reject decisions, the contradiction is unimportant. Our wealth-maximization rule says, using the benefit-

Figure 3–4
Present value profile example

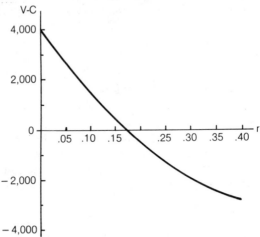

cost ratio criterion, to accept all projects for which the benefit-cost ratio is greater than 1.0 (or equivalently, for which net present value > 0) when discounted at the required rate of return, while the rate-of-return rule says to accept all projects for which the internal rate of return exceeds the required rate of return. If the required return is below r_3, both projects will be accepted regardless of which criterion is used, if it is between r_3 and r_4, only A will be accepted, and if it is above

Figure 3–5
Sources of contradiction in present value rankings

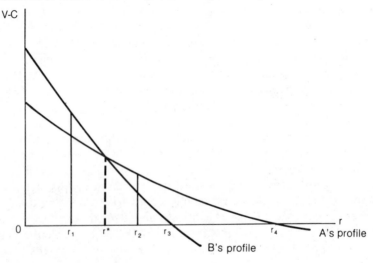

r_4, neither will be accepted. So, the choice of criteria need not affect accept-reject decisions since either leads to the same results.

Yet, the world is not always so simple. Some people feel that ranking alternatives might be desirable in at least two situations. The first situation is said to occur when choosing among mutually exclusive alternatives (choice of techniques) within a project. This is incorrect. The correct approach is an incremental analysis comparison of the alternatives as described in Example 3.6.2. In fact, ranking the individual alternatives by internal rate of return in this situation is likely to lead to an incorrect choice. The second situation where rankings are alleged to be desirable is in the case known as *capital rationing*. But, under our assumptions of perfect certainty and perfect capital markets, capital rationing need never occur. Given all the necessary information regarding productive opportunities of the firm, the interaction of consumers exercising their preferences in the capital market (as described in the model of the consumption-investment process) is assumed to lead to an *equilibrium* where the ruling price of capital is the market rate of return. This presumes that all projects we represented earlier as being included in the optimal capital budget will be undertaken, and the necessary capital will be forthcoming from the market under our assumptions. This result continues to hold even under conditions of uncertainty. However, if we admit departures from our perfect capital market assumptions, as the capital-rationing argument implicitly does, it is nonsense to continue to assume perfect certainty at the same time, unless some artificial barriers to the functioning of the markets are introduced. Relaxing both assumptions together, which is necessary for the capital-rationing idea to have any content, creates a problem situation which is much more complex and for which the optimal solution is correspondingly more difficult to find than just using simple-minded rankings. Capital-market perfection is an empirical question for practical purposes. For the moment, we retain the assumption, but will consider capital rationing again in Chapter 7.

However, in spite of this argument, the reader may have the somewhat nagging feeling that there nevertheless remains an inconsistency between the presumed equilibrium in perfect capital markets and the fact that our productive opportunities frontier depicts a range of projects whose returns are clearly greater than the market return (below point y in Figure 3–3). Is this a contradiction? Should not all *excess returns* be eliminated in equilibrium, as is always the case in perfect markets? While this is true, we are only assuming that capital markets are perfect. No such assumptions are made regarding markets for other factor inputs such as labor or raw materials nor for the market for outputs. In fact, the processes of research and development deliberately pursued by firms are intended to lead to advantageous positions.

For this reason, the institutionalization of research and development or oil and mineral exploration operations by businesses is common. Furthermore, the other parts of our society acquiesce in the vesting of property rights in the resulting discoveries or inventions to encourage commercial development on the grounds that permitting excess returns leads to economic growth. By the same token, the incidence of opportunities for excess returns causes some firms to grow, while others decline when such opportunities no longer occur and new infusions of capital are not available but rather are transferred to better uses. Without such opportunities, there can only be a steady state at best. Thus, we argue that far from being a contradiction, it is the possibility of excess returns (positive net present value) that endows the capital-expenditure decision with real significance and justifies the effort to study and understand it thoroughly.

Another basis on which net present value and internal rate of return are contrasted is with respect to differing implicit assumptions regarding the rate of return on reinvestment of positive net cash flows during the lifetime of a project.[25] The net present value method contains the implicit assumption that positive net cash flows can be reinvested at a rate of return equivalent to that used for discounting, that is, the (market) required rate of return under our present assumptions. This is illustrated by the following example.

Example 3.14.2:

Required: Find the net present value for a project having an immediate outlay of $1,000 and generating net cash flows of $500, $1,000, and $200 in years 1, 2, and 3 respectively, when discounted at 5 percent.

Calculations:

Year	Cash flow	PV factor @ 5 percent (Appendix A)	Present value
1	$ 500	0.952	$ 476
2	1,000	0.907	907
3	200	0.864	173
			$1,556
		Less initial outlay	1,000
		Net present value	$ 556

Alternatively, we may accumulate the cash flows to their terminal values at the end of the project, then find the present value of the resulting amount:

Year	Cash flow	Interest received if proceeds reinvested in		Terminal value of total cash flows at end of 3d year	Present value at time 0 of terminal value
		2d year	3d year		
1.......	$ 500	25	26	$ 551	$ 476
2.......	1,000	—	50	1,050	907
3.......	200	—	—	200	173
					$1,556
				Less initial outlay	1,000
				Net present value	$ 556

The reinvestment assumptions of the net present value method make economic sense under our assumptions of perfect certainty and perfect capital markets. Under those assumptions, any project offering excess returns should always be accepted, for such projects can always be financed. However, the existence of intermediate cash flows does *not* make possible the acceptance of any *additional* projects yielding excess returns. The use of the intermediate cash throw-off merely means that the firm can finance further projects without resorting to the capital markets. But, since such transactions are costless in a perfect capital market, the reinvested cash flow can only earn the market rate of return, so there can be no real economic gain.

The internal rate-of-return method makes a different implicit assumption about the rate of return earned on intermediate cash flows. It assumes that all the project's net cash flows can earn a return equal to the project's internal rate of return. This can be illustrated by recasting Example 3.14.2 for which the internal rate of return has been found to be 35 percent.

Example 3.14.3

Year	Cash flow	Interest received if proceeds reinvested in		Terminal value of total cash flows at end of 3d year	Present value at time 0 of terminal value
		2d year	3d year		
1	$ 500	$175	$276	$ 911	$ 370
2	1,000	—	350	1,350	549
3	200	—	—	200	81
					$1,000
				Less initial outlay	1,000
				Net present value	$ 0

Using the internal-rate-of return method is equivalent to employing a project's internal rate of return as the discount factor as the example shows. But this is equivalent to assuming that if the project in the example was not undertaken, the funds released could have been invested elsewhere at a return of 35 percent. However, as we have already emphasized, under our assumptions the opportunity cost of undertaking any specific project is measured by the going cost of funds which bears no obvious relationship to the internal rate of return of any nonmarginal project. On this basis, if we then assume reinvestment of intermediate cash flows in our example at 5 percent, the terminal values of Example 3.14.2 apply with a total of $1,801 at the end of the third year. For an initial investment of $1,000, this is equivalent to a yield of approximately 21 percent (compounded)—considerably less than the internal rate of return. This concept of return is not usually mentioned in discussions of investment criteria, perhaps because it depends on the explicit assumption of a reinvestment rate. We believe, however, that it is more meaningful economically, specifically because of that assumption. On the other hand, while it can be used for accept-reject decisions, it cannot be used for ranking alternatives along with regular internal rates of return because it is strictly noncomparable. While it should be clear that we believe net present value to be the best criterion, we suggest that if a rate of return is considered desirable, then this is the preferred measure. We will refer to this as the *modified* or *reinvestment* rate of return.

In spite of the rather tenuous assumption regarding reinvestment rates implicit in the internal rate of return, there are still some who argue strongly that it must be preferred on operational grounds.[26] The argument is that rates of return are preferred by businesses because they are more easily understood. However, the apparent similarity of the internal rate of return to the ordinary accounting rate of return may be misleading and result in incorrect decisions. It is also argued that the internal rate of return method allows the analyst to avoid measuring the required rate of return: the analyst merely generates the internal-rate-of-return data for the projects under consideration. Management then receives these data and decides where to place the cutoff rate. But the required rate of return is not ignored—it is simply introduced at a different, perhaps inappropriate, point in the evaluation process.

A further claim is made that internal rate of return allows management to adjust for risk or at least to see how much latitude exists between the apparent return and required return (somehow determined). If a substantial gap exists, then it is argued that even if things go badly, a reasonable return will still be realized. This approach implicitly discounts for risk, which may not be the best way of treating the problem. More systematic and theoretically robust methods are available (see Chapters 11 and 12).

3.15 Applicability of modified certainty criteria

As stated previously, under our assumptions of perfect certainty and perfect capital markets, there is only one required rate of return—the risk-free market rate. However, if we relax the certainty assumption a little, we will recognize that not all opportunities are equally risky. We may feel much more confident that the cash flows from one kind of project will be much less volatile than another, while recognizing that both may be variable. We might then feel intuitively that the former exhibited more possible *business risk* than the latter. We might then ask whether we could reflect this risk in the various criteria for project evaluation which we have discussed. As mentioned in the last section, the intuitive way to do this would be to attach a *risk premium*, somehow determined, to the risk-free market required rate of return and use this higher, *risk-adjusted* rate for discounting to obtain the net present value or as the standard for comparison with the internal rate of return.

A somewhat more rigorous way of viewing this would be to say that we will discount twice—once for the time value of money and once for risk. We may, however, combine this into one discount rate by defining a risk-adjusted rate of return as follows:

$$
\begin{aligned}
(1 + k) &= (1 + r)(1 + rp) \\
&= [1 + r + rp + (r \times rp)]
\end{aligned}
\tag{3.15.1}
$$

where k is the risk-adjusted rate, r is the risk-free rate, and rp is a risk premium. Disregarding the term $r \times rp$ as being of small magnitude, we see that:

$$
(1 + k) \cong (1 + r + rp)
\tag{3.15.2a}
$$

or

$$
k \cong r + rp
\tag{3.15.2b}
$$

We may then use k as our risk-adjusted discount rate in any of the criteria discussed earlier and refer to this context as *modified certainty.*

But how shall the risk premium be determined? Even though it is natural to want to "guesstimate" it on intuitive grounds, this may be less constructive than not including any adjustment at all. The way in which we may estimate rp, and thus k, also indicates the circumstances in which modified certainty may reasonably be used. Again we appeal to the market process (still assumed to be perfect) to help us, albeit by an indirect route this time. Consider a firm which is in a steady state, that is, it is operating but not growing. It has a fixed capital structure and stable profits and pays the same dividends period after period. The only capital-expenditure decisions it makes are those necessary to maintain the capital base, that is, it only makes routine replacement decisions. Then, by a set of assumptions and measurements described in Chapters 5 and 6, we may attempt to estimate the *cost of capital* to this firm. This cost may be taken as representative of the risk-adjusted required rate of return incorporating the *market price of risk* relative to this firm. The cost of capital so measured may reasonably be used as the discount rate for computing the net present value of projects for this firm which are in the same *risk class.* Any departures from the set of constraining assumptions stated earlier may mean that the empirically measured cost of capital does not represent a suitably risk-adjusted required rate of return, since under changing conditions some of the relevant costs are implicit and are not captured by the simple measurement techniques generally used. In such circumstances, we need to be much more explicit about the impact of risk.

But even if our assumptions are satisfied, or we use more sophisticated measures, our problems are not ended. For while this naive risk adjustment procedure is correct in a single-period, equilibrium context, it implies a pattern of exponentially increasing risk over time with respect to the cash flows in a multi-period context which may not accord with our beliefs.[27] To see how this arises, consider the following definition of the *risk-adjustment ratio:*

$$\alpha_t = (1 + r)^t/(1 + k_t)^t \qquad (3.15.3)$$

where the riskless rate r is assumed constant over time, and k_t is the *average* (risk-adjusted) rate of discount which applies only to period t. In order to use a constant rate of discount, k, in the modified certainty evaluation process, the average rates must be the same for all periods, that is, $k_1 = k_2 = \ldots$. From equation 3.15.3, it is apparent that this will be satisfied only if α_t is given by:

$$\alpha_t = (1 + r)^t/(1 + k)^t \qquad (3.15.4)$$

where $k_t = k$ is constant over time. But equation 3.15.4 implies that α_t *decreases* at a constant rate over time, since $k > r$. In other words, we can find some constant discount rate k which is an unambiguous measure of return under risk if and only if the risk of the expected cash flows (as measured by the ratio a_t) *increases* at a constant rate (that is, exponentially) as a function of the time at which the cash flows are expected to be realized. However, if α_t and r are assumed constant over time, then the average rates k_t must *decrease* over time. The latter might be more relevant, for example, to a mining company whose projects encompass the (contingent) stages of exploration, development, and exploitation where the risks associated with the expected cash flows clearly decrease as projects move through the stages. In general, we must conclude that a single discount rate may not be suitable to express risk as used in the modified certainty approach. However, if the analyst believes that the implicit assumption regarding increasing risk is more correct, then the modified certainty approach will lead him to decisions which reflect his beliefs.

Chapter 11 describes a *certainty equivalent* approach which uses the market price of risk derived from capital-market equilibrium under assumptions of uncertainty. There the risk adjustment derives directly from the aggregate effect of investors' risk preferences: the certainty equivalent approach uses these risk preferences directly, while the discount rate approach uses them indirectly. Although the two approaches are shown to be equivalent in the single-period context, the indirection of the discount rate approach leads to difficulties in multiperiod application.

3.16 Multiple-rate-of-return problem

In this section, we discuss one remaining and serious problem with the internal-rate-of-return criterion. Occasionally, if present values are calculated using a number of discount rates, the present value of benefits may be found to equal present value of costs at more than one of those discount rates. In other words, the project has more than one internal rate of return. As it is quite easy for the analyst to stop looking after he has found one rate, there is a possibility (indeed a strong likelihood) that in many projects for which this is true, it is overlooked. As we will see, erroneously assuming that a correct internal rate has been found may lead to incorrect decisions, and so we recommend sketching present value profiles in all cases as a form of insurance against this possibility. Several suggestions for the interpretation of multiple-rate cases have been made in the literature, but few of them make any economic sense on close scrutiny. Before examining these, however, it is desirable to understand why multiple rates may occur so that we may be on our guard.

Figure 3–6 shows sketches of present value profiles for a number of cases in which multiple rates can be found. Type B is probably the most common. What do these cases have in common? This is not very clear at first glance. Types (a) and (c) have positive intercepts on the vertical axis, indicating that *undiscounted* benefits exceed costs, but (b) and (d)

Figure 3–6
Multiple rates of return

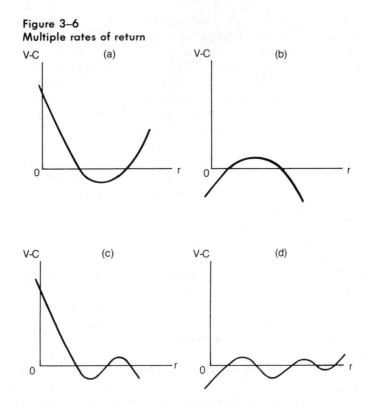

do not. Adding a requirement that undiscounted benefits must exceed costs for a project even to be considered is a device that will eliminate some multiple-rate cases, including the most common, but it will not eliminate others and is wrong anyway. One example of a well-behaved type of project (in that it has only one rate of return) is a normal loan contract. Since the amount of money eventually to be repaid to the lender exceeds the amount borrowed, benefits of the loan are exceeded by the undiscounted costs and the present value profile looks like Figure 3–7. The rate of return in the normal loan case is more familiar as the interest cost of borrowing. It makes no more sense to exclude multiple-rate projects having negative net present value from consideration than it does to exclude the possibility of borrowing. They are, in fact, an equivalent to (or more accurately, a substitute for) borrowing, as we shall see presently.

If we consider cash outflows as negative and cash inflows as positive, the typical single rate investment has a cash outflow succeeded by a stream of inflows, as shown in Figure 3–8. Net present value is thus really the *sum* of the discounted values of the stream (after we adopt the sign convention just suggested). In the normal case, we can

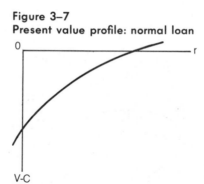

Figure 3-7
Present value profile: normal loan

find a positive rate of return if undiscounted benefits exceed costs
because as *r* is increased, benefits lying further in the future than costs
are reduced by a proportionately greater amount than costs so that for
some finite value of *r* they are reduced to equality. Since this is the
process used in finding a rate of return by trial and error, its success
depends on the alteration in sign between the initial outflows and the
succeeding inflows. If there were no alteration in sign, we could never
reduce the present value of the income-outlay stream to zero. One
alteration in sign is mathematically a necessary condition for the existence of a single, finite rate of return.

Similarly, the existence of two reversals in sign is a necessary condition for the existence of two rates, three for three rates, and so on.
These conditions are not sufficient, however. The mathematical conditions for the existence of multiple rates are discussed in some detail in
Appendix 3.A.

Are multiple rates really a problem? Since they require an income
stream such as that shown in Figure 3-9, would it not be simpler to

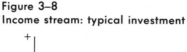
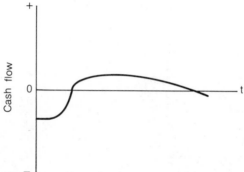

Figure 3-8
Income stream: typical investment

Figure 3–9
Income stream: dual-rate case

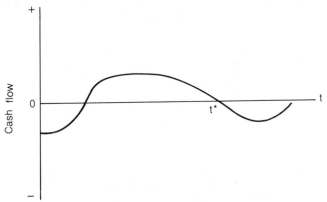

discontinue the operation at time t^* and thus avoid the subsequent losses and incidentally the multiple-rate problem?[28] Unfortunately, things are not so simple. Many projects involve positive abandonment costs. Old buildings must be torn down, abandoned oil wells plugged, strip mines filled, and so on. Failure to do so is apt to incur the penalties of the law and result in even larger terminal costs. The firm is committed to the abandonment costs at the moment it undertakes the project.

Even if it were not, the problem of choice among mutually exclusive alternatives involves calculation of the rate of return on the incremental investment in more expensive alternative. The cash flow in such cases is found by subtracting that of the less expensive alternative, period by period, from that of the more expensive. Such a process can easily lead to a multiplicity of sign reversals, as shown in the following:

| | Cash flows | | Incremental |
Year	Project A	Project B	cash flow (B−A)
0	$(10,000)	$(15,000)	$(5,000)
1	6,000	4,000	(2,000)
2	5,000	5,000	0
3	4,000	6,000	2,000
4	3,000	7,000	4,000
5	3,000	8,000	5,000
6	3,000	8,000	5,000
7	3,000	2,500	(500)
8	3,000	0	(3,000)
9	3,000	0	(3,000)
10	3,000	0	(3,000)

Another way in which sign reversal can occur in practice would be in cases involving periodic major overhauls of equipment or major replacements.

The existence of multiple rates raises a problem concerning their interpretation. Are all equally valid, or are some more valid than others? There are three basic possible interpretations. The first attempts to distinguish between *genuine* and *spurious* rates. The second treats all rates as equally valid, but it recognizes the internal rate criterion must be supplemented in cases where multiple rates exist. The third interpretation is that all rates are equally irrelevant and that the wrong question is being addressed.

Several authors have chosen to define as genuine those rates at which the net present value is decreasing as r increases.[29] A convention has also been offered for deciding which among the genuine rates is to be regarded as the rate.[30] The reason for regarding these rates as genuine is "because for higher rates of interest . . . the project is unprofitable. That is, it is the highest rate of interest it would be worthwhile to pay on borrowed money."[31]

Making a distinction on this basis would require that only rate r_3 in Figure 3–10 be accepted as genuine, for this is the only rate which is

Figure 3–10
Three-rate case

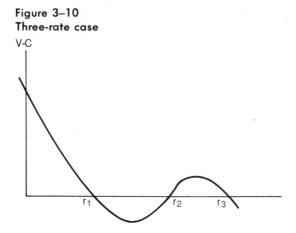

genuine in accordance with the verbal basis for distinguishing among rates. Yet this is not the procedure followed by Wright, who identified r_3 and r_1 as genuine, and r_2 as spurious.[32] McLean offers no reason for his requirement, while Massé offers a convention which requires consideration of the net present value at the company's cost of capital rate. While his procedure will generally lead to correct results, it really is equivalent to making a decision using the net present value criterion and subsequently picking a rate of return which justifies it.

Another solution proposed in the literature uses the cost of capital to discount negative portions of the income stream to a point where they can be deducted from positive flows and succeeds in producing a single rate.[33] Alternatively, we might compound the cash flows to their terminal value at the company's cost of capital, as in Example 3.14.2, then calculate an overall compound return for the initial outlay (if any), but there is no guarantee that a positive return will be found. The *return on invested capital* described below is a variation on these approaches. In any case, the rate produced by the approaches discussed here is not the equivalent of the rate found by the regular discounting process for normal single-rate projects in either a mathematical or economic sense and thus cannot be used to rank multiple-rate projects along with the others. These approaches are, therefore, rather useless except for accept-reject decisions, for which they are unnecessary.

Mathematically speaking, no grounds are available for distinguishing one rate from another, as all are roots of a single polynomial equation.[34] The verbal distinction offered by Wright has no basis, is inconsistent with his practice, and would, if applied, frequently lead to inappropriate decisions. What we are interested in is reaching correct decisions, and the quest for a genuine, correct, or true internal rate of return is irrelevant unless it leads to making better decisions. As this really addresses the wrong question and thus contributes nothing to our understanding which improves our ability to make decisions and at the same time is inconsistent with out theoretical development, the concept had best be dropped. The appropriate question to be asked is not "What is the correct rate of return?" but "Under what circumstances does it pay to invest in a project exhibiting multiple rates of return?"

The answer to this is clear from an examination of the present value profiles. If net present value is positive at the required rate of return for the project, the project adds to the wealth of the stockholders and should be undertaken. If it does not, it should be rejected. This principle holds irrespective of the number of rates of return there are and irrespective of whether the undiscounted benefit-cost ratio is above or below 1.

To see why this is so, consider the case of an investment which costs $6.00, returns $100.00 after one year, and involves a terminal outlay of $100.00 at the end of the second year. This project has an undiscounted net present value of *minus* $6.00 and two rates of return, 6.8 percent and 1443 percent. Its present value profile is sketched in Figure 3–11. If the required rate of return is 10 percent, the net present value is $2.26, and the project is profitable. This project is not dissimilar to borrowing $100.00 for a year, but paying $6.00 interest a year in advance of

Figure 3–11
Dual-rate case

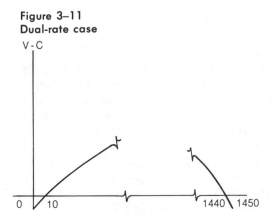

receiving the loan. It pays, if the required rate of return, that is, the cost of funds from the capital markets, is 6.8 percent or higher, because it can be viewed as an alternative temporary source of funds during the period for which cumulative inflows exceed cumulative outflows.

An analysis based on reasoning similar to this example has lead to the development of a concept of *return on invested capital* which considers the return on funds only when they are actually invested in the project, that is, when the cumulative outflows exceeds the cumulative inflows.[35] Definition of this concept is rather complex, leading to a procedure for its calculation which is quite cumbersome, and requiring computer solution in any realistic case.[36] While this analysis might be of interest in understanding the structure of the multiple-rate problem, it is too lengthy to include here. This is especially the case because as an operational tool, return on invested capital offers no advantages over net present value, and in any case, still requires prior knowledge of the required rate of return on which it is functionally dependent. Further, like the other earlier attempts, it is not equivalent to the single-rate concept, so it cannot be used for ranking, but only for accept-reject decisions. The extra complication seems to us to be unnecessary and hardly cost-effective.

To summarize this lengthy discussion for accept-reject decisions, if any multiple-rate cases are present, the internal rate of return cannot be meaningfully defined, thus it cannot give an unequivocal answer. Further, none of the alleged alternatives, however cleverly argued, is equivalent for use in ranking decisions either. The net present value criterion and correspondingly the discounted benefit-cost ratio are quite satisfactory, however.

3.17 Variant rates of return

For reasons outlined earlier, net present value measures are the preferred measures of merit for capital-expenditure decisions. The analyst
should learn to use them and obtain sufficient familiarity with them that
they may be regarded as old friends. However, some decision makers
continue to prefer a rate-of-return measure. They know that they receive one rate on their savings accounts and pay a somewhat higher
rate on their mortgages and thus feel more able naturally to relate to a
rate-of-return measure. For such persons, a measure is available which
is, in effect, a benefit-cost ratio, disguised as a rate of return and which
avoids the difficulties associated with the internal rate of return which
render it less than useful as an analytical tool.

The measure is most easily expressed as:

$$R_a = r_0 + \left[\frac{\sum_t Q_t(1 + r_0)^{N-t}}{\sum_t C_t(1 + r_0)^{N-t}} \right]^{1/N} - 1 \qquad (3.17.1)$$

where N is the life of the asset, or alternatively, a common terminal
date chosen to cover all investments under consideration, and r_0 is the
cost of capital or any other rate at which it is assumed net proceeds can
be reinvested. The benefit-cost ratio with the brackets is accumulated
forward to the terminal date, then the Nth root is taken to obtain an
annual rate of change in value, from which the rate of return is calculated.[37]

Note, however, that if we divide the bracketed term, top and bottom, by $(1 + r_0)^N$ we get the more familiar discounted benefit-cost
ratio, to which the accumulated benefit-cost ratio is equivalent,
that is:

$$\mathrm{BCR} = \frac{\sum_t Q_t(1 + r_0)^{-t}}{\sum_t C_t(1 + r_0)^{-t}} \qquad (3.17.2)$$

Thus it will suffice to find the Nth root of the discounted benefit-cost
ratio.

While this measure retains the dimensionality of an annual percentage and thus appears in somewhat familiar sheep's clothing, the analyst
(at the very least) should be aware of what it is and what it is not. It is

not a true internal rate of return, since its value is dependent on the (external) discount rate used in computing the benefit-cost ratio. Larger values of r_0 will, providing the project still produces a positive benefit-cost ratio, tend to produce higher values of R_a because of the more rapid growth of the reinvested proceeds after recovery of the initial outlays. Nor is it invariant with the choice of terminal date N. Long horizons will tend to force R_a down to its limiting value r_0, since most of the action will be in the accumulation at r_0.

Because it is variable in this fashion, it should not be viewed formally as a true rate of return, but as an annualized benefit-cost ratio added to the cost of capital rate. The discount/accumulation rate r_0 used in calculating it must always be specified, as should the term over which it is annualized. With these precautions taken, it can be a valuable device, particularly for communicating the properties of projects to senior managers whose financial sophistication is suspect.

The remaining issue is whether N should be chosen to correspond to the life of the project or to a common terminal date. Note that the benefit-cost ratio is invariant, whether discounted to the date of origin or accumulated to the project terminal date, and that further accumulation beyond that point involves multiplication of the numerator and denominator of the bracketed term in 3.17.1 by a common factor. If project life is chosen, a larger R_a will be found for the shorter lived of two projects which produce identical lifetime net benefits and equivalent present values. Getting there first is preferable only if there are above normal investment opportunities for the earlier cash flow thus generated; if the cost of capital defines the reinvestment opportunity rate, this is not the case, and it is preferable to relate all projects to a common terminal date. In certain capital-rationing situations, getting there first may be important. In general, the somewhat more formal techniques described in Chapter 7 offer a preferred basis for decision making in capital-rationing situations. It may, however, be useful for communication purposes to describe the get-there-first property in terms of the higher rate resulting from use of the (shorter) project life for the calculation, rather than a common terminal date. As it is cash throw-off during the first few years which is most relevant in a capital-rationing situation, the analytical usefulness of the measure is apt to be limited.

As suggested earlier, we believe this measure to be of primary use for purposes of communicating properties of projects to individuals who prefer to discuss financial matters in rate-of-return terms. It does, however, have the other properties associated with benefit-cost ratios which were discussed in Section 3.11.

3.18 Multiple rates and the double-switching and capital-reversing debate

Our discussion of multiple rates in the last section in the context of the choice of techniques problem (choosing among mutually exclusive alternatives) has lead us into an area where we may show a connection with a recent controversy in capital theory, described as the *double-switching and capital-reversing debate*.[38] In the (received) neoclassical capital theory, it was presumed that in the aggregate choice of techniques problem (that is, the choice of the technology to be represented in the aggregate production function for an economy), that one technology would be preferred at low equilibrium rates of return up to a point where a switch would be desirable to an alternative technology for all higher equilibrium rates of return. In our terms, a normal present value profile for the aggregate stream of incremental benefits and costs was presumed. What we there defined as the internal rate of return where the profile cut the horizontal axis is identified in capital theory as the rate of return for the economy as a whole at which the switch in technologies would occur.

The debate arose because the development of certain aggregate production functions under plausible assumptions lead to a situation which implied the existence of two such equilibrium rates, rather than a single, unique rate as had been presumed. This was interpreted as implying *double switching* or *capital reversing* where a particular technology would be preferred at low equilibrium rates, the alternative over some intermediate range of rates, but for higher rates the original technology would again be the preferred alternative. The debate was concerned with whether this made economic sense or was an artifact induced by overly simplistic assumptions in the foundations of the theory. The consensus from further inquiry seems to be that the result stands up under less restrictive assumptions, that it can be rationalized under plausible scenarios, and thus makes economic sense.

The niceties of this debate need not concern us here. We may, however, consider the description of the problem in the context of an example concerning *reswitching in a durable-machine model*.[39] Suppose we have two possible machines, both capable of performing the same technical function, and each costing the same amount to purchase (in the context of the economic model, this is in terms of the number of units of labor needed to produce either machine). Machine A yields a stream of benefits of 18 units at the end of period 1 and 54 units at the end of period 3. Machine B yields 63 units at the end of period 2. Which is preferred? The incremental stream of benefits for the comparison of

A to B is 18, −63, and 54, at the ends of periods 1, 2, and 3, respectively. To answer the question, we may tabulate the present value of this stream for various discount rates:

Discount rate (percent)	Present value
0	9
50	0
66	−0.2
100	0
200	2

From these data, we see that there are two rates, 50 and 100 percent, that give a present value of 0 (as we would expect because there are implicitly two sign reversals in the stream). Alternative A is preferred between 0 and 50 percent, switching to alternative B between 50 and 100 percent, and then back to A again above 100 percent.

Such a possibility is familar to us at the level of individual projects. The debate in capital theory seemed to result from economists being somewhat surprised that the same situation arose in the simplified models of the choice of technology for the economy in the aggregate.

3.A Appendix/Conditions for multiple rates of return

The simplest case in which multiple rates can exist is one in which the investment produces income in the two succeeding periods. In this case, finding the internal rate of return involves solving the following expression for r:

$$\frac{Q_1}{(1 + r)} + \frac{Q_2}{(1 + r)^2} - C = 0 \qquad (3.\text{A}.1)$$

where C is the cost and Q_1, Q_2 the respective receipts.

This is a quadratic equation in r, which may be rewritten in more familiar form:

$$-Cr^2 + (Q_1 - 2C)r + (Q_1 + Q_2 - C) = 0 \qquad (3.\text{A}.2)$$

Like any other quadratic, this has two roots which can be found from:

$$\frac{-(Q_1 - 2C) \pm \sqrt{(Q_1 - 2C)^2 + 4C(Q_1 + Q_2 - C)}}{-2C} \qquad (3.\text{A}.3)$$

Roots may either be real or complex and positive or negative. The only roots which admit to an economically meaningful interpretation as internal rates of return are positive real roots. By Descarte's Rule of Signs, the number of possible roots is given by the number of changes in sign between the successive coefficients of r in 3.A.2. For the normal investment project, in which C is positive, the sign of the first coefficient is negative. The sign of the second is uncertain and dependent on the numerical values in the given case, as is the sign of the third. Where the undiscounted benefits exceed the costs, however, the third coefficient is positive, which means that the sequence of signs must be either $- - +$ or $- + +$. As both of these contain only one reversal, there is only one real, positive root. In the two-period case with positive C, an excess of undiscounted benefits over costs is a necessary and sufficient condition for the existence of a single internal rate of return.

For a dual rate to exist in this two period case, it is necessary that undiscounted benefits be less than costs, that is, that the constant term in 3.A.2 be negative. As this could imply either $- - -$ or $- + -$, it is not a sufficient condition for dual rates. Unless $Q_1 > 2C$, there will be no roots at all. Where $Q_1 > 2C$, there will be an outlay, a substantial inflow of funds, and a subsequent outlay, but the availability of funds from period 1 to period 2 may make the whole venture profitable at certain rates of discount. The present value profile of this case is sketched in Figure 3–6B.

In the loan case, the conditions are reversed, and the present value profile is sketched in Figure 3–6A.

In the general case, we have:

$$\frac{Q_1}{(1 + r)} + \frac{Q_2}{(1 + r)^2} + \cdots + \frac{Q_n}{(1 + r)^n} - C = 0 \qquad (3.A.4)$$

which reduces to:

$$-Cr^n + \cdots + \left(\sum_{t=1}^{n} Q_t - C \right) = 0 \qquad (3.A.5)$$

Here there can be as many as n roots. For there to be at least one positive real root, that is, one internal rate of return, it is sufficient that the undiscounted benefit-cost ratio be greater than 1.0.

Notes

[1] G. Terborgh, *Dynamic Equipment Policy* (New York: McGraw-Hill, 1949), p. 271.

[2] E. F. Fama and M. H. Miller, *The Theory of Finance* (New York: Holt, Rinehart & Winston, 1972), p. 122.

[3] This section is based primarily on D. Bodenhorn, "A Cash-Flow Concept of Profit," *Journal of Finance* 19 (March 1964), pp. 16–31.

[4] Bodenhorn, "Cash-Flow Concept," p. 16.

[5] The following discussion is based largely on that given by C. W. Haley and L. D. Schall, *The Theory of Financial Decisions,* 2d ed. (New York: McGraw-Hill, 1979), pp. 45–53, where the reader may find a more extensive discussion.

[6] We will later encounter *stochastic dependence* among benefits and costs when we explicitly introduce uncertainty, but we leave that out of consideration until Chapter 12.

[7] Haley and Schall, *Theory of Financial Decisions,* p. 47.

[8] Haley and Schall, *Theory of Financial Decisions,* p. 48.

[9] See James T. Porterfield, *Investment Decisions and Capital Costs* (Englewood Cliffs, N.J.: Prentice-Hall, 1965), pp. 38–41, for further discussion of this criterion, as well as an example of where discounting at multiple rates of return does not give the same results as compounding at those rates.

[10] J. M. Keynes, *The General Theory of Employment, Interest and Money* (London, Macmillan and Co., 1936), pp. 135–36.

[11] Irving Fisher, *The Theory of Interest* (New York: Macmillan, 1930), p. 168. Professor Alchian disputes this identification claiming that Fisher, elsewhere, uses the concept to measure return on an opportunity cost basis, starting with the cheapest project and expanding its size only if the incremental returns on the additional investment meet the usual tests. The alternative to the cheapest investment is not investing at all, and the procedure outlined here appears to be consistent with Fisher in all respects. See A. A. Alchian, "The Rate of Interest, Fisher's Rate of Return over Costs [Sic] and Keynes Internal Rate of Return," *American Economic Review* 45 (December 1955); p. 938.

[12] The payback reciprocal, while limited in value as an investment criterion as we will see, may be helpful in picking an initial estimate.

[13] This is a bad selection for this particular example. The payback reciprocal works best for long-lived projects having relatively stable cash flows.

[14] H. M. Weingartner, "Some New Views on the Payback Period and Capital Budgeting Decisions," *Management Science* 5 (August 1969): pp. 594–607.

[15] M. J. Gordon, "The Payoff Period and the Rate of Profit," *Journal of Business,* reprinted in E. Solomon, ed., *The Management of Corporate Capital* (New York, Free Press, 1959), pp. 48–55.

[16] For further discussion see M. J. Gordon and E. Shapiro, "Capital Equipment Analysis: The Required Rate of Profit," reprinted in Solomon, *Management of Corporate Capital,* pp. 141–49.

[17] We do not intend to imply that they are used solely by accountants or that they have the endorsement of the accounting profession in general or any responsible group of accountants.

[18] See the similarly depressing discussions in the United States Congress and the Canadian Parliament of bills requiring the disclosure of the true rate of interest on installment contracts.

[19] Which follows from the relationship $C = \Sigma_t D_t$. In fact, proper treatment of economic depreciation and capital cost allowances is rather more complex than this simple-minded example suggests and is discussed in more depth in Chapter 4.

[20] This is the customary definition in which if $C_t > 0$, $Q_t = 0$, and vice versa. There are some merits in using an alternative definition which does *not* net out the cash flows but simply gives a ratio between total expected inflows and total expected outflows.

[21] J. C. Van Horne, *Financial Management and Policy,* 4th ed. (Englewood Cliffs, N.J.: Prentice-Hall, 1977), pp. 87–88.

[22] See B. Schwab and P. Lusztig, "A Comparative Analysis of the Net Present Value and the Benefit-Cost Ratio as Measures of the Economic Desirability of Investments," *Journal of Finance* 24 (June 1969): pp. 507–11.

23 This is sometimes referred to as the annual capital charge method. See A. J. Merrett and A. Sykes, *The Finance and Analysis of Capital Projects* (London, Longman, 1963), pp. 39–42.

24 We have already noted the relationship between net present value and discounted benefit-cost ratio in Section 3.11 and so leave the latter out of explicit consideration here.

25 See also E. Solomon, "The Arithmetic of Capital Budgeting Decisions," reprinted in Solomon, *Management of Corporate Capital*, pp. 74–79.

26 Merrett and Sykes, *Capital Budgeting*, pp. 158–63, in spite of admitting technical difficulties where no meaningful internal rate of return can be defined, as we discuss in Section 3.16.

27 A more extended version of the following discussion may be found in A. A. Robichek and S. C. Myers, *Optimal Financing Decisions* (Englewood Cliffs, N.J.: Prentice-Hall, 1965), pp. 83–86.

28 C. S. Soper, "The Marginal Efficiency of Capital, A Further Note," *Economic Journal* (March 1959), p. 175.

29 J. G. McLean, "How to Evaluate New Capital Investment," *Harvard Business Review* 36 (November–December 1958), p. 59; J. F. Wright, "Notes on the Marginal Efficiency of Capital," *Oxford Economic Papers* N.S. Vol. 15 (July 1963), p. 125.

30 P. Masse, *Optimal Investment Decisions* (Englewood Cliffs, N.J.: Prentice-Hall, 1962), pp. 21–23.

31 Wright, "Marginal Efficiency of Capital."

32 Wright, "Marginal Efficiency of Capital," p. 128.

33 E. Solomon, "Measuring a Company's Cost of Capital," reprinted in Solomon, *Theory of Financial Management*, pp. 128–40; Merrett and Sykes, pp. 162–65.

34 The only roots capable of interpretation as rates of return are, of course, those which are real numbers, and negative rates are of little economic interest.

35 This concept was originally developed by D. Teichroew; A. A. Robichek; and M. Montalbano, "Mathematical Analysis of Rates of Return Under Uncertainty," *Management Science* 11 (January 1965), pp. 395–403, and "An Analysis of Criteria for Investment and Financing Decisions under Uncertainty," *Management Science* 12 (November 1965), pp. 151–79. It was subsequently elaborated by J. C. T. Mao, "An Analysis of Criteria for Investment and Financing Decisions Under Uncertainty: A Comment," *Management Science* 13 (November 1966), pp. 289–91, and *Quantitative Analysis for Financial Decisions* (New York: Macmillan, 1969), pp. 197–212.

36 A. F. Herbst, "A FORTRAN IV Procedure for Determining Return on Invested Capital," *Management Science* 20 (February 1974), p. 1022.

37 Merrett and Sykes, *Capital Budgeting*.

38 An extensive literature exists, but we mention only two key articles: P. A. Samuelson, "A Summing Up," *Quarterly Journal of Economics* 80 (1966), pp. 568–83; and L. L. Pasinetti, "Switches of Technique and the 'Rate of Return' in Capital Theory," *Economic Journal* 79 (1969), pp. 508–31.

39 Adapted from Samuelson, "A Summing Up," pp. 573–74.

Problems

1. Assuming the required rate of return is 12 percent, calculate the net present value and internal rate of return for the following projects:

	A	B	C	D	E
Initial Cost..........	$10,000	$12,000	$15,000	$11,000	$20,000
Benefits:					
Year 1	6,000	3,000	6,000	2,000	5,000
Year 2	4,000	4,000	8,000	4,000	5,000
Year 3	3,000	5,000	9,000	6,000	5,000
Year 4	2,000	6,000	9,000	8,000	5,000
Year 5	1,000	7,000	9,000	10,000	5,000

2. For the projects of problem 1, and again assuming the required rate of return is 12 percent, calculate benefit-cost ratios and annual benefits and costs.

3. *a.* Sketch present value profiles for the following projects:

	A	B
Initial Cost	$10,000	$10,000
Benefits:		
Year 1.................	2,000	7,000
Year 2.................	4,000	5,000
Year 3.................	6,000	4,000
Year 4.................	8,000	2,000

b. What is the internal rate of return for each project?
c. For what range of required rates of return is project A preferable to project B? Why?

4. Projects C and D are mutually exclusive. If the required rate of return is 15 percent, which project should be chosen?

	C	D
Initial Cost	$20,000	$30,000
Benefits:		
Year 1.................	8,000	8,000
Year 2.................	9,000	9,000
Year 3.................	10,000	11,000
Year 4.................	10,000	13,000
Year 5.................	10,000	17,000

5. A mining company calculates that by continuing operations at the present rate, ore reserves will be exhausted in ten years, with an annual net cash

flow, after taxes, of $10,000 during this period. By introducing a mechanized digger, it can double output and raise the annual net cash flow to $20,000 after taxes. The digger costs $30,000. (Assume for this problem that any investment tax credits or tax credits for depreciation are taken into account in reckoning the net cash flow.) The company estimates its required rate of return to be 8 percent.

a. Calculate the cash flow stream resulting from installing the digger.
b. Should the company install the digger?
c. What is peculiar about this project?

6. Cash flows for projects A, B, and C are as follows:

	Project		
Year	A	B	C
0	$-100	$-100	$-100
1	0	100	0
2	200	0	0
3	-100	100	300

a. Calculate the payback period and net present value for each project, assuming a required rate of return of 10 percent.
b. If projects A and B are mutually exclusive, while C is economically independent, which project, or combination of projects, would be preferred using the two criteria? What do your results tell about appropriate choice of criteria for selecting projects for inclusion in a capital budget?

7. A firm has been established with an initial capital subscription of $20 million. No additional funds can be brought into the firm, but cash flows may be reinvested in the business. The stockholders have a required rate of return of 10 percent for this business and have mutually agreed that the firm will be wound up at the end of three years. In that event, the stockholders' welfare will be maximized by having the firm attain the greatest possible terminal value at that time.

Two projects are available for investment at the time the company is formed. Each project costs $20 million and provides cash flows as follows:

	Project	
Year	1	2
1	$10,000,000	0
2	10,000,000	0
3	10,000,000	$35,000,000

a. Calculate the net present value and internal rate of return for each of the projects. Which of the projects should be accepted?

b. Assuming cash flows may be reinvested at 14 percent, recalculate the net present value and internal rate of return for each project. On the basis of the new calculations, which project should be accepted?

c. At what reinvestment rate would you be indifferent between the two projects?

8. A mining firm is contemplating opening a strip mine at an initial cost of $8.8 million. The mine will be operated for only one year, providing a net cash flow of $55.4 million to be received at the end of the first year. Due to environmental regulations, the company has to guarantee to return the land to its natural state at a cost of $50 million, payable at the end of the second year. Find the internal rates of return for this project. (Hint: Make a graph that approximates the project's present value profile by calculating its net present value at 0, 9.2, 80.5, and 420 percent). If the required rate of return is 8 percent, should the project be accepted? What about 14 percent? Explain.

9. "A firm which maximizes the rate of return on its assets does not thereby maximize its profits." Is this proposition correct? Explain.

10. "A firm which seeks to maximize its long-run profits should seek to maximize the ratio of its receipts stream, suitably discounted, to its discounted stream of expenditures." Is this proposition correct? Explain.

Measuring and evaluating private benefits and costs

4.1 Some basic rules

The evaluation of projects involves estimating the benefits and costs which will result from the undertaking of these projects and then using these estimates to evaluate project desirability. Alternative measures of desirability have already been discussed; in this chapter we will examine their application to the data of specific cases. We will not be concerned here with the mechanics of estimation, which is a problem requiring the special skills of engineers, market researchers, economic forecasters, and other specialists, but with the conceptual problems involved in deciding which costs and benefits are to be considered in the analysis. There are a number of possible concepts of costs and benefits, but many of these are inappropriate for decision-making purposes. Decisions as to what should be included are difficult enough in the context of the firm; in the public sector, they are still more complex. It is here that the judgment of the analyst is critical, for once estimates are prepared, application of the decision criterion is almost routine.

The basic principles to be applied in the analysis are relatively simple. They may be summarized as follows:

1. The analysis should embrace all costs and benefits resulting from the adoption of the proposed project, from the standpoint of the optimizing unit, that is, the firm in the case of private-sector decisions and society or the economy as a whole in public-sector decisions.
2. It should be on an incremental basis, taking the difference between the resulting streams of costs and benefits with and without the project, respectively.
3. External effects, that is, indirect benefits or costs, should be taken into account to the extent appropriate to the decision-making unit.
4. In general, total benefits and costs should be calculated and compared. Netting costs against benefits is formally correct, but this can be misleading where risk is present.
5. Double counting should be avoided.

6. Opportunity costs are the relevant standard.
7. An appropriate period should be considered.

Application of these principles is best illustrated by the examination of certain rules.

4.2 Depreciation and other noncash items

The appropriate cost of an asset to be charged against operations during any given period is the opportunity cost of using it during that period, or technically, its *user cost* for that period. Obviously, when we are considering a new capital expenditure, the relevant cost to be considered is the entire capital cost, to be regarded as an outlay in the period the asset is acquired, minus its residual value on disposition, to be regarded as a cash receipt at the time it is disposed of. Depreciation or depletion should not be charged against the income produced since provision for this is implicit in the procedure of comparing or equating the discounted benefit and cost streams. To deduct it again would involve us in counting the same cost twice.

In the case where assets are already owned and their continued use is involved in the decision, the appropriate cost is user cost, that is, the reduction in disposal value resulting from the continued use of the asset for the period in question. This is particularly relevant in the replacement problem, which involves other complications and will be discussed in Sections 4.11 and 4.12. It also enters other decisions such as the following.

Example 4.2.1: A firm has a plant which was used for the manufacture of a discontinued line. The plant equipment has been disposed of, and the plant is currently vacant. The plant itself is fully written off on the firm's books, but the land is carried on the books at its original cost of $10,000, incurred 40 years ago. The property could be sold today for $150,000 net after taxes. It is estimated that the remaining life of the building is 10 years, after which it will be a candidate for demolition. Because of this, and because of its location in a declining neighborhood, its estimated (after-tax) value 10 years from now is only $70,000. The firm is considering using this property to house a new manufacturing operation, equipment for which costs $70,000 and which is expected to produce income having a *present value* of $140,000 after taxes. The cheapest alternative location would cost $100,000. Should the process be housed in the old plant or should it be undertaken at all?

If one adheres to accounting conventions, the project is highly desirable. On a conventional accounting basis, it will show a profit, since no charge will be made for the fully depreciated plant nor for the land which is, of course, not depreciable. It is clear, however, that a decision to undertake the process in this location involves a rejection of the $150,000 which could currently be realized on the sale of the property, so that an opportunity cost is incurred. Besides this, there is an outlay of $70,000 for the equipment bringing the opportunity cost of the venture to $220,000, against which we have the present value of income of $140,000 and the future value of the property, $70,000, which must be further reduced to a present value basis. On this basis, it is clear that the project as a whole is unprofitable, when the alternative of selling the property is taken into account. If the analysis is to lead to the appropriate decision, these costs must be taken into account in the evaluation process, although they are not out-of-pocket costs or costs which will appear on the books.[1]

Example 4.2.2: In other circumstances, depreciation may appear on the books but should be ignored. A mining company has a mill which costs $2 million and was installed three years ago on a concession in a remote corner of South America where the ore body unexpectedly petered out. Its estimated life was 20 years, and it has been depreciated on a straight line basis, so that its book value is $1.7 million. The company's new geologists have found another ore body which would, if developed at a cost of $500,000 after allowing for tax credits, produce concentrates having a present value of $1.4 million, after taxes. The scrap value of the mill in its present location is nil.

Should the company proceed to develop the new ore body? Some of the company's management thought not, arguing that it was silly to throw $500,000 in good money after $1.7 million of bad in order to recover ore with a net present value of $1.4 million. After this group had convinced the board of directors not to proceed with development of the mine, the accountant quit and incorporated a company of his own. Several months later he was able to convince the management to sell him the concession, complete with mill, for $50,000. After all, they had analyzed it and concluded it was worthless. Having obtained title to the property, our intrepid hero approached a member of the board and offered to sell the concession back to the company for $500,000. He was able to convince the board that the purchase would be extremely profitable, since although they would pay $500,000 for the property and an additional $500,000 to develop the mine, the present value of the ore was $1.4 million, offering a discounted benefit-cost ratio of 1.4. After due consideration, the board decided to buy the concession from him, and offered him a job as president of their company. The former incumbent had suddenly been taken ill.

In this case, the company's initial decision was wrong. Because the mill had no value in any alternative use, no opportunity cost was involved in utilizing it to develop the new ore body. No provision should have been made for depreciation in the benefit-cost analysis because no outlay was involved, and no opportunity sacrificed. This is, of course, an instance where the classic adage "Sunk costs don't matter" applies. The loss has already been incurred by building the mill. While it would not pay to build the mill to develop the new ore body, it does pay to use it if it is already there and cannot be used for anything else or disposed of. The fact that the loss will appear as annual losses in future income statements is merely one of the vagaries of the accounting process. They will, however, be less than if the ore body had not been developed. If desired, they could be avoided by writing down the book value of the mill immediately. While this is probably preferable, it might not be desired for tax reasons.

4.3 Basis for comparison—total benefits and costs

This rule is frequently ignored in practice. In theory, ignoring it is unlikely to lead to incorrect decisions, if all projects showing positive net present values, benefit-cost ratios in excess of 1.0 or rates of return in excess of the cost of capital can be adopted. Netting will not make a desirable project appear either desirable or undesirable. However where risk is present but not explicitly provided for in the evaluation process, it may make projects which are in fact quite different appear virtually identical. While explicit analysis of risk along the lines suggested in Chapters 11 and 12 is desirable, keeping benefits and costs separate may provide a useful feel for the situation in cases where no such analysis is made.

Example 4.3.1 (narrow versus wide margins): Project A has an initial cost of $250,000. It produces revenues of $55,000 annually for ten years, from which annual operating costs of $5,000 may be deducted, giving net benefits of $50,000 per year. Project B also costs $250,000, but produces annual benefits of $200,000 for ten years. Operating costs are $150,000 per year, so net benefits are once again $50,000 per year.

If future costs are deducted from future benefits, and net benefits are used in the evaluations, the two projects appear equally desirable. At a required rate of return of 10 percent, the discounted benefit-cost ratio is 1.23, the internal rate of return is 15 percent, and the net present value is $57,230. But are they equally desirable?

There are some reasons for preferring project A. Its adoption implies the commitment of resources having a present value of $280,723 (initial cost plus present value of operating expenses) to the production of output having a present value of $337,953. The discounted benefit-cost ratio on this gross basis is 1.20. Adoption of project B, on the other hand, implies the commitment of resources having a present value of $1,171,690 to produce output worth $1,228,920. Its benefit-cost ratio on a gross basis is only 1.05. The *relative* gain from the resources committed to A is greater than from those committed to B. Using net benefits overstates the true benefit-cost ratio in both cases, but the overstatement is greater in the case of the marginal project. The whole rationale of the internal-rate-of-return calculation is based on netting benefits against costs and finding the rate of discount which equalizes them. On this basis, both projects appear equal. This is a clear case of a situation where its power to discriminate (if discrimination is desired) is inferior to that of the discounted benefit-cost ratio.

But, as we argued earlier, if the firm is operating on a profit-maximizing basis, it should accept both projects. If there is a capital-rationing problem, however, and the firm chooses to rank projects on the basis of benefit-cost ratios it may prefer to adopt project A, because of the lower implicit commitment to future expenditures. Strictly speaking, however, both projects make the same addition to the firm's present value and are equally desirable uses of this year's budget. This is the wealth-maximizing decision.

At a more practical level, consider the effects of risk. If risk is present, we are presumably using certainty equivalents of benefits and costs, to be discussed more systematically in Chapters 11 and 12. Benefits and costs are estimated separately and may fluctuate to some extent independently of one another (though there may be some correlation between the two). If the variability of benefits and costs is proportionate to their size, then B is absolutely a much more risky venture than A, although relatively the same. Suppose revenues have been overestimated by 10 percent, as the result of unforseen competition. Then A's gross benefits drop to $50,000 per year, but the project remains profitable. If B's annual revenues were cut to $181,819, the present value of benefits would be only $1,117,205, and it would be clearly unprofitable. We will subsequently discuss more formal means of evaluating the risks of such alternatives. For an impartial ranking, it is desirable to estimate benefits and costs as two separate streams and compare their present values.

Example 4.3.2 (Deduction of borrowing costs and benefits):   A second case in which the netting process can lead to inappropriate results is the situation where the effects of borrowing (real or notional)[2] are netted against the results of the investment itself.

Consider two projects (machines), both costing $37,900, producing cost savings of $10,000 per year for five years. Project A, however, can be financed in part with a $30,000 loan at 8 percent repayable in 5 annual installments of $7,513. Project B can be financed with a $20,000 loan at 6 percent repayable in 5 annual installments of $4,748. If the sum borrowed is deducted from the cost of the machine and the repayments from the cost savings, the cash flows appear as follows,

Year	Project A	Project B
Initial	$(7,900)	$(17,900)
1	2,487	5,252
2	2,487	5,252
3	2,487	5,252
4	2,487	5,252
5	2,487	5,252

Internal rates of return calculated on these cash flows are approximately 17 percent and 14 percent respectively. Benefit-cost ratios, at a 10 percent assumed required rate of return, are 1.19 and 1.11. Yet, the machines themselves produce indentical outputs. On a gross basis, the rate of return is 10 percent and the benefit-cost ratio 1. In this case, netting has distorted both the rate of return and the benefit-cost ratio.

The decision to acquire the asset should be distinguished from the decision with regard to its financing and made separately. Usually there will be a difference between the riskiness of the projects which can only be obscured by lumping consideration of the projects and their financing into the same calculation. Where projects differ in risk, then different risk-adjusted required rates of return, as in our discussion of modified certainty, are necessary. If capital markets depart from our perfect market assumptions, then it may well be that this will be reflected in an incorrect market required rate of return for one project, or perhaps downright unwillingness of suppliers to provide funds at all. In that case, investment and its financing must be considered jointly. However, if the required rate of return for both projects is 10 percent, both are on the margin of indifference and might just as well not be adopted at all, a fact which is obscured by the inappropriately calculated rates of return and benefit-cost ratios.

Example 4.3.3 (Treatment of associated costs): In many public-expenditure decisions, there are not only costs incurred by the public treasury but other costs incurred by individuals or firms in the private sector in utilizing the facilities made available through the public investment. For example, where public investment is made to develop an irrigation scheme, farmers must also make substantial investments to shift to more capital-intensive agriculture. Occasionally, financing for the project itself comes from several levels of government. Our criterion would require that all costs, both public and private, go into the denominator, and all benefits into the numerator of the benefit-cost ratio.

Different practices in this regard are followed by different government agencies. In the United States, for example, the rule stated earlier is followed by the Department of Agriculture, but other agencies follow different rules. The Bureau of Reclamation deducts associated costs (in the private sector) from the benefits, as does the Army Corps of Engineers, although the latter includes contributions to project cost from local sources on the cost side.[3] The differences in results may lead to serious incomparabilities in the comparison of projects undertaken by different agencies and, even worse, may lead to inconsistent selection of priorities among projects having a different mix of federal and state costs. Differences in evaluation resulting from the different approaches are illustrated by the following example:

		Present Worth
Direct federal cost		$10 million
Direct state and local cost		2 million
Associated private cost		3 million
Benefits		20 million

Benefit-cost ratios:

a. Department of Agriculture basis $\dfrac{20}{10 + 2 + 3} = 1.33$

b. Army Corps of Engineers basis $\dfrac{20 - 3}{10 + 2} = 1.41$

c. Bureau of Reclamation basis $\dfrac{20 - 5}{10} = 1.50$

Both (b) and (c) overstate the correct benefit-cost ratio and tend to make the projects more attractive than they really are.

Eckstein has recommended that the relevant denominator be the costs incurred by the agency making the appraisal and that all other costs be considered as deductions from benefits.[4] This rule is derived by considering the size of the budget as fixed and attempting to maximize benefits subject to the agency's fixed budget constraint.[5] In our view, this is incorrect.

One cannot take the budget as fixed and independent of the available projects. The evaluation process can go a long way toward determining the size of the budget itself, as can be seen in Chapter 8. All projects meeting the target benefit-cost ratio when an appropriate discount rate has been used should be adopted. To do less leads to misallocation of resources. A similar approach, deducting subsidies from cost, may be justified in the private sector, where selfish considerations are valid. It is not acceptable in government where the criterion is supposedly the general welfare.

The use of this approach is allegedly justified by the fact that it leads to the maximum benefit for a given level of federal government expenditures (in the examples used). This ignores and treats as virtually irrelevant costs borne by the private sector and other levels of government. Even if capital rationing is necessary, it is unacceptable because it will lead to the acceptance of inferior projects simply because a larger portion of their costs will be borne by other agencies. Consider the following projects (all benefits and costs are stated on a present value basis):

	A	B
Federal cost	$ 5 million	$10 million
Private cost	5 million	
Benefits	14 million	15 million
Benefit-cost ratios		
Eckstein basis	$\dfrac{14 - 5}{5} = 1.8$	$\dfrac{15}{10} = 1.5$
Recommended basis	$\dfrac{14}{10} = 1.4$	$\dfrac{15}{10} = 1.5$

While use of the Eckstein criterion might not lead to serious misallocation of funds by the federal government (though one may be forgiven for skepticism), it can lead to particularly bad decisions at lower levels of government, where the socially inferior project may be eligible for federal grants of 90 percent. Compare the following:

	A	B
Local costs	$ 1 million	$10 million
Federal costs	9 million	
Benefits	11 million	15 million
Local benefit-cost ratio		
Eckstein criterion	$\dfrac{11 - 9}{1} = 2.0$	$\dfrac{15}{10} = 1.5$
Recommended criterion ...	$\dfrac{11}{10} = 1.1$	$\dfrac{15}{10} = 1.5$

Application of the Eckstein criterion under capital-rationing conditions will generally lead to the acceptance of projects part of whose cost is borne elsewhere in lieu of socially equal or better projects whose cost is borne wholly by the government in question. It is equivalent to attempting to evade the budget constraint by inducing other people to spend their money to supplement it, giving the spending authority control, albeit indirect, over more funds than have been appropriated to it. Not only does it lead to a misallocation of resources on an economy-wide basis, but it also tends to undermine the fundamental control of the legislature over the purse strings which is a basic necessity in a democratic society.

4.4 Comparisons on an incremental basis

While it is important to include all benefits and costs resulting from the project in the analysis, as the earlier examples show, care must be taken that the benefits and costs included are on an incremental basis and actually result from the project. Thus, care should be taken to avoid the use of fully distributed costs which may overstate the true costs.

Consider the case of a company considering a small expansion in plant capacity to produce subassemblies which were formerly purchased. On a discounted basis, the following present values are relevant to the decision:

Savings on subassemblies formerly purchased	$1,500,000
Direct operating cost of producing subassemblies	1,000,000
Cost of plant expansion	200,000

The comptroller derived a benefit-cost ratio of 1.13, after allowing for income taxes estimated at $150,000 on a present value basis. The plant manager, who may have had enough headaches already, claimed that the expansion would be unprofitable, as it had not been allocated its fair share of overhead, which the comptroller was in the habit of passing on to operating departments at 32 percent of their direct costs. His calculations showed:

Saving on purchases	$1,500,000
Direct operating costs	1,000,000
Overhead	320,000
	$ 180,000
Plant cost	200,000
Benefit-cost ratio	0.9

He made no allowance for taxes since on a distributed cost basis the project was unprofitable.

In a case such as this, it is unlikely that overhead will be increased at all. Thus, it should not be taken into account in the decision. If the plant manager is paid on the basis of results, and if he is to be held accountable for the overhead allotted to his department, his position is understandable. Of course, he would not be in such a position under a rational system of allocating responsibility.

There may be other instances when overhead will be increased. For example, when a new branch plant is established which will require additional traveling and other communication costs for senior executives who must oversee it, a charge for overhead is quite appropriate. If such a charge is to be made, it must be the best available estimate of the actual additional costs likely to be incurred and not some rule-of-thumb allocation. Generally, projects of the cost-reducing or replacement variety will not involve additional overheads, but major expansions of capacity will.

Another frequently included and often arbitrary provision is an allowance for working capital. Here again the use of a company-wide average based on sales or expenses cannot be justified. Any such allowance must be based on a careful analysis of the effects of the project on required cash balances, inventory, and receivables and take into account the funds provided by expense accruals. Since some projects may have the effect of reducing working capital requirements (for example, by reducing required inventories), it is impossible to establish any rule. Where the projects are small, and the amount involved insignificant, working capital may as well be ignored. In other cases (for example, major capacity expansions), the effect on working capital will be considerable and must be taken into account. Still other projects (for example, a warehouse network or materials-handling systems) may be justified primarily on the basis of their effect on working capital.

4.5 Treatment of taxes in a private context

It goes without saying that any appropriate measure of benefits and costs in the private sector must take account of the effects of taxes on property and incomes. In theory, this can be done equally well by considering either benefits and costs on a before-tax basis, using a required rate of return suitably adjusted on a similar basis to complete the evaluation, or by making all calculations on an after-tax basis. In practice, however, because of accelerated depreciation and other factors, the appropriate adjustment to the required rate of return for various projects may be difficult to understand, so that it is much simpler to make all evaluations on an after-tax basis. Further, since cash flow to the owners is after tax, the market evaluation must be on that basis as well.

The incremental effect on the tax bill resulting from proposed projects should be carefully calculated at the company's marginal tax rate and included in the cash flows. While depreciation must not be directly included in the cash flows, it affects tax liability by providing a tax shield which must be considered in the tax calculation. For this purpose, the basis of the depreciation charge should be that actually used for tax purposes, not that used for financial reporting purposes. Where accelerated depreciation is available for one project but not another, this should be recognized in the evaluation, both from the point of view of stockholders, legitimately interested in maximizing after-tax profits, and from that of society, which presumably established the accelerated rates to provide an incentive to investment which can only be effective if calculations are made on this basis. Tax liability should thus be stated on the basis of the tax actually payable as a result of the project. The method of reporting is of little or no consequence. Where accelerated allowances are available in early years, the tax liability in later years is increased, relative to that which would be incurred in later years under normal depreciation practices. The net result is to increase the discounted benefit-cost ratio, net present value, or internal rate of return by shifting benefits to the earlier years which are most heavily weighted under these criteria. It is in their ability to deal with subtleties of this kind effectively that these criteria derive their principal advantage over the older, simpler methods of evaluation.

Where there are external effects within the firm (that is, on other divisions, as discussed in Section 4.6), the tax implications of such external effects must, of course, be taken into account. The treatment of taxes in public-expenditure decisions is an area fraught with controversy. Government operations as such are usually tax exempt, so there is no tax liability to be considered in a formal sense. There may be taxes on the other side, that is, in the form of user charges, but these are seldom an appropriate measure of benefits and are best ignored. (The only exceptions are projects designed to improve the tax-collecting machinery. Additional collections may be a measure of benefits.)

However, implicit taxes cannot simply be ignored in government expenditure decisions. One of the things we hope to get from our evaluation of public-expenditure projects is some indication of the optimum size of government budgets, or the extent to which resources should be devoted to the different activities for which government is responsible, and we cannot do this unless we can make evaluations on a basis comparable with that used in the private sector.

It is theoretically quite feasible to make allowance for implicit tax payments out of the benefits estimated for public-sector expenditures. This may be the appropriate policy for commercial and quasicommercial government enterprises (for example, the post office and publicly owned power plants) and a number of Canadian federal government enterprises go through the ritual of making notional book entries for an implicit tax on income, allegedly to ensure that they compete with private enterprises on a fair basis.

For most government operations, where the benefits are not marketed, any attempt to reduce benefits by some notional tax allowance is likely to be a futile exercise in make-believe. Just as it is most natural to consider benefits in the private sector net of tax and to use an after-tax required rate of return in their evaluation, it is most natural to consider benefits in the public sector on a nontaxed basis, using a before-tax cost of capital for evaluation purposes. The problem of selecting an appropriate cost of capital which will place public projects on a basis comparable with those in the private sector will be discussed in Chapter 8.

4.6 Treatment of external or spillover effects

The external effects of a project are those benefits and costs which do not accrue to the decision-making unit. While they occur both within the private sector and the public, their relative importance is usually greater in the public sector; indeed the importance of external effects is one of the major reasons for the incorporation of certain activities, for example, the provision of police and fire protection (which are so-called public goods) within the public sector. Where they occur within the private sector, they may lead in the absence of government intervention to troublesome discrepancies between private and social costs which prevent the attainment of an efficient allocation of resources through the functioning of the market mechanism.[6]

Ideally, from the point of view of welfare economics, all decision-making units should take account of the external consequences of their acts and behave accordingly, for it is only in such conditions that an ideal allocation of resources will be attained. As a practical matter, however, there are important differences between the ability of firms or individuals and that of the government to take account of external factors and in the extent to which they should. External effects of a firm's projects are those which affect other firms or other members of the community. Where a firm is decentralized and decisions are made at the divisional level, there may be external effects on other divisions of the firm. Where this type of external effect is involved, optimum behavior at the level of the firm will only result if they are included in the decision-maker's calculations, just as optimum performance at the economy-wide level requires consideration of external effects by all firms. Such external effects at the divisional level, however, affect the firm's profits and losses so are not external from the point of view of the firm itself but have direct financial consequences and should normally be taken into account. If negotiation between divisions fails to reconcile problems created by divisional externalities, top management may have to impose a solution.

It is not always so with true external effects—those which are felt outside the firm. While these are of many possible types, classic examples are those involving pollution. Pollution usually imposes costs on the rest of the community far beyond those it imposes on the polluter. For the firm to prevent pollution may require costly additional equipment or a change in location. Pollution is usually regarded as antisocial behavior and roundly, perhaps justifiably, condemned at least in the aggregate. Where the industry is purely competitive, so that profit margins are merely normal, the financial ability of its members to provide protection against pollution is determined by the most antisocial firm (see Chapter 2). If the latter is able to avoid the costs of preventing pollution and is otherwise efficient, the ruling price for the product will be one which does not cover the social costs of producing it, if we included pollution among the social costs. If other firms are to prevent pollution, they can do so only at the expense of their customers and/or stockholders, to the possible detriment of their ability to raise additional capital. If there are extra social costs involved in producing a product, they should, at least at first glance, be borne by those who benefit by consuming the product. The only way out of such an impasse is for the state to intervene and require all firms to prevent pollution. (A private cartel might accomplish the same objective but might also be tempted to pursue less altruistic goals. Cartels are thus not regarded as an acceptable type of regulation in North America.)

A firm which has a sufficient degree of monopoly power could take account of such external effects. However, to the extent that the exercise of such power leads to a reduction in output and an increase in price from the competitive level, consumers presumably are already paying for pollution prevention, although they may not be getting it. To the extent that costs are taken into account, prices raised, and output reduced further, socially responsible behavior of this type is no clear guarantee of ideal output. If, however, the firm is following a price-output policy consistent with that of a competitive industry,[7] such costs should be taken into account. It is, perhaps, not possible to do more here than suggest that firms having substantial market power should behave in a socially responsible fashion on both counts. What the incentives are for them to behave in this socially desirable way is not clear, however. The element of political risk, mentioned earlier, may not be recognized or considered.

Appropriate behavior in the public sector can be more easily defined. The government, as custodian of the general welfare, should take into account all external effects except possibly those costs borne by foreigners such as downstream pollution of international rivers. (Presumably these can be the subject of international negotiations; to abstain from the threat of harming your neighbor while he is in a position to harm you may be virtuous, but it passes up a good opportunity to protect yourself against his future misdeeds.)

The problem, however, becomes more complex when several levels of government with differing jurisdictions are involved. The seriousness is shown by the extent to which municipal sewage disposal plants are involved in water pollution problems. Most regional and local governments are under no consitutional obligation to consider benefits and costs external to their jurisdiction, nor do they in practice. Again it is easy to suggest that they should consider such effects, but in practice here, as in the private sector, the lowest common denominator may set the standard. A city which installs expensive sewage treatment facilities may be handicapped in its ability to attract population or industry compared with a suburb which is a flagrant polluter, whether such treatment is financed by user charges or out of the general tax revenues.

Where there is widespread disregard of external effects, and the offenders are local governments having powers granted by charter from a senior government, a tolerable solution can often be obtained by negotiation and agreement between individual government units. Where it cannot, it can be imposed by the senior government either via charter provisions setting conditions on behavior or by the establishment of specialized authorities having taxing powers and geographical jurisdiction coterminous with the extent of the external economies or diseconomies.[8]

Where the offending governments have sovereignty within a federal system, as have the state governments or the provincial governments in Canada, difficulties are compounded. Some solutions may be attainable by interstate compact, but the small number of such agreements is indicative of the difficulty of reaching them. Since the activity is within the jurisdiction of the regional government, constitutional difficulties usually prevent the federal government from applying an imposed solution, although it may take the lead in attempting to bring the states together and may be able to use its financial strength and the promise of funds, virtually its only weapon in such a case, to encourage resolution of the problem. The Tennessee Valley Authority is perhaps the leading example of this approach.

A constitutional amendment to place the activity within the sphere of the federal power is, of course, another alternative, but it is a cumbersome device. However, there is always the heartening experience of prohibition to look back on as a reminder of its possibility.

Since most public-sector decisions will involve external benefits and costs, we will not look at special examples here. We will examine, however, external effects within the firm.

Example 4.6.1 (Economies external to the division): The pipeline subsidiary of a major oil company is considering the extension of its line to a new field and the construction of a gathering system within the field. The field produces 2,000 barrels per day, of which 1,000 are produced by the parent company and the balance by competitors. Crude from the field is currently carried by a nonaffiliated trucking company to the existing pipeline terminus at a cost of $0.30 per barrel.

The line is under regulation which limits its return to 7.5 percent on a depreciated rate base. Anticipated cost of the line is $200,000, salvage value nil. Output is prorated and is expected to remain at 2000 b/d for 10 years, at the end of which time the field will be depleted. Operating expenses are estimated at $40,000 per year.

Estimated tariff to be charged users is a flat rate of $0.103 per barrel, calculated to produce an accounting rate of return of $7.5 percent after taxes, over the life of the line, calculated as follows:

	Cost per year
Operating expenses	$40,000
Depreciation	20,000
Return (7.5 percent of average investment)	7,500
Income taxes (50 percent)	7,500
Total required	$75,000 = 0.103 per barrel

From the pipeline's point of view, the investment will produce a cash flow of $27,500 per year for 10 years on an investment of $200,000, giving an internal rate of return of 6.3 percent. This rate of return is respectable enough for a pipeline investment, but it is below the parent company's cost of capital of 13 percent. If this were all that was considered, there is a good chance the proposal would be rejected.

But the line also affects the earnings of the parent company, saving it 19.7 cents per barrel in transportation charges, increasing wellhead prices by an equivalent amount. This is a gross flow of $72,000 per year, reduced by income tax calculated as follows,

Gross earnings from price increase	$72,000
Less depletion allowance (23 percent)	16,500
Taxable earnings	$55,440
Tax (50 percent)	27,720

Total annual cash receipts to the firm as a whole are as follows:

	Pipeline subsidiary	Producing department	Consolidated
Receipts:			
Trucking charge saved	—	$109,500	$109,500
Pipeline charge	$75,000	(37,500)	37,500
Total receipts	75,000	72,000	147,500
Outlays:			
Pipeline operating	40,000	—	40,000
Income tax	7,500	27,720	35,220
Total outlays	47,500	27,720	75,220
Net receipts (after tax)	$27,500	$ 44,280	$ 71,780

which provides a handsome rate of return of 34 percent on the pipeline investment of $200,000. In this case, the external savings form the major portion of the benefit. This is one of the factors which have led oil companies to extend pipeline systems aggressively rather than wait for other investors to do so.[9] Prospective returns to them are much greater than they are to outside investors. As a consequence, nearly all crude oil pipeline systems are owned by oil company subsidiaries.

By providing this line, however, an equal external benefit is provided for other operators in the field. If these can be induced to share its cost 50:50 by setting it up as a joint venture, the company can reduce its investment to $100,000 while its annual receipts fall only to $58,030, boosting its internal rate of return on the venture to about 60 percent.[10] Since its incremental rate of return on the $100,000 extra investment required for full ownership is only 6.5 percent, it will prefer, if possible, to negotiate such a deal. Such a deal would have the incidental advantage of eliminating the likelihood of squabbles from nonintegrated producers over alleged tariff discrimination, secret rebates, and so on. For both parties, it offers the additional attraction of being able to cut the tariff below the regulated level, so that no return is earned on the pipeline, where it is taxable at the full rate, thus augmenting the price by an equivalent amount, of which only 77 percent is taxable, thanks to the depletion allowance.

Example 4.6.2 (External diseconomies within the firm):   The Feline Division of the Universal Motor Car Company is considering the introduction of a sports model, tentatively named the Cheetah. Market surveys indicate unit sales at a manufacturers net price of $4,000 growing as follows:

First year	15,000
Second year	25,000
Third year	35,000
Fourth year	40,000
Fifth year	45,000
Thereafter	50,000

Labor and materials cost is estimated at $2,000 per unit. Some assemblies can be produced in the division's existing plants, but new plant space costing $40 million will be required. This can be written off for tax purposes at a straight-line rate of 5 percent. Initial tooling cost is estimated at $40 million of which $16 million can be written off at once, as it relates to the current year's model, the balance over a ten-year period. Costs of annual model changes are estimated at $6 million for the second year, $10 million in the third, and $20 million in the fourth year, a pattern which is expected to repeat itself indefinitely. An advertising campaign costing $40 million will be required to establish the new line, while $20 million annually is expected to be sufficient to maintain its market position at the projected level of sales. The company is subject to a 50 percent marginal tax rate. Its required rate of return is 12 percent after taxes. For investment decision purposes, it does not carry analyses beyond the tenth year, as an arbitrary protection against risk.

Table 4–1 shows the estimates of cash flows derived by the division from this data. It appears reasonably profitable on this basis, with an internal rate of return of approximately 31 percent and a discounted benefit-cost ratio of 1.08.

Table 4–1
Cash flows from new model, Feline division ($000)

Year	Revenue	Labor and materials	Plant and tooling	Advertising	Tax outlays	Net Cash Flow
1	$ 60,000	$ 30,000	$80,000	$40,000	$(15,200)	$(74,800)
2	100,000	50,000	6,000	20,000	9,800	14,200
3	140,000	70,000	10,000	20,000	17,800	22,200
4	160,000	80,000	20,000	20,000	17,800	22,200
5	180,000	90,000	6,000	20,000	29,800	34,200
6	200,000	100,000	10,000	20,000	32,800	37,200
7	200,000	100,000	20,000	20,000	27,800	32,200
8	200,000	100,000	6,000	20,000	32,800	39,200
9	200,000	100,000	10,000	20,000	32,800	37,200
10	200,000	100,000	20,000	20,000	27,800	32,200

Internal rate of return = 30.8%
Benefit-cost ratio ($k = 0.12$) = 1.08

The analysis carried out by the division ignores, however, that the Canine Division of the same company produces another sports model, the Mongrel, which currently has 40 percent of the market for this type of car. Of the sales achieved by the Cheetah, at least one third will be achieved at the expense of the Mongrel. This will lead to a reduction in sales of the other division, to a reduction in their expenses for materials and labor, and to a reduction in taxes, as shown in Table 4–2.

The full analysis indicates that the proposed addition to the Feline Division's product line is unprofitable for the corporation as a whole, if its required rate of return is 12 percent. The profit-maximizing solution for the company as a whole requires that such effects, external to the division, but internal from the point of view of the firm, be taken into account. Ensuring that they are so taken into account is a major problem in the design of a decentralized capital-budgeting system where capital-expenditure decisions are delegated to the divisions. This can be accomplished either by subjecting divisional budgets to a central review or by limiting the delegation to types of projects not likely to have external effects. Specifying these *a priori* may be somewhat difficult, as even cost-reducing projects may have external effects.[11]

Since many firms have decentralized decision-making systems which do not take full account of such external effects, some comment on the results of such failure should be added at this point. Such external effects on the revenue side only exist where the firm is sufficiently large for the sales of one division to have some impact on the other divisions, so they may be presumed to be limited to firms having some

Table 4–2
Analysis of new model, at corporate level, incorporating external effects on division
($000)

Year	Canine division — Lost sales (units)	Lost revenue	Reduced expenses	Reduced taxes	Net cash flow	Feline division net cash flow	Total corporate net cash flow
1	5,000	$20,000	$10,000	$ 5,000	$(5,000)	$(74,800)	$(79,800)
2	8,333	33,333	16,667	8,334	(8,332)	14,200	5,868
3	11,667	46,668	23,333	11,667	(11,666)	22,200	10,534
4	13,333	53,333	26,667	12,333	(12,332)	22,200	9,868
5	15,000	60,000	30,000	15,000	(15,000)	34,200	19,200
6	16,667	66,667	33,333	16,667	(16,666)	37,200	20,534
7	16,667	66,667	33,333	16,667	(16,666)	32,200	15,534
8	16,667	66,667	33,333	16,667	(16,666)	39,200	22,534
9	16,667	66,667	33,333	16,667	(16,666)	37,200	20,534
10	16,667	66,667	33,333	16,667	(16,666)	32,200	14,534

Internal rate of return = 11.0%
Benefit-cost ratio (k = 0.12) = 0.98

degree of monopoly power. In such a firm, failure to consider such effects will lead to an expansion of output beyond the profit-maximizing output in the conventional price theory textbook analysis of monopolistic competition. In the language of the latter, discounted benefits are (long-run) marginal revenues and discounted costs are (long-run) marginal costs. Failure to take full account of internal "external" effects will lead to incorrect estimates of both. While there is no general way of predicting the outcome, an examination of the most likely types of error leads to the surmise that, in the limiting case, the competitive output and price will be attained. The examination of market concentration at the corporate level is likely to give an overestimate of the extent of monopolistic influences in the market to the extent that such practices persist. Insofar as continuation of the practice is likely to lead to price-output results more nearly approximating the competitive ideal, it is socially desirable that it be continued. We are concerned here, however, with laying down the conditions under which the firm, whether possessed of monopoly power or not, can maximize its profits, not with whether it should. Therefore, we need not pursue the matter further.

External effects can, of course, also exist on the cost side. Here their existence is independent of market structure. Such effects arise when the realization of economies of scale by one division is affected by the output decisions of another. Some degree of transfer price manipulation from higher levels may be necessary to ensure optimal decisions.

4.7 Some observations on environmental impacts

Legislation requiring environmental impact assessments (EIAs) prior to starting a variety of projects is now in force in many jurisdictions. The preparation of such statements involves an analysis of the ecology of the area within which the project will be located and of how the ecology will be disturbed by the project. The project can be held up indefinitely or modifications required by the agencies enforcing such legislation. Similar delays can be imposed in urban or other areas where historical site preservation becomes an issue. Clearly, such legislation requires more careful evaluation of projects in new dimensions by new groups of professionals who were largely absent from the business scene a generation ago. They also create enormous potential for delay and frustration and can turn profitable projects into unprofitable ones.

The existence of such legislation does not alter the fundamental criteria for project selection by private firms. It does, however, create a need for environmental analyses at the project design stage, to ascertain whether the project can be redesigned or relocated to avoid environmental objections. Often, if this is done early enough, no extra costs will be incurred in doing so. But this will not always be the case, and trade-offs between environmental and other social goals sometimes have to be made. Where possible conflict exists, a social valuation of the project and alternatives prepared along the lines indicated in Chapters 8 and 9 may be helpful in pointing out a way to a resolution which is not only profitable to the firm but beneficial to society. Failure to provide such information leaves an invitation to environmental absolutists to push for rejection of the project whether there are any significant social costs involved or not. Just how valuable to society is the furbish lousewort anyway?

4.8 Mutually exclusive projects

Whenever there are two or more ways of achieving some objective, the decision maker is faced with the problem of choosing between alternative techniques. In practice, such decisions often incorporate problems of choice of scale, as for example, the choice between dams of different size with different generating capacity on the same site; however, this added complication does not seriously affect the decision process.

In the pure technique case, benefits are identical. The decision problem resolves itself into one of picking the alternative for which gross discounted costs are the lowest.

In cases where problems of both scale and technique are involved, the decision requires consideration of a series of fictitious projects constructed in the following manner. Suppose we have three alternative projects, A, B, and C, listed in order of increasing cost. Substitute for the latter two the fictitious projects B' and C'. The cost of B' in each time period is the excess of its cost over the cost of A; the cost of C' is the excess of its cost over the cost of B'. Benefits may be similarly defined in the mixed case, although these will be identical in the pure choice-of-technique situation. Project A and the fictitious projects B' and C' are included in the list of budget proposals and the latter processed in the normal manner. If the accepted budget includes both A and B' and not C', then project B should be constructed. If, it includes all three, proceed instead with C. If only A is included, this is the appropriate choice. (For other problems involving mutually exclusive projects, see Section 4.9.)

Example 4.8.1 (Mutually exclusive projects—the pure technique case):   A company intends to manufacture a minor part which it now purchases from an outside supplier at a cost of $20,000 per year. Three processes, having the following characteristics, may be adopted.

	Initial cost	Annual operating expenses (including taxes)
A	$ 8,000	$15,000
B	12,000	14,000
C	20,000	12,000

At the company's required rate of return of 12 percent, the present value of benefits over ten years is $130,000 in all three cases. The present value of costs for the three projects is:

A	$92,750
B	91,100
C	87,800

Project C should be adopted. Internal rates of return for the three projects are 62 percent, 49 percent, and 38 percent respectively. Note that use of the internal rate criterion gives misleading results in this case, as we earlier discussed. C is preferable despite its lower rate of return because the yield on the additional investment required is in excess of the cost of capital.

Example 4.8.2 (Mutually exclusive projects, mixed scale and technique case): A government agency is considering two proposals for the development of a dam for irrigation purposes. Project A will cost $1 million initially, $50,000 per year to operate, will irrigate 5,000 acres, and will produce annual benefits of $200,000 for 50 years. Project B will cost $1.5 million initially, $150,000 per year to operate, and will irrigate 10,000 acres including some which are not cultivable for other reasons. It will produce annual benefits of $320,000 for 50 years. The agency's cost of capital is 10 percent. Which alternative should be chosen?

Project A has a benefit-cost ratio of 1.48, and project B a ratio of 1.12. Both are acceptable, but only one site is available, so the question is how intensively it should be developed. The following estimates can be derived for the fictitious project B'.

	Project B	Project A	Project B' (B − A)
Initial cost	$1,500,000	$1,000,000	$500,000
Annual operating	150,000	50,000	100,000
Annual benefits...............	320,000	200,000	120,000

B' has a benefit-cost ratio of only 0.39 and would not be built if it were a separate, individual project. Therefore, project A should be chosen.

4.9 The problem of horizons

The choice of a horizon refers merely to the selection of the time period which the decision maker will consider in evaluating benefits and costs. Some projects have a well-defined life and are dependent on physical or legal circumstances, for example, the construction of a service station on a leased site. Others have indefinitely long lives and may still be yielding benefits 300 years from now.

Is there any rule for establishing a horizon? In general, we must answer no, whether we are considering the private sector or the public sector. There is no reason for attaching any higher or lower weight to future benefits, other than that implicit in the discounting process. Even if the owners of a firm plan to retire in five years, maximizing the market value of their holding at that time probably requires that it be sold on a going-concern basis, and its market value will be dependent on present value of expected cash flows past that point. However, as a practical matter, at the rates of discount which required rate of return considerations require us to use, benefits and costs do not count for much if they occur very far in the future. At 8 percent, a dollar to be received 25 years from now is worth only $0.15 today, one due in 50 years only $0.02. The most practical way of resolving the horizon problem is to let the discount rate take care of it.

In practice, many firms impose a shorter limit on benefits and costs to be considered for many types of projects. The argument for the practice is that the future is uncertain, that forecasts beyond a certain length are unreliable, so that benefits beyond a certain point are largely conjectural. The short horizon is imposed as a crude limit on risk. Recall that this was one rationale given for the use of payback as a criterion (see Section 3.8).

Most analyses prepared by federal agencies in the United States use a 50-year horizon, though 100 years is used in some cases.[12] The former limit has been criticized as favoring present generations to the exclusion of the future. However, the importance of the difficulty is also related to the choice of a discount rate. This problem and the implicit horizon problem in the public sector are considered later in Chapter 8.

The analysis of projects with lives considerably shorter than the effective planning horizon contains a built-in horizon which may hamper the application of particular criteria to arrive at appropriate decisions. Which is better, to invest $10,000 in a project lasting five years and promising an internal rate of return of 17 percent or to invest it in a project lasting ten years and promising an internal rate of return of 15 percent? The two projects have built-in horizons, of five and ten years respectively and cannot be directly compared. To see why, it is necessary to review the sense in which the internal rate of return is a rate of return on the sum invested.

Consider project A which costs $10,000 and returns, net of taxes, the following amounts at the end of the years listed.

First	$2,700
Second	3,530
Third	4,190
Fourth	2,680
Fifth	2,340

This project has an internal rate of return of 17 percent as verified by the calculations in Table 4–3.

The internal rate of return is the return earned *on that portion of the investment which has not yet been recovered*. It is the true rate of return

Table 4–3
Internal rate of return: Project A (5 years, r = 17 percent)

Year	Unamortized balance of investment January 1	Cash flow December 31	Of which	
			Return 17%	Recovery of capital
1	$10,000	$2,700	$1,700	$1,000
2	9,000	3,530	1,530	2,000
3	7,000	4,190	1,190	3,000
4	4,000	2,680	680	2,000
5	2,000			
6	0			

on the unrecovered investment in that it is the largest amount which can be withdrawn each year and allow recovery of the initial investment by the expiry of the project. As a measure of profitability, it is merely an index of the profitability of the remaining investment in the project and not of the contribution of the project as a whole to the profitability of the firm.

Depending on the available opportunities for investing the funds set free, such a project may contribute less to the firm's ultimate profitability than another which offers a lower rate of return but ties up funds for a longer period.[13] This was discussed in Section 3.14 in connection with what we there called the modified or reinvestment rate of return.

To see how this may happen, consider project B, which offers a 15 percent internal rate on a $10,000 investment having the cash flow indicated in Table 4–4. From the second year on, there is more still invested in project B than in project A, and it is producing a rate of return of 15 percent on this amount, whereas A is producing 17 percent on a smaller amount.

Because of the rapidly shrinking amount still invested in project A, the portion of cash receipts from Project B which can be regarded as return on the remaining investment is larger than the portion of A's cash flow which can be so regarded, from the third year forth. If the opportunities for profitable reinvestment of the funds which are recovered from the two projects are limited, it may well be that B is to be preferred to A. To make a direct comparison of their effects on the profitability of the firm, it is necessary to examine what reinvestment

Table 4–4
Internal rate of return: Project B (10 years, $r = 15$ percent)

			Of which	
Year	Unamortized balance of investment, January 1	Cash flow December 31	Return 15%	Recovery of capital
1	$10,000	$2,500	$1,500	$1,000
2	9,000	2,350	1,350	1,000
3	8,000	2,200	1,200	1,000
4	7,000	2,050	1,050	1,000
5	6,000	1,900	900	1,000
6	5,000	1,750	750	1,000
7	4,000	1,600	600	1,000
8	3,000	1,450	450	1,000
9	2,000	1,300	300	1,000
10	1,000	1,150	150	1,000

opportunities are available and to consider what funds could be accumulated by the firm to a common terminal date or horizon, which must be no sooner than the expiry of the longer project.

If the estimated reinvestment rate is sufficiently low relative to the internal rate of return, the longer project will be chosen, despite its lower internal rate of return. This may be expected to happen quite frequently if the cost of capital is used as the reinvestment rate, if only because neither project will be regarded as acceptable if its internal rate of return is not greater than the cost of capital. Occasionally, however, the expected reinvestment rate may be above the internal rate of return of the longer-lived project because of potentially higher returns on anticipated future projects. In such a case, the shorter-lived project is to be preferred as its quicker cash throw-off makes funds available for reinvestment sooner. This will be especially attractive if the firm is in a capital-rationing situation with respect to the external financing of new projects.

While our example is in terms of projects having definite longer and shorter lives, it also appears in those cases where there is a marked difference in the time shape of the receipts stream, so that in one case, for example, half the investment is recovered in two years, while in the other it takes eight.

If the firm is pursuing a policy of maximizing long-run profits and accepting all those projects for which the internal rate exceeds the cost of capital, it should, of course, accept both projects unless they are mutually exclusive, in which case a careful analysis of the reinvestment situation should be carried out.

4.10 Double-counting problems

This warning should be unnecessary. But unfortunately, there are some fairly subtle traps into which the analyst may fall. It would be impossible to catalog all of the possible errors of this variety.

Perhaps the most common is that of charging interest on the investment as an expense, then calculating an internal rate of return or benefit-cost ratio on the remaining profits. Such imputed interest is not a cash flow (if it is, the project and its financing are hopelessly scrambled up and should be separated), and its inclusion as an expense results in an understatement of the desirability of the project. The appropriate allowance for interest is included in the analysis when cost of capital is considered as part of the decision process. Putting it in anywhere else counts it twice.[14]

Closely related is the practice of including interest during construction as part of the capital cost of a project. If all outlays are dated and appropriate discounting takes place, this item is automatically provided for. When it is desired to treat outlays as if they took place at a single point in time, that is, at the beginning of the receipt stream, earlier expenditures should be accumulated with an allowance for interest at this point. Where this is done, however, the appropriate interest rate to use is not the bond rate, which is frequently used for this purpose, but rather, the required rate of return.

A similar practice is that of charging depreciation as an expense, then applying benefit-cost analysis or computing the internal rate of return. The internal rate criterion, as has been shown, calculates the return on the unrecovered capital invested in the project and makes full provision for the recovery of capital in this way. Capital recovery in benefit-cost analysis is provided for by the requirement that the benefit-cost ratio exceeds 1. Further depreciation charges are not only unnecessary but incorrect in either case. Again, depreciation is only considered in connection with estimating cash flows because of its tax implications.

Other ways of counting the same tricks twice should also be avoided. A project which improves the earning power of a service station increases its value to the company owning it. The increase in value is entirely the result of the increased earning power, and an analysis which takes into account both the increased earnings and the increased value is clearly wrong as it involves double counting. Where the residual value at time of planned disposition is affected (by an increase in earning power subsequent to the time of disposition) and earning power prior to disposition is increased, there is, of course, no double counting if both are included.

4.11 Analysis of replacement chains

Another type of horizon problem arises when we consider replacement situations. For the most part, we have examined projects on the assumption that their lives were known beforehand. While this is true of certain types of assets, such as oil wells, peat bogs, and dams subject to silting at a predictable rate, it is an oversimplification in most cases. Machines do not simply fall apart at the end of their life span, instead they become more expensive to repair and more intermittent in the character of service which they render and probably obsolescent as well. Determining the appropriate time for the replacement of an existing facility is a capital-budgeting problem, while determining the economic life of an asset is a closely related one. Even if we can predict the economic service lives of various machines, these may differ for different alternatives, that is, one machine may be more durable than the other. This is a special type of mutually exclusive project situation. To make a fair comparison between the more durable and less durable assets, it is necessary to place them on the same footing with respect to the period of analysis to be considered. If they are associated with a particular operation which has a known terminal date, discounted costs prior to that date should be minimized. Where there is no terminal date, it is usually preferable to assume an infinite chain of replacements.

The simplest problem is one of determining the economic life of a single machine. More frequent replacement means more capital is tied up in the machine, while less frequent replacement means higher repair costs and out-of-service costs.

Further, resale price of the asset falls as its age increases, but the user cost of continuing to use it for an additional year normally drops from year to year. In practice, resale price can be deducted from the appropriate replacement cost when incurred, that is, treated as a trade-in. As life increases, capital cost per period falls, while operating expense per period increases. The optimum life is chosen at the point where the increase in operating expenses is equated with the decrease in capital cost. This problem is considered in the following example.

More difficult problems arise where the pace of technological change is considered such as in the case of computers. Here, the productivity of new machines increases, so that, presumably, subsequent machines will either cost less to buy or to operate. Where this situation exists, it will be a factor tending to postpone replacement slightly in order to get a more productive replacement.

Some problems also involve planning for expanded capacity at the time of replacement. It is impossible to deal with all such problems here, for a comprehensive treatment of them would be too involved mathematically.[15] It should be noted that the calculated economic life at the time of installation does not determine the appropriate time of replacement. The former was a forecast and was undoubtedly subject to forecasting errors. The search for investment proposals should involve a systematic review of the performance of equipment, beginning some time well in advance of its originally forecast retirement age and a search for possible replacements.

Replacement should take place only after the point at which the present value of the future stream is reduced by replacement, and then only if a further delay in replacement will not produce an additional gain in present value. As the operating inferiority of existing equipment is intensified with age, the point will be reached where no further delay can be accepted without loss; replacement investments improve with age.

Example 4.11.1 (Life of a truck):   A trucking company has the following estimates of data on the cost of running a truck costing $5,000:[16]

Year	Operating expenses	Trade-in value at end of year
1	$1,000	$3,000
2	1,100	1,800
3	1,250	1,000
4	1,500	700
5	1,900	500
6	2,500	300
7	3,500	200

If its required rate of return is 10 percent, at what age should it replace the truck?

Costs per *replacement cycle,* which we will consider first, consist of the capital outlay made at the beginning of the cycle, less any trade-in received, plus operating expenses during the cycle. For convenience in the analysis, these can be regarded as occurring at the beginning of the cycle if we take their present values at that point. As a first step in our

calculation, therefore, calculate the present value of operating expenses for the various possible lives:

Year	Operating expenses	Present value at 10 percent	Cumulative PV from year 1
1	$1,000	$ 909	$ 909
2	1,100	910	1,819
3	1,250	938	2,757
4	1,500	1,025	3,782
5	1,900	1,180	4,962
6	2,500	1,410	6,372
7	3,500	1,790	8,162

Cost of a one-year replacement cycle is the present value of operating costs, $909, plus the capital outlay of $5,000 for the initial cycle and
$2,000 for subsequent cycles, after deducting the trade-in of $3,000.
Cost of a two-year replacement cycle is $1,819 in present value of
operating costs plus $5,000 for the initial cycle and $3,200 for subsequent cycles, crediting the trade-in from the previous cycle against the
cost of the replacement. Costs calculated in similar fashion for replacement cycles of greater length are as follows:

Life	First cycle cost (initial year)	Subsequent cycle cost (beginning of cycle)
1	$ 5,909	$ 2,909
2	6,819	5,019
3	7,757	6,757
4	8,752	8,082
5	9,962	9,462
6	11,372	11,072
7	13,162	12,962

Providing the service indefinitely with a one-year replacement cycle
will require an initial outlay worth $5,909, and subsequent annual out-
lays of $2,909 in perpetuity. Replacing every second year will require
an initial outlay of $6819, with subsequent outlays of $5,019 every
second year and so on.

The present value of the cost of each alternative can be regarded as
the sum of the initial cycle cost and the present value of a perpetuity of
the amount of the subsequent cycle costs incurred at appropriate inter-

vals at the cost-of-capital rate. Factors for this can be calculated simply from the formula $1/kn$, where k = the annual discount rate, and n = number of years in the replacement cycle.

Substituting in the formula, the present value factor to be applied to subsequent cycle costs is for a one-year cycle $1/0.10$ or 10.00; for a two-year cycle, $1/2(.10)$ or 5.00; and so on.

Using these factors, we can calculate the present value of costs for alternative replacement cycle lengths (see Table 4–5). To find the economic life of the truck, we choose the replacement cycle which minimizes the present value of costs.

Table 4–5
Least cost solution to truck replacement problem

Life	Cost/subsequent cycle	Present value factor	Cost of future cycles	Initial cycle	Total cost
1..........	$ 2,909	10.00	$29,909	$ 5,909	$34,999
2..........	5,019	5.00	25,095	6,819	31,914
3..........	6,757	3.33	22,501	7,757	30,258
4..........	8,082	2.50	20,205	8,752	28,957
5..........	9,462	2.00	18,924	9,962	28,886
6..........	11,072	1.67	18,453	11,372	29,825
7..........	12,962	1.43	18,536	13,162	31,798

The economic life of the truck, that is, the age at which it should be replaced, is five years in this case.

As noted earlier, replacement analysis should begin before the originally estimated asset life has expired; data may change and alternative replacements may be available. The analysis should compare immediate replacement with replacement postponed for another year and should compare total income or expense streams under the two alternatives. In this connection, it seems appropriate to consider future replacement at intervals corresponding to the life of the asset at the time replacement is contemplated, although different assumptions may be appropriate in particular cases.

In applying year-by-year analysis to the truck problem, we assume that we already have a truck and that data have not changed from those given earlier. Consider replacement at the end of three years. The initial replacement cycle will cost $6,757 (after trade-in) while subsequent cycles cost $22,501, giving a present value of $29,258. Delaying replacement until the fourth year will give rise to an initial cycle replacement cost of $8,082, subsequent cycle costs of $20,205, plus operating costs of $1,500 during the year ahead. These total $29,787 but because of deferral they have a present value of $27,079. Deferring replacement till the fourth year will reduce the present value of the expenditure stream by $2,179, and, therefore, replacement should be deferred.

After four years, the initial and subsequent replacement cycles cost $28,287. Delaying replacement until the fifth year will give rise to an initial cycle cost of $9,462, a subsequent cycle cost of $18,924, and $1,900 in operating costs. The total is $30,286, but present value, allowing for one year deferral of the expenditures, is only $27,533. A further year's deferral gives a present value saving of $754.

However, when we consider a further postponement at the end of five years, we face an initial plus subsequent cycle cost of $28,386. Postponement leads to an initial cycle cost of $11,072, plus subsequent cycle costs of $18,453 and operating costs during the postponement at $2,500. These total $32,025, and have a present value of $29,114. Postponement of replacement beyond the fifth year leads to a present value loss, rather than a saving, and should be avoided. The year-by-year analysis thus leads to the same conclusions as the economic life calculation, as long as the basic data remain unchanged.

4.12 Incorporating technological change into replacement analysis

Example 4.11.1 involves the replacement of an asset with a like asset, on the implicit assumption that a truck is a truck. This is far from the usual case, however. Even if the replacement is a truck, it will usually be a better truck, since technological improvement in successive vintages of capital goods has been a pervasive feature of the societies which emerged from the industrial revolution. As we noted earlier, the fact that the replacement will usually be better than the original affects optimum replacement decisions in two offsetting ways. Because the replacement is superior, an incentive to earlier replacement is created. However, by waiting until next year to replace, instead of replacing now, an even better replacement will be available. Should we wait for it? In order to decide, we must incorporate an evaluation of these offsetting effects in our analysis.

This is perhaps most easily done with respect to the immediate replacement. Indeed, to the extent that improvement is reflected in a lower initial cost or lower operating costs, it has probably found its way into the analysis already. If the improvement is in capabilities rather than cost, the value of the improved capabilities to the prospective user must be taken into account. Prospective replacements may be available in a range of discrete sizes, and the improvements may not be such as to permit substitution of a smaller, cheaper unit; the replacement may provide expanded capacity for which there is no requirement. If this is, in fact, the case, then, of course, no extra benefit is created, and there is no need, strictly speaking, to account for one. But greater capabilities offer flexibility which was absent before and which may prove to be valuable even if no need is currently foreseen.

Benefits from improvements in subsequent replacements are harder to forecast. While they may accrue in any of the forms discussed earlier, these may most conveniently for analytical purposes be converted into the equivalent of lower costs per replacement cycle. Thus, to go back to Example 4.11.1, if productivity can be expected to grow at the rate p percent per year, the costs in successive n-year cycles should be multiplied by the reduction factor $1/(1 + p)^n$ to account for productivity change. This yields the following, assuming 2 percent productivity gains:

Life	Unadjusted subsequent cycles cost	Adjustment factor	Adjusted cycle cost
1	$ 2,909	.9804	$ 2,851
2	5,019	.9612	4,824
3	6,757	.9423	6,367
4	8,082	.9238	7,466
5	9,462	.9057	8,570
6	11,072	.8880	9,832
7	12,962	.8706	11,284

These must be incorporated, along with the first-cycle cost, into an analysis of the indefinite replacement cost similar to that performed in Section 4.11. In this instance (see Table 4–6), the optimum cycle is still five years, as it was in the initial case.

Table 4–6

Life	Initial cycle cost	Subsequent cycles cost	Total cost
1	$ 5,909	$28,510	$34,419
2	6,819	24,120	30,939
3	7,757	21,223	28,980
4	8,752	18,665	27,417
5	9,962	17,144	27,102
6	11,373	16,387	27,759
7	13,162	16,120	29,282

While the offsetting effects have canceled each other in this case, insofar as any practical impact on the decision is concerned, the analyst will not always be so lucky—where significant technological change is characteristic of the asset whose acquisition is being considered, it should be taken into account in the analysis.

4.13 Optimal timing considerations

Appropriate values of the benefit-cost ratio, net present value, or the internal rate of return indicate that a project is acceptable in that it makes a positive contribution to the current market value of the firm. It does not follow, however, that the latter will be maximized if all projects passing the acceptability test are incorporated into this year's capital budget, as is suggested in most of the standard treatments of the capital-budgeting problem.

The current market value of the firm, which management seeks to maximize, is (according to our theory) the sum of (*a*) the present value of cash flows from existing operations; (*b*) the present value of additions to cash flows resulting from projects in this year's budget; (*c*) the current present value of additions to cash flows resulting from projects in next year's budget; and (*d*) the current present value of additions to cash flows resulting from projects in subsequent budgets.

Market values reflect not only items (*a*) and (*b*) but the market's estimate of (*c*) and (*d*) as well. In the case of growth firms, (*c*) and (*d*) may account for a significant fraction of total value, and they are primarily responsible for the high price-earnings ratios observed for the shares of such firms.

The basic reason why the set of all projects meeting acceptable profitability standards does not maximize net present value is that some projects which are acceptable may make a greater contribution to net present value if included in next year's, or a subsequent year's budget, by virtue of exploiting output market opportunities that will become available, thus enhancing cash flows. Current production would tend to have lower marginal revenue because of depressed prices in the implicit model of monopoly or monopolistic competition. If they do, they should be postponed rather than included in the current budget. The current budget should, therefore, include only those projects which are acceptable and which should not be postponed.

Present values of projects may be enhanced in future periods for a variety of reasons. Many projects involve replacement of existing equipment as discussed in Sections 4.11 and 4.12 and are justified because new equipment offers lower operating costs or lower mainte-

nance costs. The advantage of new equipment tends to grow as maintenance costs on existing equipment rise, suggesting that replacement
investments may well merit postponement beyond the time replacement first appears profitable. Postponement may also be profitable if
the market for output of a given project is growing (assuming that
competitors do not capture it in the meantime.)

Determining whether a project should be postponed is accomplished
most simply in a net present value context. An *index of postponability*
may be constructed for each project by comparing the current net
present value of the project delayed one period with the net present
value if done this period. Present values are taken at the current date
and not at the date the project is to be undertaken. Postponement is
desirable only if the net present value grows between this period and
the next by a factor of $(1 + k)$.

Postponement results in substituting the cash flow stream

$$Q_1^* - C_1^*, Q_2^* - C_2^*, \ldots, Q_{n+1}^* - C_{n+1}^*$$

for the original stream

$$Q_0 - C_0, Q_1 - C_1, \ldots, Q_n - C_n$$

(Q_0^* and C_0^* are, of course, equal to 0). Net present value for the
postponed project is given by:

$$\text{NPV}_p = \sum_t (Q_t^* - C_t^*)(1 + k)^{-t} \qquad (4.13.1)$$

Unpostponed net present value is:

$$\text{NPV}_u = \sum_t (Q_t - C_t)(1 + k)^{-t} \qquad (4.13.2)$$

while the index of postponability is given by the ratio of equation 4.13.1
to 4.13.2.

Note that if neither the benefit nor the cost stream is changed as a
consequence of postponement, so that $Q_t^* - C_t^* = Q_{t-1} - C_{t-1}$ in 4.13.1
reduces to

$$\text{NPV}_p = \sum_t (Q_t - C_t)(1 + k)^{-t-1} \qquad (4.13.3)$$

and the postponability index becomes simply $1/(1 + k)$. Since this is
less than 1.0, postponement does not pay.

Our postponability index applies to single-period postponements. It
is, of course, possible that some projects should be deferred for a longer
time. The single-period index, however, will identify those projects

which should be excluded from this year's budget and tentatively assigned to next year's. If they should be thrust further into the future, it will become evident when next year's budget is prepared, as they will once again be postponed. While multi-period postponement indexes can be constructed, they are rarely needed.

The profit-maximizing budget then consists of all projects meeting basic acceptability standards which do not have postponability indexes greater than 1.0. Many companies do not, in practice, carry investment to this margin for a variety of reasons. Before succumbing to any of the reasons for such failures to maximize market value, management should recognize the extent of the profits being foregone by adhering to alternative policies.

The most frequent departure from the maximization policy is one which sets a maximum limit on the budget, because of some real or imaginary limit on the funds available, or because limited managerial skills and shortages of personnel limit the capacity of the firm to digest growth (which may be viewed as a form of human-capital rationing). While the operative restrictions are different, both situations have in common a more or less arbitrary upper limit on capital expenditures, within which management must do the best they can.

Notes

[1] A thorough accounting analysis will reveal that nonrecurring profit on the sale of the asset will be reduced by holding it. Unless present values are taken into account, however, it may still show the project to be profitable, for example, if the undiscounted operating profits total in excess of $150,000.

[2] As in the approach suggested by E. Solomon, "Measuring a Company's Cost of Capital," *Journal of Business* (October 1955), reprinted in E. Solomon, ed., *The Management of Corporate Capital* (Glencoe: Free Press, 1959), p. 140, where borrowing power contributed by a project is deducted from its cost and amortization of the loan is deducted from the benefits. Again we emphasize that under our assumptions of perfect certainty and perfect capital markets, investment and its financing are separable decisions.

[3] O. Eckstein, *Water Resource Development: The Economics of Project Evaluation* (Cambridge: Harvard University Press, 1961), p. 65.

[4] Eckstein, *Water Resource Development*, chap. 3.

[5] Eckstein, *Water Resource Development*, p. 75ff.

[6] For the classical treatment of these problems, see A. C. Pigou, *The Economics of Welfare*, 4th ed. (London: Macmillan & Co. 1932). A more contemporary treatment may be found in D. K. Whitcomb, *Externalities and Welfare* (New York: Columbia University Press, 1972).

[7] W. J. Baumol, *Business Behavior, Value and Growth* (New York: Macmillan, 1959), chaps. 6–8.

[8] See also the discussion in K. J. Arrow, *The Limits of Organization* (New York: W. W. Norton, 1974).

[9] For other factors, see L. Cookenboo, *Crude Oil Pipelines and Competition in the Oil Industry* (Cambridge: Harvard University Press, 1955).

[10] Pipeline receipts fall by 50 percent to $13,750, producing department receipts are unchanged.

[11] See J. Hirshleifer, "On the Economics of Transfer Pricing," *Journal of Business* 29 (January 1956); pp. 172–84; "Economics of the Divisionalized Firm," 30 (April 1957); pp. 96–108.

[12] Eckstein, *Water Resource Development*, pp. 83ff.

[13] E. Solomon, "The Arithmetic of Capital Budgeting Decisions," *Journal of Business* (April 1956), reprinted in Solomon, *Management of Corporate Capital*, pp. 74–79.

[14] We should note that evaluation of the rate of return to the underlying equity interest is common practice in the real estate industry, where mortgage financing of individual projects is the usual form of financing. This does not involve double counting, nor does it create problems of the type we have referred to in Section 4.3 since all the alternatives are similarly treated.

[15] These are discussed at length by Birger Rapp, *Models for Optimal Investment and Maintenance Decisions* (New York: Halsted Press, 1975).

[16] For a more comprehensive treatment, see G. Terborgh, *Dynamic Equipment Policy* (New York: McGraw-Hill, 1949); or P. Massé, *Optimal Investment Decisions* (Englewood Cliffs, N.J.: Prentice-Hall, 1962), chap. 2. Compare also M. J. Gordon, "The Optimal Timing of Capital Expenditures," in H. Levy and M. Sarnat, eds., *Financial Decision Making under Uncertainty* (New York: Academic Press, 1977), pp. 83–94.

Problems

1. The XYZ Corporation is considering a project which has a three-year life and costs $12,000. It would effect an annual saving in operating costs of $3,600 and increase annual revenue by $2,000. The project would be financed by a three-year loan, with interest at a 5 percent annual rate and having the following repayment schedule:

Year	Payment	Interest	Repayment of principal	Balance
1	$4,406.50	$ 600.00	$ 3,806.50	$8,193.50
2	4,406.50	409.70	3,996.80	4,196.70
3	4,406.50	209.80	4,196.70	0.00
		$1,219.50	$12,000.00	

   If XYZ's after-tax cost of capital is 10 percent, its marginal tax rate is 50 percent, and it uses straight-line depreciation, what is the net present value of this project?

2. An automobile manufacturer must install a new automated engine-boring, transfer-machine facility to produce small, fuel-efficient engines. Two machine tool manufacturers have bid on the installation. The S machine costs

$50 million and will require cash operating expenses of $20 million per year. The P machine costs $75 million, but operating expenses are expected to be only $15 million per year. Both machines have an estimated useful life of ten years with no salvage value and would be depreciated on a straight-line basis. If the company's marginal tax rate is 50 percent, and its after-tax required rate of return is 10 percent, which bid should it accept? Would the decision be affected if the required rate of return was 8 percent? 12 percent?

3. Suppose now that for the machines of problem 2 it is estimated that the machines could be converted to other use at the end of their present useful life so that the salvage value of the S machine would be $5 million and that of the P machine $10 million. Which bid should the manufacturer accept under these new assumptions?

4. The cost of planting a particular variety of rubber trees is $2,400 per acre. Yields from an acre of rubber trees of this type vary according to the following pattern:

Age, years	Annual yield, lbs.
0– 5	0
6– 10	1,000
11– 15	2,000
16– 20	3,000
21– 25	2,500
26– 30	1,500
31– 40	1,000

Estimating harvesting costs are $400 per acre per year. Planting costs are deductible for tax purposes in the year in which they are incurred.

a. Assuming a rubber price of 80 cents per pound, a marginal income tax rate of 50 percent, and a required rate of return of 10 percent, at what age should the rubber trees be replaced?

b. What is the effect of changes in (i) rubber prices, (ii) harvesting costs, (iii) marginal tax rates, and (iv) the required rate of return on the optimum age for replacement?

c. If we assume that rubber prices will increase at 2 percent per annum, that harvesting costs will increase at 5 percent per annum, and that an annual improvement of 1 percent in productivity is available through improved planting stock, what happens to the optimum age for replanting?

Costs of capital from specific sources

5

5.1 Which cost to consider

Cost of capital is one of the fundamental cornerstones of financial theory. While there is a fairly general agreement concerning the usefulness of this concept and how it should be applied, there has been a fundamental lack of agreement on exactly what it is or how it should be measured, although some recent progress has been made. So long as this remains so, any estimate of the cost of capital requires, at some point, the exercise of informed judgment. The contribution of theory, in its present state, is to narrow the range of possible estimates within which judgment must be exercised.

As we saw in Chapter 3, an estimate of the cost of capital, or the required rate of return as we called it there, is necessary in the application of the more sophisticated and satisfactory measures of desirability, including net present value and internal rate of return. We have also seen that it is necessary to consider the cost of capital at the project design stage. These are the primary reasons for its consideration here. While, in addition, it may be useful to management in making decisions between alternative financing proposals, we do not consider such policy issues here, except in the case of lease financing (see Section 5.5). In fact, for the reasons stated in Section 1.6, it is not only possible, but desirable, to consider the capital-expenditure decision independently of the question of financing projects. Detailed examination of financing policy decisions is beyond the scope of this volume. Even within our narrower framework, however, cost may not be the deciding factor as questions of control or of avoiding risk may be more important.[1]

We must tread warily, however, for there are several different concepts of the cost of capital, only some of which may be appropriate for use in the decision-making framework.

For decision-making purposes in general, it is the *future* costs and not the historical ones which are relevant. Capital-expenditure decisions, involving the weighing of future benefits against present outlays, are no exception to this rule; indeed, extra care should be taken to ensure that this standard is being applied.

The most intuitively appealing concept of the cost of capital is simply the cost associated with the use of a particular block of funds raised from a single source, either by a single security issue or a package of securities. We will refer to this concept as the *specific cost* of capital (from a specified source).[2] However, no firm, except perhaps one that is on the point of being set up, relies exclusively on funds from a single source. As a result, generally speaking, the specific cost of funds from a particular source is not the same as the *inclusive cost* of funds from all sources.

The use of different amounts of funds from one source alters the terms on which they are available from other sources, so that it is generally incorrect to associate the inclusive cost of funds with the marginal cost *from a specific source*. The appropriate cost concept for all expenditure decisions is the inclusive concept.[3]

We may also distinguish between *spot costs,* that is, those prevailing in the market at any given moment, and *normalized costs,* those that reflect, by some averaging process, an estimate of costs from which the cyclical element, that is, the variation attributable to the fluctuation in interest rates and security prices over the business cycle, has been abstracted. While spot costs should only be considered in financing decisions, the normalized cost figure is relevant for expenditure decisions, since it more nearly represents the capital market's evaluation of the firm's prospects. In this chapter, however, we shall be concerned with the estimation of spot costs only.

5.2 Relation of capital cost to valuation

The notion of capital cost is intimately related to the problem of valuation. Although some progress has been made, the absence of a fully satisfactory theory of the valuation of the firm is responsible for the lack of a truly operational capital-cost theory. As we have seen, a meaningful notion of profit maximization requires that present stockholders' funds be employed within the firm only if they are worth as much to the stockholders within the firm as they would be if handed over to them in cash. Outside funds should be used only to the extent that they do not detract from the market value of the (current) stockholders' holdings. The (inclusive) cost of capital is simply the amount of earnings (cash flow) that extra funds must produce to justify their use within the firm in the light of this profit (market value) maximization concept. If we knew exactly how the market was going to value additional cash flows, we would know exactly how much additional cash flow would have to be produced to justify any given increase in the volume of funds used by the firm, that is, the cost of capital. While theory does provide some insight into this issue, it is not complete, so that at some point we must rely on judgment rather than arithmetic. Part of the reason for treating the theory is to gain some understanding of where that point may lie.

Cost of capital as used for investment decision purposes is thus an opportunity cost concept. As it is the rate of return which must be earned on assets to justify their acquisition, it might be more appropriate to refer to it as the required rate of return. But the term cost of capital has become entrenched in the literature and will be retained here, at least until we begin discussing risk-adjustments.

It is possible to attempt to measure inclusive costs directly or to synthesize an estimate of inclusive costs from estimates of specific costs. The latter approach, while less direct, has the merit of bringing out certain important interrelationships (see Chapter 6).

5.3 Specific costs: general principles

The most general formula for specific costs is similar to the formula for the internal rate of return. It can be found by solving the following expression for k:

$$Q_0 - \sum_{t=1}^{n} \frac{C_t}{(1 + k)^t} = 0 \qquad (5.3.1)$$

where Q_0 is the sum received, net of all underwriting costs, and the C_t represents the cash earnings necessary to pay interest, dividends, sinking fund contributions, and so on, in subsequent periods after deduction of the appropriate tax credits. It will sometimes be convenient to use the continuous form:

$$Q_0 - \int_0^\infty C(t)e^{-kt}dt = 0 \qquad (5.3.2)$$

The formal relationship between the cost of capital and the internal rate of return has already been discussed, and the present value profile associated with a typical source of funds was shown in Figure 3–4. Use of the formula is shown in Example 5.3.1. There are, however, conventional formulas for calculating costs of capital from different sources which are more convenient for calculation and which produce close approximations to the value of k.

However, we are concerned with the anticipated future cost of capital and not the historical cost. Thus, it is important to use the estimated receipts from a new issue of the security in question in calculating the cost of capital funds from this particular source. This is no problem when a new issue is being prepared and the issue price and the underwriting costs are known, but there is a problem, for example, in computing the cost of debt when no new issue of debt is being contemplated. Historical costs have no relevance in such a circumstance, and the cost calculation must be based on what the issue could be sold for now. This may be most easily calculated from the present market price less estimated underwriting costs.

Example 5.3.1. (using general formula): Five percent bonds of 1989 of the XYZ Manufacturing Company may be sold for a net price to the issuer in 1979 of $95. It is required to calculate the cost of an issue of $1,000,000 (par value) of these bonds, bearing a sinking fund commitment of $80,000 annually for the first five years and $120,000 annually for the last five. The marginal tax rate is 50 percent. The first step is to calculate the annual cash outlay, which is comprised of three elements: (a) the interest payments; plus (b) the sinking fund payments; minus (c) the tax credit on the interest payments and the amortization of discount, which for this example will be taken on a straight line basis. Table 5–1 shows these calculations.

The next step is to find the present value at the varying rates of discount and sketch the present value profile. Table 5–2 shows the necessary calculations, while Figure 5–1 shows the resulting part of the present value profile. The cost of capital is found at the intersection of the $V - C$ curve with the rate-of-return axis. By interpolation, the cost is 3.04 percent. The same result can be found using a computer program for calculating the internal rate of return.

Table 5–1
Cash flow for debt service, XYZ Manufacturing Company

Year	Sinking fund payment	Interest payment	Less: tax credit (50 percent) Interest	Less: tax credit (50 percent) Amortization	Cash flow
1980	$ 80,000	$50,000	$25,000	$2,500	$102,500
1981	80,000	46,000	23,000	2,500	100,500
1982	80,000	42,000	21,000	2,500	98,500
1983	80,000	38,000	19,000	2,500	96,500
1984	80,000	34,000	17,000	2,500	94,500
1985	120,000	30,000	15,000	2,500	132,500
1986	120,000	24,000	12,000	2,500	129,500
1987	120,000	18,000	9,000	2,500	126,500
1988	120,000	12,000	6,000	2,500	123,500
1989	120,000	6,000	3,000	2,500	120,500

Table 5–2
Calculations: present value of debt service charges,
XYZ Manufacturing Company

Year	Variable	Cash flow	Present value at 2.50%	Present value at 2.25%	Present value at 3.00%
1980	C_1	$ 102,500	$ 99,999	$ 99,753	$ 99,517
1981	C_2	100,500	45,656	95,194	94,731
1982	C_3	98,500	91,467	90,797	90,137
1983	C_4	96,500	87,419	86,580	85,740
1984	C_5	94,500	83,529	82,517	81,516
1985	C_6	132,500	114,255	112,598	110,296
1986	C_7	129,500	108,935	107,097	105,296
1987	C_8	126,500	103,819	101,820	99,859
1988	C_9	123,500	98,886	96,750	94,650
1989	C_{10}	120,500	94,135	91,869	89,664
$-\Sigma_t C_t$		$-$1,125,000	$-$978,100	$964,975	$952,079
	Q_0	950,000	950,000	950,000	950,000
	$V - C$	$-$175,000	$-$28,100	$-$14,975	$-$2,079

5.4 Specific costs: bonds or notes

In the case of borrowing, where the borrower receives the full face value of the bonds or notes, the cost is simply the interest rate, adjusted for the tax deductibility of interest, or:

$$k = (1 - T)R \qquad (5.4.1)$$

where T is the marginal tax rate, and R is the nominal or coupon rate of return.

Figure 5–1
Present value profile: XYZ bond issue

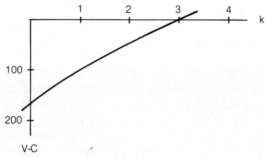

Most frequently, however, bonds are sold at a price differing from the par value at which they must be repaid. The approximate cost of bonds sold at a discount or premium is given by:[4]

$$k = \frac{(1 - T)\left[R + \dfrac{1}{n}(P - Q_0)\right]}{(1/2)(Q_0 + P)} \qquad (5.4.2)$$

where P is the par value of the bond, and n is the number of years to maturity, the other terms having the definitions already given.

The second half of the term in brackets in the numerator represents the amortization of premium or discount and is negative in the case of an issue sold at a premium. The denominator reflects the average amount outstanding during the life of the loan. The principal drawback of the formula is that it takes no account of differences in the size or timing of sinking fund payments, which may be crucial factors in some cases.

In the case of perpetual bonds, equation 5.4.1 simplifies to:

$$k = \frac{(1 - T)R}{Q_0} \qquad (5.4.3)$$

Example 5.4.1: Formula 5.4.3 may be used to calculate an approximate cost of capital for the XYZ bond issue described in Section 5.3. Substituting in equation 5.4.2, the cost is:

$$k = \frac{(1 - 0.50)5.00 + \dfrac{1}{10}(100.00 - 95.00)}{(1/2)(95.00 + 100.00)}$$

$$= 2.82\%$$

This approximation understates the true rate calculated from equation 5.3.1 because it does not take account of the specific period-by-period timing of the outlays for sinking fund payments nor of the annual compounding implicit in equation 5.3.1.

5.5 Specific costs: leases

Installment purchases and the acquisition of assets by leasing pose some problems in the estimation of the cost of capital regarding both whether they should be considered and, if so, how their costs should be measured. In cases of these kinds, it is easy to get the asset-acquisition part of the transaction mixed up with the funds-acquisition (financing) part, with confusing results. There may also be some charges other than interest which are also considered part of the cost of funds from these sources. For example, when insurance is part of the transaction, the insurance costs may be omitted only if the insurance is required anyway, and the premiums are no greater than those which would have been paid through other channels in any event. Where insurance is not ordinarily required (for example, if the firm generally self-insures), but is accepted merely as one of the conditions of obtaining the loan or lease, the premiums should be included as one of the costs. So should any excess of premium over the normal commercial premiums for similar risks. Service charges should also be included in the cost.

Because of the possibility of confusing asset acquisition and financing decisions in both the installment purchase and leasing situations, it is best to remember that purchase for cash is generally an available alternative (with funds coming from general corporate sources, and except in the few cases where a particular asset is available only by leasing). Thus, as in all other circumstances, two decisions need to be made: first, whether to acquire the asset and second, how to finance the acquisition. Failure to follow this rule results in the use of net cash flow estimates which almost invariably overstate the desirability of the acquisition. The decision to acquire the asset must be made on its own merits using the appropriate required rate of return. Installment purchase or leasing may then be compared with the general corporate pool of funds as sources of financing on the basis of explicit costs and savings. As we will see, there may be bona fide, special circumstances which endow lease financing in particular with tax savings not available in ordinary debt or equity financing arrangements. Since lease financing is the more complex, and frequently surrounded by an array of incorrect and/or specious arguments, we will concentrate our discussion on that alternative, for the most part.

We distinguish here between an operating lease and a financial lease and, in the latter instance, the special case of a leveraged lease. An operating lease is cancelable by either the lessee or the lessor upon due notice to the other party. This type of lease is, therefore, an arrangement of indefinite (for the most part, short) duration. Among the assets frequently acquired through operating leases are vehicles, computers, copiers, fixtures, and furniture. Such leases may be net or may be maintenance leases. In *net leases,* the payment is only for the asset and not for keeping it in operating repair. A *maintenance lease,* on the other hand, requires the lessor to provide maintenance services and is frequently used in leasing vehicles, computers, copiers, and other technical equipment which require expert service. Clearly, the cost of such service will be included in the lease payments.

A *financial lease* is a contractual commitment under which the lessee makes payments to the lessor over a specified period of time in exchange for the use of the leased asset. A strict financial lease is one that does not provide for maintenance services, is not cancelable, and is fully amortized (that is, the payments received by the lessor equal the full price of the leased equipment). A financial lease will ordinarily provide a means for the lessee to continue possession of the property after the expiration of the initial lease either through a renewal option or a purchase option. Financial leases are most commonly used in connection with office equipment, railroad cars, aircraft, and construction equipment.

With outright purchase of an asset either for cash or through an installment purchase, the depreciation tax shield must be calculated in the usual way, as we discussed earlier. By contrast, the full amount of the lease payments is deductible for income tax purposes provided the taxing authorities agree that a particular contract is a genuine lease and not simply an installment purchase called a lease. Thus, it is important that any lease contract fall within the acceptable guidelines and be carefully drawn up as to form. The differential tax effects on cash flows make each alternative form of financing more or less attractive in particular circumstances.

While we have been discussing leases as dealing implicitly with the acquisition of new assets, a firm may also sell an asset it already owns to another party and then lease it back from the buyer in a *sale and leaseback* arrangement. By these means, the firm can obtain the cash proceeds from the sale and still have the use of the asset. Similarly, if the firm wants to lease an asset it does not own, it may purchase it, sell it to another party, then lease it back. Either way, sale and leaseback arrangements are almost always financial leases rather than operating leases. Again, the incentive for such arrangements would be to obtain cash and/or to share in some tax-reducing benefit not otherwise available, as we will discuss later.

Finally, we consider a *leveraged lease* or *third-party* lease. In contrast with the two-party involvement in the contracts previously discussed, there are three parties involved in leveraged leasing (as the alternate name implies): (a) the *lessee,* (b) the *lessor* (or *equity participant*), and, (c) the *lender.* For the lessee, there is no difference between the leveraged lease and any other type of lease. The lessor, however, plays an *intermediary* role. As required by the terms of the lease arrangement, the lessor acquires the asset, financing this acquisition partly with his own funds with the balance provided by long-term lenders. The loan is generally secured by a mortgage on the asset, as well as by assignment of the lease (and thus the lease payments). Note, however, that in these circumstances, the *lessor* is both the borrower and the owner of the asset.

The benefits which may accrue to each party may help to explain why each would want to enter into a leasing arrangement. As owner of the asset, the lessor is entitled to claim the depreciation tax shield in respect of that asset and any interest expense in the case of a leveraged lease (and the entire investment tax credit, where applicable). In recent years, high-tax bracket individuals have formed partnerships for the purpose of purchasing equipment and then leasing it to firms. The tax shield from depreciation and interest expense is more valuable to them than to any firm leasing the asset. As a result, to the extent some part of this saving may be bargained for, both lessor and lessee may benefit (at the expense of the taxing authorities). Note that is not the existence of taxes per se that imparts economic benefits to leasing arrangements, but rather the fact that the marginal rate of tax differs among different firms, intermediaries, and individuals creating a differing ability to realize the benefits of the tax shields associated with owning the asset. Such differences arise from (a) differences in tax rates among the various parties and (b) different levels of past and current income among them. A firm with a tax loss carry forward will have little or no current tax liability, thus the tax shield (and investment credit) available from purchasing an asset may be of no value. If, however, that same firm is able to lease an asset from some other party that would ordinarily pay high taxes, it may be able to capture part of the tax benefits associated with ownership through lease payments that are lower than they would otherwise be. The lessor, in turn, is able to use the full tax shield benefits which he might not otherwise be able to use, and as a result, both parties gain.

We emphasize that a lease contract and its required payments are a fixed obligation of the lessee and, as with interest payments on debt, failure to make scheduled lease payments may induce the same results, that is, deemed technical insolvency and possible bankruptcy proceedings. While the lessor's claim against the lessee in the event of bankruptcy is less stringent than that of most creditors, nevertheless the lease contract will generally provide for repossession of the leased asset, and at least partial compensation for the lease payments owing under the remaining term of the lease. Perhaps more relevant is that a financial lease, like debt, involves both the advantages and disadvantages of financial leverage. Since leases involve a fixed charge similar to interest on debt, fluctuations in operating income will be absorbed by the lessee.

As a point in favor of leasing, it is frequently argued that leasing an asset rather than purchasing it imposes less of a current demand on the firm's cash balances, thus freeing capital for other productive purposes. If it is valid at all, this argument would only be true in some sort of absolute capital-rationing situation where the firm could lease the asset, but could not borrow further to buy it, nor use installment purchase (although it is not clear that this would be the case because the particular class of asset is not financed that way, or because the firm's credit standing is so poor that no one wishes to make the implied loan). In the latter event, leasing is likely to be inaccessible as well. But firms do not ordinarily face such an impenetrable barrier (if so, we would question the assumptions in the analysis of the decision to acquire the asset in the first place as being unrealistic). There need be no net cash outflow if the firm can borrow the purchase price of the asset. Under either a leasing arrangement or purchase using debt, the firm has the asset for use and a fixed commitment to make future payments (either to the lessor or the lender).

While it is generally accepted that too much debt in the firm's capital structure will restrict the firm's capacity to borrow further, it is sometimes argued, at least implicitly, that leasing somehow is a method of obtaining assets through implicit borrowing without reducing debt capacity. Clearly, a lease imposes fixed charges on the firm and thus is equally likely to lead to technical insolvency as debt. The question is whether lenders (or investors) view leases this way, or whether they merely ignore any outstanding leases in computing fixed charges (and coverage) of the firm? Given that lease obligations frequently are revealed only as notes to the financial statements, it would seem that their implications may not be captured by the calculation of standard ratios, for example, and thus may not properly be considered in evaluating the actual extent of financial leverage. To the extent that this is the case, it would then appear that financing asset acquisition by leasing rather than borrowing may have less of an impact on the firm's apparent debt capacity. More recently, however, due both to increasing lender sophistication and to the activities of professional accounting groups regarding disclosure of lease obligations, leases have come to be treated as similar to debt and are now more frequently taken into account in appraising the firm's capital structure and determining its debt capacity.

Another alleged advantage of leasing, at least in the case of operating leases, is that the lessee can escape the risk associated with the possibility that the asset may become technically and economically obsolete. Whether the asset is economically obsolete would be decided by replacement analysis (see Chapter 3). An operating lease is cancelable, and even a financial lease can be written with a term sufficiently short that the lessee cannot be compelled to continue using an obsolete asset. But, since the lessor may be presumed to know his business, the risk of obsolescence will have been appraised and impounded into the lease payments. There are some cases of leasing, particularly in computers and certain industrial equipment, where the lessor is well able to manage the obsolescence problem. Since it is not usually the case that an asset becomes totally obsolete and economically useless instantly, the lessor may make it part of his service to find an economic use for a slightly outdated asset. When he can, the economic cost of obsolescence will be less under leasing than under purchase, and some of that advantage may be expected to be passed along to the lessee (in the form of lower lease payments) as potential lessors compete for his business.

To this point we have discussed differences in effective taxes paid by lessors and lessees and differences in bearing the risk of obsolescence as being factors that impart economic value to leasing. We now consider the differences in protection afforded to the lessor and lessee in event of bankruptcy. These three factors are the only ones of relevance in determining whether lease financing is appropriate.

As we mentioned earlier, the lessor has a superior position in bankruptcy and liquidation because he owns the asset and may quickly repossess it if the lessee defaults on his lease payments. While it is also true that a lender can secure his loan against the asset with a mortgage bond, it is considerably more difficult and costly to seize the asset. In addition to the direct costs of initiating bankruptcy litigation, there are opportunity costs because of delays in obtaining judgments. To the extent that any of these anticipated costs of bankruptcy may be avoided or reduced by leasing, then these savings may be passed along in part to the lessee. In fact, some suppliers of capital may act either as lenders or as lessors, the choice depending upon the perceived riskiness of the firm seeking accommodation. There have even been situations where loans have been converted to leases where the lender has perceived that the risk of default has increased significantly.

In Chapter 1, we began our analysis by assuming that capital markets were perfect: no transaction costs, information costlessly and readily available to all market participants, infinitely divisible securities, no bankruptcy costs, and no taxes. It can be shown that under these simplifying assumptions the debt and lease obligations of a firm will be valued in the capital market by lenders and lessors in exactly the same manner.[5] Since the costs of debt and lease financing consequently will be the same, the firm should be indifferent between the two methods of financing. Thus, if lease financing is a significant source and a material part of the firm's capital structure, it should be considered to have the same specific, after-tax cost as debt, as discussed in Section 5.4.

Although we claim that the specific, after-tax cost of leasing can be taken to be the same as that of long-term debt, we emphasize that this is not the correct rate to use for comparing debt and lease financing alternatives as is frequently claimed.[6] Since we have argued that the decision to acquire an asset should be considered independently of how the acquisition is to be financed, and since the acquisition decision will be analyzed (see Chapter 3) using the firm's overall required rate of return or the required rate of return for projects in the risk class for which the asset is being acquired (see Chapter 6), then that same rate (the inclusive cost) must be used to compare financing alternatives. Financing the acquisition from the general pool of capital funds whose sources cannot be identified, but which have some aggregate cost (the overall required rate of return) is always an alternative. To then compare a specific source of financing, such as debt, with the leasing alternative using the specific cost of debt as the standard is both inconsistent and incorrect. The reason for this is that, since both alternatives absorb debt capacity, they both involve *implicit* costs (see Chapter 6). For this reason, the same required rate of return must be used in both the asset acquisition and financing decisions. The benefit to the firm of choosing leasing instead of borrowing as a form of financing must flow only from the explicit cash (tax) savings.

As we relax the assumptions of perfect capital markets and introduce transactions costs, information costs, less than infinite divisibility of securities, taxes, and bankruptcy costs, then debt and lease contracts may not be valued in quite the same manner. Their costs to the firm may differ, but market imperfections may create or induce impediments to arbitraging between financial instruments. If arbitrage is impeded, then specialized institutions may develop to take advantage of the situation and make available one or the other form of financing preferred by the firm. We have examined three special circumstances which may make leasing advantageous.

To the extent that leasing is preferred, it must be because the cost to the firm is lower than debt, and thus our argument for using the after-tax cost of debt may be disputed as overstating the cost of leasing. This may be checked by performing an internal rate of return calculation to determine the after-tax cost of leasing by solving the following equation for r.[7]

$$A_0 - ITC - \sum_{t=0}^{n-1} \frac{L_t}{(1 + r)^t} + \sum_{t=1}^{n} \frac{T(L_{t-1} - P_t)}{(1 + r)^t} = 0 \qquad (5.5.1)$$

where A_0 is the cost of the asset to be leased; ITC is the investment tax credit (where applicable); n is the number of periods to the end of the lease; L_t is the lease payment at the end of period t; T is the corporate tax rate; and P_t is the depreciation in period t that would be applicable if the asset were owned. The only problem with attempting to make this calculation is that the pattern of cash flows will have at least one reversal in sign at the end which leads to the possibility of multiple rates of return (as discussed in Chapter 3).

In the special case of an asset which can only be leased and is not available for purchase, the cost of the asset, A_0, cannot be determined directly. The cash-equivalent price of the lease can be inferred by finding the present value of the lease payment stream, but since this requires the choice of a discount rate, it makes no sense to then apply equation 5.5.1 to the resulting price. If the lease is to be capitalized for disclosure purposes, then the after-tax cost of debt would be a suitable capitalization rate, since it converts the lease payments into a present value or debt equivalent. This should be noted so that it will not be confused with a market-determined value for A_0.

We conclude the discussion of this section with two examples which compare an installment purchase with a lease arrangement.

Example 5.5.1: ABC, Ltd., a Canadian corporation, is considering the acquisition of a forklift truck to improve materials handling in their warehouse. It is estimated that the truck will save $5,000 per year in labor costs and $1,000 in inventory carrying costs. The estimated life of the truck is six years. Scrap value is assumed to be nil. Maximum rate of depreciation for income tax purposes is 33.33 percent on a declining balance basis. The truck can be bought for $10,000 cash or for a down payment of $3,000 with the balance in 16 quarterly installments of $437.50 plus interest at 3 percent per quarter on the unpaid balance. The wrong way of examining this proposed purchase is to lump the whole transaction together as has been done in Table 5–3.

Table 5–3
Analysis of forklift acquisition, ABC, Ltd.* (incorrect)

Year	Cash savings	Cash outlays			Net cash flow
		Principal	Interest	Taxes	
1	$6,000	$1,750	$761	$ 953	$2,536
2	6,000	1,750	551	1,613	2,085
3	6,000	1,750	341	2,089	1,820
4	6,000	1,750	131	2,441	1,678
5	6,000	—	—	2,671	3,329
6	6,000	—	—	2,781	3,219

Initial outlay: $3,000
Rate of return: 75 percent

* Lumping the whole transaction together as is shown in this table is the wrong way to examine the proposed purchase. See Tables 5–4 and 5–5 for the correct way.

Table 5–4
Analysis of forklift acquisition, ABC, Ltd. (correct)

Year	Cash savings	Tax	Net cash savings
1	$6,000	$1,333	$4,667
2	6,000	1,889	4,111
3	6,000	2,259	3,740
4	6,000	2,506	3,494
5	6,000	2,670	3,329
6	6,000	2,780	3,219

Initial outlay: $10,000
Rate of return: 32 percent

Table 5–5
Analysis of installment loan, ABC, Ltd. (correct)

Year	Payment	Tax saving on interest	Net outlay
1	$2,511	$381	$2,130
2	2,301	275	2,026
3	2,091	170	1,921
4	1,881	66	1,815

Amount received: $7,000
Cost of capital: 5 percent

It is safer to separate the asset-acquisition and fund-raising parts of the transaction as is done in Tables 5–4 and 5–5. Table 5–4 indicates that the true rate of return on the acquisition of the asset is not the spectacular 75 percent shown by the calculation in Table 5–3, although it remains a respectable 32 percent. This is the rate of return from acquiring the asset, regardless of the way it is financed, so that if it can be financed more cheaply than through the installment purchase, there is a clear gain. Whether the asset should be acquired is a decision that should be taken on its own merits. If this decision is favorable, consideration can then be given to how the acquisition is to be financed. If the installment loan is the financing alternative which leads to the lowest cost of capital, then it should be bought on the installment plan. If not, it should be bought for cash and alternative sources of funds used. Table 5–5 indicates that the installment loan will provide $7,000 in debt financing at an after-tax cost of 5 percent.

Example 5.5.2: While the directors of ABC, Ltd., were still mulling over the proposed acquisition of their forklift truck, the finance com-

pany offered to lease them the truck for $200 per month on a six-year
lease that provided that ABC, Ltd., would assume all repair and
maintenance costs. The rental payments would be deductible in full for
tax purposes, but they would no longer be able to claim depreciation.
The resulting calculation of capital costs is shown in Table 5–6.

Table 5–6
Analysis of leasing cost, ABC, Ltd.

Year	Rental	Tax saving on rental	Tax loss on depreciation	Net tax effect on lease status	Cash outlay
1	$2,400	$1,200	$1,667	$+467	$ 2,867
2	2,400	1,200	1,111	− 89	2,311
3	2,400	1,200	741	−459	1,941
4	2,400	1,200	494	−706	1,694
5	2,400	1,200	329	−871	1,529
6	2,400	1,200	220	−980	1,420
					$11,762

Amount received: $10,000
Cost of capital: 5.5 percent

This cost seemed quite reasonable, and in view of the company's
need for funds, it was felt that it was more desirable to raise $10,000 at a
cost of 5.5 percent than to raise $7,000 at a cost of 5 percent. The
treasurer demurred, however, stating that the additional $3,000 would
cost the company a lot more than 5.5 percent and that other sources of
the funds ought to be investigated. The meeting was adjourned for 15
minutes to enable him to calculate the *incremental* cost of raising the
extra $3,000 by adopting the leasing proposal. The result of his calcula-
tions is shown in Table 5–7.

Table 5–7
Incremental cost of extra funds raised by leasing, ABC, Ltd.

Year	Cash outlay installment loan	Cash outlay leasing	Incremental outlay
1	$2,130	$2,867	$ 737
2	2,026	2,311	285
3	1,921	1,941	20
4	1,815	1,694	(121)
5	—	1,529	1,529
6	—	1,420	1,420

Extra funds received: $3,000
Cost of capital: 6 percent

5.6 Specific costs: preferred stock

It is, perhaps, necessary to explain why the dividend on preferred stock must be regarded as a cost. One may take a legalistic position and claim that such a dividend represents a distribution of earnings to owners, or the view of some accountants that because there is no binding legal obligation to pay dividends on preferreds, the dividends do not constitute a cost.[8] Such quibbles merely beg the question.

From the point of view of common stockholders, preferred stock represents an alternative source of senior funds having many of the characteristics of debt but certain advantages in particular circumstances.[9] Dividends on preferred stocks, even though they are not legal obligations to the same extent as debt-servicing charges, are a cost to the common stockholder. Few corporations would issue preferred stock without the intention of paying regular dividends and the consequences of failing to do so can be extremely serious. Frequently preferred issues gain voting rights when the dividend is passed, in fact, they often gain control. Worse, perhaps, than the danger of loss of control is the damage done to the company's credit standing. Its preferred issues, even its bonds, may cease to be eligible for trustee investment, and the accumulation of arrearages adversely affects the likelihood of being able to pay dividends on the common. As a consequence, the firm may find difficulty in raising funds on reasonable terms except by the sale of well-secured senior bonds. If its borrowing capacity in this direction is fully utilized, it may not be able to raise funds through regular channels at all and may be driven to use expensive back-door sources of credit.

For these reasons, the decision to pass a preferred dividend cannot be taken lightly. If there is no distributable surplus or if the dividend would render the company insolvent, there may be little choice. While the obligation to pay is moral, rather than legal, the cost is economically relevant.

The cost of a straight preferred issue, like that of a debt issue, is most accurately calculated using equation 5.3.1, particularly when there is a sinking fund involved, or where it is planned to call parts of the issue at specified dates. The conventional approximation treats the preferred as a perpetual obligation and the dividend as an interest payment which is not tax deductible, giving the expression:

$$k = \frac{D}{Q_0} \qquad (5.6.1)$$

where D is the annual dividend.

Equation 5.6.1 is applicable as it stands only to straight preferred issues. For convertible or participating issues, a more sophisticated approach is required (see Section 5.14). As Q_0 will be dependent on the market price of the company's outstanding preferred stock, or other companies' issues of comparable risk, k is influenced in part by the extent of prior claims and the earnings coverage available for the payment of dividends. It is thus *not* independent of capital structure as the equation might appear to suggest.

5.7 The cost of equity capital: common stock

The objections mentioned in connection with our attempt to measure the cost of funds raised by issuing preferred stock are apt to be raised again with more vehemence, when it is proposed to measure the cost of equity funds. However, management is, at any given point in time, responsible only to the existing common stockholders and is by implication concerned with maximizing their wealth. As already noted, further investment in the firm is worthwhile if, and only if, it is expected to leave them at least as well off, in terms of prospective dividend income and the market value of their holdings, as they were before. We confine ourselves for the moment to examining a firm which is constrained, for some reason, to using common stock financing exclusively.

Issuing common stock may do several things:

1. It entitles the holders of new shares to all future dividends on an equal basis with the holders of existing shares.
2. It entitles the new stockholders to a pro rata share in the undistributed profits of the company, and more generally, to a pro rata share in the assets in the event of winding up.
3. It may as a consequence result in lower earnings per share or a reduction in book value as far as the existing stockholders are concerned and may reduce market value.

Unless the earnings from a new investment requiring a new stock issue are expected to be sufficiently great to prevent *dilution* and a consequent worsening in the dividend income from or market value of their stock, the new stock should not be sold and the investment should not be undertaken. The required rate of return on the new investment is the implicit cost of funds. What is this required rate of return?

The relationships between capital structure and the cost of equity funds are complex and subject to considerable debate (see Chapter 6). For the moment, we shall retain the assumption that the company has an all-equity capital structure. Even under these restrictive assumptions, several measurement proposals have been put forward; but only two are worth serious consideration at this point in our analysis.

The first of these uses the earnings-price ratio, or, more specifically, the expected earnings-price ratio as the cost of capital. If E_A is the expected average earnings per share, and Q_0^* is the amount which would be received from the sale of a single share, cost is expressed by:[10]

$$k = \frac{E_A}{Q_0} \tag{5.7.1}$$

This proposed measure implicitly assumes that the only factor influencing market price is earnings per share and that if the new investment produces earnings per share for the new shares equal to that which would have been earned on existing shares in its absence, market price will be unaffected, and present stockholders protected against dilution. Unfortunately, new stockholders not only gain a pro rata share in existing earnings, they get a share in future earnings as well. Where the prospect of larger future earnings is an important element of value, equation 5.7.1 neglects the reduction in present stockholders' future earnings share and understates common equity costs.

The second measurement proposal is somewhat more sophisticated and regards the market price as dependent on the dividend being paid and the expected rate of growth in the dividend. The cost element is the dividend. Its growth is dependent on retained earnings. A fraction b of the earnings E_t are invested each period at an expected rate of return *on book value* of r^*. The expected dividend in period t is:

$$D_t = (1 - b)E_t \tag{5.7.2}$$

while income per share at time t is:

$$E_t = E_{t-1} + r^* b E_{t-1} \tag{5.7.3}$$

That is, E_t grows at the rate $g = br^*$, so that:

$$E_t = E_0 e^{gt} \tag{5.7.4}$$

and

$$D_t = D_0 e^{gt}$$

Substituting in equation 5.3.2 yields:

$$Q_0 = \int_0^\infty D_0 e^{-t(k-g)} dt$$

and integrating (if $k > g$):

$$Q_0 = \frac{D}{k - g} \tag{5.7.5}$$

whence:

$$k = \frac{D_0}{Q_0} + g \qquad (5.7.6)$$

The cost of equity capital using this equation is simply the current dividend yield plus the average growth rate (adjusted for issue costs).[11] Equation 5.7.6 gives the same results as 5.7.1 if $E_0 = E_n$ and if $b = g = 0$ (so that $D_0 = E_0$) and under certain more restrictive assumptions.[12] It is quite possible to express equity cost in terms of earnings rather than dividends; an appropriately formulated expression gives results equivalent to 5.7.6 and is more complex than 5.7.1.[13]

Equation 5.7.6 is a simplification, which assumes a constant rate of growth in perpetuity. For equilibrium to exist in the capital market, it is necessary that k be the marginal rate of return for all firms of equivalent risk. Values of r^* greater than k must, therefore, be regarded as resulting from unusually profitable investment opportunities, which will be limited in number for any firm, as we earlier discussed in Chapter 3. But in mature industries, or industries where r^* is subject to regulatory constraint, it may be more appropriate to consider a finite, rather than an infinite, growth period after which $r^* = k$, and no further goodwill gains accrue to stockholders from additional investment undertaken on their behalf.[14]

If the period of growth during which $r^* > k$ is finite, values will be less than those implied in equation 5.7.5, and k will be correspondingly lower. Q_0 must be equated to the present value of the dividend stream during the period of growth plus the present value of the stock price at its end. The latter is simply the capitalized value of the perpetual earnings stream at the end of the period of growth, discounted for its distance in time. Finding k involves solving:

$$Q_0 = \sum_{t=1}^{n} \frac{D_0(1 + g)^t}{(1 + k)^t} + \frac{E_0(1 + g)^t}{k(1 + k)^t} \qquad (5.7.7)$$

which is time consuming and troublesome. Except where the growth period is expected to be very short, 5.7.6 usually gives a satisfactory approximation. Tables of growth yields which permit solution of 5.7.7 are available.[15]

The cost of common equity computed using equation 5.7.6 may be viewed as being comprised of two parts. One is a pure rate of interest component which reflects the time value of money, and the second is a risk premium which is peculiar to the individual firm (or project) and reflects the additional market yield investors are able to command for accepting the residual claim position in an enterprise with given commercial (business) and financial risk characteristics. We introduce this view in the context of the capital asset pricing model briefly, discuss it in more detail in Section 6.11, and consider it further in Chapters 11 and 12. It is possible that the pure interest component may be further partitioned into a real-interest component and an anticipated-inflation-rate component. This possibility and its implications will be examined in Chapter 10. For the moment, the simple dichotomization into an interest component and a risk premium will suffice.

This has several implications. One is that it offers a convenient way to update equity cost estimates, which may be time consuming and expensive to prepare. While full analyses should be prepared regularly on a benchmark basis, the cost estimates so obtained can be updated between such studies by applying the change in the long-term government bond rate, the closest approximation to a pure interest rate of the appropriate maturity dimension, to adjust the equity cost. Thus if k_e was 0.12 when the government bond rate was 0.07, and if the latter has risen to 0.095, then $0.12 + (.095 - .07) = 0.145$ is a reasonable approximation to the current level of k_e. This treatment should be used with some caution, however, as it assumes the risk premium to be *invariant* with the interest rate. Gordon and Halpern claim that where interest rate changes are due to changes in inflation expectations there may be offsetting changes in the appropriate risk premium.[16] If so, using this approach may lead to overestimates in times of rising prices and underestimates when prices are falling.

A somewhat more elaborate use of the pure interest-risk premium dichotomy is involved in attempts to measure k_e using the capital asset pricing model (CAPM) as an alternative to the so-called Discounted Cash Flow (DCF) procedure described earlier. The CAPM (which is examined in more detail in Chapters 11 and 12) is an attempt to explain the structure of risk premia for individual securities. Specifically, it asserts that, in a one holding period context, ex-ante (expected) returns are specified by:

$$E(r_j) - r_f = \beta_j(E(r_m) - r_f) \qquad (5.7.8)$$

where $E(r_j)$ = the expected holding period return on security j;

r_f = the risk-free interest rate expected to exist during the holding period;

$E(r_m)$ = the expected rate or return on the market portfolio, the set of all risky assets as we will later define it;

β_j = a measure of systematic (undiversifiable) risk for security j.

This appears, at first glance, to offer a way around the unobservable g parameter of equation 5.7.6, and to permit the calculation of the risk premium in terms of observable variables and parameters.

But this is more illusion than reality. We really are dealing with *expectations* of three random variables, not with their observed values, and simply plugging in some average of their past values makes certain strong assumptions about the stationarity of their distributions which may not be justified. Past values of r_f can be measured. Indeed there are an abundance of contradictory observations depending on whether the implicitly assumed single-holding period is a day, a month, a quarter, or five years. $E(r_m)$, the yield on the true market portfolio cannot even be measured in the past because the portfolio includes not only publicly traded securities, but equities in privately held corporations, real property, consumer durables, and individuals' investment in human capital.[17] It is common practice to use a stock market index as a surrogate, but this is defensible more on grounds of convenience and accessibility than anything else.[18] What is required as an input is the market's expected yield on the global portfolio, which is at least as unobservable as g. It is possible to infer a value of $E(r_m)$ from an estimate of k_e by rewriting the equation, solving for $E(r_m)$.

Nor is the unobservability of $E(r_m)$ the only problem. The β_js so calculated are not stationary but tend to regress to the population mean value of 1.0,[19] and there appears also to be significant correlation between the residuals of such a regression and subsequent yields, contrary to the theory.[20] While corrections for the regressive tendency of β_j have been proposed,[21] it is far from clear that the regression tendency is a statistical artifact, as is assumed, and not a reflection of the fact that extremely risky situations tend (over time) to become less risky, while at least some extremely safe ones (for example, Penn Central) eventually deteriorate. While the model has promise, it undoubtedly has not attained its final form.[22] In our view, it should be used only with extreme caution and should be checked where possible by the more conventional *DCF* calculation.

5.8 The special case of rights offerings

When stock is not offered to the public at large but is offered to existing stockholders through the medium of a privileged subscription or rights offering, shares are usually sold at a price lower than the existing market. Use of the offering price in calculating the specific cost associated with a rights offering would indicate that this method of raising funds was more expensive than a straight public offering. That this is an incorrect conclusion is demonstrated by consideration of the results that would occur if the issue were to be taken up entirely by the stockholders. Each stockholders' pro rata share in the company would be unchanged, however, his investment will have increased by the amount subscribed. All that is needed to insure that he is as well off after the issue as he was before is for the market value of the firm to increase by the amount of cash subscribed under the new offering. This requires that the earnings from the use of the new funds must be sufficient when capitalized to increase the market value by the amount of the new funds. The appropriate specific cost estimate is thus exactly the same as that derived earlier for the general common stock case.

This conclusion is not altered if the stockholders do not subscribe to the issue but sell their rights. Here they are parting with a portion of their equity for a consideration which itself must be correctly priced while the integrity of their remaining equity is maintained by meeting the earnings standard specified.

5.9 The cost of retained earnings

There are two ways of approaching the problem of estimating the cost of retained earnings. They can be regarded as the equivalent of a fully subscribed rights offering with certain tax advantages, or the problem can be approached on an opportunity cost basis.

If we choose to approach the evaluation of retained earnings cost by the rights approach, we note, first of all, that there are no underwriting costs, so there is no need to make a deduction from the market price in the denominator if Equations 5.7.1 or 5.7.6 are to be adopted. If, however, earnings were paid as dividends and a simultaneous rights offering made, stockholders would be subject to personal income tax on the dividends and would only be able to subscribe an amount equal to $(1 - T)D_0$, where T is the marginal tax rate applicable to the individual stockholder. To be as well off as he would be under a rights offering, it is only sufficient that the value of his shares rise by an amount which after making due provision for any tax on capital gains is equal to the net dividend he would have received after tax.

For the investor subject to income tax at the rate T_y and capital gains tax at the rate T_c, Equation 5.7.6 gives and effective after-tax yield of:

$$k_t = (1 - T_y)\frac{D_0}{P_0} + (1 - T_c)g \qquad (5.9.1)$$

In the case of a corporation for which $k = .10$ and $g = .04$ (so that $D/P = .06$), the return required by a stockholder with a 75 percent marginal tax rate, subject to 25 percent capital gains tax is:

$$k_t = (1 - .75).06 + (1 - .25).04$$
$$= 2.5\%$$

However, for a stockholder with a 40 percent marginal tax rate, subject to 20 percent capital gains tax, k_t is:

$$k_t = (1 - .40).06 + (1 - .20).04$$
$$= 6.8\%$$

For the tax-exempt stockholder, the minimum required rate of return remains 10 percent. If we accept the reduced-earnings-requirement standard implied in 5.9.1, there is no apparent way for management to resolve the conflict of interest between the high-tax bracket stockholders and the tax-exempt stockholders. However, there is no need to give up quite so easily. These are minimum requirements. If the company meets the minimum return requirements of its tax-exempt stockholders on all the funds reinvested, it will exceed the requirements of the taxable stockholders, so we will have a situation where none of the stockholders will be made worse off, and some will be made better off, with the result a clear gain. This will only be possible, of course, if there is an infinitely elastic supply of investment opportunities available offering prospective rates of return at or near the tax-free stockholder's required rate. Fortunately, such a reservoir is available through the capital market. Shares will ordinarily be available in a number of companies offering yields similar to those required by the tax-exempt stockholders with roughly comparable risk. In many cases, the company can buy its own shares. These alternative investment opportunities provide a floor below which no project should be accepted. To the extent that intercompany dividends are taxable, the acceptable yield on marginal projects may be reduced slightly, but caution should be exercised here. The possibility of acquiring a sufficiently large interest in other companies to permit filing a consolidated tax return may reduce the impact of taxes, or it may be possible to find situations in which most of the expected yield is in the form of capital gains. Normally, the market rates of return on investments in other companies with similar risk characteristics should be adopted as a minimum required rate of return for reinvested earnings.

All this standard does is provide us with a cutoff rate for capital-budgeting purposes. It does not tell us whether we should reinvest funds or, if so, how much. Some comments on this problem follow.

5.10 Dividend policy

While it is possible to resolve the problem of what minimum return to require on retained earnings, management is faced with an apparent dilemma in resolving the conflicting interests of different groups of stockholders in the actual decision of how much to reinvest. If market investments are taken into account, available investment opportunities are apt to be much larger than available earnings for most corporations, and while tax-exempt stockholders may be indifferent between receiving dividends and having earnings reinvested at the market yield k, taxable stockholders will in general not be indifferent. To some degree, the issue is one of investment policy rather than dividend policy; Miller and Modigliani have shown that in the absence of transactions cost and taxes, stockholders will be indifferent between financing a given investment program out of retained earnings and financing it through new security issues.[23] In the face of transactions costs and taxes, the retained-earnings alternative will generally be preferable and investment policy in practice can seldom be taken as independent of financing, even if it should be.

While these considerations tend to suggest that taxable stockholders would be better off and nontaxable stockholders no worse off if all earnings were systematically reinvested at market yields or better, the world is not quite so simple. Several studies have suggested the existence of a positive relationship between dividends and stock prices. While the general high correlation between earnings and dividends makes interpretation of the results somewhat difficult, there appears to be a strong likelihood that dividends at least convey information about earnings expectations which is otherwise unavailable to the market. Payment of a significant fraction of earnings as dividends can be justified on these grounds alone, if not otherwise.[24]

One of the difficulties in resolving the theoretical problem lies in the fact that the supply of funds to the firm is not independent of the prospects for growth implicit in the demand for funds within the firm, a point which has already been noted. As a practical matter, however, we would suggest that funds be retained only if internal investment opportunities offer a clearly higher rate of return than the market-capitalization rate for the firm as a whole (see Chapter 6). If enough projects are available to use up the entire cash flow from depreciation accruals and earnings stream on this basis, then the entire cash flow should be retained. If this only uses a fraction of the available earnings and accruals, the balance should be paid out. If no projects meet these requirements, all cash flows should be paid as dividends or shares repurchased. This will probably give an estimate of the cutoff rate which errs on the low side, but the added complications of a correct calculation on these grounds may not be worthwhile in most practical situations.[25] We concern ourselves with estimating the cost of capital with allowances for risk on a much firmer theoretical basis in Chapter 11.

While the market-investment opportunity was noted earlier, it should only be resorted to with caution. Operating management has, in most cases, no clear mandate to turn the firm into an investment trust. The individual stockholders are probably as capable of selecting their own portfolio investments with their own money, an issue we also examine at least peripherally in Chapters 11 and 12. There may be a case for it on a temporary basis, for example, if projects meeting the retention standard are likely to be available in the next budget period. This does not apply, of course, to investments undertaken with a view to obtaining control or ultimate merger.

To the extent, if any, that dividend policy does not maximize share prices, all our estimates of equity costs will be too high. Our equations apply only when dividend policy is optimal in this sense.[26] However, since substantial deviations in dividend payout do not appear to have any clearly demonstrated effect on valuation, any error introduced is likely to be slight. Generous dividend policies may be disadvantageous to high-income stockholders, as compared with the repurchase of stock. However, there appears to be some tendency for stockholders to sort themselves out, choosing companies with dividend policies appropriate to their tax circumstances. The probable existence of this clientele effect makes it desirable to maintain a relatively predictable dividend policy, with a high or low payout rate consistently followed.

5.11 Depreciation accruals

It is an even more common, but equally fallacious, practice to regard funds released by earned depreciation and similar accruals as free. Depreciation, if earned, represents the conversion of fixed assets into cash which should not be reinvested in less liquid assets unless the effect of reinvestment is to maintain the value of the firm. If it will not, there is always the alternative of reducing debt or giving the cash back to the stockholders by purchasing shares on the market or where this is not permitted by law by a formal reduction in capital. Cost should, therefore, be taken at a minimum as the cost of the debt which could otherwise be retired. For most purposes, however, as reduction in total capital employed (in one form or another) is the alternative to reinvesting such accruals, the appropriate cost to be imputed to depreciation funds is the inclusive or overall cost of funds to the firm (see Chapter 6).

5.12   Deferred taxes

Corporate income tax regulations permit the use of accelerated depreciation at rates which may exceed those used for corporate reporting purposes. Taxable income from an asset is thus reduced in the early portion of its life by a *depreciation tax shield*. This will be balanced in later years by an increase in tax above that payable using book depreciation. In this instance, *timing* differences are created between the reporting of incomes or expenses for tax purposes and the reporting of the same items in financial statements to the stockholders. When these timing differences cause a postponement of tax payments, these will be disclosed as deferred income taxes on the firm's balance sheet. For the financial manager, at least two questions are of interest: (*a*) How (if at all) should deferred taxes be treated in the evaluation of the firm's capital structure that is, are they liabilities or equity? (*b*) If deferred tax balances represent interest-free obligations to government, are they, in fact, costless?

Should this deferred tax liability be considered as debt or equity? One argument is that it may be treated as a segregated portion of the equity (retained earnings) account because they may never have to be paid. Under what circumstances is this argument valid? There are probably two. First, if the firm continues to grow and acquire more assets or new assets to replace exactly those existing assets in respect of which the deferred tax liability arose, then the balance in the deferred tax liability account will either grow or at least remain the same as new depreciation allowances are claimed. Second, if the firm sustains temporary losses, then the balance in the tax liability account will be reduced in respect of those losses. Both of these arguments assume, of course, that the rules of the game remain the same. On the other hand, if the prospects of the firm appear dim so that continuing losses are likely, then bankruptcy may ensue. In this event, it is unlikely that any taxes would become payable. While the balance may increase or remain unchanged, there is a turnover within the account. New deferrals on newly acquired assets offset repayments on the older assets. The fact that the balance grows is no more reason to reject the debt classification in this case than it is in the case of accounts payable, which also grow in the growing firm.

From the government's viewpoint, the primary purpose of permitting accelerated depreciation would appear to be to encourage investment in real, productive assets to generate economic growth by providing what is effectively an interest-free loan during the earlier, frequently cash-poor, years of a project. As a simple calculation will show, for constant income over the life of the project, the lifetime nominal tax liability is the same regardless of the depreciation method used. But, to the extent that payment is delayed, this will be of value to the firm because of the time value of money. Thus, viewed as debt, the deferred tax liability has no specific cost. However, again viewed as debt, there are two possible sources of indirect or implicit costs. The use of deferred taxes permits the acquisition of more assets than would be available with the given conventional debt and equity base, and these permit a higher rate of activity, that is, output, sales, and so on. To the extent that there are fixed costs, operating leverage is increased. And ultimately, of course, the deferred taxes may have to be repaid.

On balance then, the existence of deferred taxes implies that the firm is more highly levered on both an operating and financial basis than it would otherwise be. To the extent that this account is of significant magnitude, we would expect it to be reflected in the specific costs of the other debt and equity sources of financing in the same way as we explain in Chapter 6. Thus there is an implicit cost associated with the use of deferred taxes as a source of funds.

5.13   Convertible preferreds or debentures

These types of securities are usually issued by the firm as an alternative to common stocks at a time when the market for common stocks is believed to be abnormally depressed so that sale of common stock would unduly dilute the holdings of the existing stockholders. Compared with regular preferred issues or debentures, they probably sell on a lower-yield basis, owing to the existence of the conversion feature. It would be a mistake, however, to regard the funds thus raised as cheap. This is because if the fortunes of the firm or the state of the market improves to that point where the common stock is selling above the conversion price, the holders of the convertible issue can exchange it for common and enjoy all the advantages of common stock ownership. Such issues contain built-in future dilution for the common stock (the extent of the dilution depending on the conversion price) as an intrinsic feature and are best regarded as an indirect way of selling common stock above the present market price. Their cost should be evaluated as the higher of (a) their cost calculated on the assumption that conversion does not take place and they remain as senior obligations in their original form or (b) their cost when considered as if they are replaced by common when conversion takes place.

The latter cost comprises two elements,[27] the annual interest payment (or preferred dividend) during the period while the issue is outstanding in its present form and the dividend payment after conversion. After conversion, the cost will be the then-payable common equity cost. The cost at any point in time is an appropriately weighted average of these two costs. The stream of payments which must be equated to the current price is simply $r_1, r_2, \ldots, D_t, D_{t+1}, \ldots, D_n$, where $r =$ the annual interest payment (preferred dividend), $D_i =$ the dividend payable in period i, and $t =$ the time of conversion. The present value of this stream is:

$$\frac{\cdot r_1}{(1 + k)} + \frac{r_2}{(1 + k)^2} + \cdots + \frac{D_t}{(1 + k)^t} + \frac{D_{t+1}}{(1 + k)^t(1 + k_e)}$$
$$+ \frac{D_{t+2}}{(1 + k)^t(1 + k_e)^2} + \cdots$$
$$+ \frac{D_n}{(1 + k)^t(1 + k_e)^{n-t}} + \cdots \qquad (5.13.1)$$

where $k =$ the cost of the convertible issue and $k_e =$ the common equity cost likely to prevail at the time of conversion. We recall that the present value of the dividend series is simply:

$$P = \frac{D_0}{k_e - g} \qquad (5.13.2)$$

Assuming that conversion takes place or can be forced once the market price of the stock exceeds the conversion value C, we can truncate the present value series thus:

$$\frac{r_1}{(1 + k)} + \frac{r_2}{(1 + k)^2} + \cdots + \frac{r_{t-1}}{(1 + k)^{t-1}} + \frac{C}{(1 + k)^t} \qquad (5.13.3)$$

In effect, we retire the convertible at the conversion date by giving the holder common shares worth C.[28] The principal problem involved in estimating convertible costs is estimating the conversion date. It is not necessary to estimate the subsequent equity costs, since these were eliminated by the substitution of C for the dividend series.

The simplest basis on which to estimate the conversion date is to use the estimate of g from the present common share equity cost estimate to estimate how long it will be before the present market price will grow to a price at which conversion will take place or be forced. Ordinarily, this will not be the first moment at which the market price of the common exceeds the conversion price, but some time later, when a premium has emerged. The magnitude of the premium is a matter of policy, but it is one which affects the cost.

Example 5.13.1: XYZ Corporation 6 percent convertible debentures are convertible without time limit into common stock at a conversion price of $12.50. The debentures mature in 20 years, and their current market price is $4.70 to yield 7.5 percent to maturity. The common stock is now $10.00 per share, and the rate of growth g is estimated at 8 percent. What is the cost of the convertible issue?

If we assume 8 percent growth, the shares will be worth $10.80, $11.66, $12.74, $13.82, and $14.93 in successive years. If we assume conversion will not be forced until the price reaches $14.93, the convertible will be retired just before its 5th-year interest payment, leading to the following series of receipts:

Year 1—$	6.00
2—$	6.00
3—$	6.00
4—$	6.00
5—$119.44	

These have a present value of $84.70 at 12.39 percent, the effective cost of the convertible issue. Note that this cost could be reduced by forcing earlier conversion.

5.14   Participating issues

Like convertibles, participating issues have a dual nature. Although the possibility of conversion does not exist, they may share in earnings just as if they had been converted. From the common stockholders' point of view, they are even less attractive, for if subsequent difficulties develop, their preferred status reemerges to claim priority on dividends. Their cost should be calculated in a similar manner to that for convertible issues, except that implicit conversion on an appropriate basis should be assumed when the common dividend has grown to exceed the present preferred dividend If participation is on a share-for-share basis, the implicit conversion price in terms of common share equivalents is the market value of one share. If they are entitled to receive ten times the dividends as, for example, in the case where the common shares are $10 par and the participating preferred $100 par, the conversion value in common stock equivalent is ten times the market value of a share of common stock.

5.15   Trade credit and related sources

This section is concerned with trade credit (accounts payable), revolving-credit arrangements, commercial bank loans, and commercial paper as possible sources of financing for capital expenditures rather than as sources of financing for working capital as they are usually regarded. In fact, since it is usual to regard the net portion of working capital as quite permanent at any given level of operations (seasonal fluctuations aside) and conventional wisdom suggests that permanent net working capital be financed long term, it may seem irrelevant to mention the opposite case at all. However, more than a few firms have resorted to financing fixed assets using current liabilities in the past decade in spite of the attendant financial risk.

What are the specific costs of such sources of finance? Consider trade credit. Assuming that the firm takes all cash discounts, there is no explicit cost to this source. But since the availability of credit is of economic value to the firm, this cost must be borne by someone since the use of funds over time is not free. The burden of the cost may fall on the firm, its suppliers, or partly on both. In the case of a product for which demand is elastic where there is considerable competition among sellers, the supplier may be reluctant or even unable to pass along the cost in the form of higher prices and thus may end up absorbing most of the cost of the trade credit. This implies that it may be borne indirectly by the supplier's stockholders because they need to provide more working capital than otherwise. Under other circumstances, the supplier is able to pass some or all of the cost on to the buying firm.[29] If the buying firm is able to discover the amount of the cost that is being passed along, then that is a specific cost and may be used to judge whether it is worthwhile to continue with that source of financing or to switch to some alternative short- or long-term source. Since this is a choice of the source of financing, the decision does not affect asset acquisition decisions any more than did the choice of installment purchase versus lease financing.

A revolving credit agreement represents a legal commitment on the part of a commercial bank to extend credit up to a certain, specified amount based upon the bank's assessment of the credit worthiness of the borrower and upon his credit needs. Because of the standby nature of any unused portion of the credit, the bank is precluded from making alternate loans, thus the borrowing firm is usually required to pay a commitment fee on the unused portion. In addition to charging interest on the portion of the credit actually borrowed, commercial banks (in the United States) generally also require the borrower to maintain demand-deposit balances, known as *compensating balances,* at the bank in proportion either to the amount borrowed or the amount of the commitment. To the extent that this compensating-balance requirement forces the borrowing firm to maintain balances greater than it would ordinarily, the effective cost of borrowing is increased. The specific costs of the revolving-credit agreement include the interest cost and the commitment fee. In addition, there is the opportunity cost of the compensating-balance requirement.

Many large, well-established corporations will borrow on a short-term basis in the money markets by using unsecured, short-term, negotiable promissory notes known as *commercial paper*. Because these notes are unsecured, only the most credit-worthy corporations are able to resort to this means of financing, at least in principle. Further, because of the fixed cost of issuing commercial paper and the need to roll it over frequently, the issues are of considerable size. Large sales finance companies are major suppliers of paper to this market.

The specific cost of this source is based on the yield implied by the difference between the selling price and the redemption price. This yield on prime commercial paper is generally lower than the prime bank lending rate to the highest-quality borrowers. This spread will increase when money market conditions are easy and decrease when they are tight. Under normal market conditions, the yield-to-maturity increases with increasing time to maturity implying that the specific cost of short-term debt is less than long-term debt for the same borrowing firm. Thus there is an apparent incentive to borrow short term. However, the implicit cost is that commercial paper must be renewed or replaced at maturity, and in tight money market conditions, it is quite possible for required short-term yields to be higher than long term. There is also the possibility that funds will not be available at all, since the supply of short-term loanable funds to the money market can be quite volatile depending upon relative yields and risks elsewhere and on other economic and political factors as well. This suggests that the strategy of using commercial paper to finance capital expenditures leaves the firm vulnerable to the possibility of a sudden, large cash outflow—normally considered to be very risky financially. Such exposure will likely have the effect of increasing the cost of funds from other sources.[30]

Regardless of which of these three sources of short-term financing is used to finance capital expenditures, there are at least two related implicit costs. First, the net working capital position is reduced, implying a reduction in liquidity. Second, as a result, the risk of technical insolvency, perhaps even bankruptcy, is increased. Both of these implicit costs will be reflected indirectly in the specific costs of other sources of financing.

Nevertheless, there are recent cases of utilities undergoing expansion who have been "leaning on the trade," using relatively large amounts of trade credit. They have been able to do this because their cash inflows are both increasing and are of low variability partly because of the nature of the industry and the fact that generally it is regulated. At least while these firms are continuing to grow, the implication of their cash flow pattern is that they need carry less net working capital, that is, larger current liabilities relative to their current assets, than otherwise.

While *asset matching,* that is, matching the maturity structures of assets to those of liabilities, is not necessarily a good financial management strategy, nevertheless it is wise to consider the maturity structure of the firm's assets and liabilities when making financing decisions and to impose limits on the degree of exposure through mismatching. Any firm whose assets are mostly fixed, but whose liabilities are current, may be heading for a liquidity crisis at best and technical insolvency or bankruptcy at the worst.

5.16 Guarantees and their implicit costs

Sometimes a corporation will be formed which is both an operating company and a holding company in that it may own all the shares or at least a controlling interest in a range of subsidiaries or affiliates. The parent firm may believe that the investment opportunities open to its subsidiaries are not being correctly evaluated and that the market tends to view them as being riskier than the firm believes them to be. To counter this, when the subsidiary issues debt in its own name, the firm will offer some form of guarantee of the payments of interest and principal of this debt on behalf of the subsidiary in order to reduce the capital market's perceived default risk and thus lower the required yield on the debt.

An implied consequence of this action would be that the consolidated earnings (long-run profit) of the firm and its subsidiaries would be greater than otherwise, and thus the wealth of the stockholders of the parent firm would be increased. In perfect capital markets, the potential of the subsidiaries projects would be correctly valued, and the required rate of return would be correctly estimated. If, however, imperfections can be found in the capital market, then the guarantee can be viewed as a form of *reinsurance,* and there will be some anticipated cost to providing it. Otherwise it would be of no economic value.

An important consideration is whether this cost is reflected in the cost of financing of the parent firm, thus having an implicit cost. In principle, if the guarantee does have economic value, then we would expect it to have some impact. In practice, however, whether this cost would be impounded in the financing costs would seem to depend on two factors. First is the manner in which the *contingent liability* is reported in financial statements and whether sophisticated investors consider this information. Presumably this guarantee implies that the debt capacity of the parent is, in fact, less than a superficial examination of the balance sheet would indicate. As in the case of lease financing, the question is whether and/or how this is valued by the capital markets. The second factor is whether this guarantee is material in the sense that the total amount of such guarantees is significant relative to the total liabilities of the parent firm.

In principle, there is no doubt that guarantees have an implicit cost. What this cost might be is an empirical issue about which we have no data and thus can offer no explicit measure. Since it appeared to take a long time for the implicit costs of lease financing to be correctly recognized and to the extent that guarantees are much more obvious and immediate in their consequences, we would be inclined to think that their actual (implicit) cost is really quite small—but this does not imply that their potential impact should be overlooked.

5.17 Specific and implicit costs

One of the most common fallacies in the analysis of capital-budgeting decisions is to regard the cost of debt financing as identical with the marginal cost of capital. The confusion arises because traditional capital theory, dealing with aggregate investment, assumes perfect certainty and perfect capital markets, then prescribes that aggregate investment should be carried to the point where the marginal productivity of capital equals the market rate of interest as the condition of equilibrium in the capital market. The reader may recall that we showed essentially the same result in Chapter 1. But we also showed that under the assumptions made, there was no distinction between various forms of financing instruments and that all had to yield the same return for the capital market to be in equilibrium.

The theory is perfectly valid on its own terms, granted these assumptions. The fallacy arises in attempting to apply it without alteration in practical situations. Doing so can lead to absurd results, as the following example will illustrate.

Firm A had, in three successive years, the same set of investment opportunities given in Table 5–8. All projects are equal in risk. It began in year 1 with a 100 percent equity capital structure. The treasurer, a persuasive man who had just heard of marginal cost, indicated to the management that they could raise $900,000 by issuing debentures at 5.5 percent and convinced his colleagues that the whole package should be approved.

Table 5–8

Investment opportunities: firm A

Year 1		Year 2		Year 3	
Amount of investment	Rate of return	Amount of investment	Rate of return	Amount of investment	Rate of return
$100,000	20	$100,000	20	$100,000	20
200,000	15	200,000	15	200,000	15
200,000	10	200,000	10	200,000	10
200,000	8	200,000	8	200,000	8
200,000	6	200,000	6	200,000	6

The second year, convinced of his wisdom, the management accepted the first four projects when he told them that he could borrow a further $700,000 at 7.5 percent or $800,000 at 9 percent, rejecting the fifth project as promising a yield below the marginal cost of capital.

When budget time came around the third year, the treasurer was somewhat mystified to learn that the firm's investment bankers refused to issue more debt for him, suggesting that he also issue equity at an estimated cost of 19 percent. He had beaten the bushes carefully in an effort to find more debt money, but so far had only been able to come up with a possible finance company loan of $100,000 at 18 percent. Since the marginal cost of funds had risen to 18 percent, he recommended that the budget be cut back sharply and only the first project be adopted. He had not made up his mind about the financing, but he was inclined to go along with the finance company loan as it was cheaper, although there were certain onerous conditions attached by the finance company which he was not happy about.

Confronted with this presentation at the budget meeting, the production manager got out an envelope and started figuring. He noted that the average return on the investments made over the three years, if the current budget were adopted, would be 12 percent, whereas the same amount could have been invested to earn an average of 13.3 percent, if they had not been in such a hurry to commit funds in the first year (his calculations are shown in Table 5–9). Furthermore, he noted that several trade creditors had refused to lengthen their credit lines and one or two friends had kidded him about firm A being overextended. He said he thought the treasurer owed them an explanation of how this new system had gone wrong.

What the treasurer had overlooked was that debt capacity is a function of earning power and the equity base supplied by the stockholders. Unless the equity base is enlarged, a firm will sooner or later exhaust its

Table 5–9
Prospective return on investment: firm A

	Actual budgets			Production manager's alternative	
	Spent	Percent		Spent	Percent
Year 1	$ 100,000	20	Year 1	$ 100,000	20
	200,000	15		200,000	15
	200,000	10		200,000	10
	200,000	8	Year 2	100,000	20
	200,000	6		200,000	15
Year 2	100,000	20		200,000	10
	200,000	15	Year 3	100,000	20
	200,000	10		200,000	15
	200,000	8		200,000	10
Year 3	100,000	20		200,000	8
Totals	300,000	20	Totals	300,000	20
	400,000	15		600,000	15
	400,000	10		600,000	10
	400,000	8		200,000	8
	200,000	6		$1,700,000	13.3
	$1,700,000	12.0			

borrowing capacity and be forced into the equity market. Even if the financing is done in blocks consisting of debt or equity, using the debt rate as a marginal cost leads to the preemption of the available capital supply by low-yielding projects, eventually forcing higher yielding ones out, unless some provision in the calculations is made for the equity financing which will have to be done sooner or later to preserve borrowing power.

It also means that budgets are larger than they should be, and if financed by debt, more debt is incurred than would be desirable if a more conservative policy were followed. Had firm A followed a policy which took explicit account of the need for further equity, using an appropriate overall required rate of return, they would not only have been able to increase their profitability, but they would have had a debt of only $1 million at the beginning of year 3 instead of $1 million.

When the capital structure is changed by an issue of debt, the relevant cost is not only the out-of-pocket cost of the debt itself, but it includes the implicit cost of the increase in the cost of equity resulting from the higher-risk premium attached to the shares as a result of the debt. Arguments surrounding this issue are discussed in Chapter 6.

For example, consider a firm with an income of $100,000 after taxes and a current market value of $1 million. If the firm issues $200,000 in 6 percent debentures and as a result the price-earnings multiplier drops to 8.0, the additional earnings which must be obtained to maintain the value of the stockholders' investment are as follows:

Net income required for stockholders ($1,000,000 ÷ 8).............	$125,000
Interest on debt...	12,000
Less tax credit	6,000
Required earnings	131,000
Present level of earnings	100,000
Required increase...	$ 31,000

The *required rate of return* on $200,000 investment is 15.5 percent ($31,000/$200,000), not the 3 percent out-of-pocket cost of the new funds. Unfortunately, this rule is not simple to apply in practice because of the difficulty of knowing beforehand what effect a change in debt will have on the capitalization rate (price-earnings ratio) which the market will apply. If we have a reliable valuation model, the answer may be calculated easily. In Chapters 11 and 12, we describe extensions to our model, alluded to in Section 5.7, which allow us to introduce the notion of the *market price of risk* into the evaluation. A complete solution would also require inclusion also of the risk of bankruptcy and reorganization, implying the need to consider the firm's liquidity position. Such a complete treatment has only been partly developed in the financial literature, so we are forced to approach the problem by a more indirect route.

Notes

1. See J. F. Weston and E. F. Brigham, *Managerial Finance,* 5th ed. (Hinsdale, Ill.: Dryden Press, 1975), parts IV and V for a balanced discussion of the issues relevant to financing decisions.
2. The term *out-of-pocket cost* might be preferable in certain cases, but in others, as we shall see, there may be no actual outlay of funds associated with this cost.
3. The question of whether the short-run or long-run variety is to be employed is discussed further in Chapter 6.
4. Equation 5.4.2 implicitly assumes that issue expense and the amortization of premium or discount is taxable or deductible, respectively, as it is under U.S. law. If the latter are not deductible, as is the case in Canada, the equation must be modified as follows:

$$k = \frac{(1 - T)\left[R + \dfrac{1}{n}(W - Q_0)\right] + \dfrac{1}{n}(P - W)}{(1/2)(Q_0 + P)} \qquad (5.4.2a)$$

Where W is the price received before deducting issue expense.

[5] J. C. Van Horne, *Financial Management and Policy,* 4th ed. (Englewood Cliffs, N.J.: Prentice-Hall, 1977), p. 512.

[6] For example, as in Van Horne, *Financial Management,* p. 502.

[7] Van Horne, *Financial Management,* pp. 505–7.

[8] As expressed, for example, by M. W. Davenport in his discussion of D. Durand, "Costs of Debt and Equity Funds for Business: Trends and Problems of Measurement," in *Conference on Research in Business Finance* (New York: National Bureau of Economic Research, 1952), p. 254, reprinted in E. Solomon, ed., *The Management of Corporate Capital* (Glencoe, Ill.: Free Press, 1959), p. 121.

[9] See G. Donaldson, "In Defense Of Preferred Stock," *Harvard Business Review* 40 (July–August 1962); pp. 123–36. The point is elaborated further in his *Corporate Debt Capacity* (Homewood, Ill.: Richard D. Irwin, 1971). See also J. F. Childs, *Long-Term Financing* (Englewood Cliffs, N.J.: Prentice-Hall, 1961).

[10] For a defense of this view, see E. Solomon, "Measuring a Company's Cost of Capital," *Journal of Business* (October 1955), reprinted in Solomon, *Management of Corporate Capital,* pp. 128–40. See also Childs, *Long-Term Financing,* p. 322.

[11] M. J. Gordon and E. Shapiro, "Capital Equipment Analysis: The Required Rate of Profit," *Management Science* 3 (October 1956); pp. 102–10, reprinted in Solomon, pp. 141–49.

[12] See Gordon and Shapiro, "Capital Equipment Analysis," pp. 145–46.

[13] For the equivalence of the dividend and earnings approaches, see M. H. Miller and F. Modigliani, "Dividend Policy, Growth and the Valuation of Shares," *Journal of Business* 34 (October 1961), pp. 411–33.

[14] Consider the yield on holding stock for one period:

$$k = \frac{(1 - b)E_0 + P_1 - Q_0}{Q_0} \qquad (5.7.6a)$$

Growth in earnings at the constant rate br^* implies

$$P_1 = (1 + br^*)Q_0$$

Substitution in 5.7.6a gives

$$Q_0 k = (1 - b)E_0 + br^* Q_0 \qquad (5.7.5a)$$

whence

$$Q_0 = \frac{(1 - b)E_0}{k - br^*} \qquad (5.7.5b)$$

which is equivalent to 5.7.5.

If, however, $k = r^*$, 5.7.5a becomes

$$Q_0 k = (1 - b)E_0 + bkQ_0$$

whence

$$k = \frac{E_0}{Q_0}$$

Under these circumstances, expansion neither hurts nor helps stockholders, since earnings on the funds needed for expansion merely equal the cost of raising them.

[15] R. M. Soldofsky, and J. T. Murphy, *Growth Yields on Common Stocks: Theory and Tables* (Iowa City: Bureau of Business and Economic Research, State University of Iowa, 1964). Also, R. M. Soldofsky, "Growth Yields," *Financial Analysts Journal* 17 (September–October 1961); pp. 43–47.

[16] M. J. Gordon and P. Halpern, "Bond Share Yield spreads Under Uncertain Inflation," *American Economic Review* 66 (September 1976), pp. 559–65.

[17] R. Roll, "A Critique of the Asset Pricing Theory's Tests," *Journal of Financial Economics* 4 (March 1977), pp. 129–76.

[18] T. E. Copeland and J. F. Weston, *Financial Theory and Corporate Policy* (Reading, Mass.: Addison-Wesley, 1979), pp. 183–85.

[19] M. Blume, "On the Assessment of Risk," *Journal of Finance* (March 1971), pp. 1–10.

[20] M. H. Miller and M. Scholes, "Rates of Return in Relation to Risk: A Re-examination of Some Recent Findings," in M. C. Jensen, ed., *Studies in the Theory of Capital Markets* (New York: Praeger, 1972), pp. 47–78.

[21] O. B. Vasichek, "A Note on Using Cross-Sectional Information in Bayesian Estimation of Security Beta," *Journal of Finance* (December 1973), pp. 1233–39.

[22] See also the alternative proposed by A. Kraus and R. H. Litzenberger, "Skewness Preference and the Valuation of Risky Assets," *Journal of Finance* (September 1976), pp. 1085–1100, and I. Friend and R. Westerfield, "Co-Skewness and Capital Asset Pricing," Working Paper No. 10–79, Rodney L. White Center for Financial Research, Wharton School, 1979.

[23] Miller and Modigliani, "Dividend Policy."

[24] See, for example, J. E. Walter, "Dividend Policies and Common Stock Prices," *Journal of Finance* 11 (March 1956), pp. 29–41, and "Dividend Policy: Its Influence on the Value of the Enterprise," *Journal of Finance* 18 (May 1963), pp. 280–91; J. Lintner, "Dividends, Earnings, Leverage and the Supply of Capital to Corporations," *Review of Economics and Statistics* 44 (August 1962), pp. 243–70; I. Friend and M. Puckett, "Dividends and Stock Prices," *American Economic Review* 54 (September 1964), pp. 656–82; J. A. Brittain, *Corporate Dividend Policy* (Washington: Brookings Institute, 1966); and E. F. Brigham and M. J. Gordon, "Leverage, Dividend Policy and the Cost of Capital," *Journal of Finance* 23 (March 1968), pp. 85–104.

[25] See M. J. Gordon, *The Investment, Financing and Valuation of the Corporation* (Homewood, Ill.: Richard D. Irwin, 1962), pp. 46–54; and E. M. Lerner and W. T. Carleton, "Capital Budgeting and Stock Valuation," *American Economic Review* 54 (September 1964), pp. 683–702.

[26] More strictly, the capital budget, the optimum dividend, and the financing plan are interdependent when we admit departures from perfect capital market assumptions and should be determined simultaneously. For the practical objections to this approach, see the discussion in Section 2.9.

[27] This treatment is derived from that presented by E. F. Brigham, "An Analysis of Convertible Debentures: Theory and Some Empirical Evidence," *Journal of Finance* 21 (March 1965), pp. 35–54.

[28] See G. D. Quirin and W. R. Waters, "Treatment of Deferred Taxes in Regulated Industries," a paper presented to the Southern Finance Association, November 9, 1978, for a fuller treatment.

[29] In the case of consumer goods, Canadian Tire Corporation, Ltd, a Canadian franchise dealer in tires and automotive parts, hardware, and sporting goods, offers customers a 4 percent discount in merchandise coupons for paying in cash instead of using credit.

[30] None of this seemed to deter the financial managers of Penn Central from using this source of financing nor the money markets from accepting their commercial paper. For a somewhat journalistic account of the ensuing financial debacle, see J. R. Daughen and P. Binzen, *The Wreck of the Penn Central* (New York: New American Library, 1971).

Problems

1. What is the after-tax cost of borrowing funds for a firm whose marginal tax rate is 50 percent contemplating the following bond issues?

	Offering price	Net to issuer	Coupon rate	Maturity
1.	98.00	96.00	4.50	20
2.	97.50	95.00	5.00	10
3.	103.00	100.00	3.75	15
4.	105.00	102.00	3.50	10

2. What is the cost of equity capital for the following firms?

	(a)		(b)		(c)	
Year	Earnings per share	Dividends per share	Earnings per share	Dividends per share	Earnings per share	Dividends per share
1	1.17	0.60	2.57	1.23	1.48	0.85
2	0.31	0.60	2.65	1.40	1.49	0.90
3	0.33	0.45	3.07	1.40	1.56	0.95
4	0.45	0.40	3.18	1.60	1.71	1.00
5	0.24	0.40	3.62	1.60	1.81	1.10
Price, latest	$14.38		84.00		34.00	

3. The B Corporation has an outstanding issue of convertible subordinated debentures 4½ percent of 1996, convertible into 26.72 common shares per $1,000 par value at any time. The debentures sell for $128.00, the shares at $43.00. The debentures are callable at $102.375. Earnings and dividends on the common shares have been as follows:

Year	Earned per share	Dividend per share
1976	1.58	1.00
1977	1.42	1.00
1978	1.15	1.00
1979	1.38	1.00
1980	1.17 (9 months)	1.00 (est.)

What is the cost of funds represented by these convertible debentures?

4. A firm is contemplating the installation of a packaging machine which will save $6,000 per year in labor, in reduced damage to goods, and in packaging materials after deducting all operating costs. Life of the machine is

estimated at six years, at the end of which time net scrap value is nil, after taking account of removal costs. The firm uses sum-of-the-years'-digits depreciation.

The machine may be purchased for $10,000 cash or on monthly install-ments totalling $1,930 per year, of which the interest component is $460, 390, 310, 230, 140, and 50 in the first through sixth years. Alternatively, the machine may be leased for $2,400 per year.

a. What is the internal rate of return on the machine?
b. What is the cost of funds raised under the installment loan?
c. What is the cost of leasing the asset?
d. If the firm's required rate of return (after-tax) is 10 percent, which action would you recommend? Why?

Cost of capital to the firm

6.1 Uses in capital budgeting

This chapter will examine the problems encountered in attempting to estimate the overall cost of capital (required rate of return) to the firm, as well as its application in capital-budgeting decisions. For the present, we disregard the question of whether it is necessary to distinguish required rates of return at the level of the firm, the division, other subunits, or the individual project because of differences in their risk characteristics. We shall, however, return to this question later in this chapter and consider it in detail in Chapters 11 and 12. If we consider the firm as an aggregation of assets, we may properly use an overall cost of capital as a standard of comparison only if the investment proposals being considered have also the same business risk characteristics as existing assets. That is, for routine capital-budgeting decisions which involve only changes in scale or do not otherwise affect the business risk profile of the firm, the overall cost of capital may properly be used to make the net present value calculations or as a hurdle rate for internal rate of return calculations as described in Chapter 3. On the other hand, strategic capital-budgeting decisions usually involve changes in the business risk characteristics of the firm and cannot properly be evaluated for acceptance or rejection using the cost of capital of the existing firm. In that case, a much more detailed analysis will be required, as we later discuss.

The main advantage of using a single, overall required rate of return is simplicity. Once measured, it may be provided to analysts who may use this single rate to evaluate all proposed projects. This rate will not change unless the conditions underlying its computation change. The problems and costs involved in computing individual required rates of return for each investment proposal are avoided. In practice, it may well turn out that a compromise will be needed in determining the point at which it no longer pays to discriminate. Thus, while it may not be formally correct to use an individual rate across all projects in the firm, it may be sufficient to identify homogeneous subunits (such as divisions, for example) within the firm and apply different rates at that level, subject to the same caveat regarding business risks.

6.2   Regulatory applications

It may be inefficient economically or difficult to impossible physically to permit two or more firms to compete in one locality in the production or distribution of goods or services, such as electricity, natural gas, telephone, community-antenna television, public transportation, and other so-called public utilities.[1] Such goods and services are usually considered to be natural monopolies, and where competition has been attempted, the costs tend to be high, and one firm usually emerges as dominant while the others go bankrupt. As a result, either some level of government will establish a publicly owned utility or will award an exclusive franchise to a private firm, subject to continuing regulation by a government agency which may be established for the purpose. Regulation, which is intended to protect consumers against the adoption of monopoly pricing tactics by the private firm, necessarily includes some form of control over the prices the utility may charge for its goods or services. The object is to produce pricing behavior comparable to that which would result in a competitive marketplace, if competition could be maintained.

The regulatory price-fixing process as usually applied in North America involves two interrelated steps: (*a*) determining the revenue requirements of the utility, or how much it will be allowed by way of revenues to cover operating expenses plus permitted earnings and (*b*) setting individual rates for individual services in such a way as to produce the desired level of revenues. In the determination of revenue requirements, the usual procedure is to allow for operating expenses plus a return on investment component which is usually expressed as the product of the amount of capital employed or considered to be employed times a rate of return. The former component is usually called the *rate base,* and the latter, the *fair rate of return* or simply *allowed rate of return.*

Regulators operate under statutory authority and are also bound, at least in the United States, by constitutional limits on their authority and in particular by the due process clauses of the 5th and 14th amendments, which bring regulators' actions within the scope of judicial review. Most jurisdictions use prudent-investment or original-cost rate bases in which the rate base is defined essentially as the book value of the assets used in providing the service; assets which are unused or unnecessary, such as excessive working capital, may be excluded.

The courts have over the years set forth certain standards which must be applied in determining the allowable rate of return. In *Bluefield Waterworks* v. *West Virginia Public Service*[2] the U.S. Supreme Court said:

A public utility is entitled to such rates as will permit it to earn a return equal to that generally being made at the same time and in the same general part of the country on investments in other business undertakings which are attended by corresponding risks and uncertainties; but it has no constitutional right to profits such as are realized in highly profitable enterprises or speculative ventures.

The return should be reasonably sufficient to assure confidence in the financial soundness of the utility and should be adequate, under efficient and economical management, to maintain and support its credit and enable it to raise the money necessary for the proper discharge of its public duties.

This rule was further delineated in 1944 in *Federal Power Commission* v. *Hope Natural Gas Company*[3] where the court prescribed:

Rates which make the company to operate successfully to maintain its financial integrity, to attract capital, and to compensate its investors for the risks assumed. . . .

From the investor or company point of view it is important that there be enough revenue not only for operating expenses, but also for the capital costs of the business. These include service on the debt and dividends on the stock. By that standard the return to the equity owner should be commensurate with returns on investments in other enterprises having corresponding risks. That return, moreover, should be sufficient to assure confidence in the financial integrity of the enterprise, so as to maintain its credit and to attract capital. The condition under which more or less might be allowed is not important here. Nor is it important to this case to determine the various ways in which any rate base is on which the return is computed might be arrived at. For we are of the view that the end result in this case cannot be condemned under the act as unjust and unreasonable from the investor or company point of view.

There is at least a family resemblance between these concepts and the required rate of return or cost of capital concept we employ in financial analysis. The link is provided by the capital attraction requirement laid down in *FPC* v. *Hope;* ability to attract capital is prima facie evidence that those providing it think the terms fair. It is really the latter which counts. If investors do not regard the terms as fair, they will not provide capital, whether the terms are regarded as fair by regulators and judges or not.

In the long run, the allowed rate of return and the capital-attraction requirement are critical factors in the regulatory process and not just in price fixing. Many franchises or certificates of convenience and necessity under which utilities operate impose an obligation to serve all customers. To fulfill this, a regulatory agency may order a utility to make certain capital expenditures, but in practice it cannot (in free market economies) similarly order the capital markets to provide the necessary financing unless the utility is able to earn the market required rate of return.

The regulatory agency's objective is to determine a price above the cost of producing the utility's output that provides the utility with the least rate of return on its capital consistent with attracting the real capital base sufficient to meet the public interest requirement. This translates into a minimum revenue figure which is the product of the measured rate base and the allowed rate of return.

The major difference between the capital-attracting rate of return used for financial analysis purposes and that used for regulatory purposes is that the latter need not measure marginal costs of funds in the current market. Much of the capital used by utilities is raised in the form of long-term debt and invested in long-lived physical assets. This makes it possible for the regulatory body to discriminate between sources of funds. Thus holders of an old bond issue who contracted for a 6 percent coupon are fairly treated if they receive 6 percent on their money. They might not invest on those terms today, but that is quite irrelevant. It is thus possible to adopt a rule whereby 6 percent is allowed on the capital raised by 6 percent bonds, 8 percent on that raised by selling 8 percent bonds, and so on. As long as it is understood that, if the utility needs to pay 12 percent for debt capital in the current market, future earnings will be provided to cover that, the firm will be able to attract debt financing on a continuing basis. This leads to the concept of *embedded debt cost,* which is simply the weighted average cost using book value weights, of the outstanding debt securities. It is appropriate to use book value weights because these will, when applied to the appropriate share of the book value rate base, generate enough earnings to service the debt. This concept differs from the current debt cost used for the purposes of financial analysis. Of course, if interest rates rise, current costs of debt will exceed the contracted for or embedded cost of funds raised in earlier periods at lower cost rates. Until the old, low-cost debt is retired and has to be replaced, there is a windfall gain available. Using embedded debt costs in the regulatory process passes the windfall along to the consumers, whereas using current debt costs would pass it along to the stockholders of the utility firm.

It is also usual practice to apply the embedded cost criterion to preferred stock funds. Deferred tax funds are usually either deducted from the rate base or included as a zero cost source of capital—procedures which are equivalent for most purposes.

The embedded cost standard cannot be applied in the common stock equity portion of the capitalization. Unlike bonds or preferreds of different series, shares of common stock cannot be distinguished. Consequently, regulators cannot discriminate between those stockholders who may have bought their shares when an 8 percent return was deemed ample, and those who bought them yesterday at an expected holding period yield of 15 percent. Nor could the company divide its earnings up so as to give the former an equity in the earnings equivalent to 8 percent while the latter got 15 percent. If 15 percent is required to attract capital now, it must be allowed on all of the common stock equity funds in the business.

The appropriate measure of the allowed rate of return on common equity is the cost of equity capital formula developed in Section 5.7. Note, however, that it is being applied in this case to the book value of common equity. It will tend (if earned) to generate earnings which will keep market value roughly equivalent to book, although price will increase to reflect additions via retained earnings. This is sometimes held to impose a special disadvantage on utility stockholders in that the price of their stock will not rise to reflect inflation in the replacement cost of the assets. It is not clear that this happens with any degree of regularity outside the regulated sector either; even if true it does not mean utility stockholders cannot be compensated for inflation within the context of the traditional regulatory mode. Anticipated inflation changes required yields, increasing them, and the utility stockholder who is faced with an increase in the inflation rate should have an increase in allowed earnings as compensation. Particularly since the inflation rate took off in 1974, many regulatory commissions in an attempt to fight inflation impose allowed rates of return on equity which were significantly below those demanded in the marketplace. As a result, many utility stocks dropped in value and sold well below book. There are severe limits on the ability of firms in this position to attract capital on a continuing basis.

6.3 Macroeconomic considerations

Occasionally, we may wish to move from the microeconomic theory of investment (decisions of the individual firm) to that part of macroeconomic theory which explains the investment behavior of the entire private business sector. Microeconomic theory is constructed to deal with partial equilibrium in particular markets using frequent appeals to *ceteris paribus* assumptions. Indeed, one of the main underpinnings of the contemporary theory of finance is the notion of equilibrium within the capital market. On a broader scale, the effect of other markets, such as, the market for real capital assets or the markets for products or factors other than capital, may need to be taken into account in examining macroeconomic theory. For a broad class of firms whose securities trade on the organized securities markets, there is considerable evidence that the markets are efficient, which may be considered an operational form of the perfect market assumption. Such markets may also be quite effective at transmitting the implications of policy initiatives. However, in the presence of a significant minority of firms facing imperfect capital markets, it will become necessary to understand the nature of the imperfections and how they may affect the implementation of economic policy. We will look specifically at market imperfections, particularly of a time-dependent nature, later in this chapter.

Economic policy makers usually seem to think of themselves as being able to manipulate two main policy levers: monetary and fiscal. *Monetary policy* appears to be viewed historically as affecting interest rates or credit available, while *fiscal policy* affects taxes and subsidies. Manipulation of taxes will affect the cash flows available to firms through changes in the tax shields from depreciation or depletion allowances, for example. But, as we have seen in Chapter 3, capital-expenditure decisions are based on the combination of both cash-flow and required-rate-of-return considerations. Interest rate changes will be reflected in the cost of capital to the firm, but under ordinary circumstances they may have only a minor influence, depending on the mix of capital used by the firm. Since fiscal policies may be applied selectively and may have a more direct impact on the cash flows from projects of particular types, they may sometimes be more effective in influencing decisions.

Business firms can generate cash flows from which investments may be made from only three sources: operations, liquidation of assets, and external sources. Inflation, and attempts to eliminate it, have led to curious (and serious) effects on business investment. To the extent that price increases are suppressed, as they are when direct price controls are applied, profits (and thus after-tax cash flows) are reduced in both nominal and, especially, real terms. To the extent that depreciation allowances are based also on historical costs without allowance for replacement costs, for example, real capital will be transferred through excessive tax payments from the private sector to the public sector, and the real capital base of the private sector will be eroded.[4] When monetary policy restricts the availability of financing, another source of cash is constrained. Thus, inflation because of its own effects and the policy actions apparently necessary to attenuate it all tend to reduce the amount of aggregate investment and thus lower the rate of real economic growth in the economy below its potential.

Chapter 10 will consider how inflationary effects must be incorporated into capital-expenditure decisions, both in respect of cash flows and required rate of return. For the present, inflation is disregarded in order to keep the discussion as uncomplicated as possible.

6.4   Alternative methods of combining

The selection of projects for inclusion in the market-value maximizing budget requires that all projects having positive net present values, or discounted benefit-cost ratios in excess of 1.0, be accepted when the discount rate used is the required rate of return for the firm. We have seen in Section 5.17 that it is not appropriate to use, for example, the specific cost of debt as the required rate of return, even if only debt financing is currently contemplated. More generally, increasing the relative level of debt may increase the market-required rate of return on the common shares, and this additional cost on the equity component of the existing capital structure should be imputed as part of the cost of debt.[5] While most students of the problem agree this far, disagreement breaks out at the next step, that is, making the actual imputations or presenting alternative methods of calculating marginal costs.

One alternative to using specific contractual costs of debt as a marginal cost is to impose an earnings coverage requirement similar to that used by investment analysts in rating bonds. Thus if the minimum earnings coverage acceptable is four times interest charges, then if the before-tax cost of debt is 5 percent, the coverage cost, that is, earnings necessary to provide the desired coverage is 20 percent (also before taxes).[6] This approach certainly has practical merit in that it will prevent the more naive errors of the type discussed in Section 5.17. However, it does not explicitly consider the effect of altered debt levels on the required return on equity and, as such, is neither the appropriate imputed cost of debt nor an accurate measure of the marginal cost of funds (except by accident).

Some of the approaches do not specifically attempt to measure marginal cost or at any rate are not claimed to do so by their proponents. Thus an average of specific costs, weighted by their respective shares in the total capital structure, has been advocated by Childs, who proposes book value weights, and by Bierman and Smidt, who use current market values as weights.[7] Weston and Brigham use book value weights but derive a separate approximation to marginal costs.[8]

An alternative weighting scheme uses the anticipated additions to capital over some not specified horizon as weights.[9] Costs of these incremental funds are not identified as marginal costs, however. Solomon has rejected weighted averages of this type and has proposed what amounts to a separately weighted average for each project, with the debt component weighted by the imputed borrowing power of the project in question. This is to be considered in relation to a rising supply curve for equity funds in determining the budget. Solomon has suggested that the debt charges should be netted against the cash flows from the project to give a rate of return on equity. Equity requirements will be determined by the projects included in the budget and debt requirements by the imputed borrowing power. So the process determines both the capital budget and the plan for financing it. While it is possible to apply this approach consistently, to do so requires considerable sophistication both on the part of the analyst and the management who must use it. Borrowing power is, of course, a function of risk, and this scheme will alter the capital structure in response to changes in the business risk of the operation. The drawback is that it scrambles together and confuses the analysis of projects and that of their financing, which we have sought to avoid. Furthermore, it is apt to lead to the adoption of projects on the basis of the financing available as part of the package and to excessive use of high-cost debt, through leasing and installment purchases, unless a standard of debt capacity other than that of the lenders is applied.[10] Solomon has suggested a weighted average approach based on market value weights[11] as an approximation to the marginal cost we are seeking.

Lindsay and Sametz have suggested an alternative approach based on a segmented supply curve having successive components of debt, depreciation accruals, retained earnings, and new equity, with additional chunks of debt thrown in at appropriate intervals to balance the capital structure, which they have named sequential marginal costing.[12] This implies that the firm faces a rising supply curve of funds, and that there is an optimum capital structure for the firm.

Faced with this range of suggested approaches, the would-be analyst is apt to be bewildered at least. Two major points of difference exist between the different schools of thought. The first relates to the assumed shape of the cost function for funds facing the firm. Does the cost rise as a function of the volume of funds raised, or is it flat or nearly so as is implicit in the average costing approach? A second and slightly more subtle question is also involved: Is the cost of capital dependent on the capital structure or not? If it is, and if there is an optimum capital structure, then average costing will give incorrect results unless the firm is at this point, and then only if the proposed increment is also optimal in structure, and cost is independent of the amount raised.

These are essentially questions of valuation. How will additional earnings be valued? How does capital structure affect value? We shall examine the latter problem first as it has been the source of a great deal of confusion and has generated "more passion than reason."[13]

6.5 Traditional notions of capital structure optimality

Traditionally the effect of leverage on capital structure has been that certain amounts of debt can be raised at a cost less than that of equity, either at constant cost or at a cost increasing slightly as the debt-equity ratio rises. Small amounts of debt are also claimed not to affect the price-earnings ratio, or capitalization rate applied to the equity share of earnings, so that overall costs can be reduced by using some debt. Beyond a certain debt-equity ratio, costs of both debt and equity rise

Figure 6-1
Traditional views of optimum capital structure

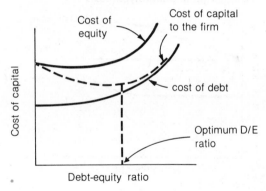

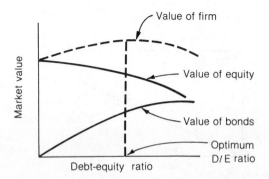

SOURCE: G. David Quirin, *The Capital Expenditure Decision* (Homewood, Ill.: Richard D. Irwin, 1967), p. 126.
© 1967 by Richard D. Irwin, Inc.

owing to the increasing riskiness of each, so that eventually the rising cost of debt raises the average cost of capital for the two sources combined. At some point, average cost is at a minimum. The location of this point indicates the optimum debt-equity mix for the firm.[14]

This is equivalent to another proposition to the effect that the market value of the firm is maximized at that same debt-equity ratio. The propositions are shown graphically in Figure 6–1.

6.6 The Modigliani-Miller theorem

In an article published in 1958, Modigliani and Miller suggested that the traditional view of capital structure optimality is incorrect and offered

**Figure 6–2
The Modigliani-Miller hypothesis**

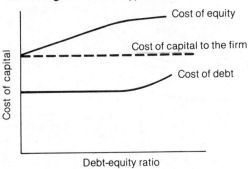

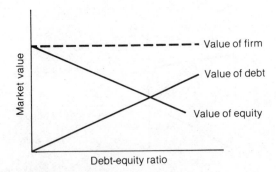

SOURCE: G. David Quirin, *The Capital Expenditure Decision* (Homewood, Ill.: Richard D. Irwin, 1967), p. 127. © 1967 by Richard D. Irwin, Inc.

theoretical arguments as well as empirical evidence against it.[15] The Modigliani-Miller position is that, irrespective of the effect of the debt-equity ratio on interest rates, the capitalization rate on equity will rise by an amount just sufficient to offset any possible saving, so that the overall cost of capital and the value of the firm as a whole are independent of the leverage employed. This relationship is illustrated graphically in Figure 6–2.

The way in which this adjustment is argued to be brought about is as follows. Suppose we have two firms with identical business risk characteristics. Expected operating income of the two firms is identical at $1 million per year. Suppose further that there is no income tax and that all profits are paid as dividends. The only difference between the two firms is in their capital structure. Firm A is financed entirely by equity, and has 1 million common shares outstanding. Firm B has $5 million in 6 percent debentures and 500,000 common shares outstanding. Suppose the market value of shares of firm A is $10, so that the market value of firm A is $10 million. The optimum capital-structure theory asserts that B's value (the market value of all claims on B's income) will be greater than that of A (unless the debt is so excessive that it is lower). Partial income statements and per share dividends are shown in Table 6–1.

Table 6–1
Income statements, A and B

	A	B
Operating income	1,000,000	1,000,000
Interest	—	300,000
Earnings and dividends	1,000,000	700,000
Shares outstanding	1,000,000	500,000
Dividends per share	1.00	1.40

SOURCE: G. David Quirin, *The Capital Expenditure Decision* (Homewood, Ill.: Richard D. Irwin, 1967), p. 128. © 1967 by Richard D. Irwin, Inc.

Suppose first of all that the value of B were higher, say $11 million (per share earnings of B have higher risk because of the existence of leverage and will sell at a lower price-earnings ratio). Suppose for simplicity's sake that the debentures sell at par so that the fraction of the value attributable to the common shares is $6 million or $12 per share.

Now examine the case of an investor who holds 1,000 shares of B. His annual dividend income is $1,400, and he must bear $1/500$ of the risk of fluctuations in B's income. He can sell his holdings for $12,000 and buy $20,000 worth of shares in A by borrowing $8,000 on private account. His income would be:

Dividends	$2,000
Less: interest	480
Net	$1,520

He would own $1/_{500}$ of the shares of A so that his risk would be unchanged, but he can increase his income if he makes the switch. It will pay him to sell B and buy A. The selling pressure in the market from investors seeking to make this switch will drive the price of B's shares down and A's shares up, and the opportunity for profit which leads to this selling pressure will continue as long as B is valued at a price above A (disregarding transactions costs as we also do in assuming a perfect capital market).

Suppose, on the contrary, that the value of B was below the value of A, say $9 million so that the price of B's shares was only $8. The investor holding 1,000 shares in A could sell these for $10,000, buy 500 shares of B, leaving the variability of his income unchanged, and buy $6,000 worth of B's bonds as well. His income will be increased from $1,000 to:

Dividends	$ 700
Interest	360
	$1,060

Again switches of this type will be profitable as long as B is valued below A. Thus, in equilibrium, the value of the two companies must be equal, their costs of capital equal, and the cost of capital independent of capital structure.

Several criticisms of the Modigliani-Miller theorem have been advanced on theoretical grounds. Durand has argued that personal leverage is not equivalent to corporate leverage because corporate leverage is typically in long-term form and is held at arm's length by the investor through the medium of limited liability, whereas personal leverage (buying on margin) is typically in the form of demand loans subject to margin calls and carries full personal liability. Further, all investors are subject to limits on the amount of margin commitments and many institutional investors are not permitted to buy on margin at all. It is thus argued that it is questionable empirically whether there is enough arbitrage of the sort described to provide for the value equilization.[16] Attainment of the results is thus not certain, but it will also depend upon the risk preferences and aversions of individual investors as well as institutional constraints on their behavior. Leverage at the portfolio level can, of course, be increased by more sophisticated methods than margin borrowing. Selling bonds out of portfolio holdings and using the proceeds to buy stock can be just as effective as the sale of newly created claims and can have the same arbitrage effects. It still remains a question of fact whether enough investors do so to bring about the result predicted by the theory.

Before looking at the empirical evidence, it should be noted that the predicted result is, strictly speaking, applicable only in a world where there are no taxes on corporate incomes, or at least where there is no double taxation of the earnings on equity. Where interest is tax deductible but dividends are not, the model predicts a slight decrease in the cost of capital with higher debt-equity ratios. The decrease is due solely to the tax treatment of the interest expense, which will provide a tax-shield cash flow which increases the market value of the firm and yet not lower the specific cost of the debt. Indeed, according to the model, if debt were interest free, there would be no advantage to using it as it would be indistinguishable from equity (it has to earn some rate of return otherwise it could not be sold). The optimum capital structure where interest can be claimed as a tax-deductible expense is one incorporating the maximum amount of debt obtainable or otherwise acceptable.

Argument over the Modigliani-Miller theorem continues; empirical evidence has been presented on both sides.[17] Unfortunately, there are formidable econometric problems involved in testing the model and the results are not particularly compelling. The empirical issue must still be regarded as open. A priori arguments against it persist, mostly based on the nonequivalence of personal and corporate leverage. Both the interest rates and the maturity structure of the borrowing options open to individual investors is different from that facing corporations. However, if we allow for the sale of bonds out of existing portfolios, equivalents are available. More serious perhaps is the inability of individual investors to acquire effective limited liability. Again, such inability is far from universal, and the only recourse must be to the facts of the marketplace. Unfortunately these have spoken equivocally. The Modigliani-Miller theorem relates to equilibrium; firms may well be able to take advantage of temporary disequilibria to the benefit of their existing stockholders.

6.7 Bankruptcy costs

This section considers two related possibilities which may distinguish the positions implied by the Modigliani-Miller theorem on the one hand and traditional views of optimum capital structure on the other. These include risky debt and bankruptcy costs. *Risky debt* is that debt where there is some probability that the coupon payments may not be met or the bonds themselves may not be redeemed. This situation is clearly more likely to occur in the highly levered firm. *Bankruptcy costs* occur if there are fees or other costs to be paid to third parties, such as trustees and lawyers, which costs must be borne and thus lower the value of the firm from what it would otherwise be if it could be reorganized costlessly. Do these possible costs imply an optimal capital structure?

The Miller-Modigliani theorem states that in perfect capital markets it does not make any difference to the overall market value of securities how the stream of cash flows from operations is split up among security types. The proportion of debt or equity does not change the valuation of the cash flows provided by the productive investments of the firm. Thus, so long as there are no bankruptcy costs, the fact that debt is risky is not sufficient to induce an optimal capital structure.[18]

This suggests we must turn to bankruptcy costs themselves if we are to find any basis for postulating the existence of an optimal capital structure. With bankruptcy costs, the value of the firm in bankruptcy is reduced by the fact that cash payments must be made to third parties other than the firm's bondholders or stockholders. These payments (trustees' fees, legal fees, and other costs) are deducted from the proceeds of sale of the firm or its assets which would otherwise go to the bondholders. These costs may be viewed as deadweight losses associated with the bankrupt condition and may therefore cause the value of the firm for which there is some possibility of bankruptcy to be less than the value when such costs do not exist or may be disregarded. Since we can think of the firm as passing from negligible to significant bankruptcy probability with increasing proportions of debt to equity, significant bankruptcy costs might be able to explain the existence of an optimal capital structure.[19]

Figure 6–3 summarizes the implications of significant bankruptcy costs. The dotted lines are the familiar Modigliani-Miller results where the cost of capital (weighted average) declines with increasing leverage in the presence of (only) corporate taxes. The solid lines show what might happen if bankruptcy costs are significant. As the proportion of debt increases, the probability of bankruptcy also increases, and the

Figure 6–3
Optimal capital structure in the presence of bankruptcy costs

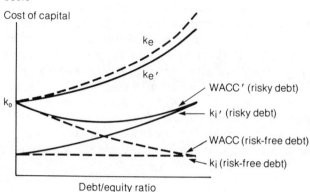

rate of return required by bondholders increases as a consequence. This implies a U-shaped weighted average cost of capital curve and an optimal capital structure. The optimum leverage may be found by increasing the proportion of debt until the marginal gain in value from increased leverage is equal to the marginal expected loss from higher bankruptcy costs.

The key question for deciding whether bankruptcy costs are a sufficient explanation for optimal capital structures in practice is whether such costs are significant or negligible. The empirical evidence bearing on this question is somewhat limited and equivocal.[20] Direct costs consisting of professional fees (such as for lawyers and accountants) and the value of managerial time devoted to bankruptcy-related tasks appear to be trivial and average only about 1 percent of the market value of the firm prior to bankruptcy. Furthermore, as a proportion of value, direct costs appear to decrease with increasing firm size. Possibly more significant could be indirect costs to bondholders, such as opportunity losses on funds tied up during legal proceedings and/or losses in security market values from resultant forced changes in capital structure. Other indirect costs to stockholders could result from loss of sales to customers anticipating bankruptcy and/or disruptions of output during reorganization if facilities must be liquidated and production rationalized. On the whole, the evidence does not appear to us sufficiently compelling to lead us to search very far for optimal capital structures in practice. This does, however, disregard the personal costs associated with possible stigma attaching to individual managers who may be held responsible for leading their firms into bankruptcy, even if no real costs accrue to the firm's security holders.

6.8 Debt capacity

At the end of the previous section, we alluded to the attitudes of managers and the costs that might have to be borne by them personally if the firms in their charge experience bankruptcy. Since we have shown that, in principle, the effects of bankruptcy on the market value of the firm are most likely negligible, concern for the question of debt capacity appears to mostly on the part of managers.[21]

What is meant by *debt capacity?* It is a perceived limit to issuing debt which depends on the willingness of the market to lend (at a price) and the willingness of managers to borrow (at a cost). One way conveniently to view this notion in a familiar context is shown in Figure 6–4.

Figure 6–4
Debt capacity

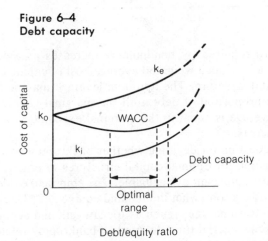

Here the cost of debt is shown as being constant until it becomes risky at which point the market's required rate of return begins to increase at an increasing rate (it cannot exceed the cost of equity since they become indistinguishable in the limiting case). This increasing cost may be interpreted by managers as signaling the market's view that the debt has become risky, and consequently, there is some probability of bankruptcy. "A level of debt may be reached at which the debt burden is as much as can safely be carried, and the prudent executive will not add more burden to endanger the company's solvency."[22] The firm has reached its debt capacity. The question really is, however, prudent from whose viewpoint? There may still be a substantial tax-shield cash-flow incentive from further increases in leverage which would increase the value of the firm, but which will remain unrealized if a debt capacity limit is imposed. The stockholders' and the managers' objectives are potentially in conflict. How this conflict might be resolved is beyond the scope of this book, and in any case, the detailed study of financing policy decisions is not our main concern.[23]

6.9 Market imperfections

We can examine a number of supply curves of capital to the firm, depending on the flexibility of the options open to the company and the extent and speed of adjustments in the market's valuation of the firm and its prospects. The firm, at any point in time, will be at a point on or above the supply schedules, which relate not to the funds to be added to those at its disposal, but to the total funds at its actual or potential disposal.

In the short run, we assume that the firm is limited in additional financing to the funds it can raise from privately negotiated short-term or term loans on the debt side and to retained earnings on the equity side.[24] It can reduce the funds at its disposal by prepayment or purchase of outstanding debt in the open market to the extent that cash is generated from operations during the period, but equity cannot be reduced. The only short-run information about these activities generally available to the market is any change in the dividend rate, and this is, accordingly, the only factor capable of affecting the market valuation of the common shares. New investments made do not affect earnings expectations immediately.

Under these conditions, we can draw a set of cost curves, one for each level of equity investment, showing the cost of debt for various levels of debt *at the given level of equity*. These will have the shape shown in Figure 6–5, with the following characteristic features:

1. A vertical portion at the left, representing the minimum level to which debt may be reduced by devoting all available cash to debt retirement.
2. A fairly flat portion to the right of the lower limit, showing the average cost of the various quantities of debt. This portion will rise, slowly at first, then more steeply as debt capacity is approached, the credit position of the borrower impaired, and the firm driven to seek borrowed funds from more expensive sources.
3. Another vertical portion at the right, representing the nonavailability of further credit at the existing level of equity.

For each level of equity, cost is not affected in the short run by the increase in debt, so that the average cost of capital obtained by weight-

Figure 6–5
Debt cost function (equity fixed)

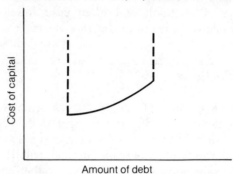

SOURCE: G. David Quirin, *The Capital Expenditure Decision* (Homewood, Ill.: Richard D. Irwin, 1967), p. 131. © 1967 by Richard D. Irwin, Inc.

ing the respective costs by the market-value proportions of debt and equity in the capital structure behaves as indicated in Figure 6–6 because initially debt is cheaper than equity and increasing the amount of debt in the debt-equity mix lowers cost. As the proportion of debt rises, so does the cost of debt, and the average cost of capital eventually turns upward.

Figure 6–6
Debt cost and cost of capital functions (equity fixed)

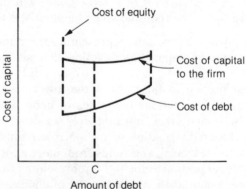

SOURCE: G. David Quirin, *The Capital Expenditure Decision* (Homewood, Ill.: Richard D. Irwin, 1967), p. 132. © 1967 by Richard D. Irwin, Inc.

Under these conditions, there is an optimum capital structure at point *C,* where the average cost of capital is lowest. We can show the short-run cost of capital for the firm in a three-dimensional figure as a function of debt and equity. To do so, draw a curve similar to that of Figure 6–6 for each attainable level of equity (equity cannot be reduced in the short run and cannot be increased beyond a limit imposed by 100 percent retention of earnings). Imagine that the curves for each level of equity have been cut out and placed in an appropriate position as sketched in Figure 6–7. If we keep adding sections parallel to the debt axis in this fashion until we have filled in the spaces for every attainable equity level, we will have the short-run cost of capital represented by a surface in a three-dimensional figure.

Figure 6–7
Cost of capital (debt and equity variable)

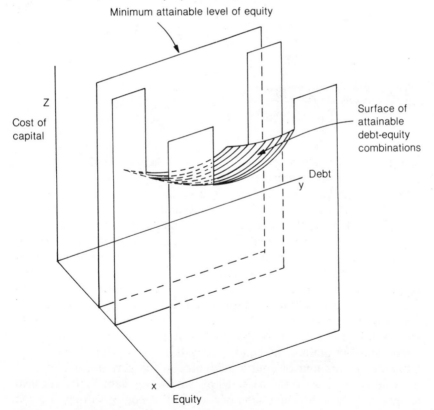

SOURCE: G. David Quirin, *The Capital Expenditure Decision* (Homewood, Ill.: Richard D. Irwin, 1967), p. 133. © 1967 by Richard D. Irwin, Inc.

A cross section through this surface parallel to the *y* (debt) plane gives us Figure 6–6, as is obvious from the method of construction. A cross section parallel to the *x* (equity) axis gives us the alternative profile of Figure 6–8.

**Figure 6–8
Cost of equity (debt fixed)**

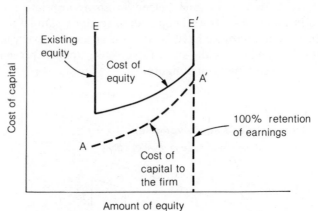

SOURCE: G. David Quirin, *The Capital Expenditure Decision* (Homewood, Ill.: Richard D. Irwin, 1967), p. 133. © 1967 by Richard D. Irwin, Inc.

Equity investment in the short run can be increased only by increasing the portion of earnings retained. Other things being equal, this will either reduce the price-earnings ratio or increase the cost of equity capital so that we have for each level of debt a curve similar to *EE'* in Figure 6–8 showing the average cost of capital for the firm as a whole.

Because it is rather difficult and clumsy to work with three-dimensional figures, we can map the surface on a two-dimensional figure using contour lines to indicate the locus of all points on the surface having identical capital costs. This construction is analogous to the use of isoquants to map a production surface or the use of indifference curves in price theory. Such a two-dimensional representation is shown in Figure 6–9, where the amount of debt is measured along the *y*-axis and the amount of equity along the *x*-axis. Upper and lower limits on the amount of equity attainable in the period are shown as lines perpendicular to the axis. Upper and lower debt limits are also shown, but these are functions of the level of equity so they are not perpendicular to the *y*-axis. Within these boundaries, the average cost of capital is represented by contour (isocost) lines.

Figure 6–9
Cost of capital surface (short run)

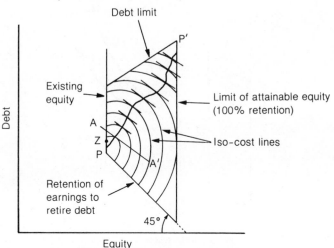

SOURCE: G. David Quirin, *The Capital Expenditure Decision* (Homewood, Ill.:
Richard D. Irwin, 1967), p. 134. © 1967 by Richard D. Irwin, Inc.

On this diagram, the various combinations of debt and equity which
give the firm a fixed volume of funds can be represented by a 45° line,
such as *AA'*, intersecting the respective axes at the amount fixed. We
can pick the lowest-cost combination for financing a desired volume of
funds by selecting the point on the lowest indifference curve tangent to
a 45° line such as *AA'*. This can be connected with the lowest cost
points for other amounts to give the expansion path *PP'*, which must
pass through the upper right-hand corner point *P'* but is not otherwise
constrained. This expansion path connects all the points for which
capital costs are at a minimum for the respective supply of funds and
can in turn be used to construct the short-run average cost of capital
curve in Figure 6–10.

The curve may be U-shaped with a minimum point such as *Q*, or
the cost of capital may increase from the outset. We can also draw a
marginal cost curve *MC* corresponding to the average cost of funds
PP' in Figure 6–10.

Referring back to Figure 6–9, the existing capital structure of the
firm may be represented by a point *Z* somewhere on the diagram. It
must lie on the lower equity limit, but it may not coincide with point *P*.
If it does not, it will pay the firm to alter its capital structure by changing its short-term debt level until *P* is reached.

In the intermediate term, the range of financing options is increased.

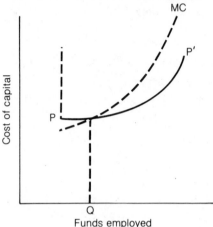

SOURCE: G. David Quirin, *The Capital Expenditure Decision* (Homewood, Ill.: Richard D. Irwin, 1967), p. 135. © 1967 by Richard D. Irwin, Inc.

Long-term debt and equity securities may be issued. As these will be public knowledge, the market valuation of the firm will adjust to reflect the prospective earnings from the new investment. The new investment will not have been fully digested by the firm, and its exact effect on the earnings will not be fully known so that the revaluation of the new situation will not be complete. The possibilities of reducing capital employed in either form or in total are also broadened, as equity may be increased to refund debt, or what is less common, but equally feasible in many cases, debt may be increased to obtain the funds to effect either a formal reduction in capital or in jurisdictions where it is permissible, to buy back the company's stock on the open market.

We may sketch cost curves for the various types of capital as was done in the short-run case. The resulting curves will lie either on or below the short-run curves (they cannot be above as the short-run options remain). There is now an upper limit on debt but no lower limit owing to the refunding possibility. The upper limit will be somewhat higher, since funding a portion of the debt in long-term form will reduce the risk associated with any given level of debt.

There is no theoretical upper limit on equity and no lower limit except that resulting from the borrowing limit and the implications of possible insolvency and bankruptcy discussed earlier. As the proportion of equity is increased, the dilution effect is likely to overbalance the earnings anticipation effect, thus reducing the market valuation and increasing the costs of equity.

Without drawing the curves for individual security types, which will be similar to those in Figures 6–5 through 6–8, we can proceed to sketch the overall function, which is shown in Figure 6–11.

Figure 6–11
Cost of capital surface (intermediate run)

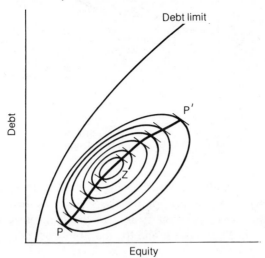

SOURCE: G. David Quirin, *The Capital Expenditure Decision*
(Homewood, Ill.: Richard D. Irwin, 1967), p. 136. © 1967
by Richard D. Irwin, Inc.

Once more we can derive the expansion path PP', to which corresponds the intermediate term cost of funds curve shown in Figure 6–12. This curve will lie at all points on or below the short-run cost curve of Figure 6–8, shown dotted in Figure 6–12. *MCI* is the relevant marginal cost curve. As before, the existing position of the firm will be somewhere in Figure 6–11. If it is not on the expansion path PP', it will pay the firm to alter its capital structure.

In the long run, no further financing options become available, but the effects of financing on the size and stability of earnings becomes widely known and the market completes its adjustment to revised earnings expectations and to the revised risk characteristics of the firm which has completed financing.

To the extent that the financing was justified to acquire earning assets, this has become reflected in earnings expectations, so the dilution effect disappears. As a result, the cost of capital becomes independent

Figure 6–12
Average and marginal cost of funds
(intermediate run)

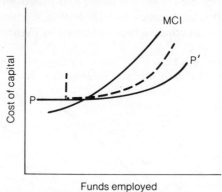

SOURCE: G. David Quirin, *The Capital Expenditure Decision* (Homewood, Ill.: Richard D. Irwin, 1967), p. 137. © 1967 by Richard D. Irwin, Inc.

of the volume of funds employed, being determined the market valuation of earnings of the appropriate risk category as described earlier.

At least for a given capital structure, the long-run cost of capital curve is flat as in Figure 6–13, and the marginal cost curve is necessarily coincident with it.

But capital structure affects the risk of fluctuating earnings as far as the common stockholder is concerned. It is necessary to consider

Figure 6–13
Average and marginal cost of funds (long run)

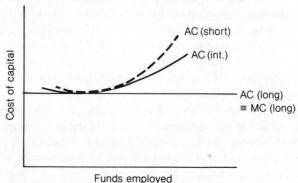

SOURCE: G. David Quirin, *The Capital Expenditure Decision* (Homewood, Ill.: Richard D. Irwin, 1967), p. 138. © 1967 by Richard D. Irwin, Inc.

whether there is an optimum capital structure in the long run as the traditional view appears to suggest. If there is, the marginal cost of capital in the long run, which is the relevant criterion for investment decisions purposes, is the weighted average cost of capital at the optimum capital structure, which we may not know with any degree of confidence. If there is not, then the weighted average cost of capital in the long run will be the same irrespective of what the capital structure is. Furthermore, in the long run, the firm does not face a rising supply curve of funds. The empirical evidence for this is the experience of a relatively large number of Canadian mining and oil firms which have increased the capital at their disposal several times over at no apparent increase in cost. The cost of capital from the viewpoint of the firm is also the required rate of return from the viewpoint of the market. Where it is clear that a firm can profitably employ several times its existing capital to earn at least the required rate of return, the capital can usually be raised. Cross-sectional studies do not indicate that the average cost of capital for large firms is above that of small; if anything they indicate the opposite, which would be expected, given the relative risks. The barriers to corporate long-run growth are not to be sought or found in a rising supply curve of funds, except in the short or intermediate term as already indicated, but in the inability to generate sufficiently attractive investment proposals and/or to build an organization capable of carrying them out at a sufficient rate.

Even if we grant that in the long run knowledge of the prospective profitability of added investment may make the supply curve of funds horizontal with respect to the amount raised, this does not necessarily imply that there is no optimal capital structure. The isocost lines might, for example, take the form sketched in Figure 6–14.

However, the arbitraging process envisaged by Modigliani and Miller is, in our view, more likely to be effective in the long run than the short, and in our judgment, it is likely to take place, although it may not show up in statistical analyses. If so, it is safe to use the weighted average cost of capital at the existing capital structure as a measure of the long-run cost of capital. This does not mean that the firm cannot or should not seek to finance in a way that takes advantage of a temporary disequilibrium in the capital market. It does suggest, however, that any gains thus made will be revalued rather quickly and will accrue to the existing stockholders as capital gains rather than from the ability of the firm to undertake marginal projects which its less financially astute competitors might reject.

Does anything remain of the optimum capital structure notion? Yes, but in the short and intermediate term only. For practical reasons, it is essential that financing be done in blocks of debt or equity or, less

Figure 6–14
Possible cost of capital surface (long run)

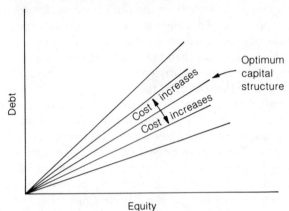

SOURCE: G. David Quirin, *The Capital Expenditure Decision*
(Homewood, Ill.: Richard D. Irwin, 1967), p. 139. © 1967 by
Richard D. Irwin, Inc.

frequently, both together. As a consequence, the expansion path actually followed will not be the smooth idealized expansion path *AA'* of the
intermediate-term case, for example. Rather, as shown in Figure 6–15,
it will be stair-shaped, "sequential marginal cost" path, *ABCDEFGA'*.
AB, CD, EF, and *GA'* represent additions to equity; *BC* and *FG* addi-

Figure 6–15
Expansion path

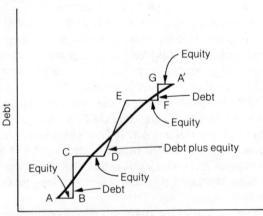

SOURCE: G. David Quirin, *The Capital Expenditure Decision*
(Homewood, Ill.: Richard D. Irwin, 1967), p. 140. © 1967 by
Richard D. Irwin, Inc.

tions to debt, and *DE* is a simultaneous offering of debt and equity. The extent of the rising cost as the amount of funds raised increases will depend on the extent to which the market takes account of the earnings prospects of the new investments being financed by the firm.

6.10   Estimating the marginal cost of capital

As was argued earlier, the firm which successfully exploits the departures of the capital market from long-run equilibrium can expect to have any resulting savings valued rather quickly so that they are realized essentially at once rather than over some indefinite future. If this is so, the applicable marginal cost of funds for investment-decision purposes is the long-run marginal cost which, in the model we examined, is equal to the long-run average cost.

This must be measured by using the weights of the existing capital structure at market values which reflect opportunity costs rather than at book values which reflect historical costs and are irrelevant for decision-making purposes. Use of the structure of intended financing cannot be supported if this will change the overall structure. Specific costs of debt, preferred stock, and common equity will all shift as required to produce the long-run cost equal to that resulting from using the weights implicit in the present structure.

Some adjustments are necessary, however. The capitalized value of leases should be added to the other outstanding long-term obligations at market value. In using this standard, equity is valued at market price times the number of shares; this figure replaces the capital and surplus item in the balance sheet. The common share specific cost is used for all, while the specific costs for depreciation and retained earnings do not enter the calculation. The following example will illustrate the calculations involved.

Example 6.10.1: Canadian Pacific Limited had the following consolidated capital structure as of December 31, 1979:

	Par/Book value ($ millions)	Market value* ($ millions)
Funded debt	$2,424.8	$1,963.1
4 percent consolidated debenture stock	292.5	103.8
7.25 percent preference series A	22.0	18.8
4 percent preference	15.7	7.5
Common stock (71,662,280 shares)	2,950.2	3,000.9

* May 1980 estimated, based on issues for which quotations available.

The outstanding debt includes a large number of privately placed issues for which no quotes are available; quotations are available for some $960 millions worth (at par value) which sell to yield, on average, approximately 13.6 percent. The 4 percent consolidated perpetual debenture stock sells at a deep discount to yield 11.28 percent. Like the funded debt, the carrying cost of the debenture stock may be expensed for tax purposes.

The two series of preference stock sell on an 8.4 percent yield basis, approximately. The common stock sells at $41.875, offering an indicated dividend yield of 4.30 percent. The major difficulty in arriving at a cost of capital estimate for Canadian Pacific is in assigning a reasonable growth rate to the earnings available to the common stock. The earnings record on a per share basis is as follows:

1965	1.12	1970	0.85	1975	2.40
1966	1.21	1971	0.94	1976	2.62
1967	0.99	1972	1.26	1977	3.31
1968	1.03	1973	1.62	1978	4.72
1969	0.98	1974	2.48	1979	7.06

The estimated 1980 earnings are $7.50 per share. The 15-year growth rate for 1965–80 is 13.5 percent. If the growth is measured from the 1966 peak to the (possible) 1980 peak, the growth rate drops to 13.0 percent. Measured over shorter periods, the growth rate is higher; in the 10 years since 1970, it is 24.3 percent and in the 5 years since 1975, 25.5 percent. Historically the earnings have been subject to fairly wide cyclical swings; experience in 1968–70 and 1974–75 suggests that these persist although they are virtually swamped by the strong growth trend. The retention rate is in excess of 75 percent; rates of return realized are, on average, not too high, but this reflects heavy, low-yielding investment in rail facilities and equipment; incremental rates of return on investment in nonrail activities have been large enough to produce the growth rates indicated.

As a minimum, the 15-year growth rate of 13.0 percent can be used. Adding it to the 4.3 percent dividend yield gives a common equity cost estimate of 17.3 percent. Using the 5-year growth rate of 25.5 percent, the equity cost becomes 29.8 percent under 1980 conditions. While this may seem high, even with inflation, the resulting "br" estimate of growth, based on the indicated 1980 retention rate of 76 percent, is 22.6 percent which accords reasonably well with the observed growth rate.

To avoid overestimating, we take the average of the 17.3 percent and 29.8 percent figures, or 23.6 percent.

Applying market-value weights, and the effective average 1980 tax rate of 48.9 percent, the estimated cost of capital becomes 16.74 percent as follows:

	Dollars (millions)	Percent	Cost ratio Before taxes	Cost ratio After taxes	Weighted cost (percent × after taxes)
Funded debt	1,963.1	38.5	13.6	6.95	2.68
Debenture stock	103.8	2.0	11.3	5.77	.12
Preference shares	37.7	0.7	8.4	8.40	.06
Common stock.............	3,000.9	58.8	23.6	23.60	13.88
	5,094.1	100.0			16.74

The cost of capital which results from these calculations is a long-run cost in the sense that it makes allowances for all the expected market adjustments. It is, however, a spot cost, corresponding to a particular moment in time. Several general factors affect the level of spot costs generally, although not the spot costs of any particular company. These include shifts in savings habits affecting the supply of funds and the demand for funds arising from changing business demands due to changing opportunities and the impact of government fiscal and monetary policies as earlier discussed.

Although the point has been ignored for the sake of simplicity in exposition, the discounting procedures discussed in Chapter 4 are formally correct only when the appropriate spot rate is used for individual time periods in the future. In general, it is quite sufficient to use an average of expected spot rates (a geometric average to be strictly correct). However, the existing spot rate may not fill the bill in this regard as it may be unduly influenced by current factors. It may be felt that an average of historical spot rates ought to be used. This can merely be an average of rates experienced over the past five or ten years, or some more sophisticated smoothing scheme may be employed. Both are illustrated in the following example.

Example 6–2: Corporation A's debt cost, dividend yield, and growth rate are shown on an annual average basis together with capital structure at average market prices and the annual estimates of the weighted cost of capital in the following table:

	Debt		Equity				
Year	Percent-age of market value	Cost	Percent-age of market value	Divi-dend yield	Annual growth rate	Cost	Weighted average cost
1	30	0.030	70	0.05	0.03	0.08	0.065
2	35	0.028	65	0.06	0.01	0.07	0.055
3	37	0.027	63	0.07	0	0.07	0.054
4	32	0.031	68	0.05	0.03	0.08	0.064
5	29	0.033	71	0.04	0.05	0.09	0.074
6	31	0.032	69	0.05	0.05	0.10	0.079
7	34	0.029	66	0.06	0.02	0.08	0.063
8	33	0.032	67	0.06	0.02	0.08	0.064
9	28	0.037	72	0.04	0.08	0.12	0.097
10	30	0.030	70	0.03	0.07	0.10	0.079

As will be seen from Figure 6–16, besides the cyclical pattern of changes in the cost of capital, there is an apparent upward trend.

The analyst in year 10 may decide to use the current spot rate as his best estimate of future costs, he may use the 10-year average of 6.9 percent shown by the solid line in Figure 6–16, or he may decide to use exponential smoothing, for example, which is an averaging process

Figure 6–16
Long-run cost of capital: corporation A

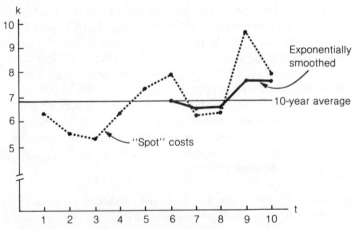

SOURCE: G. David Quirin, *The Capital Expenditure Decision* (Homewood, Ill.: Richard D. Irwin, 1967), p. 143. © 1967 by Richard D. Irwin, Inc.

giving more weight to recent years and perhaps more indicative of the trend.[25]

In this case, the results do not differ appreciably from the spot figure for year 10, but year 10 appears to be part of the way down from a cyclical peak and this would probably be a fairly good estimate for the next few years. The long-term average is probably less suitable if there really is a trend. Other weights can be used, of course, and will give different results. Despite the apparent precision of the calculation, it must be remembered that it is only an estimate and is to be used with discretion. While it would be appropriate for corporation A to use a discount rate of 8 percent in calculating net present values, management must be prepared to scrutinize carefully those projects with net present value only slightly greater than zero. Should the appropriate rate turn out to have been 9 percent instead of 8, some of those marginal projects should not have been accepted, and the market price of the shares may be slightly depressed relative to what it would be if the projects had not been undertaken.

6.11 Risk and the cost of capital—the capital asset pricing model

So far in this chapter, our discussion has been focused on the cost of capital for a given firm. Implicit in this discussion is the premise that the operating risk of the firm is unchanging with new investment; in the Modigliani-Miller terminology, the firm is assumed to remain in a given *risk class*. If either the underlying risk or the way underlying risk is perceived by the capital market changes, the cost of capital will change in response to the change in the required rate of return for the new risk class, just as the cost of equity was argued to respond to changes in financial risk resulting from changes in leverage. The relationship between degree of risk and required yields is one of the oldest observed regularities in the financial world, although attempts to describe its theoretical basis and to measure it are more recent.[26]

For many practical problems where capital-expenditures decisions are of the routine kind, it is unnecessary to consider the effect of changes in risk on the cost of capital; the projects under consideration are either too small or too similar in nature to have any observable impact on the riskiness of the company. Where the possibility of a significant change in risk is involved, as in the case of what we have described as strategic decisions, it is, of course, necessary to take into account the effects of such a change in the decision process. Problems of this type are examined in Chapters 11 and 12.

The cost of capital computed for a firm in a given risk class is, in effect, composed of two elements. One is an interest rate which discounts only for the pure time value of a cash flow to be received with certainty at some known future time. The other factor is usually referred to as a *risk premium* and discounts for the risk and uncertainty of the amount but not its timing.

Several authors have objected to the practice of using a discount rate in which a risk premium is embodied.[27] In principle, they argue, future cash flows should first be reduced to certainty equivalents, that is, discounted for uncertainty, and the resulting data should be discounted at a risk-free rate of interest with no risk premium to determine its present value. It can be shown that unless the risk (as measured by variance) of the elements in the stream of future cash flows can be viewed as increasing exponentially at an appropriate rate, a fixed risk premium would be incorporated only when the risk-free rate is expected to decrease. It is difficult to imagine circumstances under which such an assumption would be valid.

The argument is partly the result of trying to extrapolate the use of the simple tools of analysis developed under conditions of certainty to the uncertainty case with minimal changes. It does not work out quite as anticipated. Many implicit assumptions need to be made explicit, and when this is done the nature of the problem can be appreciated.

One of the major accomplishments of the theory of finance over the past decade or so has been to provide the analytical treatment needed to understand and cope with issues of this kind.[28] In particular, the capital asset pricing model shows that in a single-period, equilibrium framework, there is no distinction between the risk-premium and certainty-equivalent adjustments. The first adjusts the required rate of return, while the second adjusts the cash flow. One treatment can be derived from the other, but the net result is the same either way. However, when we move into the context of multiple periods, the correspondence breaks down.[29] Whether we choose to use the certainty-equivalent treatment described can be shown to depend on the assumptions we make regarding our knowledge of the evolution of the cash flow stream.[30] We consider the risk-premium approach to be the most appropriate in our judgment. We will describe its actual implementation in Chapters 11 and 12.

Notes

[1] Useful discussions may be found in E. Solomon, "Alternative Rate of Return Concepts and their Implications for Utility Regulation," *Bell Journal of Economics and Management Science* (Spring 1970), pp. 65–81, C. F. Phillips, Jr., *The Economics of Regulation,* rev. ed., (Homewood, Ill.: Richard D. Irwin, 1969), Chap. 9. An extensive

empirical study has been reported by M. J. Gordon, *The Cost of Capital to a Public Utility* (East Lansing: Division of Research, Graduate School of Business Administration, Michigan State University, 1974). For general background on the economics of regulation, the reader may wish to consult Richard A. Posner, *Economic Analysis of Law* (Boston: Little, Brown, 1972).

[2] 262 U.S. 679 (1923).

[3] 320 U.S. 591 (1944).

[4] J. A. Tatom and J. E. Turley, "Inflation and Taxes: Disincentives for Capital Formation," *Federal Reserve Bank of St. Louis Review* (January 1978), pp. 2–8, and A. C. Neal, "Immolation of Business Capital," *Harvard Business Review* (March–April 1978), pp. 75–82.

[5] See R. Lindsay and A. W. Sametz, *Financial Management: An Analytical Approach,* rev. ed. (Homewood, Ill.: Richard D. Irwin, 1967), chap. 18, for an elaboration of this point.

[6] The coverage cost concept was introduced and discussed in P. Hunt; C. M. Williams; and G. Donaldson, *Basic Business Finance,* 3d ed. (Homewood, Ill.: Richard D. Irwin, 1966), pp. 440–41.

[7] J. F. Childs, *Long Term Financing* (Englewood Cliffs, N.J.: Prentice-Hall, 1961), p. 378.

[8] J. F. Weston and E. F. Brigham, *Managerial Finance,* 3d ed. (New York: Holt, Rinehart & Winston, 1969), pp. 352–58.

[9] J. Dean, *Capital Budgeting* (New York: Columbia University Press, 1951), p. 50, R. W. Johnson, *Financial Management,* 2d ed. (Boston: Allyn & Bacon, 1959), p. 216; and W. G. Lewellen, *The Cost of Capital* (Belmont, Calif.: Wadsworth, 1969), p. 87.

[10] E. Solomon, "Measuring a Company's Cost of Capital," *Journal of Business* (October 1955), reprinted in E. Solomon, ed., *The Management of Corporate Capital* (New York: Free Press, 1959), pp. 128–40.

[11] E. Solomon, *The Theory of Financial Management* (New York: Columbia University Press, 1963), p. 88.

[12] Lindsay and Sametz, *Financial Management,* chap. 20.

[13] A. J. Boness, "A Pedagogic Note on the Cost of Capital," *Journal of Finance* (March 1964), p. 99.

[14] Among the many references may be cited B. Graham and D. L. Dodd, *Security Analysis,* 2d ed. (New York: McGraw-Hill, 1941), pp. 541–42.

[15] F. Modigliani and M. H. Miller, "The Cost of Capital, Corporation Finance and the Theory of Investment," *American Economic Review* (June 1958), 261–97.

[16] D. Durand, "The Cost of Capital in an Imperfect Market; A Reply to Modigliani and Miller," *American Economic Review* (September 1959), pp. 639–55.

[17] See also Durand, "Cost of Capital"; A. Barges, *The Effect of Capital Structure on the Cost of Capital* (Englewood Cliffs, N.J.: Prentice-Hall, 1963), R. F. Wippern, "Financial Structure and the Value of the Firm," *Journal of Finance* (December 1966), pp. 615–34; M. H. Miller and F. Modigliani, "Cost of Capital to the Electric Utility Industry," *American Economic Review* (June 1966), 333–91, M. J. Gordon, "Some Estimates of the Cost of Capital to the Electric Utility Industry," *American Economic Review* (December 1967), pp. 1267–77; and M. Davenport, "Leverage and the Cost of Capital, Some Tests Using British Data," *Economica* (May 1971), pp. 136–62.

[18] This result has been demonstrated by analyses beyond the scope of this book by J. Stiglitz, "Some Aspects of the Pure Theory of Corporate Finance: Bankruptcies and Takeovers," *Bell Journal of Economics and Management Science* (Autumn 1972), pp. 458–482, and M. Rubenstein, "A Mean-Variance Synthesis of Corporate Financial Theory," *Journal of Finance* (March 1973), pp. 167–81.

[19] Detailed discussions may be found in N. Baxter, "Leverage, Risk of Ruin and the Cost of Capital," *Journal of Finance* (September 1967), pp. 395–403; Stiglitz, "Aspects of the Pure Theory of Corporate Finance"; A. Kraus and R. Litzenberger, "A State-

Preference Model of Optimal Financial Leverage," *Journal of Finance* (September 1973), pp. 911–22; and E. H. Kim, "A Mean Variance Theory of Optimal Capital Structure and Corporate Debt Capacity," *Journal of Finance* (March 1978), pp. 45–64.

[20] The major studies, limited to U.S. railroad data, appear to be J. Warner, "Bankruptcy Costs: Some Evidence," *Journal of Finance* (May 1977), pp. 337–47; and J. Warner, "Bankruptcy, Absolute Priority, and the Pricing of Risky Debt Claims," *Journal of Financial Economics* (May 1977), pp. 239–76. There is also some data in W. B. Hickman, *Corporate Bond Quality and Investor Experience* (Princeton: Princeton University Press, 1958).

[21] The most comprehensive study of this issue is by G. Donaldson, *Corporate Debt Capacity* (Boston: Division of Research, Graduate School of Business Administration, Harvard University, 1961).

[22] P. Hunt; C. M. Williams; and G. Donaldson, *Basic Business Finance: A Text* (Homewood, Ill.: Richard D. Irwin, 1974), p. 442.

[23] See, for example, E. H. Neave and J. C. Wiginton, *Financial Management: Theory and Strategies* (Englewood Cliffs, N.J.: Prentice-Hall, 1981), chap. 14.

[24] Compare G. Donaldson, *Strategy for Financial Mobility* (Boston: Division of Research, Graduate School of Business Administration, Harvard University, 1969).

[25] The basic formula is:

$$K_t = wk_t + (1 - w)K_t - 1$$

where K_t is the normalized value, k_t the value in year t, and w is a weighting factor between 0 and 1.

Using $w = 0.4$, and setting K_5 equal to the average of the first five years, applying the formula gives the value of 0.078 for year 10.

[26] W. F. Sharpe, "Risk Aversion in the Stock Market: Some Empirical Evidence," *Journal of Finance* (September 1963), pp. 416–22.

[27] See also A. A. Robichek and S. C. Myers, *Optimal Financing Decisions* (Englewood Cliffs, N.J.: Prentice-Hall, 1965), chap. 5; and J. Lintner, "The Valuation of Risk Assets and the Selection of Risky Investments in Stock Portfolios and Capital Budgets," *Review of Economics and Statistics* (February 1965), pp. 13–37.

[28] Neave and Wiginton, *Financial Management,* Part II.

[29] E. F. Fama and M. H. Miller, *The Theory of Finance* (New York: Holt, Rinehart & Winston, 1972), chap. 8.

[30] E. F. Fama, "Risk-Adjusted Discount Rates and Capital Budgeting under Uncertainty," *Journal of Financial Economics* (August 1977), pp. 3–24.

Problems

1. Using the following data, calculate the cost of capital for Amalgamated Tree Farms, Inc.

AMALGAMATED TREE FARMS, INC.
Capital Structure
($000)

5¼ First Mortgage Bonds, due 1998 (market price 98.00)	18,500
5¾ Debentures, due 1993 (market price 97.50)	57,000
Common Stock, 10,400,000 shares no par value	

AMALGAMATED TREE FARMS, INC.
Selected Financial Data

Year	Earned per share	Dividends per share	Common stock price range
1975	2.26	1.50	29–38
1976	2.36	1.50	26–36
1977	2.64	1.50	31–38
1978	3.46	1.50	33–42
1979	3.52	2.00	37–53
1980	3.98	2.00	52–73
Latest price $53.00			

2. Using data from *Moody's* or *Standard and Poor's* and current quotations, calculate costs of capital for the following companies:
   a. General Dynamics Corp.
   b. International Business Machine Corporation.
   c. Sears, Roebuck and Co.
   d. United States Steel Corporation.
   e. Xerox Corporation.

3. How would you determine what cost of capital to use in setting capital budgets for a firm which had no publicly held securities?

Optimal budgets under modified certainty

7.1 Static and myopic optimality

The analysis of selection of projects for inclusion in optimum capital budgets is based on a *static,* equilibrium model which also assumes certainty and perfect capital markets. While we relaxed the certainty assumption slightly in Chapter 3, like much else in economic theory, we are faced with a dilemma in coping with the inherently dynamic nature of our world when we seek practical decisions. The dynamic element is reflected both in the fact that the anticipated cash flows will actually be generated at several future points in time and that these cash flows are uncertain. We wish to examine more closely the multi-period aspect of these cash flows.

The analysis used to this point can be extended to the multi-period case so long as we may assume that the real capital goods which are the objects of choice can be bought and sold in perfect (primary and resale) markets. Under this assumption, the selection of the optimal level of investment in each period of the planning horizon (and particularly the first period) is merely a sequence of independent, single-period decisions that can be taken exactly.[1]

If the market for real capital goods were perfect, the firm could buy or sell as many units at the beginning of any particular period as it might wish at a known, fixed price, with no transactions costs. Operationally, no transactions costs means that the firm would receive from selling the asset exactly as much as it would expect to pay for its purchase.[2] Under these conditions, to determine whether the firm should acquire an asset, the analyst need only compare the current outlay with the forecast cash flow, including the resale market price of the asset, one period later, using one of the criteria already described.

This one-period horizon property of the decision may be considered *myopic* and may also be thought paradoxical because of the durability of the assets and the number of periods for which cash flows are anticipated. However, if the markets for real capital assets were perfect, the firm could adjust its capital stock to any desired level at will. No matter what stock it currently holds, it can sell the whole lot and then buy back whatever quantity it wants to have to operate through the next period. No costs are incurred in such a rollover, so the firm will not be worse off by deciding one period at a time.

Many investment decisions can be made one period at a time even if there are some minor imperfections in the secondary or resale markets. If the firm acquires the asset, the worst possible outcome it may expect is to receive its one-period cash flow and the net salvage value of the asset after the first period. If the asset is acceptable on this basis, it should be acquired, since the firm can only gain by the opportunity to retain it and continue operating it for additional future periods. Problems arise when we consider those many, possibly worthwhile, projects whose salvage value at the end of one period poorly reflects future earning power. In such cases, further periods may need to be considered in arriving at a capital-expenditure decision.

Even this would not be necessary if the ownership claims (securities) against the assets and their attendant cash flows traded in a perfect market, and if the assets involved were those of the whole firm. In these circumstances, the claims will be valued correctly even though the assets themselves only trade in imperfect markets. Unfortunately, even with perfect financial (capital) markets, if securities giving title to particular assets cannot be sold separately by the firm, explicitly multiperiod analysis will be necessary.

7.2 Explicit multi-period optimality

As indicated, the problem of dealing explicitly with multi-period optimality arises because of uncertainty,[3] because (1) the market for physical capital is imperfect and (2) claims against these assets cannot be sold separately by the firm to be traded in perfect financial capital markets (and implicitly that the various assets the firm might be considering are not all in the same risk class). We have not yet explicitly introduced uncertainty into our analysis, although we have suggested using risk-adjusted discount rates. Making explicit statements regarding multi-period optimality which are correct in principle is more complex than our treatment to this point.[4] Nevertheless, it is necessary to consider the problem briefly in order to understand the issue of *capital rationing* which is our main topic of concern in this chapter. We can sketch what a correct approach to multi-period optimality would need to include and use this as a basis for addressing practical questions.

For a n-period project life, it is convenient to proceed by backward induction from the last period to the first. For the last time period, the value of a project at time n will be just the (final) cash flow to be received at that time. In the next-to-last period $(n - 1)$, we have a single-period problem as before, but conditional on whatever state-of-the-world will be existing at time $(n 1)$.[5] We may then proceed to solve a series of single-period problems successively, using the preceding results for subsequent periods as data, so that we find both a general solution and a solution for the first period.

Finding a solution in this way involves solving an n stage stochastic dynamic programming problem. In principle, this approach shows us how to value assets that can be traded only in imperfect markets and thus how to make economically optimal asset acquisition decisions. Unfortunately, even if we imagine only a few possible states-of-the-world, the dimensionality of the problem multiplies and makes it difficult and costly to solve.[6]

Knowing what the correct solution must be in this situation is not always helpful operationally. Let us see how far we can go in using some of our other knowledge. If the productive activities of the firm are similar in business risk, then the assets (and the firm) belong to a homogeneous risk class in the Modigliani-Miller sense. This implies that some proportion of the firm's securities may be notionally ascribed to the individual projects in proportion to their market values. Again, so long as the securities (claims) trade in perfect capital markets, the important separation principle that permits us to separate operating (investment) from financing decisions still applies.

For the moment, let us assume that we will continue to recommend making investment decisions as already described. Cash flows must be estimated period by period as accurately as possible. These cash flows are then discounted using the long-run weighted average cost of capital, as discussed in Chapter 6, to obtain either the net present value or discounted benefit-cost ratio to determine whether the project should be accepted or rejected. The aggregate of all such acceptable projects constitutes our current capital budget.

If we accept this capital budget, we must arrange financing in order to ensure all economically profitable projects are undertaken. However, for many reasons, we may choose not to accept all projects that will yield a positive net present value and thus increase the value of the firm. All of these reasons involve us in capital rationing. While some are valid, others are specious from an economic viewpoint. We will attempt to indicate which is which and also an operational approach to the problem of deciding the necessary financing.

7.3 Capital-rationing problems—their origin

Capital-rationing situations arise when the firm must operate within a fixed budget, rather than accepting all projects which increase the value of the firm according to the decision rules outlined in Section 3.9. They also occur in the public sector, when an overall constraint is imposed on the size of the budget, so that it is not possible to accommodate all projects showing an excess of social benefits over costs.

Within the private sector, the constraints which lead to a decision to hold capital expenditures to a fixed sum may arise due to market conditions, or they may be entirely self-imposed.[7] Market constraints may be effective because, while the long-run supply curve of capital to the firm may be perfectly elastic, the short- or intermediate-run curve will ordinarily slope upward. Beyond limits, it may become perfectly inelastic. The rising supply price is probably the result of market imperfections and the information lag discussed in Chapter 6, but it is none the less real for a firm which is attempting to add assets at a rate faster than the market is valuing its earning prospects. Presumably, a firm in this position could finance temporarily with some of the more expensive forms of short-term debt, replacing this source with lower-cost permanent funds once the market values the augmented earning power. Since there is a limit to the profitability of this type of financing, it is not without risk for any firm. It is particularly dangerous for a firm which expects to maintain a high rate of asset growth for the indefinite future, since it is likely to find itself in a situation in which it is forced to depend almost continuously on such treacherous sources of funds.[8]

Many firms in a high-growth situation are apt to restrict budgets to the amount they believe they can raise from "reasonably priced" sources, which do not lead to excessive leverage and resulting high levels of risk. For such firms, there is an optimum capital structure. It is not dependent on the cost of capital situation but determined by the maximum probability of default on debt which is acceptable to management.[9]

A somewhat less defensible capital-rationing policy is one imposed by a decision to restrict investment to the funds available from depreciation accruals plus current earnings less dividends, that is, to cash flow generated from operations. Such a policy may reflect extreme risk aversion on the part of the management to the detriment of stockholders. If so, it overlooks the possibility of financing greater expansion with equity raised by way of a rights offering, the judicious use of long-term debt, and/or convertible senior issues. It is more likely that such a policy originates from a combination of risk aversion with a concern for retaining control on the part of an insider group who, for reasons of their own, do not wish to increase their own investment. They may have more profitable opportunities elsewhere or simply not have the required funds. Whatever the reason, they may be quite willing to sacrifice not only their own extra profits from the firm, but those of other stockholders, in order to retain control.

Capital rationing may, of course, be adopted as a temporary measure in any given year if a firm is normally able to handle all profitable projects from internal sources, expects to do so in the future, and wishes to maintain the dividend rate by postponing a few projects until next year. There is certainly a prima facie case for borrowing under these conditions. However, if investment opportunities are so limited, one might wish to scrutinize management's research and development activities and their ability to generate profitable projects in general.

The need for capital rationing may also arise where there is no effective funds constraint, but where the rate of growth must be restrained because of shortages of skilled personnel or of critical materials. While this type of bottleneck problem can be handled by imposing an overall expenditure constraint, this will ordinarily prove to be an inefficient way to do so. The inputs of scarce materials and talents will not ordinarily be proportional to project cost. Furthermore, most such resources can be obtained at a price. Some projects, such as data processing systems, may find their primary justification in the way in which they enable the firm to economize on scarce managerial talents. Problems of this type, particularly those in which there is more than one scarce factor, are most satisfactorily handled by the use of programming models of the type to be discussed in Section 7.8.

Governments may wish to impose a limit on the sizes of their budgets for reasons similar to those used by private firms. They may have manpower constraints or be faced with debt limits imposed either by the market or by constitutional requirements. Central governments with control over the money supply will seldom face market-imposed constraints because they can create all the credit they need or want. However, they may wish to constrain expenditures for fiscal policy reasons to reduce inflationary pressures or to improve the balance of payments. In developing countries, there may be a need to consider foreign exchange requirements, along with other scarce factors, such as managerial skills, in a programming budget model.

7.4 Alternative solutions to the single-period capital-rationing problem

The simplest capital-rationing situation is one in which the expenditure constraint lasts for a single period only. This simple case indicates some of the properties of the solution of the more general case. It is also of practical as well as theoretical interest because many if not most firms do not have sufficient knowledge of their future investment opportunities to apply the more sophisticated models to be discussed later in this chapter. In any event, we need only to decide on the first period's budget.

The easiest way of selecting projects, assuming they are of similar risk, for inclusion in a limited budget is to rank them in descending order of attractiveness then to accept projects beginning at the top of the list and work downward until the funds are exhausted. Mutually exclusive projects are handled by breaking them into a basic project and supplementary projects, in the manner described in Section 4.8.

However, as we saw in Chapter 3, projects may be ranked in several different ways, which do not always give the same results. Consider, for example, a firm which seeks to select a set of projects costing no more than $500,000 from among the opportunities listed in Table 7–1.

Table 7–1

		Benefit-cost ratio when discounted at						Internal
	Cost	20 percent	18 percent	16 percent	14 percent	12 percent	10 percent	rate of return
A	100,000	0.9	1.0	1.1	1.3	1.5	1.7	18%
B	100,000	1.0	1.1	1.2	1.3	1.4	1.5	20
C	100,000	0.8	0.9	1.0	1.1	1.1	0.9	11,16
D	100,000	0.8	0.9	1.0	1.1	1.2	1.3	16
E	100,000	0.5	0.7	0.9	1.0	1.1	1.2	14
F	100,000	0.1	0.2	0.5	0.7	1.0	1.4	12
G	100,000	0.3	0.5	0.7	0.9	1.1	1.2	13

Note that project C is a multiple-rate-of-return project, which has a benefit-cost ratio below (negative net benefits) at rates of discount below 11 percent or above 16 percent, but a ratio above 1 at discount rates in between these values.

Suppose that the firm's cost of capital, calculated according to the criteria established in Chapter 6, is 10 percent. If it ranks projects in order of benefit-cost ratios calculated at 10 percent (or, since costs of all projects in the example are equal, in order of the present value of net benefits) it will select projects as listed in Table 7–2.

If, on the other hand, the firm selects in order of descending internal rates of return, it will select in the order shown in Table 7–3.

Differences in the ranking and in the set of projects selected are obvious. Using the internal-rate-of-return criterion leads to the adoption of project C, which was not only rejected on the basis of benefit-cost ratio rankings, but it would be rejected if the firm adopted a

Table 7–2
Selection using benefit-cost ratios
(10 percent)

Project	Benefit-cost ratio
A	1.7
B	1.5
F	1.4
D	1.3
E or G	1.2

Table 7–3
Selection using internal rate of return

Project	Internal rate of return
B	20%
A	18
C and D	16
E	14

profit-maximizing strategy and carried investment to the point where the marginal rate of return was equal to the cost of capital, since it would be removed when the discount rate fell below 11 percent. When we have a constraint, however, we have an implicit opportunity cost of funds, which is associated with the constraint. The implicit opportunity cost is equal to the rate of return on the best project excluded from the final budget, that is, the return which can be earned on funds in their best alternative use. In nearly all cases, this will be higher than the firm's cost of capital calculated in the usual way. In this case, it is 13 percent, the rate of return on project G. Using the internal-rate criterion for ranking is equivalent to selecting projects on the basis of their benefit-cost ratios, calculated at the opportunity cost rate, rather than on the regular cost of capital basis, which is inconsistent with our recommendation in Chapter 6. In our example, project C has a benefit-cost ratio in excess of 1.0 at the opportunity cost rate of 13 percent and, therefore, is in the adopted budget.

If we select projects initially on the basis of benefit-cost ratios (see Table 7–2), we must recognize that there is an opportunity cost here also. Depending on whether we reject G or E, which have identical

Table 7–4
Selection using benefit-cost ratios
(13 percent)

Project	Benefit-cost ratio
A	1.40
B	1.35
D	1.15
C	1.10+
E	1.05

benefit-cost ratio rankings, the implicit opportunity cost is either 13 percent or 14 percent. If we recalculate benefit-cost ratios at the former rate, we get the ranking shown in Table 7–4.

Project F, included in the initial selection, has been deleted because its benefit-cost ratio falls below 1.0 when discounted at 13 percent, while project C has been included. Although differences in ranking remain, the list of adopted projects is identical to that derived by ranking the projects by internal rates of return.

The changes in benefit-cost ratio ranking, as discount rates change, reflect crossing present value profiles in the case of normal investment projects (see Figure 3–5) and the presence of a multiple-rate project. (As a useful exercise, sketch the present value profiles of projects in Table 7–1.) These occur, of course, because of different time shapes in the income streams of different projects. For normal projects characterized by an initial outlay of funds followed by an inflow, one project (such as A) will have a higher benefit-cost ratio than another (such as B) at high discount rates and a lower ratio at low discount rates only if it has a relatively higher cash flow in earlier periods and lower cash flow in later periods. The most frequent type of multiple-rate-of-return project is the income-acceleration project, which may not increase overall cash flow from a project at all but which results in it being earned more quickly. It is clear that using the higher rate alters the selection set in favor of projects which produce a relatively greater immediate cash flow.

In the case where the budget constraint is temporary and market-imposed, this is a desirable type of alteration in the adopted project set. It produces cash more rapidly, thus directly reducing the impact of any constraint in future periods. Because the resulting higher earnings[10] will add to market value and the higher apparent growth rate may have a favorable effect on investor expectations, the intermediate-term funds supply schedule may shift more to the right, further easing the constraint and hastening the day when it will cease to be binding.

Even in cases where the budget constraint is not due to market factors but is self-imposed, so that the opportunity cost is merely a measure of self-imposed loss, this alteration will lead to a more rapid expansion in cash flow. In cases where the constraint is tied to reported earnings, their more rapid growth will diminish the impact of the constraint in subsequent periods. This is, we feel, a strong argument for ranking projects in order of descending rates of return in many capital-rationing situations and allocating funds from the top of the list until exhausted. In the case of multiple-rate-of-return projects, the listing should indicate not only the rates at which such projects enter the budget but the rates at which they should be deleted from it. Table 7–5 gives such a ranking for the projects listed in Table 7–1.

Table 7–5
Schedule for project adoption

Budget	Implicit opportunity cost	Projects added	Projects deleted	Projects in budget
$100,000	20%	B	—	B
200,000	18	A	—	B,A
400,000	16	C and D	—	B,A,C,D
500,000	14	E	—	B,A,C,D,E
600,000	13	G	—	B,A,C,D,E,G
700,000	12	F	—	B,A,C,D,E,F,G
600,000	11	—	C	B,A,D,E,F,G

One difficulty with this approach is apparent from inspection of the table. There are two budgets which just exhaust an allocation of $600,000. This is a direct result of the multiple-return project C, and similar results will emerge whenever there are not enough other projects which enter the budget at a rate at which a multiple-return project leaves it. In actual practice, such problems may not occur frequently since we would expect to find opportunities increasing in number and amount as we reach lower rates of return—it is, after all, only high-return projects which are scarce. What should be done when it does occur and coincides with the budget constraint is less certain. Following this reasoning, we would be inclined to work down the table until the constraint was encountered for the first time but only if the constraint was completely inflexible. Such a situation should call for a careful reappraisal of the projects and, more important, of financing alternatives which may have been neglected in setting the constraint. Adoption of project C in this context is in a sense equivalent to borrowing at 11 percent to finance some of the projects. If alternative financing is available below this rate, serious consideration should be given to changing the constraint. We will see later how this may be handled in a mathematical programming framework.

The procedure outlined earlier does not maximize the present value at the company's cost of capital added to the firm as a result of this year's budget. It has, therefore, been criticized by some authors.[11] Its advantage is that it leads through time to a more rapidly growing cash flow and the relaxing of the constraint.

One alternative to this procedure, which maximizes the present value added by this year's budget, is simply to rank in order of descending benefit-cost ratios. To some extent, this is an unsatisfactory solution, which arises from considering the problem in a one-period setting. Many projects could be postponed until next year, but postponing those with the lowest benefit-cost ratios may not be the most satisfactory way of resolving the problem.

We prefer to regard the acceptance of all projects having benefit-cost ratios in excess of 1.0 as the ideal which would be attained in the absence of the constraint and to select for postponement those projects which cause the smallest possible reduction (in present value added) from this profit maximizing ideal. In effect this provides and uses an objective measure of urgency.

Projects to be postponed using this criterion need not be those at the bottom of the benefit-cost ratio list. Although these contribute the least to the long-run profitability, they may not be the most postponable. The profitability of some projects as measured by internal rates of return may be unaffected by postponement; some, such as projects to cash in on volatile fashions, may be entirely dissipated. Some, such as replacement of machine tools, may be enhanced. The latter should be removed from the provisionally accepted list for this period even if there is no funds constraint for their contribution will only be enhanced by the delay.[12]

If the profit-maximizing budget exceeds the maximum attainable supply of funds, the implicit opportunity cost of the constraint should be evaluated as the internal rate of return of the best extra-marginal project. Next, the list of available, but rejected, projects should be combed for income-acceleration projects having multiple rates of return which will be profitable at this opportunity cost rate. These should be added to the budget to help increase the supply of funds in subsequent periods.

Next, an index of postponability should be constructed by comparing the net present value of each project in the original maximizing budget on the assumption that it is constructed next year with its present value evaluated at the cost of capital rate. Subtracting next year's value from this year's value gives a measure of the reduction in present value which will result from postponement of the project. This may be divided by the funds the project would require to obtain an index of present value of losses,[13] resulting from postponement per dollar of funds freed by postponement. Using this index, the projects may then be ranked in descending order and selected for postponement by working from the top down until the budget has been reduced by a sufficient amount.

Where the benefit-cost ratios of projects are not sensitive to timing, this procedure will (except for the inclusion of multiple-rate projects) give the same result as ranking by means of benefit-cost ratios. It does introduce another element into the calculation, however, and thus operates to minimize the reduction in present value from its maximum level which is necessary to meet the budget constraint.

Example 7.4.1: Suppose we have the group of projects listed in Table 7–6 and a budget constraint of $500,000.

Table 7–6

Project	Initial cost ($000)	Benefit-cost ratio	Internal rate of return, (in percent)	PV now of net benefits if done	
				This year	Next year
A	$100	1.7	18%	100	91
B	100	1.5	20	90	87
C	100	0.9	16,11	−10	−9
D	100	1.3	16	75	60
E	100	1.2	14	30	26
F	100	1.4	12	50	55
G	100	1.2	13	30	10

We start off by ranking the projects in terms of their benefit-cost ratios. This gives us the following ranking:

	Benefit-cost ratio	Net PV this year
A..............	1.7	100
B..............	1.5	90
F..............	1.4	50
D..............	1.3	75
E..............	1.2	30
G..............	1.2	30
C..............	0.9	−10

Taking the first five, we have a budget tentatively consisting of projects A, B, F, D, E. The internal rate of return on the marginal excluded project, G, is 13 percent. Since the dual-rate project C has a positive present value at the 13 percent opportunity cost rate, we adopt it to ease the budget constraint next year.

We next proceed to calculate the losses resulting from postponement for the projects (excluding C which we have decided to adopt anyway). These are as follows:

	(a) PV this year	(b) PV next year	Loss by delay (a) − (b) divided by cost
A...................	100	91	0.09
B...................	90	87	0.03
D...................	75	60	0.15
E...................	30	26	0.04
F...................	5	55	−0.05
G...................	0	10	0.20

Some of the projects do not change much as a result of postponement, merely showing a loss reflecting the one-year deferral of the income; some show less loss than this amount, while F shows a gain. Presumably it is a project which is just becoming profitable this year and should be postponed even if there is no funds constraint. G, on the other hand, shows a substantial loss as the result of deferral. In order to bring our budget down within the constraint, we must delete projects F and B, which leaves us with a budget consisting of A, C, D, E, and G as the final budget. To see why this is preferable to the initially selected group, compare the present value of the latter, with G delayed till next year:

	Initial selection	Final selection
A	100	100
B	90	87*
C	—	−10
D	75	75
E	30	30
F	50	55
G	10*	30
	355	367

* Delayed one year

Next year, of course, the projects which have been deferred from this year's budget must compete with the other projects for the available funds. If other projects are better, these projects may again be postponed for another year; they may, in fact, never be accepted, depending on what other opportunities become available. If we do not know what will be available next year, this is a rational method of making the allocations on a year-by-year basis.

Setting a fixed budget constraint is a poor way of approaching the capital-budgeting problem. Even where it is forced on the firm by market conditions, it is apt to be rather an elastic barrier, which can be pushed back to some extent by squeezing funds out of working capital, either by reducing current asset accounts or by increasing current liabilities. Alternative forms of financing should be carefully examined; some assets may be leased and term loans may finance the acquisition of others.[14] There are limits to all of these, but they are seldom rigid limits. The firm which appears to have a capital-rationing situation on its hands should explore carefully any avenues open to it which will make it possible to adopt as large a proportion of the projects which are acceptable out of the unconstrained profit-maximizing budget.

The one-period constraint is often unduly artificial. Some large projects take several years to complete, and expenditures may be rescheduled within wide limits between various years' budgets. In resolving the problem in a one-year setting, we introduced implicit assumptions concerning future opportunities and constraints. To get away from these artificial restrictions, it is possible to consider several periods at once using the models in the next section.

7.5 Multi-period problems—linear programming solution

An interesting approach to the solution of a multi-period capital-rationing problem is that developed by Weingartner.[15] This approach treats the problem as one in linear programming. This section examines the Weingartner model and certain extensions of it which may provide for greater realism.

The model seeks to maximize the present value, as of the current date, of the excess of present values over costs resulting from the adoption of a particular budget. This is expressed in the objective function which is to

$$B = \sum_i X_j b_j \qquad (7.5.1)$$

Table 7-7
Projects available for three-period capital-budgeting problem

Project j	b_j	c_{j1}	c_{j2}	c_{j3}	Y_{j2}	Y_{j3}
			Present values of benefits and costs ($000)			
1	70	100	0	0	20	20
2	50	100	0	0	30	25
3	−10	100	0	0	60	60
4	30	100	0	0	10	8
5	20	100	0	0	6	4
6	40	100	0	0	8	9
7	20	60	36	0	3	5
8	64	0	91	0	0	18
9	45	0	91	0	0	27
10	−9	0	91	0	0	54
11	27	0	91	0	0	9
12	18	0	91	0	0	5
13	36	0	91	0	0	9
14	18	0	54	33	0	2
15	158	0	0	183	0	0
16	141	0	0	183	0	0
17	25	0	0	83	0	0
18	18	0	0	83	0	0
19	15	0	0	83	0	0
20	14	0	0	83	0	0

$$C_1 = 380$$
$$C_2 = 345$$
$$C_3 = 314$$

where X_j is the fraction of the jth project undertaken and b_j is its net present value when discounted at the cost of capital (market required rate of return).

Each project is expected to involve cash outlays having present values C_{jt} in one or more of the periods t under consideration. These are regarded as fixed and not subject to alteration, that is, by rescheduling the project. There are fixed budget constraints C_t, the present value today of the actual constraint in the tth period. This gives us a set of budget constraint inequalities:

$$\sum_j X_j C_{jt} \le C_t \qquad (7.5.2)$$

one for each period being considered.

It is impossible to construct a negative project or to construct a project more than once so we have a third set of constraints:

$$0 \le X_j \le 1 \qquad (7.5.3)$$

This is the basic model. While we shall consider an example, we cannot devote space here to the basic theory of linear programming, computation of solutions, or geometric illustrations of simple cases, and the reader must be referred elsewhere.[16]

Example 7.5.2: As an example, suppose we have the projects listed in Table 7–7. The cost of capital is 10 percent. Projects 1 to 7 correspond to projects A to G in Table 7–1, while projects 8 to 14 are similar projects, deferred for one period. While they are similar, they are independent; adoption of project 1 does not preclude adoption of project 8. Projects 7 and 14 differ from G in that their expenditures are spread over two periods. Projects 15 to 20 are different projects which become available in the third period. The columns headed Y_{j2} and Y_{j3} may be ignored for the present example. Budget constraints are set at $380,000 per period in this example, which is the amount of the earnings from other operations which will be left after paying the desired dividend. This constraint has present values of 380 and 345 and 314 for the respective periods (present values in thousands of dollars).

Our problem, expressed in the linear programming format, is to maximize

$$B = 70X_1 + 50X_2 - 10X_3 + 30X_4 + 20X_5 + 40X_6 + 20X_7 + 64X_8 + 45X_9$$
$$- 9X_{10} + 27X_{11} + 18X_{12} + 36X_{13} + 18X_{14} + 158X_{15} + 141X_{16} + 25X_{17}$$
$$+ 18X_{18} + 15X_{19} + 14X_{20}$$

Subject to

$$100X_1 + 100X_2 + 100X_3 + 100X_4 + 100X_5 + 100X_6 + \qquad 60X_7 \le 380$$
$$36X_7 + 91X_8 + 91X_9 + 91X_{10} + 91X_{11} + 91X_{12} + 91X_{13} + 54X_{14} \le 345$$
$$33X_{14} + 183X_{15} + 183X_{16} + 83X_{17} + 83X_{18} + 83X_{19} + \qquad 83X_{20} \le 314$$

$$(7.5.3a)$$

and

$$0 \le X_j \le 1 \qquad \text{for } X_j = 1, 2, \ldots, 20 \qquad (7.5.3b)$$

The optimum solution for this problem is given by the following values of X:

$X_1 = 1.0$	$X_6 = 1.0$	$X_{11} = 0.791$	$X_{16} = 0.716$
$X_2 = 1.0$	$X_7 = 0$	$X_{12} = 0$	$X_{17} = 0$
$X_3 = 0$	$X_8 = 1.0$	$X_{13} = 1.0$	$X_{18} = 0$
$X_4 = 0.800$	$X_9 = 1.0$	$X_{14} = 0$	$X_{19} = 0$
$X_5 = 0$	$X_{10} = 0$	$X_{15} = 1.0$	$X_{20} = 0$

Added present value totals $609,297.

There are fractional values of several variables in the solution, but there will be only one fractional project per period in any solution. These can be interpreted as directions to try a smaller version of the same project or consider adjusting the budget constraint by an amount sufficient to complete the project. Integer programming[17] provides a technique which will give simple accept-reject decisions; that is, all Xs will be zero or one, although it will not ordinarily exhaust the available budget. Consideration of both integer and noninteger solutions will undoubtedly suggest ways in which either the projects or the constraints can be modified profitably, as we will later discuss. Use of linear programming models should be considered as a management decision support tool, that is, an aid to, rather than a substitute for, managerial judgement.

Most of the projects in this example require expenditures in a single period only. This is only an accident of its construction; it is quite capable of dealing with projects requiring expenditures in every period.[18]

If we compare the projects selected for the first period's budget, we find that they agree with the results which would be obtained by ranking in order of benefit-cost ratios. This is hardly surprising since they use net present values. The method is, in fact, the equivalent of benefit-cost ratio ranking which takes into account interperiod relationships (most of which have been suppressed in this example by the choice of data in order to bring the equivalence out more clearly).

7.6 Dual variables in the linear programming model

Any linear programming problem has a dual problem which is closely related to it. The original problem may be referred to as the primal problem, and if the primal problem has a solution, so does the dual.[19]

The dual of the capital-rationing problem may be written:

Minimize

$$\sum_t P_t C_t + \sum_j U_j \tag{7.6.1}$$

subject to

$$\sum_t P_t C_{jt} + U_j \geq b_j \tag{7.6.2}$$

$$P_t \geq 0 \quad t = 1, 2, \ldots, T \tag{7.6.3}$$

and

$$U_j \geq 0 \quad j = 1, 2, \ldots, n \tag{7.6.4}$$

P_t and U_j are called *dual* variables, and the definition of the other variables remains unchanged. We may write the dual problem corresponding to the problem in our example as follows:

Minimize

$$380P_1 + 354P_2 + 314P_3 + \sum_{j=1}^{20} U_j \qquad (7.6.1a)$$

subject to

$$
\begin{array}{rrrrr}
100P_1 & & + U_1 & \geq & 70 \\
100P_1 & & + U_2 & \geq & 50 \\
100P_1 & & + U_3 & \geq & -10 \\
100P_1 & & + U_4 & \geq & 30 \\
100P_1 & & + U_5 & \geq & 20 \\
100P_1 & & + U_6 & \geq & 40 \\
60P_1 & + 36P_2 & + U_7 & \geq & 20 \\
& 91P_2 & + U_8 & \geq & 64 \\
& 91P_2 & + U_9 & \geq & 45 \\
& 91P_2 & + U_{10} & \geq & -9 \\
& 91P_2 & + U_{11} & \geq & 27 \\
& 91P_2 & + U_{12} & \geq & 18 \\
& 91P_2 & + U_{13} & \geq & 36 \\
& 54P_2 + 33P_3 & + U_{14} & \geq & 18 \\
& 183P_3 & + U_{15} & \geq & 158 \\
& 183P_3 & + U_{16} & \geq & 141 \\
& 83P_3 & + U_{17} & \geq & 25 \\
& 83P_3 & + U_{18} & \geq & 18 \\
& 83P_3 & + U_{19} & \geq & 15 \\
& 83P_3 & + U_{20} & \geq & 14 \\
\end{array}
$$

$$P_t, U_j \geq 0 \qquad (7.6.2a)$$

$P_1 = 0.300$	$P_2 = 0.297$		$P_3 = 0.770$
$U_1 = 40.0$	$U_6 = 10.0$	$U_{11} = 0$	$U_{16} = 0$
$U_2 = 20.0$	$U_7 = 0$	$U_{12} = 0$	$U_{17} = 0$
$U_3 = 0$	$U_8 = 37.0$	$U_{13} = 9.0$	$U_{18} = 0$
$U_4 = 0$	$U_9 = 18.0$	$U_{14} = 17.0$	$U_{19} = 0$
$U_5 = 0$	$U_{10} = 0$	$U_{15} = 0$	$U_{20} = 0$

These dual variables have several properties, which follow from the duality theorem in linear programming.

1. Each is associated with a particular constraint in the primal problem. The P_t are associated with the C_t and the U_j with the X_j.
2. The dual variables have nonzero values if, and only if, the corresponding constraint in the primal problem is binding, that is, fulfilled as an equality, and have zero values otherwise.

Dual variables have a well-established economic interpretation as marginal productivities, opportunity costs, or "shadow prices." This interpretation can be extended to this problem. The P_t obtained in the dual solution are the opportunity costs associated with the budget constraints and are the amount by which net present value could be increased if a given constraint were relaxed to permit the investment of an additional dollar in that period.[20] They are, of course, related to the marginal productivity of the project which is fractionally adopted in that period. As noted earlier, it is a condition of the model that only one project is fractionally adopted in each period.

The U_j are associated with the constraints on the X_j, specifically with the requirement that $X_j = 1$, and are a measure of the marginal productivity of each project, that is, of the increased profit which could be earned if the project would be duplicated.

From 7.6.2 we derive

$$U_j \geq b_j - \sum_j P_t C_{tj} \qquad (7.6.5)$$

for adopted projects which gives us the optimal values of U_j and P_t. U_j is a measure of the amount by which the net present value of the jth project exceeds the sum of the products of the outlays on it times the opportunity cost associated with outlays in the respective period.

The dual variables may be useful as evaluators in making adjustments in the budget. If P_2 exceeds P_1 by a substantial margin, it may pay to shift funds from period 1 to period 2 by not utilizing them fully in the first period. This procedure is not permissible in the model as outlined earlier but is incorporated in one of Weingartner's variants on the original model, which we shall examine later. On the other hand, if P_1 exceeds P_2, the firm may wish to reconsider its constraints and borrow in period 1, thus increasing C_1, for repayment in period 2, and reducing C_2. Furthermore, the firm may wish to examine projects with high U_j values with a view to increasing their scale. (This is relatively insignificant; these projects have the highest benefit-cost ratios and this factor alone should have led to a reevaluation without reference to U_j.)

An alternative use of the dual evaluators is to perform sensitivity analysis on the solution and compare the results with the short-, intermediate-, and long-run supply of funds schedules discussed in Chapter 6. Particular attention should be paid to financing the current capital budget from short-run sources in order not to forego any profitable opportunities, but it will also aid in developing a schedule of financing needed in future periods both to refund the short-term financing and as well to meet the future cash outlays implied by the current capital budget.

In practice, the solution of the dual problem of linear programming will be obtained as a result of solving the primal problem, which is then examined by parametric analysis of the constraints.[21] Starting from the initial, optimal solution, the funds constraints may be relaxed conceptually. Supposing the first period funds constraint to be binding, the dual evaluator will apply only until a new basis for the linear program is obtained by notionally increasing the funds availability. The implied opportunity cost of funds for the current period can be found by calculating the difference between the dual variable on the funds constraint for the current period and the corresponding dual variable for the next, subsequent period. This procedure of relaxing the constraint should be carried on until either the dual variable for the current period equals zero, or at least the calculated difference is less than the previously determined long-run weighted average cost of capital. The result will be a demand schedule for incremental short-term financing which may be compared to the short-run marginal cost of capital schedule (see Figure 6–10), as shown in Figure 7–1.[22] Of course, this short-run incremental financing should be added to any intermediate financing plans to roll-it-over into suitable debt and equity financing as soon as is practicable.[23]

Figure 7–1
Incremental short-funds requirement

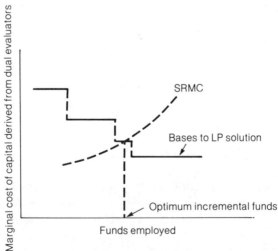

7.7 Handling externalities and mutually exclusive opportunities in the basic linear programming model

This may be done in two ways. One is by using the fictitious project approach which was outlined earlier, that is, if projects 6 and 8 are mutually exclusive, we may replace project 8 by project 8* which has the following characteristics.

$$b_8^* = 64$$
$$C_{18}^* = -100$$
$$C_{28}^* = 91$$
$$C_{38}^* = 0$$
$$Y_{28}^* = -8$$
$$Y_{38}^* = 9$$

Substitution of the appropriate values in equations 7.5.1a and 7.5.2a will give the desired solution. Alternatively, it is possible to leave 7.5.1a and 7.5.2a unchanged, but replace

$$0 \le X_6 \le 1$$
$$0 \le X_8 \le 1$$

with

$$X_6 + X_8 \le 1$$
$$X_6 \ge 0$$
$$X_8 \ge 0$$

in the constraint set 7.5.3a. This ensures that only one project will be adopted. This can be generalized to any set J of mutually exclusive alternatives by using

$$\sum_{j \in J} X_j \le 1$$

and retaining the nonnegativity conditions.

The only problem that may arise is that the solution may suggest the adoption of fractions of two or more mutually exclusive projects. This is in fact useful as it may suggest an alternative, midway in capital intensity, among the several projects, which is preferable to any of them.

If a project has one value contingent on the adoption of another project, and a lower value if the other is not adopted, we can handle this by setting up two projects m_1 and m_2, which can be treated as mutually exclusive, as before. If m_1 is the higher value contingent on the adoption of project n, we can add a further constraint

$$X_{m1} \le X_n$$

which will ensure that it is not adopted unless n is also adopted.[24] Similar formulations can be developed for other types of interrelationship between projects.

7.8 Nonfinancial bottlenecks

Within the private sector, labor costs are a cost to the firm, so they must be included in the costs of a project, and any financial constraints may still apply. What is needed is an additional constraint or constraints to handle the limitations of scare labor of a given type.

For this purpose, we can use the same basic model developed in section 7.5, for which equations 7.5.1–7.5.3 still apply, adding to it an additional set of constraints of the form

$$\sum_j X_j d_{jt} \le L_t \qquad (7.8.1)$$

where d_{jt} is the number of man-hours of input required for project j in period t and where L_t is the number of such hours available in the period.

The dual of this problem becomes

minimize $\qquad \sum_t P_t C_t + \sum_t w_t L_t + \sum_j U_j \qquad (7.8.2)$

subject to $\qquad \sum_t P_t C_{jt} + \sum_t w_t d_{jt} + U_j \ge b_j \qquad (7.8.3)$

$$P_t, w_t, U_j \ge 0$$

The new dual variable, w_t, is a shadow price reflecting the marginal productivity of the type of labor subject to constraint in the period in question, expressed as the addition to output resulting from the addition of an hour of the labor input. The w_t may be used to evaluate the desirability of adding to the labor force. Additions may not be possible in the short run, as training or seasoning may be needed before the addition becomes effective, but the multi-period structure of the model enables future requirements to be evaluated against training costs. Material bottlenecks may be handled in a similar manner.

7.9 Shifting funds (or projects) between periods

The model developed so far has assumed that funds cannot be carried over from one period to the next. This is a rather artificial restriction which we are better off without, and we can eliminate it by altering the budget constraints in a simple fashion. The objective function remains unchanged, but the constraints become

$$\sum_j \sum_{t=1}^n X_j C_{jt} \le \sum_{t=1}^n C_t \qquad (7.9.1)$$

Because the C_{jt} are on a present value basis, this formulation implicitly assumes that funds carried over can be invested until needed at the cost-of-capital rate.

To alter our example to permit shifting funds between periods, we form the new constraints

$100X_1 + 100X_2 + 100X_3 + 100X_4 + 100X_5 + 100X_6 + 60X_7 \qquad\qquad \le 380$

$100X_1 + 100X_2 + 100X_3 + 100X_4 + 100X_5 + 100X_6 + 96X_7 + 91X_8$
$\quad + 91X_9 + 91X_{10} + 91X_{11} + 91X_{12} + 91X_{13} + 54X_{14} \qquad\qquad \le 725$

$100X_1 + 100X_2 + 100X_3 + 100X_4 + 100X_5 + 100X_6 + 96X_7 + 91X_8$
$\quad + 91X_9 + 91X_{10} + 91X_{11} + 91X_{12} + 91X_{13} + 87X_{14} + 183X_{15}$
$\quad + 183X_{16} + 183X_{17} + 83X_{18} + 83X_{19} + 83X_{20} \qquad\qquad \le 1039$

$$(7.9.2)$$

Using these revised constraints gives us the new optimum solution:

$X_1 = 1.0$	$X_6 = 1.0$	$X_{11} = 0$	$X_{16} = 1.0$
$X_2 = 1.0$	$X_7 = 0$	$X_{12} = 0$	$X_{17} = 1.0$
$X_3 = 0$	$X_8 = 1.0$	$X_{13} = 1.0$	$X_{18} = 0$
$X_4 = 0.17$	$X_9 = 1.0$	$X_{14} = 0$	$X_{19} = 0$
$X_5 = 0$	$X_{10} = 0$	$X_{15} = 1.0$	$X_{20} = 0$

Added present value in this case totals \$634,100.

Using this version of the model, funds will not be shifted from period 1 to period 2 to ease the period 2 constraint unless there is a project in period 2 which would have been rejected using the simple constraint which represents a more productive use of funds than one of the projects adopted in the earlier period. Here, funds are shifted into period 3 to complete projects 16 and 17.

Another artificial feature of the model is that the timing of expenditures appears to be fixed. However, this is not really the case since all conceivable schedules for the construction of a project can be shown as separate but mutually exclusive projects. Thus provision for shifting project 1 between periods 1 and 2 can be made by considering the projects shown in Table 7–8.

If these projects are included as mutually exclusive alternatives, that is, subject to

$$X_1 + \sum_{j=21}^{30} X_j \le 1$$

Table 7–8
Shifting projects between periods

i	b_j	c_{j1}	c_{j2}	c_{j3}	Y_{j2}	Y_{j3}
1	70	100	0	0	20	20
21	69.4	90	9	0	18	20
22	68.8	80	18	0	16	20
23	68.2	70	27	0	14	20
24	67.6	60	36	0	12	20
25	67.0	50	45	0	10	20
26	66.4	40	54	0	8	20
27	65.8	30	63	0	6	20
28	65.2	20	72	0	4	20
29	64.6	10	81	0	2	20
30	64.0	—	91	0	0	20

the solution will tell within 10 percent how much of the project should be shifted from one period to the next. Similar sets of alternatives can be constructed for each project that can be rescheduled. While this process seems relatively cumbersome, a linear programming formulation requires the use of a computer in any event, and the desired degree of budget flexibility can be considered at relatively little added cost.

Here again, the project will not be shifted unless doing so frees funds for more profitable employment. Allowing for such shifts, to the extent that construction schedules can be rearranged, is a way to minimize the difficulties resulting from solutions which direct the construction of fractional projects in the simpler model.

As mentioned in Section 7.5, the model is the multi-period equivalent of the benefit-cost ratio ranking discussed in Section 7.3 and ignores the possibility of reinvesting proceeds from earlier periods at rates of return in excess of the cost of capital. This being the case, it is not surprising that multiple-rate-of-return projects were ignored. Cash throw-off can easily be incorporated into the analysis, however. The present values of the cash throw-off in periods 2 and 3 are shown in Table 7–7 as Y_{j2} and Y_{j3} respectively. Our objective function remains unchanged, but we incorporate net cash outlays instead of capital expenditures into the budget constraints which take the form:

$$\sum_j X_j(C_{jt} - Y_{jt}) \le C_t \qquad (7.9.3)$$

Treating the constraints in this fashion and continuing to permit funds to be carried forward, we replace 7.9.2 with

$$100X_1 + 100X_2 + 100X_3 + 100X_4 + 100X_5 + 100X_6 + 60X_7 \qquad \leq 380$$

$$80X_1 + 70X_2 + 40X_3 + 90X_4 + 94X_5 + 92X_6 + 93X_7 + 91X_8$$
$$+ 91X_9 + 91X_{10} + 91X_{11} + 91X_{12} + 91X_{13} + 54X_{14} \qquad \leq 725$$

$$60X_1 + 45X_2 - 20X_3 + 82X_4 + 90X_5 + 83X_6 + 88X_7 + 73X_8$$
$$+ 64X_9 + 37X_{10} + 82X_{11} + 86X_{12} + 84X_{13} + 85X_{14}$$
$$+ 183X_{15} + 183X_{16} + 83X_{17} + 83X_{18} + 83X_{19} + 83X_{20} \qquad \leq 1039$$

$$(7.9.4)$$

Our new optimum values are:

$X_1 = 1$	$X_6 = 1$	$X_{11} = 1$	$X_{16} = 1$
$X_2 = 1$	$X_7 = 0$	$X_{12} = 0$	$X_{17} = 1$
$X_3 = 0$	$X_8 = 1$	$X_{13} = 1$	$X_{18} = 0.4$
$X_4 = 0.8$	$X_9 = 1$	$X_{14} = 0$	$X_{19} = 0$
$X_5 = 0$	$X_{10} = 0$	$X_{15} = 1$	$X_{20} = 0$

Comparing this solution with the previous one, which permitted funds to be carried forward, it will be seen to have directed an increase in the investment in project 4 and to have added project 11 out of the funds flow from earlier projects.

7.10 Some practical difficulties

In our discussion of linear programming models, we have only considered some of the simpler formulations possible. More complex models can be built which are not confined to the capital-rationing case and which take into account various types of borrowing opportunities. These models permit simultaneous selection of optimal budgets and plans for financing them under conditions of certainty. While this problem is complex enough, it is still exceedingly simple in relation to the difficulties of operating in an uncertain world. Their use in practical situations to date has been limited.

One of the chief obstacles to their use in multi-period situations is that they require a complete specification of the projects which will be available for consideration in future periods. While there are some industries such as public utilities where long-run planning is sufficiently advanced to permit such specification, there are others for which it is simply not feasible. The projects to be considered next year and the year after may still lie a long way back in the research pipeline, from which the form of their eventual emergence, let alone its timing, is virtually impossible to predict.

This need not be a fatal flaw for rational behavior in the face of uncertainty merely requires that we make the best estimates possible and recalculate our strategies as more information comes to light.[25] If our expectations of the future are sufficiently well formed and of such a nature that interperiod relationships are of sufficient importance that systematic incorporation into a comprehensive model seems necessary, then they should be used.

Casual interperiod relationships can be handled without resort to such models. If a firm is giving serious consideration to building a new plant in five years time, this should be taken into account in any decisions to spend money on improving facilities in the present plant. Urgency criteria, such as those discussed in Section 7.3, can be used to select projects for postponement and otherwise adapt the single-period model to cover many situations.

7.11 Concluding remarks

Before leaving the topic of capital rationing at least as it applies to private-sector firms, we reemphasize that our concern has been with solving managerial problems. In that context, capital rationing arises from either of two possible sources: management's imposition of expenditures ceilings or absolute upper bounds on funds availability imposed by the capital markets.

Self-imposed expenditure limits, either for working capital or for capital expenditures, may arise either where preservation of corporate control plays a dominant role or where management is concerned regarding debt capacity because of unequal distribution of the costs of risk of financial failure between owners and managers. In the former case, the controlling owners may prefer to forego benefits to be derived from obtaining capital funds under conditions which may imply actual or potential diminution of control. They will prefer less wealth (and consumption) in order to maintain control. The theory which underlies our analysis assumes that only wealth is valued. Alternatively, rather than selling the business piecemeal to permit faster growth, the owners may decide quite realistically to sell the whole firm later when they believe the market will have correctly valued it. To the extent that there does exist a difference between the market's valuation of the firm and that of the controlling owners, these may reflect different expectations regarding future earnings, possibly based on unequally distributed information between the owners and outsiders.

Externally imposed capital rationing, if it does exist, is a different matter. As we have suggested, in these circumstances, the short-run marginal supply schedule of funds may be sharply upward sloping. When monetary policy is aimed at restricting credit, as discussed in Chapter 6, the commercial banks which are the primary source of short-term funds may consider themselves to be loaned up, that is, under pressure not to add new loan commitments and to urge customers to hold down their borrowings under existing lines of credit. This may be represented as a vertical line segment on the funds supply curve.

For a given firm, the short-run supply of funds schedule may also be upward sloping because substantial increases in incremental financing require tapping different sources.[26] Higher information costs which arise from unequally distributed information will increase the costs of obtaining funds from different kinds of sources.

Incomplete markets affect at least the intermediate-term ability of the firm to sell hybrid types of securities, such as preferred stock, income bonds, and convertibles of various sorts, another form of contingent strategy on the financing side.[27] This would tend to imply an upward sloping supply schedule on intermediate-term sources of funds. Whether this apparently otherwise normally functioning supply of and demand for loanable funds should be regarded as capital rationing is a moot point, however.

Notes

[1] E. F. Fama and M. H. Miller, *The Theory of Finance* (New York: Holt, Rinehart & Winston, 1972), pp. 122–26, discuss this issue at some length.

[2] This question is discussed at length by M. C. Bogue and R. Roll, "Capital Budgeting of Risky Projects with 'Imperfect' Markets for Physical Capital," *Journal of Finance* (May 1974), pp. 601–13.

[3] For, under the assumptions of perfect certainty, all future cash flows and the market required rate of return will already be known, thus there is no real problem.

[4] In fact, discussions of multi-period investment decisions under uncertainty are near the leading edge of developments in the economic theory of finance. Bogue and Roll, "Capital Budgeting," have provided the pioneering treatment. E. F. Fama, "Risk-Adjusted Discount Rates and Capital Budgeting under Uncertainty," *Journal of Financial Economics* (August 1977), pp. 3–24, has discussed the need for further restrictions on their analysis. A systematic development may be found in E. H. Neave and J. C. Wiginton, *Financial Management: Theory and Strategy* (Englewood Cliffs, N.J.: Prentice-Hall, 1980), chap. 10.

[5] Discussion of states-of-the-world analysis may be found in Neave and Wiginton, *Financial Management,* chap. 7.

[6] For further discussion, the interested reader may consult, for example, H. M. Wagner, *Principles of Operations Research* (Englewood Cliffs, N.J.: Prentice-Hall, 1975).

[7] H. M. Weingartner, "Capital Rationing: n Authors in Search of a Plot," *Journal of Finance* (December 1977), pp. 1403–31, discusses the ambiguity of the term capital rationing.

[8] Compare the position of the Penn-Central railway before its bankruptcy, as described in J. R. Daughen and P. Binzen, *The Wreck of the Penn-Central* (New York: Mentor, 1971).

[9] This is the debt capacity argument discussed earlier in Chapter 6. We again refer the

reader to G. Donaldson, *Corporate Debt Capacity* (Boston: Division of Research, Graduate School of Business Administration, Harvard University, 1961).

[10] This is perhaps exaggerated in impact by the conventions of depreciation accounting.

[11] For example, J. H. Lorie and L. J. Savage, "Three Problems in Capital Rationing," *Journal of Business* (October 1955), pp. 229–39.

[12] This point was originally made by G. Terborgh in his *Dynamic Equipment Policy* (New York: McGraw-Hill, 1949). See also M. J. Gordon, "The Optimum Timing of Capital Expenditures," in H. Levy and M. Sarnat, eds., *Financial Decision Making under Uncertainty* (New York: Academic Press, 1977), pp. 83–94.

[13] Some may be gains.

[14] Again, we recommend G. Donaldson, *Strategy for Financial Mobility* (Boston: Division of Research, Graduate School of Business Administration, Harvard University, 1969).

[15] H. M. Weingartner, *Mathematical Programming and the Analysis of Capital Budgeting* (Englewood Cliffs, N.J.: Prentice-Hall, 1963), and, "Capital Budgeting of Interrelated Projects: Survey and Synthesis," *Management Science* (March 1966), pp. 485–516. An alternative dynamic programming approach, which we do not discuss, is referred to as the knapsack problem, described in Wagner, *Principles of Operations Research*, chap. 10.

[16] For example, ibid., chaps. 2–5.

[17] Wagner, ibid., chap. 13.

[18] See also Weingartner, *Mathematical Programming*, pp. 17–18, for such an example.

[19] See Wagner, *Principles of Operations Research*, chap. 5.

[20] As such, they are more akin to benefit-cost ratios (on a net basis) than to interest rates, contrary to Weingartner's assertion in *Mathematical Programming*, p. 26.

[21] Most contemporary, commercial, large-scale linear programming computer systems provide this as a standard feature.

[22] The intersection of the demand and supply curves may occur for a particular basic solution as shown or at a basis change shown by the dashed vertical line segments of the demand curve.

[23] If longer-term options for financing appear limited, then our strategy must be reconsidered. As argued in Chapter 6, however, we do not believe this to be the case. Our strategy may be compared with the recommendations of Fama and Miller, *Theory of Finance*, pp. 136–37, where they remark that models with financial constraints may have valid uses, provided the constraints are viewed provisionally as planning estimates. That is, examination of the model as we recommend may be used to highlight when future funds are likely to be inadequate to the need and thus provide a basis for a program of external, intermediate to long-term financing to overcome the anticipated binding financial constraints.

[24] For further discussion, see Weingartner, *Mathematical Programming*, pp. 39–44.

[25] This is an instance of a contingent strategy, as described in Neave and Wiginton, *Financial Management*, chap. 15.

[26] See also Donaldson, *Strategy for Financial Mobility*.

[27] Neave and Wiginton, *Financial Management*, chap. 19.

Problems

1. A company is considering the construction of a new plant which can be built in one year at a cost of $1 million. It can be completed in six months on a "crash-program" basis at a cost of $1.1 million, or stretched out over

two years at a total cost of $1 million. Benefits from the new plant are worth $1.8 million if it is constructed in one year's time at the company's 14 percent cost of capital. What items should appear (*a*) in the objective function and (*b*) in the constraint set of a linear programming model to reflect these alternatives?

2. Project 1 costs $100,000 and has a present value of $155,000 if completed this year, $165,000 if completed next year. Project 2 costs $20,000 and has a present value of $28,000 if completed this year, $31,000 if completed next year. Which project should be postponed if the firm insists it is operating under capital-rationing conditions?

3. ABC Corporation has $300,000 of internally generated cash flow which may be used for capital expenditures. The company's estimated cost of capital is 10 percent. The company has plans for major new financing in the near future and so does not wish to resort to the capital markets at this time to raise funds for minor projects because transactions costs would make funds so raised more costly than need be. The following set of projects, all of which are regarded as equally risky by the firm's management, are available:

A.   Cost, $100,000. Cash flows: $55,066 per year for three years.
B.   Cost: $100,000. Cash flows: $23,006 per year for ten years.
   Note that projects A and B are mutually exclusive.
C.   Cost: $100,000. Cash flows: $33,434 per year for five years.
D: Cost: $120,000. Cash flows: $33,287 per year for five years.
E.   Buy bonds yielding 8 percent.
   Which projects should be included in ABC's current capital budget? Explain. Note that partial projects may not be accepted. Each project must be accepted in its entirety or otherwise rejected.
   Suppose that project D above had a cost of $300,000 and cash flows of $83,218 per year for five years (this has the same internal rate of return as above). How would this change affect your recommended capital budget?

Cost of capital in the public sector and the social cost of capital

---

8.1 Introduction

The procedures required to make constructive decisions about public-sector investments are, in principle, the same as those required in the private sector. Future flows of benefits and costs must be estimated, an appropriate adjustment made in respect of risk, and the whole reduced to a common time basis by present value calculations. While there has been a great increase in the extent to which public-sector expenditures have been subjected to formal analysis of this general variety over the past generation, it is not clear that the expenditure process has been brought under better control as a consequence.

There are several reasons for harboring doubts on this score. In many cases, it is not clear that analytical procedures have been applied at the appropriate stage in the decision process. The effective decision point is often buried deep within the bureaucracy, which determines what gets to the Budget Bureau or Treasury Board. There is a further stage of legislative scrutiny and approval, but, with rare exceptions, this is largely a formality.[1] U.S. practice permits Congress to delete certain items and add others, but in Britain and other countries which follow the British procedure, even this gesture has been eliminated, and the budget must be accepted or rejected in its entirety. Ideally, the analysis should be undertaken before the de facto decision is made, but there is at least a suspicion that many departments use benefit-cost analysis in the same way as a drunk uses a lamppost, that is, for support rather than illumination.

A second difficulty is that analytical procedures themselves are much less well defined in the public-sector context than in that of profit-seeking private enterprise. As we will see, for every proposed rule, there are enough exceptions that there are few projects for which at least a superficially plausible case could not be made by a moderately skilled analyst familiar with the literature. The analytical procedures tend to have been imposed upon preexisting or slightly rearranged bureaucracies. The latter continue to have their own organizational thrust and internal value systems. Objectivity, as viewed from the outside, may be subordinated to advocacy, if only because departmental insiders may have difficulty in identifying the point at which objectivity (as viewed from the inside) ceases and advocacy begins. The analyst, if he is sufficiently intelligent to perform the job, will seldom have little difficulty in recognizing that his next promotion depends on his contribution to the advocacy process, rather than on his adherence to external criteria of objectivity. The apparent exceptions are those departments in which analytical procedures have been developed from within. These will usually be found to be precisely those which have found the procedures useful in an advocacy context. Bureaucracy is, of course, endemic in the large-scale industrial society in that it generates similar pressures in both the private and public sectors.[2] However, in the private sector, objectives are more clear-cut, rules are simpler, and exceptions are fewer. As a consequence, it is more difficult to use the analytical procedures embedded in the control system as a lever with which to manipulate that system in the private sector.

It is perhaps here, in the structure of the overall control system, that differences between the two sectors become most obvious. It is in these differences in control systems, and not in the analytical procedures which are only a small part of them, that the difficulty appears to lie. In the private sector, budgetary decisions, and the actions taken in response to them, manifest themselves rather quickly, via the accounting process, on the bottom line of corporate financial statements. Capital-market institutions, in turn, translate these developments into unequivocal valuations in the marketplace. The process is short, swift, continuous, direct, and largely beyond the reach of the decision makers. It is the objective reporting of the results and the appraisal thereof in the marketplace which provides the ultimate control over capital expenditures in the private sector. Capital-expenditure analysis is useful as a control device precisely because it assists decision makers in predicting the response of the ultimate control system.

In the public sector, the ultimate control system is indirect, episodical, diffuse, and often slow acting. Furthermore, it is subject to the intervention at several levels of the decision makers themselves who are not bound by any externally imposed obligation to provide full, true, plain, and prompt disclosure. Financial accounting within the public sector remains largely in a conceptual stone age, where it confines itself to recording sums spent in various ways and indicating how they were (or sometimes were not) legally authorized. The nearest conceptual equivalent to the corporate income statement is in the public-sector component of the national income accounts. But public-sector output, while it may have to be paid for, does not have to be sold. Because of this, market evaluation of its worth is usually unavailable. This is particularly so when the nonmarket nature of that output caused it to be in the public sector in the first instance. A substitute valuation of public-sector output would be needed to provide a true counterpart of the private-sector income statement and an indication of whether the public sector of the economy operated at a social loss or generated a social profit. No doubt there are difficulties, even serious ones as we shall see when we come to consider estimating benefits, but the problem has been resolved at the national income accounting level by assuming it away, eschewing all value judgments and adopting the convention that public-sector output is worth exactly what it costs so that neither profit nor loss results. As a consequence, there is no financial statement bottom line in the public sector. The recently fashionable quest for social indicators represents an attempt to fashion one and incorporates the important consideration that the well-being of society cannot be completely reduced to monetary terms. Whatever the conceptual merits of such an approach, its practical usefulness is suggested by the inability of its advocates to decide whether to incorporate the divorce rate, as a measure of the prevalence of freedom in the society, or its reciprocal, as a measure of the stability of the family as a social institution.

A public-sector counterpart of the capital-market evaluation process is provided by the sporadic electoral process with intervening bid-and-ask quotations in the form of opinion poll results. In parliamentary systems, there are also occasional odd-lot transactions in the form of by-elections. These valuations are not always as easy to interpret as those available to the private sector and may in fact be highly ambiguous.

A government's expenditures are, of course, only a part of its overall policy, although it should be noted that implementation of most policies involves resource use and thus expenditures. The basic objectives of governments are different than those of corporations, involving as they must considerations of equity and popularity as well as efficiency. The primary duty of a government or an opposition party that wishes to form a government in a democratic society is to get elected or reelected; whatever it may stand for has little hope of attainment if it remains in perpetual opposition. The entire expenditure program may be judged in political terms on the extent to which it contributes to that objective.[3]

At first glance, it would appear that such political objectives preclude economic analysis. It is far from clear that they do so. While instances can be found or constructed in which the political process generates apparently irrational or economically perverse results,[4] more recent work in the theory of public choice suggests that appropriately structured political choices may well tend to produce decisions which are economically efficient at least with respect to certain types of expenditures.[5] Unfortunately, we have neither the space nor the competence to explore these matters fully here; the interested reader may wish to consult the works cited.

Instead, we make the assumption that the objective of government is to maximize social welfare in the sense in which that term is employed in the literature of welfare economics. Such an assumption has frequently been adopted on the idealistic premise that maximizing social welfare is what government ought to be doing. Whether such a precept is compatible with democratic theory is up to the reader to decide. The alternative justification deriving from the public-choice literature is that, at least outside of particular short-run situations, governments which do not take care of social welfare will not be reelected. Both have ample precedent; we believe the main message of Proposition 13, passed by California electors in 1977, is that the electorate does indeed expect tax revenues to be used in general welfare enhancing ways or taxes to be reduced.

Analyzing rational expenditure decisions in a public-sector context involves basically the same steps as in a private-sector context, namely, the estimation and measurement of benefits and costs and the conversion of these estimates into measures of merit which will be of assistance in the decision-making process. They are, however, more complex, and while the private-sector techniques provide a point of departure, that is all they do provide in many cases. In this chapter, we examine the question of what constitutes a valid cost-of-capital measure for purposes of social valuation, and in Chapter 9 we consider some of the problems that arise in estimating social benefits and costs. For the moment, we assume that we, in fact, have such measures and that our only problem is how to convert numbers, which represent benefits and costs incurred at different points in time, into valid measures of net benefits or benefit-cost ratios.

8.2 The role of the cost of capital in the evaluation of public investments

The cost of capital plays the same formal role in the evaluation of public-sector investment projects as it does in the private sector, that is, it is the rate of discount to be used in calculating benefit-cost ratios or to be compared with the internal rate of return. However, the latter criterion is less commonly used by government bodies.

The rationale for its use is somewhat different. In the private sector, it is used because it leads directly to the private-sector goal of wealth maximization. In the public sector, its basic function is similar, in that it should lead to a maximization of social welfare, providing its components have been appropriately measured. At a minimum, it will play a key role in determining the scale and capital intensity of projects in the public sector and in how available funds may best be allocated among competing projects.

A more controversial application is also possible, in which it is used not only to allocate funds among projects, but to determine the magnitude of the public budget. Constitutionally, the various levels of government have certain responsibilities and powers, which require the use of resources. Other resource-using activities which are not forbidden are left to the private sector. If social welfare is to be maximized, it is clear at least in principle that the marginal product of a dollar's worth of resources used as input for one government activity must be the same as that for another government activity and the same as that of the private-sector activity it displaces.

Use of economic analysis in making spending decisions within the public sector was a rarity a generation ago. Today economic analysis is widely used, if not to arrive at decisions, at least to support decisions arrived at in more traditional ways, including political logrolling and notions of necessity. Significant literature is available on the applications of economic analysis to a wide range of government activities.[6] Our purpose here is to examine the theoretical principles underlying such analyses and their relationships with similar models used in the private sector. In principle, models of the type discussed here are applicable to all resource-using activities in the public sector. Spending decisions which lead to transfer payments do not, of course, use resources (except for their incidental use in administering the program) and must rest fundamentally on political judgments about the desirability of carrying out the proposed redistribution. Such problems are not particularly amenable to analysis of the type we shall be discussing, although they do not have to be resolved in a wholly intuitive manner.[7]

Capital expenditures within the public sector yield benefits in future time periods as well as in the present. Among the important ways in which projects may differ is in terms of the intertemporal distribution of these benefits. Choices with respect to the discount rate determine the weighting given to nearby and distant benefits and thus influence the choice between benefits accruing to present and future generations. While this appears at one level to be an efficiency question, it also involves redistributional issues of a fundamental kind. These are examined in Section 8.4. But for the moment, we will consider certain objections to the use of economic analysis in public-sector decision making.

8.3 The necessity criterion

Considerable opposition to the use of economic decision-making criteria remains. Some opponents reject such criteria on grounds that activities have been placed within the public sector because they are too important to be regulated by the economic criteria automatically applied within the private sector. A somewhat less extreme view is that public-sector activities should be regulated on a requirements basis; the government should determine community needs, whether in respect of national defense, environmental rehabilitation, educational facilities, or whatever, and satisfy them. There is a superficial appeal in this point of view, and it is no doubt sincerely held. Unfortunately, absolute requirements defy definition. The community requires defense, a cleaner environment, and education. People within it also require food, clothing, housing, transportation and medical care, to name only a few other absolute necessities. Given limited resources, the amount that can be provided for any one of these can only be increased by reducing the amount provided for others.

An attempt to provide maximum security with no constraints would require that all resources be devoted to defense (including such essential supporting activities as the provision of a subsistence diet and housing for those fit to bear arms or work in defense industries). While something of this nature may be required in wartime and was perhaps approached in Britain during World War II, it is not a valid policy in peacetime, as in the long run there may be nothing left worth defending.

Another area where the requirements basis is frequently invoked is in law enforcement. It is held by some to be a moral imperative that no crime or other violation should go undetected or unpunished. While we may have certain reservations about the theological validity of this proposition, let us entertain it for a moment as a guide to policy and examine the progress of law enforcement in the mythical town of Frontiersville, which had a lurid beginning as a mining community somewhere in the "Old West." Crime was rampant until the town was incorporated and a sheriff hired. Losses due to crime during the year before the sheriff arrived were $175,000. After he was hired at an annual cost of $6,000, a few badmen were run out of town, and while thievery continued at a reduced pace, some of the loot was recovered and losses dropped to $100,000. The sheriff complained that he was unable to keep up with the wrongdoing singlehanded, so the town fathers raised his pay to $7,000 and hired a deputy for $5,000, and the next year losses dropped to $75,000. In subsequent years, the law enforcement payroll grew and the town got cleaner and cleaner, but not totally crime free. The policing budget grew, and losses from crime dwindled as follows:

Year	Budget	Losses due to crime
0 (no sheriffs)	$ 0	$175,000
1	6,000	100,000
2	12,000	75,000
3	18,000	60,000
4	24,000	48,000
5	30,000	38,000
6	36,000	28,000
7	42,000	20,000
8	48,000	14,000
9	54,000	10,000
10	60,000	8,000

At the end of ten years, the policing budget was ten times its original size, but crime had not been totally wiped out. Burglary insurance rates had reached a new low, such insurance having been unobtainable ten years earlier. Examining the changes in the rates over the past couple of years, an enterprising lad, formerly the cashier in a gambling den but now the town clerk and tax collector, observed that had everyone in town carried such insurance the premium reductions in the past two years would have produced a total savings of only $6,000, while taxes had gone up by $12,000 to pay for two new deputies and a spare horse for the sheriff. He proposed that the size of the sheriff's department be cut and pointed out the possible savings to the townspeople. There was great indignation at this suggestion, the sheriff pointed out the clerk's former underworld connections and he was fired forthwith. Ten years later, the law enforcement budget was $600,000 and only $1,000 was stolen in Frontiersville, which by this time had the highest tax rate in the state, had lost half its population, and still had no water supply.

While the sheriff was away on a speaking tour of the East, the mine owners, who had nothing left for themselves after paying taxes the past few years, closed the mine. The former clerk, who had sought his fortune on Wall Street after being run out of town, bought it, along with much of the real estate, for a song. Concealing his identity from the town fathers by wearing a false handlebar mustache, he offered, on behalf of "undisclosed Eastern interests," to reopen the mine if the sheriff's budget was cut to $60,000. After much complaining about the Eastern money trust, this was done and Frontiersville thrived.

Revealing his identity, our hero was asked why he had cut the budget to $60,000 instead of $48,000 as he had proposed earlier. He noted that with the budget of $48,000, the marginal productivity of the sheriff's office, in terms of losses from crimes avoided, was $6,000 and equal to marginal cost. However, there were other intangible benefits from having the larger force, which were not included in the measure of benefits he had used, so that this was probably a bit below the optimum level. Extending the budget to $60,000 was in recognition of this and also a gesture in the direction of the popular view that crime must be stamped out at all costs.

8.4 Traditional views

Contemporary discussions in the traditionally oriented public finance literature accept the notion that the optimal budget is one in which the marginal utility of the last dollar spent in satisfying public wants is equal to that of the last dollar spent in satisfying private wants,[8] but it does not go very far in specifying how, in concrete cases, this is to be determined. This is really a threefold problem where capital expenditures are involved. It is, in the first instance, a problem of measuring benefits and costs, often under conditions where no market yardstick is available even for a starting point. This has received relatively scant attention in the literature generally.

Second, it is a problem of identifying and appropriately weighting the incidence of benefits on individuals to arrive at an estimate of social benefits. This problem, which raises a number of theoretical issues concerning the possibility of meaningful interpersonal comparisons of utility and the construction of social welfare functions, has been a central topic of discussion among economic theorists for many years, but it remains unsolved in any generally accepted sense.

Finally, there is the problem of the appropriate discount rate to convert future benefits into present value terms. The first two problems are discussed in Chapter 9. For the present, we will assume that the problems of measurement and weighting have been resolved and concern ourselves with the third problem only. There are a number of suggestions in the literature. Musgrave indicates that pay-as-you-go finance assesses the out-of-pocket interest cost as a cost and implies that benefits should exceed costs when discounted at the prevailing government borrowing rate.[9] Elsewhere, however, he indicates that the difference between the yield of benefits from public projects and that of proviate projects foregone as a result of the shift of capital from the private sector through government borrowing is one of the elements in the burden of the public debt.[10] This suggests the use of the marginal efficiency of capital, or internal rate of return in the private sector (at the margin, abstracting from risk differences) as an appropriate measure of the cost of capital to the public sector. Exponents of both of these views, as well as others, may be found. Much of the classical literature has actually assumed the problem away, since with perfect markets throughout and an absence of risk, there will be one interest rate in the economy for both the public and the private sector, and the marginal efficiency of capital in the latter will equal the rate of return.

Unfortunately, in the real world, the multiplicity of rates which we have already observed exists, and we must decide which are appropriate if a market-determined rate is to be established.

There is a competing tradition which argues that market-determined rates are simply irrelevant in the social decision process. Individuals tend to adopt savings patterns which equate their marginal rates of time preference for present and future consumption with appropriate interest rates. Market rates thus reflect individuals' time preferences. It is claimed that people systematically undervalue future incomes and overvalue the present, so that individual time preferences as expressed in the market are a biased reflection even of the true preferences or self-interest of the individuals involved in the market.[11] Whether this is true or not empirically, market rates do reflect the time preferences of those currently participating in the market. Minors as well as Burke's "generations yet unborn" are excluded from voting in the marketplace. Since society embraces these individuals as well as current market participants, current market outcomes have no particular claim to validity for social valuation purposes even in a society that otherwise accepts individualistic valuation premises.

A further distortion is created in most modern states by the existence of income taxes. These systematically distort individual choices between present and future consumption. Figure 8–1 depicts this im-

Figure 8–1

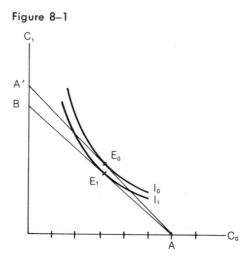

pact. In the absence of a personal income tax, the individual adjusts his consumption plans to the prevailing market interest rate, here assumed to be 10 percent and shown as the price line AA'. With a marginal income tax rate of 30 percent, the investor's rate of return opportunity drops to 7 percent, depicted on price line AB. The equilibrium choice shifts from E_0 to E_1. The sign of the change in current consumption is in principle equivocal, because of the uncertain magnitude of the income effect. With the exception of misers and ascetics, for whom current consumption may be regarded as an inferior good, it seems likely that the substitution effect will be larger and will induce a shift in favor of current consumption.

Market-determined solutions are, of course, rejected by those who consider individual preferences an invalid basis for social valuation. This is, of course, the orthodox Marxist position, although in at least one version it leads to an opportunity cost criterion which closely resembles the market criterion.

Baumol and Marglin[12] in particular argue that individuals may have one rate of time preference which they express in the marketplace but another which they are willing to accept for public-sector decisions providing the state exercises its powers of compulsion to impose it on other members of the community as well.

The other basic argument for adopting a rate below the prevailing market rate is advanced by Arrow and Lind,[13] who note that private-sector discount rates reflect the risks associated with the corporation or even the single project itself. They argue that individual project risks are irrelevant in the public sector because so many projects are undertaken in the public sector that risk is diversified away. Therefore it is appropriate to equate expected values with certainty equivalents and to evaluate public-sector investments by applying the (lower) risk-free rate to expected net benefits. This argument is suspect on two grounds.

In the first place, benefits are neither received nor costs borne by society but by individuals. Any individual is likely to benefit from at most a small subset of the projects undertaken by the public sector, and failure of the expected benefits to emerge from a project would have adverse consequences for the intended beneficiaries of the project even if the diversification argument were valid. The only apparent exception arises where the uncertainty relates to the incidence and not the magnitude of benefits, and even this is dubious. To the extent that the diversification argument has validity, it can be applied with equal logic to the *social* valuation of private-sector projects and offers no valid grounds whatever for replacing them with public-sector projects offering lower expected benefits.

The second and perhaps more fundamental objection arises out of recent work on the capital asset pricing model and related empirical work on the structure of risk. The theoretical work suggests that the degree of risk-reduction obtainable through random diversification is severely limited if returns on the individual portfolio components are (positively) correlated. Only the nonsystematic components of risk related to the individual securities can be removed.[14] The empirical work shows that high correlations in fact exist between returns on securities of firms in different lines of endeavor, presumably tied to a common business-cycle influence.[15] There is no reason to suppose that public-sector investments in general are immune. Benefits from a freeway intended to carry commuters to work will rise and fall with unemployment and those from a public power-generating plant will be related to the level of industrial output. The existence of systematic risk over large segments of the public sector provides a further reason for rejecting the proposition that risk can be ignored in public-sector investment evaluation, as Jensen[16] has pointed out. Indeed, the attraction of most transfer payment programs (as opposed to major resource-using programs) is that they are systematically, but *negatively,* correlated with business conditions generally. Risk must indeed be taken into account in public-sector evaluations. We will examine just how at a later point. For the moment, we sidestep the issue by assuming that the risk characteristics of all public- and private-sector projects are identical, and that this risk level is reflected in the private-sector discount rate. The basic issue is whether the public-sector rate should be held below the private-sector rate on grounds other than risk. It would appear that any such case must rest on Pigou's "faulty-telescopic-faculty" market failure argument, which has been resurrected and vigorously restated by some contemporary environmentalists.[17]

While the most telling objection raised by proponents of this view is the exclusion of future generations from present markets, it should be noted that, at least in the private sector, this absence is only partial in that the existence of property rights creates values tied to anticipated future markets, so that decisions of present property owners are influenced by the expected demands of future generations even if the latter are excluded from direct participation.[18] The institution of private property plays an important role in modifying market outcomes in favor of future generations, although its role is restricted by uncertainties as to the security of property rights. There is no public-sector counterpart whatever which suggests that unless procedures countervailing this bias are introduced the public sector may do an even poorer job of providing for future generations than has been apparent in the private sector.

A further argument based on risk allocation within the public sector is that presented by Stapleton and Subrahmanyam.[19] They show that if there is no systematic undervaluation of future benefits, individuals are unable to adjust their asset portfolios to reflect their own risk preferences in a society in which shares of social risk (as in Arrow-Lind) within the public sector are equally or otherwise arbitrarily allocated by the government. This being the case, costs of risk throughout the economy are increased by the government's action; this should be reflected in a higher discount rate within the public sector if social welfare is to be maximized. (The Stapleton-Subrahmanyam argument will be examined in greater detail in Section 8.8.)

8.5 The opportunity costs model

The use of differential discount rates between public and private sectors is suspect on efficiency grounds. Approaching the problem from a socialist viewpoint, Dobb[20] has argued that consumer sovereignty, particularly in respect of time preference, is suspect and should be ignored. He nevertheless argues that the effective capital-allocation rule should be the equalization of the marginal efficiency of capital or the internal rate of return. He also insists that the savings rate is too important to be left to the vagaries of individual decision and thus that it should be decided by the state but has little to offer of an analytical nature with respect to what the savings rate or the required rate of return should be.

The opportunity cost evaluation rule is perhaps best stated in the mixed economy context by Baumol.[21] The basic argument is simply that accepting low-return projects in the public sector will displace private-sector projects offering a higher social yield. This will remain true even if they are financed out of a net increment to saving, as long as the marginally excluded project in the private sector offers a higher yield than the accepted public-sector project. Baumol notes an inherent ambiguity in the definition of opportunity yield, resulting from the borrowing-lending rate differential, which is important but need not concern us here.

The essence of the problem, viewed from an opportunity cost point of view is illustrated in Figure 8–2, where OA represents a (given) volume of saving. Marginal social efficiency of capital schedules, measured in terms of internal rates of return, for the public and private sectors, respectively, are shown as GG' and PP'. The market-clearing rate, if government allocates using the private-sector discount rate, is r. The resulting public-sector capital budget is OB, while the private sector invests AB. If the government chooses to allocate using the lower

Figure 8–2
Optimizing the public-sector budget

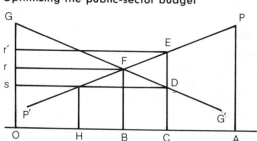

discount rate *s*, it will expand its capital budget to *OC*. It can always obtain the necessary funds by taxation, outbidding the private sector in the capital market or simply inflating the currency. Doing so will raise the marginal cost of funds to the private sector to *r'*, cut private investment to *AC*, and create a net social loss measured by the triangle *DEF*.

If *s* is really the appropriate measure of social time preference, the appropriate public-sector budget is indeed *OC*, but the correspondingly appropriate private-sector budget is *AH*. These could, of course, be accommodated if saving can be increased by the amount *CH*, thus providing the capital required to equate marginal internal rates of return to the marginal rates of time preference in both sectors. The implicitly desired additional provision for the future cannot be conjured up out of thin air, but it must be made out of real resources provided and saved in the present. Increasing the government budget to its optimum level without securing the required increment to saving merely exacerbates the problem of underprovision for the future by using the (already inadequate) savings inefficiently.

The waste may not be confined to capital alone. The newly appointed president of a Canadian government-owned oil company recently expressed the prospective contribution of his agency to an already well-populated industry in the following terms:

> I am shocked every time I look at the cost of developing frontier resources. I do believe that PetroCanada can afford to take, and should afford to take a longer look, or in fact use a lower discount rate to justify some of its expenditures in these areas where the private sector probably can't justify the long times and risks associated with development.[22]

Underprovision for the future is apparently to be remedied by the immediate exploitation of exhaustible resource deposits which the market is attempting to suggest should be left for exploitation at some future date.[23] The statement is unique only in being so clearly expressed: similar sentiments abound in government agencies everywhere.

In many cases, governments seem unable or unwilling to take measures to expand savings above the level voluntarily provided elsewhere in the economy. The failure to take such measures involves either an implicit rejection of the proposition that additional provision for the future should be made and regarded as a public good or an admission that such provision is politically unsalable to the present generation of voters. The marketplace is not the only arena in which future generations have no vote, and in the political arena there are no property values available as a substitute. As our analysis of Figure 8–2 suggests, determining the optimum level of public sector investment within a given volume of savings involves a capital-rationing problem in which funds are allocated efficiently between uses in both public and private sectors, subject to a constraint on aggregate investment. In an optimum solution to such a problem, the productivity of capital in the best excluded project plays a critical role as the shadow price associated with the constraint.[24] Thus far we are in agreement with the advocates of an opportunity cost approach.

Operationally, a number of approaches have been evolved which attempt to determine the relevant opportunity cost rate. One of the more elaborate begins by trying to determine whether the project is financed by taxation or borrowing. If the former, the incidence of additional taxes is estimated, opportunity cost estimates for different categories of taxpayers are computed, and a weighted average calculated.[25] While the result is an intellectually fascinating edifice, its validity is open to question. First of all, the taxation-borrowing classification is irrelevant. Projects may be financed out of the general revenues or may involve their own special project financing. But the magnitude of the deficit in the government budget as a whole will be determined by fiscal policy or debt management considerations and should be unaffected by how any individual project is financed. If more debt is wanted, and the project borrows, less will have to be borrowed elsewhere. If less is wanted, borrowing on the project will require offsetting debt retirement elsewhere. So any (or all) projects can with equal justification be viewed as financed by taxation or by borrowing. Given the relative uncertainty which continues to exist with respect to the average incidence of many taxes, estimates of their marginal incidence must be viewed with a certain skepticism. Even if one assumes that the results of the taxpayer identification exercise are as good as we can hope for, the discovery that a particular class of taxpayers has opportunities confined to investment in a savings account at 4 percent or paying off his mortgage at 6.5 percent tells us nothing about the value of product lost to the private sector as the consequence of it being taken from him, since the individual investment transaction may be but the first in a series of substitutions effected through intermediaries which at the other end permit a corporation to invest at either a rate of return of 25 percent after taxes or at 45 percent before taxes.

If an opportunity cost standard is to be employed, it is less apt to be misleading if prevailing rates of return in the private business sector are examined and either averaged or, preferably, weighted by the volumes of funds being invested on a current basis. These rates should be *before* tax, not after, since taxes are a cost to the taxpayer but not to society. In order that a public project yield equivalent benefits to a private project earning 12 percent after tax (20 percent before tax), the public project must earn 20 percent since if it displaces the private project the lost tax will have to be made up from somewhere else.

The chosen opportunity set should reflect commercial opportunities only, since it is the marginal productivity of private-sector capital and not its average productivity which is sought. A substantial amount of capital goes into owner-occupied housing. Its imputed yield is low, and if funds applied to this use are weighted in, the resulting rate is biased downward. There is an enormous implicit subsidy to owner-occupied housing in present tax systems in most countries. This results in enough inefficiency in resource allocation on its own account without being used as a basis for throwing good money after bad in the public sector.

While such a measure is an appropriate measure of the opportunity cost of public-sector investments in terms of foregone private-sector returns, it must be recognized that the measure itself creates serious difficulties in terms of intertemporal social choice.

Its most serious defect in the current generation-future generations context is that it discriminates between projects on the basis of the time shape of their benefit streams. If the three projects, whose benefit streams are sketched in Figure 8–3 have *ex hypothesi* equal present values at the social discount rate *s* and are evaluated at the higher

Figure 8–3
Alternative discount: rate-sensitive income streams

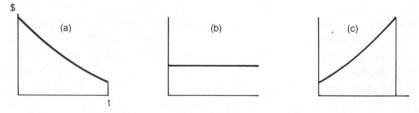

discount rate r, they will no longer be equally ranked: a will be ranked ahead of b, which in turn will be ranked ahead of c. Clearly, the use of a higher discount rate introduces a bias in favor of quick-payoff projects such as a and against delayed payoff projects such as c. Even if all are equivalently attractive at the social rate of discount, it is projects such as c which will be squeezed out first. This consideration lends credence to the views of some conservationists who claim that the discounting process leads in practice to systematic discrimination against the future.

Is there no way to preserve an operationally relevant social discount rate concept within the opportunity cost setting and so avoid this bias? Implicitly, use of a social discount rate means that the policy maximand is social wealth, or the present value of the benefit streams flowing from society's capital stock, evaluated at the social discount rate. If this is accepted and maximized subject to the savings constraint, the measure of productivity which emerges is net discounted social benefits per dollar of investment. (For an analogous treatment, which maximizes stockholder wealth at the market-discount rate, subject to an availability-of-funds constraint, see Weingartner[26] and the analysis of Chapter 7). The problem thus restated leads to a solution in which only those public-sector projects which offer expected net social benefits per dollar of investment in excess of the expected net social benefits generated by the marginal private-sector projects are accepted. The shadow price of the constraint appears as a positive net benefit-cost ratio which is required for acceptance.[27]

This concept is more difficult to apply since it requires the evaluation in social terms and at the social discount rate of a significant sample of private-sector projects rather than the mere determination of the private-sector cost of capital in order to determine the cutoff point. However, meeting this difficulty may have its own salutary effects, as it will force an explicit recognition of the social benefits of private-sector projects as compared to their public-sector counterparts, and may encourage acknowledgement of the fact that private-sector investment contributes to social well-being also.

A possible objection to this procedure is that the alleged bias toward quick payoff projects introduced by using a higher discount rate is not a bias at all, but it is a desirable response to the savings constraint. Funds thrown off quickly can be reinvested as they emerge and will lead to a higher level of benefits in future periods than will be available from the otherwise comparable project c.[28] Reinvestment assumptions underlying alternative decision criteria were discussed earlier. This argument is valid mathematically, but it is only valid economically if the benefits emerge in a form which can be reinvested, that is, cash. But benefits from many, if not most, public-sector investments are dissipated directly into the collective consumption stream without user charges and cannot realistically be viewed as available for reinvestment. Where alternative replacement chains are possible, they should, of course, be considered explicitly, as outlined in Section 4.11. This will make appropriate provision for reinvestment opportunities.

Nor should every public-sector investment meeting the proposed benefit-cost yardstick be accepted. If the net benefits per dollar invested are growing faster than the discount rates, the investment should be postponed. The basic investment timing rules discussed in Section 4.13 are as relevant here as elsewhere.

Adoption of a benefit-cost shadow price should, of course, change not only the selection of projects but the choice of optimum scale and technique for projects within the public sector. The scale decision is depicted in Figure 8–4 in which average benefits per dollar invested

Figure 8–4
Optimum scale: public sector investment with capital rationing

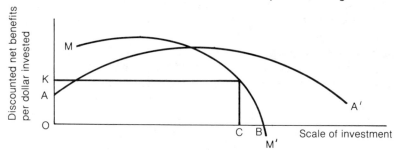

appear as AA' and marginal benefits as MM'. The unconstrained optimum is at OB, where marginal discounted net benefits just equal marginal investment cost, so that MM' crosses the scale-of-investment-axis. With a cutoff benefit-cost ratio of OK, optimum scale is reduced to OC. Similarly, in Figure 8–5, the optimum capital-labor ratio is not OD but OE. Thus the optimum expansion path for the public sector under the savings constraint will be less capital intensive than that which would have been chosen using the social discount rate in the absence of the constraint, and the optimum project scale will be smaller. These will, however, differ in turn from those which would be chosen using the higher private-sector cost of capital.

Applying this rule to the public sector alone will not by itself ensure the optimum provision for future generations. The reason is that private-sector investment decisions will continue to be made using the

Figure 8–5
Optimum technique: public sector investment with capital rationing

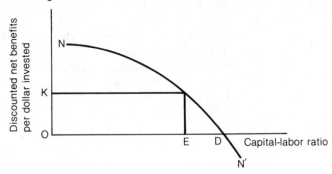

higher private sector cost of funds as an evaluator. Every accepted project, including the marginal ones for which net present value at the private-sector rate is zero, will have a positive net present value at the social discount rate. This is not only because the rate is lower but because the stream of corporate tax liabilities, which are not counted as benefits in a privately oriented calculation, must be included in the benefit stream for purposes of a social valuation. The set of projects chosen, however, will reflect the bias toward quick throw-off projects and against delayed-return projects discussed earlier. It will, however, be less serious than the corresponding public-sector problem because significant portions of the net benefit stream will be reinvested. Moreover, decisions with respect to scale and technique will be predicated upon the higher rate. It is not sufficient to apply the previously stated rule within the public sector to achieve the appropriate mix of investments, consistent with the social discount rate. The private sector must also be induced to restructure its investments. Since its decisions are influenced by the net after-tax stream of benefits, the most appropriate device short of outright subsidization is to alter the temporal incidence of taxes to reduce or eliminate the market-imposed bias. The most convenient tools for this purpose are the investment tax credit and provisions for accelerated amortization within the corporate income tax context. Depreciation rates, accelerated or otherwise, remain tied to asset lives by accounting convention (and IRS Bulletin F). To achieve the desired optimum, it may be necessary to weaken this link or even to reverse it, in order to provide higher rates of accelerated depreciation on durable assets or others with important future-oriented characteristics and eliminating acceleration for short-lived assets. Special high rates now provided for pollution-abatement investments are, of course, a step in the required direction as are provisions for expensing of research and development expenditures.

What sort of benefit-cost ratio will be required to justify a public-sector investment under this proposed criterion? The preferable method involves the analysis of a fully representative sample of private-sector projects of comparable risk, which are reevaluated by applying the social discount rate to the before-tax income stream to determine their social benefit-cost ratios.

However, an analytical approach is also possible if the marginal private sector opportunity cost rate is known. Designating the latter on an after-tax basis as k_p, and the effective tax rate, expressed as a percentage of cash flows, as T, we can determine the annual payment produced by an annuity of the same duration as our proposed public-sector project, which just yields the private-sector opportunity rate, by solving:

$$\sum_t \frac{B_t(1 - T)}{(1 + k_p)^t} - C = O \qquad (8.5.1)$$

where C is the project cost. Normalizing on an investment of $1.00, and assuming $k_p = 0.12$, $t = 20$, and $T = 0.40$, we can compute B. The after-tax annuity at 12 percent whose 20-year present value is $1.00 is $0.1339; adjusting for the tax the annual annuity is $0.2231. This annuity at an assumed 6 percent social discount rate is worth $2.56. The benefit-cost ratio which a public-sector project must earn to be worth as much as the marginal private-sector project we have defined is 2.56. If the benefit flows are level, the annual benefit must be 0.2231, the same as that of the private project. If the benefit flows are rising or falling, they may be adjusted accordingly. To find initial amounts, we make use of the relationship:

$$\sum_t \frac{S_0(1 + g)^t}{(1 + k_s)^t} = \sum_t \frac{S_L}{(1 + k_s)^t} \qquad (8.5.2)$$

where g is the rate of growth in social benefits, S_0 is the initial social benefit, and S_L is the (level payment) social benefit used above and defined as:

$$S_L = \frac{B}{(1 - T)} \qquad (8.5.3)$$

A solution to 8.5.2 may be approximated in this case by finding the annual payment to a 20-year annuity which has a present value of $2.56, using a discount rate of $k_2 - g$, where g is the expected annual rate of growth in the benefit stream (g may be negative if the stream is declining). If the stream is growing at a rate of 3 percent, then an initial annual benefit of $0.1721 will be sufficient, while if it is declining at a similar rate, an initial benefit of $0.2804 will be required per dollar of investment. This approximation may get into trouble if the growth rate is larger than k_s for long-lived projects (if $g \geq k_s$ for an infinite stream, no finite present value exists). This arithmetic difficulty is, however, nothing more than the symptom of inappropriate assumptions. If an investment exists which can generate an income stream growing at g percent per year indefinitely, it is pointless to adopt a lower social discount rate k_s. Indeed, k_s must always exceed the g available on long-lived projects in order to permit any consumption by the present generation.

In Table 8–1, we have calculated indicated marginally equivalent benefit-cost ratios for an assumed range of social discount rates, private-sector evaluation rates of 15 to 21 percent (before tax) and various lives. It will be noted that the longer the project life, the higher the benefit-cost ratio required to break even. This is simply because obtaining the higher yield over a longer period is worth more. Thus, with 15 percent available in the private sector, we need a 1.467 ratio for a 6 percent SDR if the project life is 10 years, but a 2.366 ratio if the life is 50 years. In terms of annual income streams, the amounts required are $.1993 per year per dollar of investment in the 10-year case and $.1501 per dollar in the 50-year case.

8.6 Choice of a social discount rate

In principle, one may choose any rate one selects as the social discount rate in the case where one wishes to adjust for the supposed present biasedness of the market rate. In particular, one may choose zero, which appears to weight present and future generations equally. Such a policy has indeed been proposed.[29]

There seems, however, to be a fairly strong case for using, instead of zero, a rate at least equal to the average rate of growth in real per capita output in the economy. With some interludes, the economic history of the industrialized world has been one of more or less continual growth in per capita output. As a consequence, if the average income of individuals at time t was X, their average income n periods later will be $X(1 + g)^n$ where g is the realized growth rate. There is some sense in which $1 in the earlier period is worth as much as $(1 + g)^n$ in the latter. Unless the individual can get $(1 + g)^n$ in the later period, there is no particular reason why he should sacrifice $1 in disposable income now.

Table 8–1
Equivalent benefit-cost ratios at differing social discount rates

Life of project	Private opportunity rate 15 percent			Private opportunity rate 18 percent			Private opportunity rate 21 percent		
	SDR 4 percent	SDR 6 percent	SDR 8 percent	SDR 4 percent	SDR 6 percent	SDR 8 percent	SDR 4 percent	SDR 6 percent	SDR 8 percent
1	1.106	1.085	1.065	1.135	1.113	1.093	1.163	1.142	1.120
2	1.160	1.128	1.097	1.205	1.171	1.139	1.250	1.215	1.181
5	1.328	1.257	1.191	1.424	1.347	1.277	1.521	1.440	1.365
10	1.616	1.467	1.337	1.805	1.638	1.493	2.001	1.815	1.655
15	1.901	1.661	1.464	2.184	1.908	1.681	2.477	2.164	1.907
20	2.171	1.832	1.569	2.539	2.143	1.834	2.918	2.463	2.108
25	2.417	1.978	1.651	2.858	2.338	1.953	3.308	2.708	2.261
30	2.634	2.096	1.715	3.134	2.495	2.041	3.643	2.900	2.372
40	2.980	2.265	1.795	3.567	2.712	2.149	4.159	3.161	2.505
50	3.225	2.366	1.837	3.868	2.838	2.202	4.512	3.310	2.569
75	3.552	2.468	1.869	4.262	2.962	2.243	4.973	3.456	2.617
100	3.676	2.493	1.874	4.411	2.991	2.249	5.146	3.490	2.624
1000	3.750	2.500	1.875	4.500	3.000	2.250	5.250	3.500	2.625

This case is basically intuitive, but it does have the property that in a low-income but high-growth economy, the social rate of discount will be relatively high, while as the state of satiety implicit in the classical stationary state approaches, it will indeed drop to zero. More sophisticated arguments for tying the social rate of discount to the growth rate are available; interested readers with a stomach for a strong dose of mathematics may wish to consult Ramsay and von Neumann.[30]

8.7   Social discount rates for private projects

Acceptance of the concept of a social discount rate implies that it is just that; a discount rate to be used in arriving at social valuations of all projects and not just a special low discount rate for projects located in the public sector. If long-deferred benefits (or costs) arising from public expenditures are to be given greater recognition than they would obtain under a market-discount-rate valuation, similar benefits accruing through private-sector projects are entitled to equivalent treatment. In fact, such treatment is essential if the social discount rate concept is to be useful analytically and not simply an engine for the preferential treatment of inferior projects having public-sector sponsorship.

Naturally, projects which were just marginal when evaluated at relatively high private-sector discount rates will exhibit a substantial excess of benefits over costs when evaluated at the lower social discount rate (providing, of course, that the social valuations are not adversely affected by negative externalities). For example, a $100,000 investment yielding annual benefits of $19,925 for ten years, which has a net present value of $100,000 at a 15 percent discount rate, will show a net present value of $161,611 if evaluated at a social discount rate of 4 percent. Effects on the valuation of the net benefit stream are more pronounced for long-lived projects than for short, for those with rising as opposed to flat benefit streams, and for flat as opposed to declining benefits. Thus, a similar $100,000 investment, yielding $15,056 annually for 40 years, which also exhibits a $100,000 net present value at 15 percent, has its net present value nearly tripled to $298,000 at a 4 percent rate. This selectivity works in favor of projects which create bigger benefits for future generations, which is, of course, just what it is intended to do.

The social discount rate, while an indispensible part of the social valuation process, plays but a limited role in private-sector decision making, as discussed in Section 8.5. Social valuations of private projects, however, should play an important role in defining acceptability criteria for public-sector investments, since they help define the opportunity costs of expanded public-sector investment in terms of the foregone benefits of private-sector investment.

8.8 Considering risk in public-sector investment

So far, we have avoided the problems created by differences in risk between projects by assuming all projects to be similar in risk. This is obviously not so, and taking account of such differences constitutes one of the major problems in capital-expenditure analysis. These problems are dealt with in fuller detail in Chapters 11 and 12. Those chapters deal with the problem in a private-sector context; while much of the analysis is relevant to public-sector decisions as well, it is perhaps appropriate to consider some of the peculiarities of considering risk in the public sector at this point.

We have already noted two arguments to the effect that risk in the public sector is different in character or kind from that in the private sector. The first of these is the Arrow-Lind argument that portfolio effects eliminate risk at least in the aggregate from the set of public-sector investments. As we will see, this ignores (systematic) components of risk which cannot be diversified away and overlooks the fact that benefits (and some of the costs) of public-sector investments accrue to individuals who may not have a large portfolio of them. Consequently, the conclusion that public-sector investments can be evaluated using a risk-free discount rate must be rejected. Public-sector investments should offer an appropriate risk premium for essentially the same reasons that a risk premium is demanded of private-sector investments.

The other is the Stapleton-Subrahmanyam argument that the existence of public-sector investments, in which we are all forced to share, in terms of our present and future tax liabilities if not always in the benefits, will (in general) prevent us from attaining a fully optimal portfolio of risks. Consequently, it is argued, in order to clear markets and get risks borne, the price of risk, that is, the premium in expected return per unit of risk, must rise. Further, the larger the public sector, the smaller the pool of discretionary investments, the larger the distortion and thus the greater must be the increase in the unit risk premium. Note that this higher-risk premium must be borne by all risky projects in the private sector; it will apply in the public sector only to the extent that market-determined risk premiums are used in setting hurdle rates. The existing market-determined risk premium, however, understates the marginal social cost of the risk in any public-sector investment because it ignores the effect the expanded public sector will have on risk premiums in the economy as a whole.

We believe this argument is valid, and that Stapleton and Sub-rahmanyam have uncovered a potentially important external diseconomy associated with the expansion of the public sector. However, we have as yet no idea of its magnitude and not too much to offer by way of incorporating it into decision criteria. All we can suggest is that where public-sector investments appear marginal in terms of the criteria we develop in this chapter, that is, if criteria indicate indifference, or near indifference, between acceptance and rejection, the tie should be resolved in favor of rejection. It is by no means clear, of course, that if the criteria established here were applied to all proposed public capital-expenditure projects, the public sector would continue to grow. In this sense, the problem may be of second-order importance.

We are still left with the problem of finding an appropriate method of applying a suitable risk premium to public-sector projects which are evaluated using the social rate of discount. The existence of a risk premium implies that higher expected values of benefits are required than would be in a risk-free situation. Given the law of large numbers, realized values from a group of risky projects should be greater than those from a group of risk-free projects of equal cost. The difference is the payment for bearing the risk. This difference may be shared either in terms of higher internal rate of return or a higher benefit-cost ratio. Since our analysis in this chapter utilizes the latter, the most suitable way to apply a risk premium in the social discount rate evaluation process is by requiring a higher benefit-cost ratio for acceptance.

To determine how high, we anticipate the argument of Chapter 11 to note that risk premia are primarily determined by systematic project risk (we will go along with Arrow and Lind to the extent of ignoring unsystematic risk in establishing public-sector criteria). Systematic project risk is invariant over sponsorship; it is the same no matter which firm undertakes the project, and it is the same if it is undertaken in the public sector assuming equally effective execution. We have already indicated that differences between private-sector discount rates, which reflect social opportunity costs, and the social discount rate should be taken into account by changing the required benefit-cost ratio. All that is required to give appropriate weight to project risk is to use the methods of Chapter 11 to determine the appropriate expected rate of return for the project. Table 8–1 or equations 8.5.1 to 8.5.3 can be used to determine an appropriate benefit-cost ratio, making suitable allowances for the private benefit-social benefit discrepancy resulting from income taxes.

This procedure will ensure that, apart from the necessary adjustments for the shape of the benefits stream built into the process by the use of the social discount rate, the marginal project in the public sector, like its private-sector counterpart, will generate a yield which is the sum of:

1. The (risk free) social discount rate.
2. The opportunity cost associated with the capital shortage, equal to the difference between the risk-free social discount rate and the risk-free interest rate observable in the marketplace.
3. A risk premium dependent on the risk characteristics of the project. This meets the opportunity cost equilization requirement without introducing the bias against growing income streams or future benefits generally that would be implicit in using the higher opportunity cost rate.

Notes

[1] For an entertaining view of the process from a legislator's eyes, see S. I. Hayakawa, "Mr. Hayakawa Goes to Washington," *Harper's* 256 (January 1978), pp. 39–45.

[2] J. L. Bower, *Managing the Resource Allocation Process* (Cambridge, Mass.: Division of Research, Graduate School of Business Administration, Harvard University, 1970).

[3] See also Anthony Downs, *An Economic Theory of Democracy* (New York: Harper, 1957).

[4] K. J. Arrow, *Social Choice and Individual Values* (New York: Wiley, 1951).

[5] J. M. Buchanan and G. Tulloch, *The Calculus of Consent* (Ann Arbor: University of Michigan Press, 1962).

[6] For early examples, see J. V. Krutilla and O. Eckstein, *Multiple Purpose River Development* (Baltimore: Johns Hopkins University Press, 1958); and R. N. McKeen, *Efficiency in Government through Systems Analysis* (New York: Wiley, 1958). For more recent examples, see the annual volumes *Benefit Cost and Policy Analysis* (title varies) edited by A. Harberger and others (Chicago: Aldine, 1971–74).

[7] See the evaluation of alternative transfer-payment programs by J. Bossons, C. J. Hindle, and T. R. Robinson in the National Bureau of Economic Research, *Fiftieth Annual Report* (New York: 1970).

[8] R. A. Musgrave, *The Theory of Public Finance* (New York: McGraw-Hill, 1959), pp. 55–57.

[9] Ibid., p. 560.

[10] Ibid., p. 578.

[11] A. C. Pigou, *The Economics of Welfare,* 4th ed. (London: Macmillan & Co. 1932), pp. 24–30.

[12] W. J. Baumol, *Welfare Economics and the Theory of the State* (Cambridge: Harvard University Press, 1952), pp. 91–93; S. A. Marglin, "The Social Rate of Discount and the Optimal Rate of Investment," *Quarterly Journal of Economics* 77 (February 1963), pp. 95–111.

[13] K. J. Arrow and R. C. Lind, "Uncertainty and the Evaluation of Public Investment Decisions," *American Economic Review* 60 (1970), pp. 364–78. For a similar argument that additional benefits from the existence of a public debt should be added to project benefits making the social rate less than the risk-free interest rate, see M. J. Gordon, "A Portfolio Theory of the Social Discount Rate and the Public Debt," *Journal of Finance,* 31 (May 1976), pp. 199–214.

[14] W. F. Sharpe, "Capital Asset Prices: A Theory of Market Equilibrium under Condi-

tions of Uncertainty," *Journal of Finance* 19 (1964), pp. 425–42; J. Lintner, "Security Prices, Risk, and Maximal Gains from Diversification," *Journal of Finance* 20 (1965), pp. 587–616.

[15] D. Farrar, *The Investment Decision Under Uncertainty* (Englewood Cliffs, N.J.: Prentice-Hall, 1962); B. King, "Market and Industry Factors in Stock Price Behavior," *Journal of Business* 39 Supplement (1966), pp. 179–90.

[16] M. J. Bailey and M. C. Jensen, "Risk and the Discount Rate for Public Investment," in M. C. Jensen, ed., *Studies in the Theory of Capital Markets* (New York: Praeger, 1972).

[17] B. W. Commoner, *The Closing Circle* (New York: Bantam, 1972).

[18] H. Demsetz, "Towards a Theory of Property Rights,"

[19] R. C. Stapleton and M. G. Subrahmanyam, "Capital Market Equilibrium in a Mixed Economy, Optimum Public Sector Investment Decision Rules and the Social Rate of Discount," *Quarterly Journal of Economics*, (August, 1978), pp. 399–411.

[20] M. H. Dobb, *On Economic Theory and Socialism* (London: Routledge, 1955), pp. 244, 258–60.

[21] W. J. Baumol, "On the Social Rate of Discount," *American Economic Review* 58 (September 1968), pp. 788–802.

[22] W. Hopper, in D. A. Seashore and G. Linder, eds., *Proceedings of The Conference on Government Involvement in the Energy Industry* (Calgary: University of Calgary, 1976), p. 27.

[23] See also Science Council of Canada, *Canada as a Conserver Society* (Ottawa, 1977).

[24] J. H. Lorie and L. J. Savage, "Three Problems in Capital Rationing," *Journal of Business* 28 (October 1955), pp. 229–39; H. M. Weingartner, *Mathematical Programming and the Analysis of Capital Budgeting Problems* (Englewood Cliffs, N.J.: Prentice-Hall, 1963).

[25] See also, for example, G. J. Reuber and R. Wonnacott, *The Cost of Capital in Canada* (Washington, D.C.: Resources for the Future, 1961).

[26] Weingartner, *Mathematical Programming*.

[27] S. A. Marglin, "The Opportunity Costs of Public Investment," *Quarterly Journal of Economics* 77 (1962), pp. 274–89, and M. S. Feldstein, "The Inadequacy of Weighted Discount Rates," in R. Layard, ed., *Cost-Benefit Analysis* (Harmondsworth, Essex: Penguin, 1972). pp. 311–32, have anticipated much of what follows.

[28] Marglin, "Opportunity Costs," Model I, II, III.

[29] G. Cassel, *Theoretische Sozialökonomie* (Leipzig, Wintersche Verlagsbuchhandlung, 1918).

[30] F. P. Ramsay, "A Mathematical Theory of Saving," *Economic Journal* 38 (1929), pp. 543–59; and J. von Neumann, "A Model of General Economic Equilibrium," *Review of Economic Studies* 13 (1945), pp. 1–9.

Problems

1. A hydroelectric dam in an underdeveloped country will cost $50 million, of which $35 million will be for local materials and labor and $15 million for imported equipment. Estimated annual benefits are $4.5 million, for at least 75 years.

    a. If the opportunity cost of capital is 10 percent in the local economy, should the dam be built with public funds?

b.   If the imported equipment can be paid for with a 30-year 4 percent loan from an international agency, repayable in local currency, should this alter the decision. Why?

2.   The premier of Middle Slobbovia, a thinly disguised province in Canada, recently celebrated his reelection on an antisocialist platform by introducing a bill to expropriate M.S. Power Corp. Ltd., the utility which supplies electric power and natural gas to 85 percent of the province's population. In announcing the proposed legislation, he indicated that he was acting solely to save money for the residents of the province, and that the new M.S. Hydro and Power Authority, which would own and operate the system on behalf of the government, would be able to reduce rates because

a.   As a provincial corporation, M.S.H.&P. will no longer have to pay federal corporate income taxes, which were a major element in M.S.P.C.'s cost of service.

b.   M.S.H.&P. will be able to finance not only the takeover but subsequent expansion of the utility without high cost equity funds; it will be able to borrow 100 percent of the needed money at the AA rate. The bonds will, of course, be guaranteed by the province.

Evaluate these arguments.

3.   Mr. Leitch, special advisor to the government of Poltroonia on offshore oil matters, has suggested that exploitation of concessions could be encouraged by replacing present cash bonuses, payable on acquiring the concessions, and rentals, payable annually thereafter, with an arrangement whereby a share of profits, over and above normal corporate taxes and present royalties, would be paid to the government. He proposes that the profit share be set so as to have a present value equal to the present payments which he proposes to abolish, at the social cost of capital which he calculates at 4 percent. He argues that such a substitution is cost free to society but that it will be enormously beneficial to the concession operators, whose cost of funds he calculates at 20 percent.

Comment.

Social valuation problems

9.1 Introduction

Net present value, the preferred measure of investment desirability, is nothing more or less than the present value of future operating profits to be generated by a project. The whole evaluation process can be related to the construction of a series of expected profit and loss statements for the project and their condensation via the discounting process into a lifetime profit and loss statement from which the net present value or the profitability index/benefit-cost ratio can be computed. The resemblance is shown even more explicitly in Table 9–1.

Table 9–1
Conceptual analogues between conventional accounting and present value analysis

Profit and loss statements	PV analysis
Sales	PV of revenues
Operating expenses	PV of operating expenses
Net revenue from operations	PV of net revenues
Depreciation	Asset cost
Net profit	Net present value

The only difference is that the asset cost, which is deducted in computing net present value, is the undiscounted value of the depreciation charges; this reflects the actual timing of the expenditure as opposed to the time at which the expense is recognized in the accounting system. It reflects the implicit inclusion of the cost of capital as an expense in the present value evaluation process.

In looking at social valuations and developing rules for evaluation in a social context, it will perhaps be useful to look at the links between conventional accounting (and present value analysis as related thereto) and national income accounting, which despite its defects is the most widely used social accounting system. We will then work from the national income accounts to develop an income statement analog for public-sector activities. Finally, we will examine the deficiencies of conventional accounting and national income accounting as social welfare measures and attempt to define an analytical framework which corrects for them.

National income accounting is sometimes called social accounting in that it attempts to do for society as a whole what conventional accounting does for the business firm. The conceptual basis is essentially identical to that of conventional financial accounting. While the construction of national income accounts is a major achievement, it must be observed that many of the deficiencies of corporate profit and loss accounting as a measure of social contribution carry over to national income accounts. The frequently voiced objections that GNP is not a valid measure of social welfare are true. This is quite beside the point since it was never intended to be. Even the more conceptually correct measure, national income, has a variety of deficiencies as we shall see.

9.2 Firm accounts, sector accounts, and the national income accounting framework

Just as many firms' income statements represent a consolidation of the statements of the firm and its subsidiaries, so also national income accounts are consolidated accounts. This time, however, the consolidation is effected across the entire economy. Initial consolidations are made across sectors comprising similar types of organizations. The principal sectors include business firms, governments, and households. An additional rest-of-the-world sector is used to record transactions between the national economy and foreigners. Unlike the other sector accounts, it is incomplete insofar as it considers only transborder transactions.

The other point to note is that while corporate accounts are drawn up from the point of view of the stockholders who own the firm, national income accounts are drawn up from the viewpoint of the households or individuals which comprise society and on whose behalf it is presumably run. Wages are recorded as an expense in corporate accounting, and corporate profit is the only net income category that appears. However, wages, interest, and rent also appear as income categories in the national income accounts.

Table 9–2 relates conventional income statement items for a business firm to the basic national income accounting framework. Value added, a measure of gross output, is seldom calculated in the corporate accounting process though it is reported to the *Census of Manufactures;* it eliminates the intercorporate sales needed to compute aggregate sales of the corporate sector.

Table 9–2
Corporate accounts and national income accounts

	Corporate accounts	National income accounts
	Sales	
less	Purchase from other firms	
equals	(value added)	GNP
less	Depreciation	
equals		NNP
less	Indirect business taxes (net of subsidies)	
equals		National income
consisting of		
	Wages, salaries, and so on	
	Rents	
	Interest	
	Corporate profits (before tax)	

We may record the items in Table 9–2 in the more familiar income statement format which appears in Table 9–3. All items in Tables 9–2 and 9–3 represent observable market transactions, or book entries reflecting past transactions (depreciation) or transfers of cash (taxes).

Table 9–3
Place of national income accounts in a conventional income statement

	GNP categories	Income statement
	Net purchases by others	
minus	Indirect taxes (net of subsidies)	
equals		Net sales
minus	Intermediate purchases	
	Employee compensation	
	Rents	
	Depreciation	
equals		Operating income
minus	Interest	
equals	Corporate profit	Profit before taxes

This and the fact that both sides are recorded so that cross-checks are available make the corporate sector of the national income accounts more reliable than the others.

The private owners of the corporation evaluate its performance in terms of the bottom line on the income statement, in terms of the profit it earns, or applying the more sophisticated long-run analysis we have been exploring in terms of the present values of its cash flows. Either may be related to investment.

9.3   Government accounts and national income accounts

When we come to construct the analog of Tables 9–2 and 9–3 for the government sector, whether we view it socially, as in Table 9–4, or as proprietors, as in Table 9–5, we run up against an immediate problem. Government output is not marketed, therefore, there is no objective

Table 9–4
National income accounts for a government

	Value added*	
equals		GNP
minus	Depreciation	
equals		NNP/NI
consisting of		
	Employee compensation	
	Rent	
	(Interest $= 0$)	
	(Profits $= 0$)	

* Value of output minus intermediate purchases.

way to measure its value. Instead, national income accountants adopt the convention that government operations generate neither profits nor losses (nor interest, since interest on the public debt is treated as a transfer payment and not as factor income).

This solves the national income accountant's problem of how to value nonmarketed public-sector output, but it does nothing for the proprietor of government who wants to assess its bottom line contribu-

Table 9–5
An income statement for government, using national income accounts

	Value of output	Net sales
minus		
	Intermediate purchases	
	Employee compensation	Expenses
	Rents	
	Depreciation	
equals		Profit

tion or the return it generates on investment. The assumption is justified on the grounds that our elected representatives would not have spent the money if they did not think what they were getting was at least worth it and that the electoral process provides the ultimate valuation. The formal validity of the assumption is perhaps arguable at least as far as the aggregate contribution of government is concerned. But the implied accounting system offers little guidance to the legislature seeking to decide between alternative expenditures or to the voter/proprietor attempting to decide whether the managers he has installed have done a good job.

Benefit-cost analysis is an attempt to get behind the assumptions of national income accounting to provide a bottom line for the valuation of public-sector performance. It does so in the first instance by attempting to develop market value surrogates for the evaluation of output, so that the circularity of valuing output at its cost may be avoided. This creates the possibility that gains or losses may emerge just as they might in the private sector.

GNP is, of course, not altogether satisfactory as a measure of social welfare. Nor is profit the sole measure of the corporation's social contribution. Benefit-cost analysis in its more sophisticated forms attempts to go beyond such accounting yardsticks to the underlying economic reality. While it was developed for use in the public sector, it is applicable to private-sector operations as well, where it is used to evaluate their performance from a social point of view.

9.4 Some valuation conventions and their implications

National income accounting conventions applied in the private-sector value output at market price. Regardless of whether the market is competitive or (simply) monopolistic, the market price is equivalent to the height of the demand curve for the last unit sold (see Figure 9–1). If we accept, as an approximation, Marshall's identification of the de-

Figure 9–1
Market equilibrium and the market-value rule

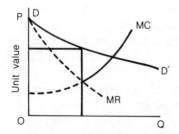
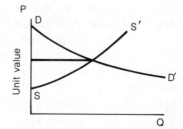

mand curve with the marginal utility curve,[1] the market price can be regarded as a measure of the marginal utility of the product being sold, expressed in money terms. This, of course, provides our basic justification for using market prices as a measure of social value in computing output.

When we come to the problem of measuring the value of public-sector output, especially that portion which is not marketed and/or for which no user charges are levied, difficulties emerge. Assuming we know the demand curve, two possibilities exist. The first is that the commodity is distributed without charge until the market is satiated and no unsatisfied demand exists. This condition, of course, corresponds to the point A in Figure 9–2 where the demand curve crosses the

Figure 9–2
Market value criteria and value of public output

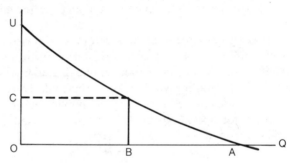

x-axis. The appropriate value for such a service, or the one which corresponds to the valuation criteria applied to the private sector, is simply zero. Individuals will demand more and more of the service until the marginal utility of the last unit is exactly equal to what it costs them, which is zero. A day spent in the surgery of a British National Health Service (NHS) general practitioner should be enough to convince anybody of the truth of this proposition, at least insofar as the marginal units are concerned.

The alternative situation is one in which output is deliberately held below the saturation point, say at OB. Here, if the demand curve is known, a value OC can be determined which corresponds precisely to the valuation concept applied in the private sector. Here, too, there will be opposition charges of insufficient service levels, and so on. Unless there are such pressures, and some demand unsatisfied, it is probable that the marginal value is nil and that excessive output is being provided. Just what output *should* be provided is, of course, the critical question at which our entire analysis is directed. To anticipate the argument which follows, the appropriate rule is to produce to the point where marginal utility equals marginal cost.

At this point, even the most savage critic of the NHS will surely spring to its defense and tell us that it is most unfair to view the *entire* output of the British medical industry as worthless. Clearly it is not; the first units of service provided are very valuable, and it is surely only the last few which may be worthless or nearly so. We are back again at that classic conundrum of the elementary economics textbook: Why are diamonds so valuable while water is free? The answer is the same as it was in that case: The marginal utility may be zero even if the total utility is very large indeed. Conventional valuation criteria reflect marginal utilities and not total utilities.

One means of avoiding the anomaly that may result from unlimited free distribution is to compute total utility, or that approximation of it that is provided by the area under the demand curve. If this exceeds total costs, then the program or the project is in some sense justified, although it should have its scale adjusted to ensure that the appropriate marginal conditions are fulfilled. This procedure, which is implicit in a number of methodologies that have been proposed for measuring unmarketed benefits[2] is equivalent to measuring benefits as the sum of the marginal valuation times the number of units, plus Marshallian consumers' surplus.[3] The resulting measure of value is useful for many purposes; it should be noted, however, that it is not comparable to the value measure used for the private sector, which is simply the marginal valuation times the number of units. Its use inevitably overstates the value of public-sector output, unless, of course, consumers' surplus is added to the private-sector output in arriving at its social valuation.[4] If public-sector output, with benefits calculated to include consumers' surplus is compared with or considered as an alternative to private-sector output for which no such surplus is included in measured benefits, an adjustment must be made.

If our purpose in valuing public-sector output is to arrive at more meaningful national income accounts for the sector which are otherwise comparable to the corresponding accounts for the private sector, consumers' surplus should be excluded. For other purposes, the formal inclusion or exclusion of consumers' surpluses from the final benefit-cost calculation is a matter of some indifference providing the cutoff ratio adopted is selected bearing in mind not only the productivity implicit in higher private-sector rates of return, as discussed in Chapter 8, but also the exclusion of consumers' surplus.

While we are hesitant on theoretical grounds to include consumers' surplus in calculating benefits from large segments of the economy such as the public sector, perhaps the most serious difficulty in any attempt to use it, even in the smaller-scale, single-industry situations where its use is more defensible theoretically, is a practical one. We know or can measure with some confidence only those small segments of the demand curve in the neighborhood of observed price-quantity pairs. But much of the consumers' surplus comes from the upper left-hand corner of the demand curve where observations are usually lacking. Extrapolating statistical evidence beyond the domain of observation is always dangerous, even if it is done all the time. It is particularly so where econometric demand evidence is involved, given the rather cavalier fashion in which many econometricians select functional forms for demand analysis. Linear or log-log (constant elasticity) forms may be satisfactory approximations over a narrow range. Both fall apart outside it, and the latter is particularly objectionable in that it implies not only that satiation is impossible but also that consumers' surplus is infinite.

Use of consumers' surplus in an incremental context is more easily defended, if only because the relevant parts of the demand curve can be estimated with more confidence. Projects, of course, may be regarded as increments to programs. While the total of consumers' surplus at the program level may be a meaningless calculation, its consideration and calculation at the project level should at least serve to ensure that there is some consumers' surplus obtainable from further expansion of the program in the direction indicated and that the appropriate efficiency criterion is respected. The same principle can be applied at the project level. Scale and/or capital intensity should be increased as long as the increment to consumers' surplus, suitably discounted at the social discount rate, bears an appropriate ratio to project costs. Here we should be operating in an area where something about the demand curve is known, so that increments to consumers' surplus can be estimated with reasonable confidence even if the total cannot. At the very least, we should know that the demand curve is downward sloping, and that additional units *per capita* are worth less than the existing ones. The only question is how much less, and this requires some estimate of the appropriate elasticity of demand.

9.5 Collective goods, public goods, and some related phenomena

One peculiarity of many of the goods traditionally associated with the public sector is that they are consumed collectively or without exhaustion so that my consumption of the good does not prevent your consumption of it at the same time or perhaps at another time. For this type

Figure 9–3
Aggregation of demand curves, pure private goods

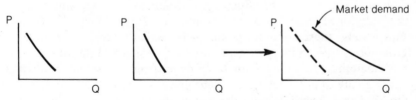

of good, aggregate demand schedules should be found, not by adding the number of units individuals will buy at a given price (adding horizontally as in Figure 9–3), but by adding the amounts that different individuals are willing to pay (adding vertically for each successive unit as in Figure 9–4).

Figure 9–4
Aggregation of demand curves, collective goods

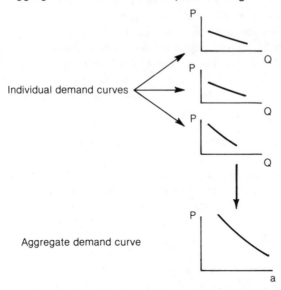

Goods of this type are often described as public goods (frequently by collectivists). In our view they should be defined as collective goods with the term *public good* more narrowly defined as it is below.

There is nothing intrinsically peculiar about collective goods except the fact that they can be consumed collectively and that demand curves may be aggregated in the manner indicated earlier. One of us may be willing to pay $14 ten times a year to take his son to see a major league baseball game, and $120 in the spring to take his wife to see Placido Domingo sing in *Figaro*. But Senor Domingo will not sing for just anybody for $120, and even the Toronto Blue Jays will not play for $14. Fortunately, there are other people with similar tastes, and among the group of us we can induce Senor Domingo to sing and the Blue Jays to play something that they claim to be major league baseball, and which occasionally approaches it, or even bliss (like getting 25 runs against the Yankees). There is a more or less public character to the consumption of collective goods; their consumption is a public event shared by a number of individuals, most of whom could not undertake the same consumption privately.

A critical element in the ability of Toronto Blue Jays to operate is the fact that they have a fence around the park. People must pay, or they do not get in. This forces them to reveal (at least enough of) their true preferences. Without a fence, at least one of us would be at every game. The team could "pass the hat" in an attempt to support the operation with voluntary offerings, while cajoling one into contributing (compare Public Broadcasting Service [PBS] campaigns for funds from viewers). The typical response would likely be to feign boredom and indifference and give just $1 as we frequently do in church when we don't particularly like the sermon. Opera houses have other problems, which need not detain us here.[5] These are nothing, however, when compared to what their problems would be if they could not charge admission or otherwise prevent people from enjoying the performance without paying.

Within the set of collective goods, as defined earlier, there is a subset of collective goods for which just this problem emerges. Everybody benefits from the fire department either directly or indirectly merely because of lower fire insurance premiums. The moral and social difficulties involved in having the fire chief determine before answering a call whether the owner of the burning premises has paid for the requisite protection are obvious.[6]

Collective goods for which it is impossible, whether for moral or merely technical reasons, to prevent nonpayers from benefiting have classically been defined by economists as *public goods*. In our view, attempts to broaden the definition to include the entire corpus of what we have defined as collective goods[7] serve only to confuse the issue and to divert the attention of an overburdened public sector from those things that only government can do to those things that it can perhaps do as well as anybody else, but which can be produced with equal efficiency by others to the detriment of the former.[8] This is not intended to suggest that the appropriate functions of government were defined 200 years ago by Adam Smith or Thomas Jefferson and remain unchanged. Technology changes and so do society's moral parameters. Exclusions that would have been accepted with equanimity a century ago are impossible on moral grounds today, and the acceptability of exclusion may delay a more significant role in defining the scope of the public sector than collectivity in consumption. Medical care is not a collective good as we have defined it. With few exceptions, benefits accrue almost exclusively to the household of the recipient. While exclusion is feasible, the proposition that it is immoral has been the driving force behind medicare, perhaps the major public-sector innovation of the past generation. While the proposition that exclusion because of the inability to pay is unacceptable has been almost universally accepted in Western countries, an intense political battle remains to be fought over the issue of whether and to what extent those well able to pay should be required to do so. A major expansion in the activities of government has resulted. In the other direction, television reception has retained a public good character for many years largely for technical reasons. Technology now permits the signal to be encoded, decodable only by subscribers to a service which includes the required attachments to the receiving unit. Exclusion is possible, and pay-TV beckons. The political debate emerging is over whether it is moral to charge for something that was hitherto free, even if it is of different quality.

While collectiveness in consumption raises technical difficulties in the determination of demand curves, nonexclusion creates others. The combination is even worse. Perhaps the most significant social role of the price system is that it forces would-be consumers to indicate their true preferences and gives no bonuses for concealment. Collective goods must be paid for as must all goods provided through the public sector. While taxes are an essential ingredient of the system, all potential taxpayers have an incentive, if asked whether they would be willing to pay X for a certain collective good, to say no, in the hope they will not be taxed to finance it and the realization that they will not be excluded from consuming it if it materializes. When asked whether they would like the good to be provided on a collective basis with no linkage to financing, their answer is apt to be dependent on what link, if any, is perceived between the provision of the service and their own tax bills. If little or none, they are apt to favor extension of the service. Under a tax system which defines liability in terms of ability to pay, low-income participants may well opt for any public-sector extension they do not regard as bad, while high-income participants may similarly be tempted to oppose all such extensions, since their share of the tax bill is likely to exceed their cost of obtaining the service privately.

The propensity to conceal true preferences when production and allocation decisions are politicized and delinked from the price system is one of the major problems of the modern mixed economy and provides a powerful rationale for the retention of the price system or taxation on a use-related basis where possible in the public sector. It also creates a need, where the lack of use-related charges encourages people to dissimulate with respect to the true value they place on public-sector goods and services, for an independent analytical methodology capable of providing answers to questions of social desirability. It is, of course, just this that benefit-cost ratio analysis purports to provide and which is its *rationale*. There is little or no need for it in the private sector, where the existence of prices forces the revelation of valuations. In applying it in the public sector, care must be taken that it does not absorb and perpetuate the very distortions that created the need for it in the first instance.

9.6 Unpriced goods and bads—externalities

The basic problem in public-sector decision making with respect to the provision of goods and services is that those who benefit do not necessarily pay, while those who pay do not necessarily benefit, so that it is difficult to appraise whether the benefits of one group outweigh the costs borne by another for a variety of reasons not the least of which are all the incentives to concealment of true valuations which underlie the whole process.

The problem, thus stated, is not altogether confined to the public sector. Many private-sector activities create costless benefits for nonparticipants, many others impose uncompensated costs on those who do not participate. Beekeeping provides pollination services for farmers of all descriptions for which the farmers do not pay. Bees may also sting passersby, some of whom may be allergic and suffer painful consequences as a result, but for which farmers do not compensate them. The reasons are similar in both cases and have to do with the difficulty of distinguishing individuals or the hives from which they came.

Costs and benefits imposed outside the market system on nonparticipants are known as *externalities* or *spillovers*. These utilities or disutilities do not enter the market-demand curve and do not affect the outcome of the market process. Because the individuals affected are as much a part of society as the market participants, effects on the farmer, for example, should be included in a social valuation. We may replace the demand curve for social valuation purposes with a *marginal social value* (*MSV*) curve, which is obtained by adding (subtracting) benefits (costs) imposed on others at the various levels of output to the valuations revealed on the demand curve. The additions are performed vertically as they are in the collective good case; indeed the classical collective good may usefully be viewed as one having nothing but external benefits. Where they are uncorrected, externalities result in market solutions which are suboptimal. Where there are no externalities MSV corresponds to the demand curve, and the competitive solution where $MSV = MC$ is optimal. The more general case is depicted in Figure 9–5, where MSV, reflecting positive externalities, is above the demand

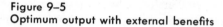

Figure 9–5
Optimum output with external benefits

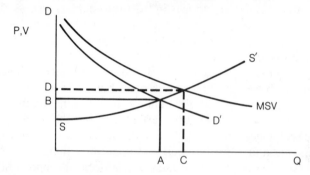

curve.[9] With the supply curve SS' representing the (horizontally summed) marginal cost curves of the producers, the market equilibrium is reached at OA with price OB. The socially optimum output is OC, which can be brought forth only by a price OD.

While there is a vast literature on devices intended to correct for externalities, once they have been identified and measured, correcting them is not our concern.[10] Our concern is, however, very much with their identification and measurement. Interdependence, or the fact that a nonparticipant in the market is affected, is not enough. It must be uncompensated. This is, of course, the equivalent of the exclusion problem in the public good case. The applegrower in a remote area may recognize interdependence and subsidize a nearby beekeeper to make sure the latter stays in business; or conversely, if applegrowing is more marginal than beekeeping, the beekeeper may subsidize the applegrower, since pollen is as necessary to bees as bees are to apple trees. Or some clever entrepreneur, recognizing the unfulfilled opportunity (sometimes identified as market failure) may simply merge the apple operation with the beekeeping operation and internalize the externalities at which point they disappear. In none of these three cases is there any externality, because the side effects are compensated.[11]

9.7 The existence of externalities

Compensation can be achieved in many ways, such as through negotiation and contract or as the result of a lawsuit, whether settled or fought to the bitter end. It may also be implicit as well as explicit. Sudbury, in northern Ontario, Canada, is a mining community which owed its early prosperity as well as its peculiar, moonlike landscape to the open-air roasting of copper-nickel sulphide ores. The resulting air pollution was extreme and affected employees in their off-hours as well as at work.[12] Whether the pollution was an externality is another matter for most of the residents. While there were some premining inhabitants, most of the population moved to Sudbury after the air pollution began. Presumably they believed the wages offered (in the case of employees) or profit opportunities (in the case of small businesses) were such as to compensate for the fouled air. (The premining inhabitants may have been uncompensated, but many were able to sell off property for residential development at windfall prices as a consequence of the mining developments and were indirectly compensated thereby.) The immigrants who came in pursuit of high wages or profit opportunities may feel, in retrospect, that they undervalued their lungs. But they cannot claim that they were not compensated to a degree acceptable to them at the time.

Other examples abound. Toronto International Airport, when built, was over 20 miles from the city and surrounded by pasture land. A community sprang up which was comprised of families of people who worked at the airport and who could save transportation costs by living close to their place of work. Later, as the airport (and the city) expanded, the surrounding area became a subpar residential suburb, attracting residents despite aircraft noise by having lower housing prices than other suburbs not so affected. Noise pollution? Yes. Externality? No. The disamenities resulting from the high noise levels were capitalized into land costs and housing prices. The buyers were compensated by the relatively lower price.

These examples are not intended to suggest that air or noise pollution are not social problems; they are. But the problem is one which goes beyond mere economic externality. It does not represent market failure so much as a broader legal failure or social failure.

One of the principal contributions of Coase[13] was to point out that there are two ways of compensating for any interdependency. Using pollution as an example, the polluters may compensate those adversely affected, as in the two cases cited. Alternatively, those adversely affected can compensate the polluters for stopping. In either case, the potential externality is suppressed. But the income distribution consequences may be, and are, grossly different. The protracted political struggle over pollution in North America is really a struggle over distribution; nobody is in favor of pollution per se, but one side of the debate wants to stick it to the polluters, irrespective of considerations like those outlined earlier, while others believe that, to the extent that society has changed its values (quite possibly for the better) those who made investments in good faith under the old ground rules should be compensated for the loss of the implied rights (to pollute) or given enough assistance to change at no cost to their stockholders. To point out the nature of this argument is not to enter it, but we note that the redistributional squabble has been a major factor in delaying solutions to pollution problems. If we are really serious about doing something about the latter, we may have to compromise on the distribution issue.

Both of the examples given earlier involve what we suggest are nonexternalities where compensation was achieved via contract. In this case, whether compensation has been effected or not is a matter requiring some degree of historical analysis. As a general principle, whoever was there first and has operated legally with no major change in the nature of the operation should be presumed not to generate an externality. Its neighbors knew it was there and accepted its presence by moving in. But the imposition of a sanitary landfill on the landscape of a resort area, or the conversion of a dairy farm with 50 cows into a feedlot with 500 cattle do create externalities unless compensation is provided.

Nor is contract the only avenue of compensation. Motor vehicle accidents create an important interdependency. Compensation is provided by the law of negligence and is usually paid for by insurance companies whose premiums are borne by vehicle owners. While it can be shown that the existing legal system does not provide for full compensation by negligent vehicle operators,[14] it is not clear that an externality exists, except for pedestrians, passersby, and owners of properties abutting streets. Participants in the activity may well be deemed to be aware of its hazardous character and of the supposed defects in the law and to have assumed the risks of participation in return for the benefits from participating. Market failure? Not insofar as other motorists are concerned. Should society intervene to change the rules of the game as Keeton and O'Connell recommend? That, in the last analysis, is an ethical judgment which society must make. Given free choice, how far should people be relieved of the consequences of their actions? This basic argument is well known in the common law doctrine of *assumpsit,* long since set aside in workmen's compensation laws and other statutes. The strongest case against it is that it ignores some real externalities.

9.8   On measuring the unmeasurable

An economist, it has been observed, is someone who knows the price of everything and the value of nothing.[15] Any student of the subject could provide examples from the literature which lend support to this observation. While one can find plenty of counterexamples, it is an observation which should be borne in mind by the benefit-cost analyst, lest he get carried away by the mechanics of his craft and fall into the trap.

One of the most frequently raised objections to the whole business of benefit-cost analysis is that it rests on monetary valuations being attached to things like beauty, health, happiness, and life itself. These are or should be from the perspective of the romantic side of our natures beyond price. Most of the supporters of benefit-cost analysis would argue that this is not the principal defect of the methodology but its chief advantage. There is a tendency on the part of decision makers to focus on the quantifiable and the quantified. Things that are priceless, and which are left out of the calculus on that account, are often treated as if they were worthless. This presumably does not apply to things of a high order of pricelessness such as national shrines. But it apparently happens all too often to things that have a lower degree of pricelessness such as the minor architectural gem that is pulled down to make way for a public housing project or the lives of teenagers burned up in a northern Ontario forest fire because they were sent out to do a controlled burn with inadequate training and negligible supervision.[16]

The fact is that decisions are made every day that involve priceless or at least unmeasurable values. Sometimes they are taken with great care and deliberation and sometimes with very little. A decision taken to build a subway system in Washington, D.C., may also be a decision to cause the deaths of a dozen workers—not deliberately, but as a probably unavoidable consequence of the construction. We could eliminate a large fraction of the highway death toll if we imposed and enforced a 25 mph speed limit and further outlawed the sale of automobiles capable of speeds in excess of 30 mph. We would reduce the consumption of energy in the process, yet we choose not to do so, basically because we value speed and mobility more than we do the lives such a change would save.

The "Treasures of Tutankhamen" collection undoubtedly qualifies as a priceless relic of the human past. Yet, it has been deliberately put at risk by being shipped around the world to be exhibited. Such a move increased its accessibility to people in Europe and North America who would never have seen the treasures otherwise, but it involved a finite, if small, probability of their loss in a transportation accident. If truly priceless, the product of an infinite loss times any finite probability of occurrence produces, as we know from Pascal,[17] an infinite expected loss, which no rational decision maker would accept. But it was accepted. Does this imply that priceless means something less than infinite value? Or is the issue moot because the exhibitions were organized to earn money to preserve other priceless antiquities in danger of perishing in ways less spectacular but of higher probability?

The issue that is forced or made explicit by benefit-cost analysis is one which many of us would prefer to sidestep, namely, that the complexity and interdependence of our society has grown to the point where possibly adverse decisions are routinely made. Some means must be found of ensuring that implicit trade-offs are not grossly inappropriate. The best way to do so is to make the valuations explicit. If they are not acceptable, they can be changed.

No one pretends or should pretend that valuations of any great precision can be attached to many of the things frequently classified as unmeasurable. In fact it is seldom necessary to do so. The true cost of a supertanker spill at sea in terms of environmental damage, clean-up costs, and so on is notoriously hard to assess. The costs per incident could be sharply reduced by using smaller tankers, although the frequency of incidents would no doubt rise disproportionately due to congestion in the shipping lanes. But the savings in transportation costs attributable to economies of scale in supertankers are greater than the most generous estimate of the added damage by orders of magnitude. The case that the environmental costs are significantly less than the transportation cost saving does not require any great precision in the estimate.[18] But all such a finding means is that we should not "throw the baby out with the bathwater." No doubt significant improvements in tanker design and navigational standards could be effected which would reduce the environmental costs by an amount greater than the transportation costs burden they would impose. One advantage of benefit-cost analysis is that it forces the search for a solution in this direction, rather than in the direction of a romantic attempt to ban the use of supertankers.

One would be tempted to dismiss such romantic solutions as quixotic were it not for their demonstrated appeal to legislators who recognize a problem but cannot grapple altogether effectively with its full complexity and so seek to abolish the problem with simplistic legislation. The Water Pollution Control Act of 1972 is a case in point. Baumol and Oates indicate that 85 to 90 percent of water pollution can be eliminated for $61 billion. A 95 to 99 percent reduction would cost $119 billion, while total elimination would cost $319 billion.[19] Benefits do not rise proportionately with costs.

9.9 The ultimate unmeasurable—human life?

First place in the list of unmeasurable values, if awarded on the basis of sheer volume of theoretical debate, would undoubtedly go to human life. This is perhaps a measure of our age. Earlier eras were more prone to assert that certain things were more precious than life itself and proved it by their actions. The present tendency to view life as the transcendent good may be nothing more than a romantic attempt at denial of mortality. But we need not inquire into its origins; taking tastes as given is traditional in economics and perhaps essential. We should, however, remind ourselves that what we are talking about is the premature taking of life and neither more or less.

One might suppose, given the rhetoric about the transcendent value of life, that life-and-death decisions would be reserved for the highest levels of government. While some are (in particular those involving the lives of persons convicted of capital offenses), in fact life-and-death decisions are made routinely by anonymous bureaucrats at all levels of government down to the smallest county road department. A decision not to straighten a particular troublesome curve probably means that at least one more person will die before it is straightened. A life cut short for an expenditure postponed—the implicit valuation is fairly straightforward and obvious.

There is a difference between these decisions and the type that are reserved to the highest political or judicial levels. The latter decisions involve known, recognizable, identifiable human beings. The former merely alter a digit or two in some not-too-well-defined mortality table and effect a minute change in the probability that any particular individual may die. Applied over enough individuals, that may be enough to condemn some proportion to premature death with virtual certainty, yet the direct causal connection is apparently severed, and we can all take such decisions with a clear conscience. For such situations are not confined to the public sector. Similar decisions are taken by managers who choose one production process over another with a different accident rate and by all of us in our individual capacities when we drive a car a bit too fast or pass on a hill or merely neglect to remove the ice from our sidewalk.

To assert the desirability, or even the need, to have a methodology to attach values to human life does not imply the lack of a proper respect for life. Quite the contrary, the purpose of such a methodology is to ensure that a proper respect for life is maintained and that lives are not sacrificed for nickel-and-dime economies. Having a methodology which assigns a finite value to life does, however, accept the implicit corollary that certain things may be deemed more valuable than life itself. Such things may represent lofty ideals or may be so prosaic as to include, as they have by implication for centuries, a supply of coal, a bridge across a river, or a tunnel under it. A finite but appropriately high value for life may, if suitable institutional controls are provided, do more to reduce industrial or other premature fatalities than any amount of rhetoric about life being beyond any price.

Several approaches to the valuation of lives exist in the literature. Perhaps the oldest is the discounted expected earnings formula:

$$^0V_L = \sum_{t=0}^{n} {}^0p_n \, Y_t(1 + k_p)^{-t} \qquad (9.9.1)$$

where

$_0$ is the year of death.

^0V_L is the value of the life at the time of death.

^0p_n is the probability that a person alive at time O will survive through year n.

Y_t is the individual's expected earnings in year t.

k_p is the appropriate personal discount rate.

which will be recognized as nothing more than the actuarially weighted, expected value of the remaining lifetime income which has been cut off at the time of death. ^0p_n is usually derived from a mortality table,[20] while k_p is usually an interest rate reflecting available yields on high grade bonds.

An improved version is the Dublin-Lotka formula[21] which uses earnings net of the individual's own consumption, or:

$$^0V_L = \sum_{t=0}^{n} {}^0p_n \, (Y_t - C_t)(1 + k_p)^{-t} \qquad (9.9.2)$$

where C_t is the individual's own consumption in period t, while the other symbols retain their earlier meanings. The rationale of equation 9.9.2 is that while the individual's contribution to the flow of output measured by earnings may cease, so does his claim on that flow of output, so that the net loss is given by 9.9.2.

Formulas 9.9.1 or 9.9.2 or close approximations thereto have been perhaps the most widely used for valuing lives in an economic context.

Yet, a moment's reflection will confirm that they tell us nothing about the most critical issue, that is, the value of the individual's life to the individual losing it. Equation 9.9.2 is perhaps a measure of the loss to the individual's heirs and, in fact, is widely used by the courts for this purpose in assessing damages recoverable by heirs in fatal accidents. Indeed, the authors of the formula were actuaries who developed the formula for the closely related purpose of helping plan appropriate life insurance coverage for an individual.[22] There are some valid reasons for using the value as a measure of the insurable interest in a life and for tying the maximum amount of life insurance that will be issued to it. There are similar reasons of public policy which suggest that heirs' rights to recovery should be limited to their economic loss, lest they be somewhat less than diligent in looking after a seriously injured victim. Equation 9.9.2 also has the unfortunate implication that the value of a life may be negative if positive values of Y_t lie too far in the future or in the past. Its too literal acceptance as a criterion could very well lead to the advocacy of infanticide or euthanasia on economic welfare grounds. The courts handle the problem by insisting on nonnegative values in such instances, and we might be wise to emulate them. But 9.9.2 is only a partial measure of the value of the individual's life being evaluated; it measures its (external) value to others, namely, the heirs and the tax collector. We are still left with the problem of finding the internal value of life to the individual.

Several ingenious attempts have been made to arrive at inferences about this value based on insurance-buying behavior. But buying insurance does nothing to alter the probability of premature death; all such studies can reveal is how diligent the person is in ensuring that his or her heirs receive the equivalent of 9.9.2. Again, the moral hazard problem with respect to buying flight insurance for amounts in excess of 9.9.2 has lead to major security problems for airlines. This suggests that at least some persons place relatively low internal valuations on their own lives.

The only way we can get any kind of grip on this value is by observing an individual's response to market alternatives carrying with them different compensation packages as well as differing risks of premature demise.[23] Presumably, this should reveal the individual's preferences and, in so doing, the implicit value put on the person's own life. Even this picture is complicated by the fact that the individual may also indulge in leisure activities that carry significant risk yet yield no income. Indeed, many such activities, like climbing in the Himalayas or skin diving in the Bahamas, can be downright expensive. That the pleasures involved in such activities outweigh the expected costs in terms of hazards to life and limb seems plausible enough, and some have suggested that the hazard itself is the source of pleasure. In any event, those complications suggest that we might have trouble in getting a price measure or in finding situations where nothing changes but the reward and risk of death. They further hint that individuals may differ widely in their valuation, and for many we will simply never get an observation. Those who we observe moving into high-risk occupations for higher pay presumably place lower valuations on their lives *ceteris paribus* than those who do not, and their valuations tell us nothing about the valuations of the intramarginal risk avoider.

There is also occasional perverse behavior in this area of which the suicide rate is only one manifestation. Some individuals may indeed place low or negative values on their lives, but "a man who would risk his life unnecessarily (or throw it away) may be a fool. For a society to take a fool's valuation (either as an explicit or probabilistic expected value) as the correct one is ridiculous."[24]

In any event, the potential statistical base from which we could derive estimates is small and subject to a variety of biases. In some circumstances, it may not matter; it may only be necessary to evaluate external effects. As Mishan observes, we do not need internal valuations for the drivers of cars nor for voluntary passengers therein. Presumably the value of the transportation service being obtained was greater than its cost, including the risk to their own lives, and they were not coerced.[25] We do need the external value to their heirs, which we can get from formula 9.9.2. But if we go off the road on a curve and kill a farmer swinging in his hammock on his porch, we need the internal value of his life as well as its external value to his heirs. We could, of course, follow Mishan and invoke the *assumpsit* doctrine once again, arguing that he knew the curve was there yet chose to sling his hammock in line with it, presumably because the added comfort he got from having his feet in the sun and his head in the shade offset the known hazard. One may be willing to swallow a small camel; but should we leave his internal valuation out of consideration if he is hit, not by a passing car, but by an airplane engine falling from 40,000 feet or a piece of a disintegrating satellite? The line must be drawn somewhere. Each day there are people deprived of their lives as the consequence of other peoples' production or consumption activities who did not willingly assume any risks beyond those thrust on them as a consequence of birth. Their lives have not been voluntarily risked, presumably because the terms were not attractive enough, yet, they are being forcibly taken. Rather significantly higher valuations would seem to be appropriate in these circumstances.

Closely related to the issue of valuation of death is the issue of pain and suffering, which is rather deliberately overlooked by economists who seem to prefer to deal only with positive values on their utility scales. Most of us are less than indifferent to the manner of our going, although we may have little choice in the matter. We can think of more comfortable ways to go than being incinerated in 5,000 gallons of spilled gasoline from an overturned tanker truck or getting bone cancer from radon given off by a landfill site. It seems quite sensible that valuations reflect not only the forcible taking of life but also the manner of its taking, so that processes and projects inflicting death in particularly gruesome forms are penalized and discouraged thereby. Economists seem again to have leaned heavily on the legal precedent. Pain and suffering claims are excluded under the Fatal Accidents Act (United Kingdom) of 1846 and its various progeny throughout the common law world, for the excellent reason that the objective of the statute is to enable heirs to recover their losses. The pain and suffering was imposed on the decedent, not the heirs, and there is no particular reason, given the intent of the act, why they should be allowed a claim for it. A far different attitude is taken to pain and suffering damages in cases where the plaintiff is a surviving victim who did suffer them. They may be hard to assess, but that of itself is no reason why they should be excluded from consideration.

Preliminary work by one of the authors on Canadian data for 1975 suggests that as of 1975 workers could expose themselves to a 0.001 increase in the probability of accidental death on the job for an increase in annual earnings of $2,800. The data are crude, and so is the analysis at this stage, but it suggests that individuals placed an internal value on their own lives of $2.8 million. This is quite apart from any external value to their heirs, which would in the circumstances be largely taken care of by Workmen's Compensation. It should be emphasized that even this may be an underestimate. It reflects mainly the trade-offs expressed by a fraction of the labor force in relatively high-risk jobs. There is no basis on which to assume that mortal risk-taking is linear, as is implicitly assumed, and the available observations cover only the extreme lower left-end of the supply curve of such risk taking. The usual assumptions about diminishing marginal utility of money suggest that the supply curve is more likely to curve upward, like B in Figure 9–6, rather than downward, implying that further supplies of lives would be offered only at higher wages. If individuals value their lives this highly, should society value them less?

The value obtained above seems high in relation to values used in many benefit-cost studies. This is no particular problem, since most of the latter are based on variations of the Dublin-Lotka technique and are conceptually incomplete; they measure only the external values which

Figure 9–6
Alternative assumptions about the
supply of mortal risk-taking

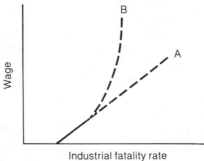

should be added to the internal value. It will no doubt be argued that the value is belied by individuals' behavior in their off-hours, as, for example, Canadians have managed to suffer nine times the number of fatal accidents on their own time than they did at work. Some of these are accidents in the home or en route to work and represent a situation of accidental death exposures which individuals must accept whether they accept more at work or not; the rest reflect voluntary exposure usually in recreational activities. Some may follow from acts of fools, as noted earlier, but not all can be so classified. The basic implication seems to be that the gross value of such activities before deducting the inevitably associated mortality costs is significantly higher than anyone believed.

In sum, the traditional Dublin-Lotka formula, while appropriate for the purposes of estimating the damages or determining insurable interests is conceptually flawed as a measure of the value of human life for benefit-cost analysis, since it measures only the external value of the individual to his heirs and overlooks the intrinsic internal value of the individual's life to the individual. This value can be estimated in terms of the compensation the individual requires to induce him to accept a higher level of risk as part of an employment package. However, such a measurement may be unrepresentative of individuals who do not choose risky occupations in spite of the differentials and incorporate no allowance for the forcible taking component of fatal injury risks not assumed voluntarily. It is probable that established values used in many studies are low by an order of magnitude.

9.10 Benefit distribution and social welfare functions

Completing a social valuation requires more than the identification and measurement of benefits and costs. It is necessary that the benefits accruing to and costs borne by different individuals and groups be traced to them, then appropriately weighted and balanced against one another in terms of a benefit-cost ratio or other suitable decision criterion. A rule which identifies the weights to be accorded to individuals' or groups' benefits and costs is referred to as a social welfare function.[26]

The specification of appropriate weights for the social welfare function is essentially a political process to which the professional economist can contribute little since it requires making interpersonal comparisons of utility which are usually regarded as ascientific.[27] While economic purists may shrink from making such comparisons, the capacity for making them is an essential part of the practicing politician's bag of tools. If the politician does not do so in a manner acceptable to the electorate, he is not apt to be elected.

Formally, social welfare functions are (weighted) sums of producers' and consumers' surpluses plus externalities. An allocation of resources which maximizes any social welfare function is said to be Pareto-optimal or simply efficient. Traditionally, welfare economics has concerned itself with defining conditions under which efficiency is realized. Much attention has been focused on the classical invisible hand model of perfect competition, which can be shown to generate an efficient solution in the absence of externalities. While this accomplishment is scarcely trivial, it does not get us very far, since there are an infinite multiplicity of Pareto-optimal states or competitive equilibria, each corresponding to a particular gross income distribution.

Out of the available multiplicity, economists have tended to single out that social welfare function in which all parties' benefits and costs are equally weighted as perhaps more equal than the rest. Strictly speaking, this is unjustified; the economist's judgment that everyone's benefits and costs should be considered equal is as unjustified as his judgment that they should not. The case for it involves an efficiency argument having a superficial resemblance to the legitimate efficiency arguments often used to define Pareto optimality. Consider states A, and B, which generate producers' and consumers' surpluses in the amounts indicated.

	A	B
Producers' surplus	100	10
Consumers' surplus	30	70

If the social welfare function assigns distributional weights of 0.1 to producers and 1 to consumers, the weighted sums for A and B are 40 and 71 respectively, and B should be chosen. However, we note that the unweighted aggregate benefits are larger under A than B, which suggests that it is possible to combine A with a tax-subsidy scheme which leaves both parties better of than they would be under B, as follows:

	Unweighted
Producers' surplus	100
Less tax	45
Producers' net	55
Consumers' surplus	30
Plus subsidy	45
	75

Because A provides this possibility and B does not it is tempting to infer that A is superior.[28] Clearly A plus the proposed redistribution is superior to B. But what the argument asks us to accept is that A is superior to B *whether or not* the redistribution takes place simply because it makes an appropriate redistribution possible.

This argument leaves us at somewhat of an impasse, although the consensus seems to be that no such inference is warranted unless the compensation payments are actually made.[29] Requiring compensation, however, imposes a unanimity rule with respect to social change and is seen by many as unduly favoring the status quo. While we can infer the superiority of A, providing compensation is paid, without express consideration of social welfare weights, this does not mean that it must be paid or that the status quo must be maintained nor even that A must be chosen. The choice depends on the political weights assigned to the affected parties. The most we can derive from compensation rules is the observation that we should always compute the equally weighted benefits and costs, as well as those weighted by the politically given social welfare function in order to be able to identify potentially preferable alternatives which might be rendered superior by appropriate redistribution.

In practice, distributional weights are used to compute adjusted benefit-cost ratios for decision-making purposes. Consider the project having the benefits and costs identified in Table 9–6. The unweighted benefit-cost ratio is 0.89, and the project is apparently undesirable in an unweighted context. However, suppose a vegetarian government attaches the welfare weights identified in Table 9–7 to the benefits and

Table 9–6
Unweighted estimates of benefits and costs

| | Present value of | |
Incidence	Benefits	Costs
Vegetarians	$100,000	$ 50,000
Pensioners	100,000	100,000
Trade unionists	500,000	300,000
Bankers	100,000	450,000
Unadjusted totals	$800,000	$900,000

Benefit-cost ratio 0.89

Table 9–7
Social welfare function weights

Incidence	Weight
Vegetarians	0.6
Pensioners	1.0
Trade unionists	1.5
Bankers	0.1

costs of the different groups. We can then compute an adjusted benefit-cost ratio of 1.48, which appears in Table 9–8. Given the social welfare function, the project appears desirable. However, if we note the unadjusted benefit-cost ratio of 0.89, we recognize that the acceptable benefit-cost ratio is produced solely by virtue of the wealth redistribution effected by the project. To get a clearer idea of this, look at the

Table 9–8
Adjusted benefit-cost estimates

| | | Weighted present value of | |
Incidence	Weights	Benefits	Costs
Vegetarians	0.6	$ 60,000	$ 30,000
Pensioners	1.0	100,000	100,000
Trade unionists	1.5	750,000	450,000
Bankers	0.1	10,000	45,000
		$920,000	$625,000

Adjusted Benefit-cost ratio 1.48

net benefits, group by group, which appear in Table 9–9. Reflecting the 0.89 benefit-cost ratio, the losses to bankers exceed the gains to vegetarians and trade unionists. While adopting the project has favorable redistributional consequences, one might prefer to juggle the tax system instead, taking only $300,000 away from the bankers, while passing $75,000 on to the vegetarians and $225,000 on to the trade unionists, thus leaving everyone better off.

Table 9–9
Incidence of net benefits

Vegetarians	$ 50,000
Pensioners	—
Trade unionists	200,000
Bankers	(350,000)

In general, when projects are justified only by their distributional impact, it will always be possible to propose a purely redistributional alternative which leaves everyone better off. While this is the case, many of the projects undertaken by any government appear to be justifiable, if at all, only on distributional grounds. This does not necessarily imply irrational behavior on the part of politicians. The explanation seems rather to be the belief that individual welfare is a function of the form in which income is received as well as its magnitude. Thus wages are intrinsically preferred to unemployment benefits, and the latter to welfare checks, even if the amounts are identical. To accommodate these preferences, governments are prone to create actuarially unsound unemployment insurance schemes that subsidize seasonally unemployed in the off-season and to spend money on job-creation programs which give the illusion of earnings, even if the marginal product of the labor supplied is well below the wage. Where such differential values are relevant to the recipients and taken into account in social decision making, it may not be possible to define a tax subsidy alternative which is preferable to a make-work project, even if the unweighted benefit-cost ratio of the latter is below 1.00.

Thus far we have considered the use of social welfare function weights, supposedly given, in a normative context for decision-making purposes. It is under certain assumptions possible to use the model in a positive context, assuming the government to have effectively maximized its social welfare function, working backwards to derive the implied weights. One such application found the following implicit weights:[30]

Low-income whites	−1.3
Other whites	2.2
Low-income blacks	9.3
Other blacks	−2.0

The assumptions in such an analysis are fairly heroic since the small sample of projects were drawn from a single program. It is by no means clear that the weights are an accurate reflection of the social welfare function of the administration in question, or even of the officials of the agency running the program. Nor, of course, is it clear that they are not. But decision makers who do not incorporate their own weights into their analyses run the risk of having weights which they would not have chosen consciously inferred from their choices.

Notes

[1] This assumes, among other things, that the marginal utility of money can be treated as a constant. For further complications, see M. Friedman, *Price Theory: A Provisional Text,* rev. ed. (Chicago: Aldine, 1962), chap. 4.

[2] See, for example, M. Clawson and J. L. Knetsch, *Economics of Outdoor Recreation* (Baltimore: Johns Hopkins University Press, 1966), pp. 217–18.

[3] We recognize the difficulties associated with the consumers' surplus concept and the ambiguities introduced by differing assumptions about starting points and the marginal utility of money. The interested reader may wish to consult J. R. Hicks, "The Four Consumer's Surpluses," *Review of Economic Studies* 11 (1943); E. J. Mishan, *Welfare Economics,* 2d ed. (New York: Random House, 1969), part 2; and E. J. Mishan, *Cost-Benefit Analysis* (London: Unwin, 1971). While we do not wish to deny the theoretical validity of these niceties, we suspect that in most practical contexts, measurement errors are large enough to dominate any error introduced due to conceptual imprecision.

[4] A partial exception exists in some instances when discriminating monopolists, for example, public utilities, capture part of the consumers' surplus in their revenues by price discrimination. In these cases, observed revenues include that portion of potential consumers' surplus which has been recaptured by the producer.

[5] Those interested may consult W. J. Baumol and W. G. Bowen, *Performing Arts: The Economic Dilemma* (New York: 20th Century Fund, 1966), for a perceptive and stimulating analysis of the problem.

[6] This does not mean that this approach was not tried, as anyone familiar with the history of fire insurance and fire services can attest.

[7] See for example, K. J. Arrow, "Political and Economic Evaluation of Social Effects and Externalities," in J. Margolis, ed., *The Analysis of Public Output* (New York: Columbia University Press, 1970), pp. 14–15. Exclusion was altogether ignored in P. A. Samuelson, "The Pure Theory of Public Expenditures," *Review of Economics and Statistics* 36 (1954), pp. 387–89.

[8] While we regard the facts cited by J. K. Galbraith in his famous "private opulence-public squalor" paradigm as understated, we expect that the overextension of govern-

ment services into ever-expanding domains since World War I has a lot to do with it. For Galbraith's explanation, see J. K. Galbraith, *The Affluent Society* (Boston: Houghton Mifflin, 1958).

[9] This treatment is arbitrary; we could as easily deduct positive externalities from the cost curve and add negative ones thereto. We prefer to perform the operation on the demand curve because of the valuation link. The opposite approach is often used. See, for example, J. Viner, "Cost Curves and Supply Curves," *Zeitschrift fur Nationalökonomie,* vol 3 (1931), pp. 23–46.

[10] But see A. C. Pigou, *Economics of Welfare,* 4th ed. (London: Macmillan & Co., 1932); W. J. Baumol, *Welfare Economics and the Theory of the State,* 2d ed. (Cambridge: Harvard University Press, 1965); J. H. Dales, *Pollution, Property and Prices* (Toronto: University of Toronto Press, 1968); E. J. Mishan, *Welfare Economics,* 2d ed. (New York: Random House, 1969) and the works cited therein; and K. J. Arrow and T. Scitovsky, *Readings in Welfare Economics* (Homewood: Richard D. Irwin, 1969).

[11] See R. H. Coase, "The Problem of Social Cost," *Journal of Law and Economics,* 3 (1960), pp. 1–44.

[12] Air pollution is now largely gone from Sudbury, having been sent hundreds of miles downwind by a tall smokestack.

[13] Coase, "Problem of Social Cost."

[14] R. E. Keeton and J. O'Connell, *Basic Protection for the Accident Victim* (Boston: Little, Brown, 1961).

[15] Actually, Oscar Wilde said it about cynics, not economists.

[16] *The Globe and Mail* (Toronto), Nov. 19, 1979, p. 11.

[17] B. Pascal, *Pensees* 194.

[18] G. D. Quirin and R. N. Wolff, "Economics of Oil Transportation in the Arctic," in L. M. Alexander and G. R. S. Hawkins, eds., *Canadian-U.S. Maritime Problems* (Kingston, R.I.: Law of the Sea Institute, 1972), pp. 32–46.

[19] W. J. Baumol and W. E. Oates, *Economics, Environmental Policy and the Quality of Life* (Englewood Cliffs, N.J.: Prentice-Hall, 1979), pp. 212–13.

[20] It should be noted that most mortality tables prepared for insurance purposes deliberately overstate the probability of dying at any given age to protect the solvency of the insurer and also to protect against epidemics and similar aberrations in normal mortality rates. Similarly, mortality tables prepared for annuity purposes typically overstate the probability of surviving for analogous reasons. For our purposes, we want neither bias, so there may be a need for a specially constructed table. For some of the issues, see for example, W. O. Menge and C. H. Fischer, *The Mathematics of Life Insurance* (New York: Macmillan, 1965), chap. 1.

[21] L. I. Dublin and A. J. Lotka, *The Money Value of a Man,* rev. ed. (New York: Ronald, 1946).

[22] See also J. H. Donaldson, *Casualty Claim Practice* (Homewood: Richard D. Irwin, 1964), Chapter 20.

[23] E. J. Mishan, "Evaluation of Life and Limb: A Theoretical Approach," *Journal of Political Economy* 79 (1971), pp. 687–705; and T. C. Schelling, "The Life You Save May Be Your Own," in S. B. Chase, Jr., ed., *Problems in Public Expenditure Analysis* (Washington, D.C.: Brookings Institute, 1968), pp. 127 ff.

[24] G. Fromm, "Comments," in Chase, *Problems in Public Expenditure Analysis,* p. 167.

[25] Mishan, "Evaluation of Life and Limb."

[26] This conforms to the sense in which the term is used by Bergson. See A. Bergson, "A Reformulation of Certain Aspects of Welfare Economics," *Quarterly Journal of Economics* 52 (1938), pp. 310–34. Arrow uses the term to define a decision rule for determining the weighting rather than for the weights themselves. See also K. J. Arrow, *Social Choice and Individual Values* (New York: Wiley, 1951); J. Blau, "The Existence of Social Welfare Functions," *Econometrica* 25 (1957), pp. 302–13; and I.

Rothenberg, *The Measurement of Social Welfare* (Englewood Cliffs, N.J.: Prentice-Hall, 1961), 3–5.

[27] L. Robbins, *An Essay on the Nature and Significance of Economic Science* (London: Macmillan & Co. 1935).

[28] N. Kaldor, "Welfare Propositions of Economics and Interpersonal Comparisons of Utility," *Economic Journal* 49 (1939), pp. 549–52; J. R. Hicks, "Foundations of Welfare Economics," *Economic Journal,* 49 (1959), pp. 696ff., and T. Scitovsky, "A Note on Welfare Propositions in Economics," *Review of Economic Studies* 9 (1941), 77–88.

[29] See also W. J. Baumol, *Welfare Economics and the Theory of the State,* 2d ed. (London: Bell, 1965), pp. 163 ff., especially p. 165, n. 1.

[30] B. A. Weisbrod, "Income Redistribution Effects and Benefit Cost Analysis," in Chase, *Problems in Public Expenditure Analysis,* p. 200.

Problems

1. The Economic Planning Department of Sarkhan is considering a proposal to build an 80-mile road from a provincial capital to a village which has hitherto only been accessible by river boat. The road will cost $2.4 million, and annual maintenance charges will be approximately $100,000. The estimated cost of capital is 10 percent. The analysis suggests that the following effects are likely to result from completion of the road:

    a. A saving of $50,000 per year on the cost of shipping agricultural produce from the village and its surrounding area.

    b. The opening up to development of an additional 50,000 acres of land. Development will cost $300 per acre, and produce, after five years, crops worth $100 per acre per year. The land will be settled by smallholders, who will move from other employment where their earnings average $150 per year. An estimated 8,000 smallholdings will be provided. Land clearing and drainage costs will be borne by the government, and each settler will receive a grant of $500 to assist in meeting relocation costs. Prior to the time the main crop becomes established, catch crops yielding $20 per acre per year can be grown.

    c. The value of land on the present developed agricultural areas is expected to increase by $500,000, while the land in the new development will be worth $38 million, an increase of $30 million from its value as timber land.

    d. Tax revenue from the area will be increased by $100,000 per year.

    e. Value of timber output will be increased by $2 million in the first year, while land is being cleared, but will be reduced by $400,000 per year after clearing has taken place.

    f. The income of boat operators on the river will be reduced by $50,000 per year. Boats costing $300,000 and scheduled for replacement in five years will not be replaced, and the labor displaced will be absorbed elsewhere at equivalent wages.

    Which of the effects listed above should be taken into account in the benefit cost analysis? Should the road be built?

2. The head of the Ruritanian Trade Commission Service, who is responsible for the commercial attachés in Ruritania's diplomatic and consular posts abroad, has asked the Ruritanian budget bureau for authority to hire another 20 attachés at an annual cost of 50,000 dinars each. These would be assigned to posts where annual exports are at least 500,000 dinars. The justification advanced is that the new representatives should easily pay for themselves since experience has shown that existing attachés increase trade in these localities by 10 percent within three years. The finance minister wants to restrict the appointments to posts taking exports of 1 million dinars annually, noting that exports have grown by 5 percent over the past three years even in localities where no representation exists.

    What do you recommend?

3. What variables would you take into account in an analysis of the desirability of expanding the state college system in your state?

4. In the province of Ontario, Canada, medical care is financed by Ontario Hospital Insurance Corp. (OHIP), a government agency which is in turn financed by premiums and general provincial revenues. It reimburses doctors and hospitals for services provided subscribers on a fee-for-service basis. In an effort to control costs, it has restricted payment to hospital services provided in approved facilities, meaning generally those in existence at the time OHIP was established or added with OHIP approval since that date.

    Wellesley Hospital in Toronto asked for permission to acquire a CAT scanner, an expensive piece of electronic diagnostic equipment, for its radiology department two years ago. OHIP refused to approve the acquisition, citing its policy of concentrating scanner facilities in other centers in the city. The hospital's directors purchased the scanner anyway, using funds donated by a private donor. It is now sitting idle because OHIP will not pay for diagnostic services performed with a nonapproved unit and the hospital has no other source of funds for operating costs. OHIP claims there is no need for the facility, citing ability of the present system to provide emergency scans within 24 hours, with an average lag of four to five days for routine cases. Some doctors on the Wellesley staff dispute these figures, citing cases where patients waited as long as three weeks for diagnosis.

    You have been asked by a friend who is on the hospital board to prepare a brief to be submitted to OHIP's political masters making a case for overruling OHIP's decision regarding payment for service provided by the scanner. Outline your argument and indicate your data requirements.

Analysis under changing price levels

10.1 Introduction

Changing price levels and depreciating currencies are endemic in the present-day world. There are differences in degree, but not in kind, between countries like the United States and West Germany, where inflation rates have for the most part been held to single-digit levels, and countries where typical inflation rates are 30 to 50 percent per year or even more. The existence of inflation means that dollars (or pounds or pesos) which will be received at some future date differ from dollars on hand today, not only in the timing of their availability, but in their purchasing power. This poses a particular problem for the capital-expenditure decision maker, for the process he is controlling, stripped of its nonfinancial features, involves nothing more than the exchange of present dollars for dollars to be received in the future, while the financing of such expenditures often involves the same type of transaction in reverse, that is, obtaining present dollars in exchange for claims to payment in future dollars. Given that the present/future purchasing power differential is an inescapable facet of all such decisions, it may seem strange that we have been able to carry our analysis to this point without explicit consideration of this problem. Our doing so was deliberate, and, for reasons we shall indicate. However, at this point it seems desirable to examine the implications of inflation more closely.

The analysis of projects in an inflationary setting is complicated not only by the existence of differences in purchasing power and uncertainty as to the rate at which they will occur, but because governments may decide to intervene at various points in the markets for goods and services in order to combat inflation. Even if inflation itself is not a politically created risk, it magnifies the political risks to which capital-expenditure projects are exposed. A further problem is that rates of inflation often differ widely among different countries and create or contribute to fluctuations in exchange rates between the currencies. This creates obvious problems for multi-national companies, but it also creates problems for stay-at-homes who are significantly involved in export or import markets or who borrow from or lend to residents of other currency areas, even in the normal course of extending trade credit. These international ramifications of different inflation rates introduce a further complication into the problem, which will be examined at a later point in this chapter. For the moment, however, let us restrict our analysis to the case of an investor operating within a single ·currency area.

10.2 Some basic considerations

A dollar buried in the backyard in 1945 and dug up today is still a dollar. It says so on both sides. It is legal tender and is equivalent, in terms of its ability to discharge a debt, to a dollar printed last week. It is a unit of account; if we debited the glass jar with a dollar on the date of burial, we could credit it with a dollar today and close out the account. In these senses, at least, a dollar is a dollar and is the same as it always was.

Yet, in other respects it is not. In 1945, the dollar would have bought a haircut, with enough change left over to tip the barber. Or it would have bought a tie for Uncle Charlie's birthday. A respectable middle-class home in many North American cities could have been bought with 6,000 of them. Today it will not buy these things. A haircut costs $6.00 or more—a bargain considering more hair is removed in the process. Uncle Charlie's tie costs $17.50, and the house costs somewhere between $40,000 and $100,000. The dollar of today is clearly something which is really quite different from the dollar of 1945, even if it is the same piece of paper. What has changed, of course, is its purchasing power.

For purposes of our analysis, it will be necessary to distinguish between dollars which are equivalent in the legal tender or unit-of-account sense and those which are equivalent in the purchasing power sense. We will follow what has become more or less established practice in calling the former "nominal" dollars and the latter "real" dollars.[1] The problem is posed by the fact that virtually all transactions, barter excepted, take place in nominal dollars, and that we can neither obtain real dollars nor claims denominated therein.[2] Real dollars are an economists' fiction. It is, however, with the real consequences of decisions that we are concerned, and decisions should be structured so as to select from among alternatives those which are most favorable in terms of real consequences.

Nominal dollars received (or paid) at one point in time can be compared with those received at another by conceptual conversion to a real basis, that is, by deflating them by an appropriate purchasing power index, to convert into dollars of equivalent purchasing power. Real dollar computations should be dated to indicate to which base period they refer. Any base period may be used, and series based on different base periods may be converted to a common base by splicing or linking the indexes. For analytical purposes, it is convenient to use either a recent year or the current year as a base for calculations. Few people are that interested in converting present-day figures to 1887 purchasing power equivalents. It should be noted that the real dollars calculated by using index numbers are, at best, approximations, since most index numbers are computed from sample data and have a variety of defects.[3]

Choosing an index number poses further problems. A dollar may be real to one individual and not to another if the costs of buying the bundle of goods and services preferred by the latter has risen more than that of the bundle normally purchased by the former. In general, it is preferable to use a broadly based index of the general price level, such as the Implicit Price Deflator of the National Income Accounts or the Consumer Price Index. The former is a weighted index of price changes of all components of gross national product, while the latter seeks to measure changes in the price of a representative sample of consumer goods used by low to middle income urban families. Neither may be strictly appropriate, but the cost of constructing a special index may be prohibitive. Since it is the investors' real income or purchasing power that we seek to preserve or enhance, there is a slight advantage in choosing an index of consumer goods' prices such as the CPI, even if it is not wholly representative of investors' spending habits. If, however, we are making decisions on behalf of a wine fanatic, we may wish to construct a special index in which the price of Chateau Latour is given a predominant weight. One course which should not be followed for this purpose is to use an index of product prices or plant replacement costs related to the industry in which the decision maker is operating. It is purchasing power in general available to investors which is relevant and not purchasing power in terms of locomotives, zinc bars, or dressed pork.

The general unsuitability of the replacement-cost criterion may be shown considering a decision to sell a barrel of crude oil now for $28 nominal or to hold it for a year, at which time it is expected to sell for $35 nominal after deducting storage costs. Use of a replacement-cost index would leave the decision maker indifferent between these choices. If the general price level is only expected to increase by 10 percent, the investor would clearly be better off to hold the oil for sale at the higher price. The use of a general price index will lead to a correct decision, while the use of a replacement-cost index will not. This is true not only in the private context of the individual decision maker but in a social context as well since relative changes in real prices have an important role to play in allocating consumption between time periods.

As we noted earlier, nominal dollars are the basic unit of account used in the economy. In recent years, the accounting profession has devoted considerable attention to the attempt to develop accounting systems which generate financial statements in real (rather than nominal) dollar terms. Several proposals for reform in this direction have been advanced by individual accountants, by the Financial Accounting Standards Board and the Securities Exchange Commission in the United States, by the Canadian Institute of Chartered Accountants, and by the Sandilands Committee in the United Kingdom.[4] A great deal of discussion has resulted, but there has been no agreement on generally accepted principles for generating real-dollar accounts. Many of these proposals involve the use of specific replacement-cost indexes for certain purposes. There are some valid reasons for using replacement costs in an accounting system which must serve a multiplicity of purposes. We do not believe, however, that they extend into the domain of capital-expenditure analysis, where the ability to convert projected cash inflows and outflows into a common real-dollar basis is required.

10.3 Costs of capital in inflationary periods

One basis for evaluation of capital-expenditure projects in an inflationary context is to forecast cash flows in real, rather than nominal dollars, and to proceed with the analysis of net present value (NPV) as if nothing else had changed. Doing so, however, involves the implicit assumption that the cost of capital to be used in making the NPV calculations is itself unchanged as a result of the inflationary expectations. If, in fact, it has been changed and incorporates an allowance for inflation, such a procedure involves doublecounting—taking out the effects of inflation twice—and can easily lead to incorrect decisions, unless, of course, the inflation rate turns out to be much higher than had been forecast.

Just what, if anything, by way of inflation adjustment is contained in cost-of-capital estimates and the market yields from which they are derived? The question of how market yields respond to anticipated price change was intensively examined by Irving Fisher as long ago as 1930, and his discussion will repay reading even today.[5] Fisher examined interest rate series and price changes in the United States and Britain as far back as 1820 and concluded that observed or nominal interest rates in fact incorporated an allowance for price-level changes expected prior to the maturity date. While his statistical work was primitive by modern standards, the theoretical rationale he proposed retains its validity.

Consider an investor who is contemplating purchase of a bond with an 8 percent coupon maturing in one year. Suppose the investor requires an 8 percent *real* return and anticipates a 10 percent increase in the price level over the year his funds will remain invested. While he will receive $108.00 (nominal) in one year's time, this will only be worth $108.00/1.10 = $98.18 in real present-day dollars. If his required real return is 8 percent, he will discount this further to $98.18/1.08 = $90.91, at which point it will yield 18.8 percent in nominal terms. In general, the nominal yield k_n on a one-year instrument will be given by:

$$(1 + k_n) = (1 + k_r)(1 + i) \qquad (10.3.1)$$

where k_r is the required real return, and i is the anticipated inflation rate.

Of course, the actual price change will be dependent in practice on the bids of other investors, who will incorporate therein their own estimates of the rate of inflation, their own required rate of return, and by the terms offered by borrowers, who will be willing to offer more in nominal terms because they anticipate shrinkage in the purchasing power which they will give up on repayment. If, however, there is no basic change in the real factors underlying the supply and demand for loanable funds, we may expect expected inflation to produce an upward shift in both the supply and demand schedules such that the required real rate is unchanged, as shown in Figure 10–1.

Figure 10–1
Inflation-induced shifts in nominal supply and demand

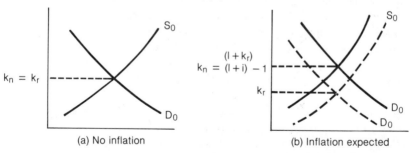

(a) No inflation   (b) Inflation expected

Because of individual differences in the rate at which inflation is expected to occur, the nominal yield will incorporate an allowance for inflation which is a consensus forecast. Investors who anticipate a high rate of inflation may only be able to participate and to place funds at their disposal if they are prepared to accept an expected real rate which is below that of other participants, while those who anticipate little or no inflation will be able to invest at expected real rates which are higher than they would ordinarily require. Expectations, of course, whether they are those of the extreme individual cases or those of the consensus, may be unfulfilled as the realized inflation rate may turn out to be something quite different.

This picture is further complicated by the fact that there may be market participants who are indifferent to real returns. Some financial intermediaries, whose liabilities are fixed in nominal dollar terms, may be quite content to invest funds available for whatever they will bring. However, the terms on which they do so will be influenced by the willingness of borrowers to offer higher nominal rates, and by the fact that if they are unable to increase the yields promised to their depositors, they will tend to lose deposits. Intermediaries with locked-in depositors, for example, certain types of trustees, life insurance companies, and the like, may be quite slow to respond, but even these should be responsive in the long run.

It is also possible that a certain fraction of participants in the market at any point in time may be suffering from *money illusion,* an irrational belief in the stability of the dollar. This term was coined to describe the behavior of workers in a situation of excess labor supply who, J. M. Keynes claimed, would not accept a cut in money (nominal) wages intended to reduce unemployment, but who were prepared to accept a cut in real wages brought about by increasing the price level with the money wage held constant.[6] The historical episodes consistent with this theory led Keynes to propose manipulation of real wages via increases in the price level as a remedy for unemployment. Recent experience, however, offers few grounds for believing in the widespread prevalence of money illusion in either the labor or capital markets. Workers, like lenders, must generally make contracts in nominal dollar terms, but there is little reason to suppose that those terms are not influenced by expectations regarding future price levels. (More than a few of these now include specific clauses relating to inflation.)

There are thus theoretical grounds for believing that on one-period instruments observed yields reflect not only the one-period real cost of money but also the anticipated inflation over that period. As we move to longer-term instruments, the analysis becomes somewhat more complex, but the conclusions are the same. Two-year instruments must sell at a yield which is competitive with the option of investing in two successive one-year instruments. The nominal yield on a two-year bond must, therefore, be a composite reflecting the current nominal yield on a one-year bond, the expected or forward nominal yield on one-year bonds a year hence, and a risk premium arising out of the risk that the attainable yield in the second year will not be the same as that which is now forecast. Thus we have:

$$(1 + {}^2k_{n1})^2 = (1 + R_2)(1 + k_{n1})(1 + {}_1k_{n2}) \qquad (10.3.2)$$

where

$^2k_{n1}$ is the two-year nominal yield in period 1.

k_{n1} is the one-year nominal yield in period 1.

$_1k_{n2}$ is the one-year nominal yield in period 2 expected as at the beginning of period 1.

R_2 is the risk premium associated with a two-year instrument.

But equation 10.3.2, which is simply the usual formula for relating current and expected nominal short-term rates to current long-term rates, used in explaining the term structure of interest rates,[7] may be decomposed into:

$$(1 + {}^2k_{r1})^2(1 + {}_2I)^2 = (1 + R_2)(1 + k_{r1})(1 + i_1)(1 + {}_1k_{r2})(1 + {}_1i_2)$$

in which

$\qquad (10.3.3)$

$_2I$ is the annual inflation expectation component of the two-year nominal rate.

i_1 is the anticipated inflation rate in year 1.

$_1i_2$ is the inflation rate in year 2 as anticipated at the beginning of year 1.

and $^2k_{r1}$, k_{r1}, and $_1k_{r2}$ are the long, short, and real rates respectively.

The risk premium, $(1 + R_2)$, also has two components, reflecting risk surrounding the future real rate, and the anticipated inflation rate, respectively. We may factor out the real component of 10.3.3 and get:

$$(1 + {}_2I)^2 = (1 + R_{i2})(1 + i_1)(1 + {}_1i_2) \qquad (10.3.4)$$

which expresses the inflation expectation component of the current long rate as a risk-adjusted function of anticipated inflation rates in the current and future periods. More specifically, $(1 + {}_2I)$ is the (risk adjusted) geometric mean of the future $(1 + i)$s. (R_{i2} is the portion of the risk premium accounted for by uncertainty as to the inflation rate.)

This analysis may be repeated for the three-period, four-period, and so on cases. We can thus regard the present term structure of interest rates as reflecting future nominal rates or as a product of future real rates and future inflation rates, with appropriate risk premiums attached to each.

In theory at least then, we can regard current yields (but not embedded costs) of debt instruments as reflecting an allowance for future inflation appropriate to the term to maturity, and a risk premium reflecting uncertainty about future inflation rates.

Or at least it should do so, if borrowers and lenders are free of money illusion. Direct tests of the proposition are impossible because anticipated inflation rates are unobservable. A number of studies have tested the joint hypotheses that (a) nominal rates reflect inflation rates and (b) expectations regarding future inflation rates are formed as a consequence of experienced inflation in some manner.

Several of these studies have found evidence in support of the joint hypotheses.[8] Others have not, but employed models of the expectation generating process which were naive and something less than compelling.[9] This seems to suggest that hypothesis a probably holds, but that expectations are generated by a complex process in which past experience of inflation does not enter in a simple manner and is not the only factor. It may also be influenced, for example, by publicity (or lack of it) about changes in the money supply, wage settlements, balance-of-payments developments, tax changes, and a myriad of such factors.

Nearly all of the empirical evidence thus far examined relates to the bond market. This has been primarily because at least some of the variables in the fixed obligation case remain constant, simplifying the analysis of what is a very complex relationship. But it means that we have very little formal evidence to rely on with respect to the response of equity costs in the face of inflationary expectations. However, there is no reason to suppose that they do not so respond. It is our view that the experience of North American stock markets since 1968 can only be explained on the premise that they do.

This does not imply that stock prices behave similarly to bond prices in the face of revised inflationary expectations. If the latter are revised upward, a more rapid rate of inflation is expected, bond prices will drop, reflecting the impact of higher required nominal yields on the fixed interest payments and fixed repayment of principal called for by the bond contract. Higher rates of inflation will generally increase nominal earnings, at least as calculated using historical cost accounting, and may even increase them more rapidly than the rate of inflation because depreciation allowances and similar expenses are fixed in nominal dollars while revenue and current operating expenses are rising. Not all of those profits are available for payment as dividends because of the need to replace inventories at higher costs (particularly if Fifo accounting is used for inventories) and because of the inadequacy of depreciation allowances for replacement. (Note that corporate income taxes do not distinguish between nominal and real dollars either, except when indexed so to the extent the real costs are understated, nominal income overstates real income, and there is a transfer of capital from the firm to government.[10] Even if dividends have to be cut temporarily, their growth rate will be increased to the point that prices may be maintained or will even rise despite the increase in required nominal yields.

It is the possibility that they will rise and at a rate at least as great as the rate of inflation that was at the root of the belief, perhaps too widely held during the 1950s and 1960s, that common stock provided a hedge against inflation. The failure of stock prices to perform in the predicted manner during the late 1960s and early 1970s should not obscure the fact that the fundamental reasoning underlying the belief was correct, as far as it went. Nor would such behavior indicate that required equity yields did not respond to inflationary expectations. Investors, however, are not the only individuals who respond. Other elements of society respond through their elected representatives. It has long been recognized that regulated utilities' stocks were an exception and could not be counted on as an inflation hedge, not only because of regulatory lags, but because original cost regulation, which is the rule in most jurisdictions, seeks merely to keep market values in excess of book values. However, partial price freezes and profit margin controls, such as those imposed in the United States during Phase II and in Canada by the Anti-Inflation Board from 1974–77, transform a large part of the corporate population into quasi-utilities. They prevent the expansion of profit margins which would normally take place. Dividends must be restricted because of replacement requirements, and there is no offsetting increase in growth rates. In such an environment, the increase in nominal yield requirements which results from increased inflation can only be accommodated by a drop in stock prices. Such drops were duly provided when the nature of the political response to inflation became clear.[11] (Note that many pension funds suffered a substantial loss in capital value during the adjustment period.)

In practical terms, we believe the indirect evidence for the adjustment of nominal equity costs to expected inflation rates is indisputable. However, it should be noted that while nominal interest rates on 3-month treasury bills contain an implicit forecast of inflation over the next 3 months, 1-year bond yields on 20-year bonds contain of price changes for the next year, and yields on 20-year bonds contain an embedded forecast of inflation over the next 20 years, those on common stocks (and those on perpetual bonds, such as Canadian Pacific's 4 percent Consolidated Debenture Stock) embody a forecast of inflation *ad infinitum*, not only to doomsday, but well into the hereafter. We should not be surprised if such forecasts, even if unbiased, were virtually worthless.

Indeed the forecasting record of the implicit forecast of price changes contained in the security yields even on a 3-month forward basis is little short of deplorable and almost as bad as that of economic forecasts generally. While bond yields may contain an implicit price level forecast, bond investors appear systematically to have under-estimated inflation rates as a matter of course in the postwar period.

Because observed costs of capital in the market are expressed in nominal terms and differ from real costs of capital by the inclusion of an implicit inflation forecast, they should not be used to evaluate projects where cash flow forecasts are expressed in real dollars. To do so would, in effect, remove anticipated inflation twice. While such an approach has an obvious conservative bias, its magnitude may differ from one project to another, because of the differences in the timing of outlays and receipts. To avoid bias, it is possible to make analyses on either of two bases, both of which are internally consistent: (a) by evaluating cash flows expressed in real dollars, using an estimate of the real cost of capital; and (b) by evaluating projected nominal-dollar cash flows using observed costs of capital.

Both methods are pure in the sense that they compare apples with apples; they may, however, not always be equivalent, even under ideal conditions. They are equivalent if inflation is expected to proceed at a constant annual rate i in which case the real dollar equivalent of a cash flow C_t due in period t is given by:

$$R_t = C_t(1 + i)^{-t}$$

and its present value at the real rate k_r by:

$$V_t = \frac{C_t(1 + i)^{-t}}{(1 + k_r)^t} = \frac{C_t}{(1 + i)^t(1 + k_r)^t}$$

If the nominal rate k_n is given by:

$$k_n = (1 + i)(1 + k_r) - 1$$

then the nominal dollar-nominal rate version is equivalent, since:

$$V_t = \frac{C_t}{(1 + k_n)^t} = \frac{C_t}{(1 + i)^t(1 + k_r)^t}$$

However, k_n embodies expectations about expected future price changes which may not be uniform, but which are expressed in a single discount rate, along with a further risk premium that arises because of the possibility of surprises in the future inflation rate. Ordinarily, we suspect, use of the nominal rate will be equivalent to attaching a growing inflation risk premium to more distant receipts, just as, in the constant price level case, the use of a risk-adjusted discount rate attaches a greater implicit risk discount to future receipts than does the use of the risk-free rate, which we will discuss in Chapter 12.

However, to attempt to choose (a) or (b) on the basis of the purity of assumptions or their correspondence to reality is to quibble. In almost any economically meaningful situation, the imprecision attached to other forecast variables will be sufficiently great to dwarf any differences due to implicit assumptions about the timing of anticipated inflation which may be made by a decision to use k_n.

Nor are there major differences in data requirements between the two approaches. Both require forecasts of the individual prices of inputs and outputs to be used in determining future cash flows. If k_n is used, these will be forecasts of absolute prices, and if k_r, of relative prices. To arrive at the forecasts of absolute prices, if using k_n, will probably require a forecast of the general price level. If using k_r, on the other hand, the observed k_n must be purged of its implicit forecast of the general price level. It is perhaps harder to make satisfactory forecasts of the general price level beyond the next two or three years than it is to predict relative price changes or to dissect k_n into its component parts. On the grounds of practical information requirements, it is perhaps a little easier to work in real dollar terms.

This advantage is, of course, lost if an attempt is made to incorporate the analyst's own forecast of general price levels into the analysis, for example, by projecting nominal prices and deflating. Doing so, or working in nominal terms with a forecast of general prices differing from that implicit in k_n amounts to pitting the analyst's forecast of future prices against the consensus forecast. This is tempting, since the latter is none too good, and since the rewards for correctly anticipating a generally unexpected price change can be handsome indeed. It is a procedure, however, which involves taking investment decisions not only on the basis of their apparent commercial attractiveness in an uncertain economic climate, but on projected price level changes which are not generally anticipated. It is thus inherently speculative in character and will lead to the taking of decisions which cannot be justified in economic terms unless the unique price level expectations of the decision maker are justified by events. As there is no reason to believe individuals' forecasts of general price level changes are better than the consensus, decision making on such a basis is hard to justify. If an individual is determined to pit his price forecasts against those of the majority, futures trading on the commodity or foreign exchange markets will generally give him more scope for his talents, offer greater leverage, and faster action.

10.4   Analysis of projects in real terms

Analysis in real terms involves the forecasting of future cash flows expressed in real dollars, usually those of the current period, and their evaluation using the real cost of capital. For small projects, it may be sufficient to simply use current prices for output and purchased inputs in order to derive estimates of real income. Such an approach, in effect, assumes that changes in relative prices will be minor and in opposite directions, so that over a group of projects, the errors in the relative price forecasts will average out. For larger-scale projects, particularly where there is any reason to believe that price movements for the product or any of the purchased inputs will differ from that of the price level in general, such an approach is insufficient. Since wages are such an input, it will ordinarily be desirable to take account of anticipated future real wage changes as a minimum in any such analysis. Real wages have risen fairly consistently over the period for which data are available, reflecting increases in labor productivity. These, in turn, reflect changes in technology, higher capital-labor ratios, learning phenomena, and a variety of other factors. Since most capital expenditures commit to a particular capital-labor ratio and at least partially freeze technology into the state of the art at the time the investment is made, the increases in productivity which affect wage increases at the national level are not fully operative at the individual project level. The real unit cost of labor may thus, in general, be expected to rise throughout the project's life. Some productivity gains may come out of the learning process, but these will ordinarily be all that can be counted on. There have been similar changes in the real prices of some raw materials and other inputs of which the energy price increases of the 1970s are merely the most conspicuous. Where these are important, it will be desirable to make a relative price forecast. Such forecasts are discussed in Section 10.7.

The other requirement in performing an analysis in real terms is to convert nominal costs of capital to a real-cost basis. Conceptually, this is easily done, by computing

$$k_r = \frac{(1 + k_n)}{(1 + i)} - 1$$

or, more roughly, by subtracting i, the expected inflation rate, from k_n the nominal cost of capital. But conceptual ease does not imply ease in practice.

There are at least two approaches. One is to attempt to model the expectations-generating process, identify the variables that appear to be influencing expectations, measure their relationships, and then to generate an estimate of current expectations by using appropriate observed values of the independent variables. This is perhaps the most intellectually satisfying approach to the problem, as well as the most complex and demanding. It is subject to the basic difficulty common to all analyses of expectational variables, namely, that expectations can seldom be measured explicitly, but it must be inferred from the behavior of the variables they are presumed to influence. There is a further complication which arises in the case of price-level expectations.

A number of models which seek or purport to explain price-level expectations (as opposed to price-level movements) have appeared in the literature. These are basically of two types, autoregressive and multivariate. *Autoregressive models* seek to explain expected future changes in a variable using the variable's own past values. The rationale underlying such an approach is that expectations, at least in part, grow out of experience. Recent changes may be expected to persist and may be extrapolated into the future, or future values may be expected to regress toward a historically established normal range. A variety of smoothing devices and lag structures may be employed to express such relationships.[12] So-called adaptive forecasting models based on such techniques have been used with a degree of success in forecasting many economic variables at least in the near term. They have been less successful in other cases. Here, however, the question is not whether they do a good job of forecasting the variables to which they are applied, but whether they produce forecasts which are a satisfactory surrogate for market participants' beliefs about the future.

In the present context, past price changes may be used to generate forecasts of future price changes which are then used to explain changes in nominal interest rates. The search is not for an autoregressive model that can predict future price-level changes, but for one which can explain contemporaneous changes in interest rates. A model that performs well in this capacity may do badly in the other. The test is, inevitably, of the joint hypothesis, (*a*) price-level expectations influence interest rates and (*b*) price-level expectations are generated by a mechanism approximated by the autoregressive model. Failure may result if either (*a*) or (*b*) is not satisfied. Some tests of the joint hypothesis have failed, and others using different expectations generating models have achieved sufficient success to suggest some empirical support for part (*a*). However, a wide range of choices remains with respect to the models used to generate measures of expectations, and there do not appear, at present, decisive reasons for choosing one or another of the contenders.

Multivariate models proceed, in this context, on the equally plausible hypothesis that price-level expectations are influenced by other factors besides past price-level changes. Such other factors may include wage rates and monetary variables. Such models may also, of course, incorporate lagged values of the price level in an autoregressive component. Again, such models have achieved some success in explaining interest rate changes. The problem, in this case, is that changes in the nominal interest rate may come about either because the underlying real rate has changed or because price-level expectations have changed. Some of the variables, such as money supply which enter into successful multivariate models, may influence both. To the extent that they do, it is difficult to use the model to estimate the implicit allowance for inflation in the nominal rate. It is, of course, possible to resolve the dilemma simply by assuming that the underlying real rate is a constant.[13] But there is little reason to believe that it should be, or that it is, although it may tend to an equilibrium value related to the real growth rate of the economy.

The use of formal models for estimating the inflation-expectation component of nominal interest rates is suspect for another reason as well. They implicitly assume an unchanging structure in the relationships which generate inflation expectations. Such unchanging relationships may or may not exist. Over the past century, students of the business cycle and of the inflationary process have stressed the psychological factor in the inflationary process. These explanations suggest that at some point an *inflation psychosis* develops, beyond which point the expectations-generating process shifts gears, creating enhanced inflationary expectations out of essentially unchanged facts. This hypothesis remains untested at least by contemporary standards of testing, but some such shift in expectations appears to be highly plausible in respect of such well-documented historical episodes as the Mississippi Bubble, the Tulip Mania in 17th-century Holland, the South Sea Bubble, the stock market boom of 1926–29, the Florida land boom of the 20s, and others.[14] Just how great a role it has played in less-publicized inflationary situations is far from clear. If this is significant, structural equations derived from experience during periods when it was largely or wholly absent may seriously underestimate the inflation expectations component in a period when it is operative, and vice versa.

A pragmatic alternative to the use of formal models is to select an historical period when cyclical conditions were comparable to the period being examined, when prices were relatively stable and inflationary expectations nonexistent or balanced by fears of deflation, and when other factors that may have influenced interest rates were of minor importance. In such a base period, discrepancies between nominal and real interest rates may be presumed to be insignificant. Differences in yields between the present period may, with appropriate modification, be attributed to changes in inflationary expectations. This approach does not assume that real interest rates are invariant over time, but it does assume that comparable real rates will prevail at comparable stages of the business cycle.

Influences due to changing levels of default risk can be eliminated by confining the analysis to senior government issues (which are presumably free of default risk). Observed differences in yields from those prevailing in the base period are attributable primarily to differences in inflation expectations.

Because of the differences in tax treatment of interest and capital gains, deep discount bonds should, if possible, be avoided. Their yields may underestimate the implicit inflation forecast because of the favorable tax treatment resulting from the discount. Similar considerations, of course, apply in determining differentials on equity issues, whether preferred or common.[15]

For an example, consider the problem of finding the real cost of common equity for Canadian Pacific Limited as of 1974. The nominal cost has been estimated at 17.5 percent, with the following components

$$D/P = 7.50 \text{ percent}$$
$$g = 10.00 \text{ percent}$$

Looking for a comparable period free of significant inflationary influences leads us back to 1956. In June 1956, Government of Canada bonds with maturities ten years and over, sold to yield 4.29 percent, on average. Corresponding issues in 1974 sold at an average yield of 9.63 percent. The difference of 5.34 percent represents the correction in yields made to adjust for the effects of inflation. As a first approximation, 12.16 percent (17.50 − 5.34) is an estimate of the required real cost.

Several assumptions can be made in this estimation procedure. It must be emphasized that the results are critically contingent thereon. In particular, the assumption that the dividend-growth split remains unchanged should be treated with some caution, and it might well be improved by an analysis of the effects of inflation on the D/P and g components in the particular company under study. Because of these assumptions, any estimate of the real cost of capital must be treated as subject to significantly larger margins of error than the nominal cost estimate from which it is derived.

A final approach which is sometimes used is simply to take the current nominal cost and deduct either the current inflation rate or the analyst's own forecast of inflation with or without an adjustment for the differential taxation factor. Such an approach is altogether too simplistic and ought to be rejected for reasons which should be abundantly clear from the earlier discussion. Rather than go through the motions in this fashion, the analyst would be better advised to carry out his evaluations in nominal terms throughout.

10.5 Analysis in nominal dollars

Analyzing capital-expenditure projects in nominal dollars is somewhat more complex at the beginning and simpler at the end. The forecasts of cash flows on which the evaluation is based must be projected in nominal dollars rather than in constant dollars. This requires not only a forecast of changes in prices relative to one another but that they be tied to a forecast of the general price level itself. Finding net present values of these cash flows is simplified, however, in that prevailing market costs of capital may be used without adjustment to real terms.

As noted earlier, in principle, analyses are identical in either real or nominal dollars providing the inflation rate used in the nominal dollar forecast is that expected in the capital market. However, evaluation in nominal dollars involves an explicit forecast of future inflation rates, which may differ from those anticipated by the market. Hence, as a practical matter, the results of the two evaluations may differ. As indicated earlier, substitution of the analyst's own forecast of the inflation rate for the consensus of the market may be difficult to justify. Although the forecasting performance of the consensus is poor, there is no evidence that any particular individual's is better.

The inflation rate forecasting problem may be rendered less acute by preparing evaluations using a set of inflation rate forecasts, as outlined in Section 10.7. These may be used to evaluate the risks associated with the variability in the inflation rate which are significant when the inflation rate prognosis is unclear.

10.6 Forecasting price levels

The difficulties associated with forecasting the price level are such as to make project analysis in real terms the preferred framework, despite the problems involved in estimating the real cost of capital. The implicit inflation rate extracted in the process of estimating the latter can be used as a forecast of inflation, but such consensus forecasts have had a dismal success record in the past, as bondholders' real losses in the postwar period demonstrate all too clearly.

Near-term forecasts, that is, for the next year or two, are possible and are produced as a part of the output of most econometric forecasting models, whether of the "Keynesian" or monetarist variety. Other less formal forecasting methods, including the use of leading indicators, can also be used to generate tolerably good forecasts of price changes in the near term. Once we go beyond the near term, however, and extend our horizon to five or ten years, the available techniques break down. The chief reason for this failure is that the factors which generate inflation are treated as exogenous variables in most of the models. Such variables are seen to influence prices through a complex lag structure over several quarters in short-term models. Because they do so, the present and recent past values of these variables will generate price-level changes over the next year or two. Existing forecasting techniques capture these relationships and use them to project short-term price changes. They do not do so perfectly, because prices may be influenced by random and essentially unpredictable events, such as crop failures, strikes, political interference with supplies, and similar events, as we have experienced. As we move further into the future, the cumulative effect of such factors becomes more pronounced. Also, the values of exogenous variables which are subject to political manipulation as *policy variables* may be changed, and as the changes work their way into and through the system, forecasts based on present data become increasingly unreliable. While the price level for next year may be determined already and is largely implicit in current values of policy and other exogenous variables, the price level five years from now will depend critically on unforeseen and unforeseeable events and on policy decisions which have not yet been made. As a consequence, it is relatively unpredictable.

The majority of econometric models which are used for forecasting were developed with a view to understanding the linkages between economic sectors and to permit the consequences of alternative economic policy measures to be examined so that appropriate policies may be selected. For this purpose, it is satisfactory, if not preferable, that the model be open such that certain variables may be treated as exogenous, unexplained by the system itself, subject to being manipulated in order to control the system as a whole. Whether they have been successful in this endeavor is not altogether clear. What is clear, however, is that a long-term forecasting model must be closed and provide a feedback loop between the values of GNP, employment, and price levels generated by the model and the policy variables which are presently outside it. Behavioral equations are needed which will indicate how money supply, government spending, tax rates, and similar policy variables are adjusted in response to given economic circumstances. It is not at all clear that stable relationships of this kind exist.

Any long-term forecast of prices or other macroeconomic variables is contingent upon an implicit or explicit forecast of policy variables and thus upon an assumed political response to economic circumstances. Even a cursory glance at the business press will serve to indicate that attempts to thus outguess policy makers absorb a considerable amount of effort and command widespread interest. Given the magnitude of government's impact on the modern economy, all but the shortest-term forecasts must be rooted in political forecasts. As the term of the forecast is extended, the political component increases in scope, importance, and (regrettably) unpredictability.

While, as a consequence, many long-term forecasts are little better than educated guesses, such forecasts are frequently made for no other reason than that they have to be. Modern industrial society requires long-lived assets, which cannot be financed with short-term liabilities. Any decision to assume liabilities with a long maturity or to lend for a similar period requires a judgment on the part of the borrower and the lender that the assets will generate enough income to service the loan or be worth enough to retire it. Such judgments are based on (implicit or explicit) forecasts about prices and a number of other economic variables. Substantial safety factors are required by both parties because of the uncertainty which must inevitably surround the forecast, but some sort of forecast is implicit in the decision itself. While the problem of forecasting price levels may be sidestepped in a capital-expenditure decision by making the calculations in real terms, it cannot be dismissed so easily if there is debt financing involved. Should product prices, wage rates, and input prices all fall by 60 percent, preserving cash flow in real terms will not be particularly comforting to an investor who has borrowed 50 percent of the purchase price and undertaken a schedule of repayments which are fixed in nominal terms and have grown by 150 percent in real terms.

Unfortunately, there is no model which can be used to generate reliable long-term forecasts of price levels. All we can provide is a basic framework. Historically, there has been a long-term tendency for price levels to rise. In the past, this was due to periodic deliberate reductions in the gold content of the monetary unit, undertaken by impecunious rulers as a means of repaying their creditors with debased coin. While there were periods of inflation due to such activities and also to major gold discoveries which augmented the money supply more rapidly than real output could be expanded, there were also periods of deflation. These occurred when wages and prices rose high enough to make goldmining unprofitable, thus cutting off further expansion in the world's monetary base. Within individual countries, the ability to sustain inflation rates in excess of those prevailing elsewhere in the world was even more restricted, since high domestic prices would create a balance-of-payments deficit to pay for imported goods, consequent upon which a loss of specie would force contraction in the domestic money supply. Thus prices moved up and down, and the notion of an equilibrium level, about which they would fluctuate in the long run, made some sense.

In our current situation, it does not. The gold standard has been progressively dismantled over the past 60 years, and its last vestiges were eliminated when the United States suspended payments in gold in 1971. All commercial nations of importance are now on managed paper currencies. Whether one applauds this fact (as a triumph of science over superstition) or deplores it, one must recognize that its chief consequence is that there is no longer a normal or equilibrium price level to which prices may be expected to return in the course of their cyclical fluctuations.

The gold standard did not collapse; it was deliberately done away with to facilitate the *political* management of the economy. The cyclical variability in prices, incomes, and employment, which it created in operation were no longer acceptable, and governments assumed responsibility for the maintenance of full employment as the primary goal of economic policy. In the United States, this commitment is expressed in the Employment Act of 1945. There is similar legislation in most Western countries. Most of this legislation also involves a (subsidiary) commitment to stable prices and balance-of-payments equilibrium. This commitment and the abandonment of the gold standard came about because of the harrowing experience of the 1930s.[16]

However, for the first 25 years following World War II, the U.S. dollar functioned internationally as a sort of paper gold. Exchange rates were fixed, under the Bretton Wooods agreement, in terms of U.S. dollars instead of gold. It constituted the major component of international reserves. Countries which did not control domestic price levels in much the same way as they would have been controlled under the gold standard lost dollar reserves and were forced to deflate or devalue their currencies. While many chose the latter course, self-restraint in the United States served to limit the world's monetary base and the retention by the United States of convertibility into gold provided a link, however tenuous, with the gold standard system. The U.S. price level provided an international reference point. For various reasons, which cannot concern us here, this system collapsed in 1971 and was replaced with a system of floating exchange rates which have largely removed balance-of-payments constraints on international currency manipulations. Despite this, and the addition of Special Drawing Rights to the list of available reserve assets, the U.S. dollar continued to be the primary international reserve asset during the 1970s until the seizure of Iranian assets by the United States (justified as it may have been) raised doubts about the realizability of U.S. dollar assets. The world of the 80s and beyond will be fundamentally different from that of the 60s and 70s as a consequence.

Some of these consequences have been implicit since the dismantling of the gold standard and the adoption of the full employment goal. The Bretton Woods system of fixed exchange rates imposed in principle a form of international discipline which would have forced countries undergoing balance-of-payments deficits to reduce their rates of monetary expansion and either to deflate their economies or moderate their inflation rates until the rest of the world caught up. During the late 40s and 50s, a number of European countries, caught in the squeeze of an apparently insoluble dollar shortage chose to devalue their currencies rather than deflate. When the U.S. balance of payments slipped into deficit in the 60s, little was done until a forced devaluation took place in 1976. The chief implication of these events is that when a clear-cut choice has emerged between maintaining employment or deflating in order to hold prices down and/or maintain balance-of-payments equilibrium, maintenance of employment has won.

In the 1930s, Lord Keynes drew attention to the fact that while attempts to eliminate real excess supply in the labor market necessitated a reduction in real wages, generalized reductions in money wages to achieve such an objective could be self-defeating if they reduced effective demand and cut prices so that real wages remained excessive.[17] Consequently, he recommended deliberate inflation, which would leave money wages constant but increase prices, as a means of achieving the needed reduction in real wages. The suggestion that monetary and/or fiscal policies could be manipulated to increase effective demand or restore full employment without any increase in the price level is an invention of later "Keynesians" and appears to be virtually devoid of any theoretical or empirical justification or support (especially from Keynes' own work). Attainment of the Keynesian solution is dependent on the prevalence of money illusion in the labor force, which is presumed willing to accept a given money wage irrespective of what happens to price levels. If money illusion is incomplete so that workers demand increased money wages because they expect inflation, labor market equilibrium can only be restored by producing more inflation than they had bargained for.

Money wages, particularly in unionized industries, are relatively sticky downwards. The Keynesian analysis suggests that this may, in fact, be relatively harmless from an employment point of view. But they are not sticky upwards. The analysis suggests that if increases in wage rates exceed productivity gains, unemployment will emerge unless an appropriate adjustment in real wages is made by increasing the price level. Similarly, any decline in the price level may increase real wages and generate unemployment.

Conceivably, prices could decline at a rate corresponding to productivity growth, providing wages remained constant, without any ill effects. In a market economy, however, it is necessary for several reasons that relative wages in different occupations change from time to time in order to redirect the flow of manpower between occupations. If wage rates are not flexible downward for whatever reason, the only way in which such relative wage rate changes can be accommodated is by letting some wage rates rise, while holding others constant. The result is *wage drift,* an upward movement in the average wage. The commitment to maintain full employment in a world in which no money wages ever decline, while some rise, is a one-way ticket to inflation. Prices may remain stable or may even decline fractionally, but these periods of stability will be punctuated by periods of deliberately induced inflation every time unemployment rises sufficiently to warrant adoption of policies aimed at creating employment. The only question becomes one of how often and how fast. With balance-of-payments constraints operating, most countries sought to hold inflation to the minimum level consistent with politically acceptable unemployment.

The Keynesian analysis suggests that the twin policy objectives of full employment and price stability are opposed, and that the former can be restored only by interfering with the latter. Since experience in the 40s and 50s seemed to confirm this conclusion, a functional relationship between the unemployment rate and the rate of inflation existed. If unemployment rates were sufficiently high, it was suggested upward pressure on wages would be moderate and price stability could be maintained. Lower unemployment rates could be achieved only by accepting a positive, but perhaps moderate, rate of inflation. The so-called Phillips curve showing this postulated relationship is shown in Figure 10–2. While price stability might not be attainable, it was at least

Figure 10–2
Phillips curve

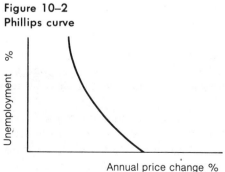

Annual price change %

plausible that a moderate rate of inflation could be found and maintained which would produce a level of unemployment which was acceptable (at least to the employed). In such a Phillips-curve world, projection of exponentially increasing future prices with a moderate rate of increase would appear to be reasonable.

Unfortunately, the Phillips curve has proven to be somewhat elusive in practice. Inflation was run up to the desired level, but unemployment failed to drop as predicted. This experience was fairly general in the industrial world. Early studies had fitted curves for the United Kingdom and United States, but by the time they had been fitted to data for other countries, the relationships were out of date. The curves, if they ever had existed, had apparently shifted to the right and continued to appear to do so. This was hardly the sort of stable relationship that policy makers thought they had discovered. When policy makers in most countries set out to restore full employment, they got *stagflation,* in which inflation rates are too high to be accepted for any length of time, while unemployment remains at levels hitherto considered unacceptably high (that is, the economy stagnates).

While it is possible that some unemployment rate exists at which wages will stabilize and inflationary pressures disappear, this rate is probably unacceptably high, since the unemployment would tend to be concentrated in the nonunionized sectors of the labor force. Reliance on massive unemployment as a means of holding prices stable is a fiscally induced, redistributive measure which penalizes the marginal members of the labor force with marginal income tax rates approaching 100 percent minus the ratio of unemployment insurance to wages in order to provide the benefits of stable prices for the more affluent portions of society. It is, perhaps, morally indefensible and marginally acceptable politically even if similar rates of tax are applied to other members of society continuously and as a matter of course. Until alternative, effective, stabilization techniques and the institutional means of applying them are found, however, it appears to be the only one we have. There will be, for good reason, a general reluctance to use the deflation weapon to defend price levels. Consequently, a credible forecast of continued inflation over the next decade or two must, we believe, project inflation at a significantly higher rate than that experienced overall during the 1955–80 period, although perhaps not necessarily at the rates experienced during the latter few years of that period which tend to reflect special factors.

Given the uncertainty about inflation rates, it seems advisable to supplement any forecast with an analysis of the sensitivity of the results to changes in the inflation rate as described in Section 10.8. Such an analysis is easily provided at little cost if the evaluation has been performed with the aid of a computer. Such a sensitivity analysis should be performed for any major project in which significant sums are involved.

10.7 Forecasting relative prices

As suggested, the price-forecasting problem be broken into two components, partly because it is only the changes in relative prices which are required if the analysis is carried out in real terms, but also because generalized inflation tends to draw attention to itself and to obscure what is happening to the relative prices which are the final determinants of commercial success or failure. Relative prices may be computed easily by deflating actual prices, or indexes thereof, by an index of the general price level. For illustrative purposes, we have computed relative prices of a number of commodities as they emerged in Canada over the period 1971–79 (see Table 10–1). If nothing else, these serve to indicate the wide dispersion in the movement of relative prices which can emerge over short periods of time. Calculating such changes, not only for output but for assorted inputs, can be instructive. The tabulated figures go far in explaining why larger proportions of consumers' budgets are being spent on food, clothing, and shelter as well as why polyethylene bags have increasingly penetrated the supermarket.

In our experience, relative price forecasts are perhaps the weakest component of many existing capital-budgeting systems. All too frequently the assumption is made that relative prices will remain unchanged or that past deviations from the behavior of general price indexes will be corrected so that some past relationship with the general price level will be restored. Ideally, the capital-expenditure analyst should have a deep understanding of the factors influencing the price behavior, not only of the company's products, but of the major inputs required for its production. Usually, he does not and relies for such estimates on specialists in marketing and purchasing, when he should be in a position to evaluate their inputs critically.

Unfortunately, we cannot in the space available provide a comprehensive introduction to the problems of forecasting prices. Several excellent textbooks are available, although most are overly concerned with forecasting more comprehensive economic aggregates.[18] The starting point for any forecasting exercise must be the careful study of the market structure and price behavior of the commodity under review.[19] Such a study may well indicate that it is impossible to forecast output prices except conditionally, because they are closely tied to prices of basic commodities which are not only highly volatile, but which appear

Table 10–1

Indexes of relative producers selling prices—selected products

	1971	1973	1973	1977	1979
Cedar shingles	100.0	168.8	144.1	175.9	176.5
Pig iron	100.0	92.7	183.7	150.2	155.6
Lumber—fir	100.0	143.2	108.2	123.2	154.7
Wool worsted	100.0	162.6	120.4	122.1	131.9
Fir plywood	100.0	130.9	124.7	106.2	130.9
Lumber—pine	100.0	135.1	107.8	100.8	128.5
Men's shoes	100.0	108.4	105.6	108.0	122.7
Dressed beef	100.0	119.9	100.0	75.0	120.7
Dressed pork	100.0	144.9	169.4	137.4	120.4
Reinforcing rods	100.0	98.4	136.7	107.9	116.6
Mixed fertilizer	100.0	98.3	148.4	108.5	113.4
Paper grocery bags	100.0	107.2	131.8	112.8	109.2
Butter	100.0	97.4	115.0	112.7	109.1
Sugar (granulated)	100.0	125.6	164.0	113.0	108.3
Hot air furnaces (oil)	100.0	93.6	95.7	98.6	99.5
Copper pipe	100.0	109.5	84.2	88.4	96.3
Tires—passenger (bias)	100.0	106.6	114.3	105.9	96.1
Synthetic yarns (man-made staple)	100.0	91.5	105.8	100.9	95.7
Poly grocery bags	100.0	94.6	112.3	90.3	91.6
Ball-point pens	100.0	87.7	100.7	85.4	89.4
Latex paint	100.0	95.2	101.6	96.3	89.2
Refrigerators	100.0	89.0	98.4	92.9	82.1
Passenger cars (standard)	100.0	89.5	79.5	75.8	78.0
Distilled liquors	100.0	94.1	85.3	76.8	76.1
Nylon carpets	100.0	81.4	75.8	65.9	60.7
CPI	100.0	112.2	137.9	160.3	190.6

SOURCE: Statistics Canada, Industry Price Indexes (1971 = 100), various years, June data, deflated by Consumer Price Index and normalized on 1971 value.

to describe a random walk when viewed as time series. Several such products appear in Table 10–1, including dressed beef, dressed pork, sugar, pig iron, and copper pipe. However, in each of these cases, the tied commodity is a raw material, and a detailed understanding of the raw material-finished product price relationship may be nearly as useful as an actual forecast of input and output prices for the purpose of evaluating capital expenditures.

Table 10–1 covers only eight years and is dominated by cyclical factors which are obscured in the original series by the general inflation (as illustrated by the CPI). It is perhaps more useful in many instances to attempt to identify secular trends in prices in the first instance and to consider cyclical influences at a later point. In general, secular trends in relative prices are dominated by the cost side of the supply-demand relationship. Costs per unit will reflect in the long run which is relevant in determining secular trends, labor costs, raw material and other input costs, and capital costs, as modified by changes in total-factor productivity. While lumber prices, along with plywood prices and shingle prices, weakened from 1973–77 due to cyclical factors, the relative prices of wood products have risen secularly over the past 50 years or more because rising labor costs have not been offset by increases in productivity. Per hour costs of labor have grown almost continuously for the past 40 years, but costs per unit of output have not in many industries, because of productivity growth. To some degree, this has reflected substitution of capital for labor, which, of course, did not take place unless unit costs were reduced thereby. Much of the observed historical increase in productivity is the result of technological change or of learning phenomena, which have reduced costs without substitution and have cut the required inputs of labor, capital, or both.

One analytical tool which is frequently used for forecasting relative prices is the input-output model of Leontief.[20] As usually computed, the coefficients are taken from a single year's observations. They do not reflect substitution possibilities nor productivity changes and thus are not, in our view, particularly suitable in the longer-term context.

A useful approach to the estimation of price relationships for a given commodity is to fit to a suitably long series of observations the equation:

$$P_t = \frac{1}{(1 + \alpha_4)^t} \left[\alpha_0 + \alpha_1 W_t + \alpha_2 M_t + \alpha_3 K_t\right] \qquad (10.7.1)$$

where

W_t = wage rate in period t.

M_t = raw material price in period t.

P_t = product price in period t.

all measured in constant dollars, and K_t = unit costs of capital in period t measured by the long-term government bond rate plus a suitable risk premium plus a depreciation allowance, expressed as a percentage of net unit costs; and where α_0 is an arbitrary constant, α_1, α_2, and α_3 are input coefficients, while α_4 is an annual rate of total factor productivity increase.

The relationship in 10.7.1 is nonlinear, and the problem of fitting it can be simplified by employing the linear counterpart:

$$P_t(1 + \alpha_4)^t = \alpha_0 + \alpha_1 W_t + \alpha_2 M_t + \alpha_3 K_t \qquad (10.7.2)$$

to a series of dependent variables generated using arbitrary values of the productivity growth rate α_4. One of these is selected on goodness of fit or other grounds.

Equations 10.7.1 and 10.7.2 simply provide a breakdown of unit prices into labor, materials, and capital-cost components, with an arbitrary overhead factor α_0 and an adjustment for productivity change. Where new products are involved or historical data to fit 10.7.2 are unavailable or insufficient, direct estimates of input coefficients derived from engineering or other data may be used in their stead and productivity changes based on productivity experience with products in the industry used to project the price trend.

The fitted values of P_t will be trend values corresponding to fully allocated costs or marginal costs at normal output levels. Residuals about the line will result from cyclical influences on prices as higher marginal cost output is supplied at demand peaks, while prices are cut to lower marginal costs in recessions. The trend values themselves abstract from demand factors and focus instead on long-run costs.

In projecting relative prices, projected trend values of real wage rates, raw material costs, and capital costs are fed into the estimated form of equation 10.7.1 to generate trend values for real prices. Ordinarily, unless prices are highly volatile, there is no need to consider the cyclical component. If volatility is serious, it may be useful to project cyclical values for the first four or five years of the project's life.

Equations 10.7.1 and 10.7.2 can be viewed as substitutes for input-output analyses which take several years' observations instead of one and which impound productivity change. They are still deficient in that they ignore substitution. In some cases, additional variables (for example, the product of energy prices multiplied by time) may be incorporated into the analysis to reflect substitution trends that are expected to persist. However, the assumption of continuing substitution at a constant rate is not much better in principle than the no-substitution assumption. This is clearly an area in which there is a great deal of scope for ingenuity on the part of the analyst.

10.8 Inflation and risk

Inflation adds an additional element of risk to the inherent commercial risks associated with capital expenditures. More precisely, the additional risk results from unforeseen deviations in the inflation rate from its expected values. If inflation proceeded precisely in accordance with a known schedule of price-level changes, it would not create any additional risk at all.

The risk of unexpected price-level changes is one that affects all projects simultaneously, along with the existing operations of the firm. It is thus a highly systematic component of risk. Other systematic risks have their roots in the business cycle, and at one time, inflation was a characteristic feature of the later stages of the business-cycle expansion phase. However, recent experience suggests that inflation rates have become divorced from their historical role and pursue a separate existence of their own. For this reason, we suggest that the systematic risks due to inflation should be analyzed separately from the other systematic risks associated with a particular venture.

Inflation has two possible effects on valuation. It increases costs and prices, thus increasing nominal cash flows. To the extent that experienced inflation alters inflationary expectations, it also changes required nominal yields and, therefore, the capitalization rate which affects the valuation process. Because of the magnitude of the inflation risk in certain situations, it may be desirable to perform a formal analysis of the impact of inflation on risk, even if no other formal risk analysis is performed. Where such analyses are performed, it will generally speaking be useful to examine a range of inflation rate possibilities for each real possibility.

The first step in such an analysis is the projection of cash flows in nominal terms at a variety of inflation rates for each real outcome of the project. These must then be converted into present value terms using the appropriate discount rates. The existing nominal rate reflects present inflation expectations. The essence of the problem is determining how inflation expectations will change in the face of changed inflation rates, or even in some cases, a continuation of the present rates. There are clearly situations where present discount rates may remain unchanged, as for example, the case in which there is a short, sharp burst of inflation, which is due to a particular known cause and which is not expected to be repeated. In general, however, we expect inflationary experience to have an effect on expectations in an amount depending on its rate, its stability, and the length of time it has persisted. The case in which increases in the inflation rate produce exactly offsetting increases in the expected rate so that no change in value results is what we would expect to be the limiting case in the long run. However, in the short run, it is possible that expectations are damped so that the full impact of the higher inflation rate does not flow through to the discount rate. In which case, values may be expected to increase. It is also possible, however, that in certain circumstances, that is, when inflation psychology takes hold, a given increase in inflation rates will generate expectations of even greater inflation rates in the future, so that values will fall.

The final step in risk analysis of a project is to specify the probability distributions of the real outcomes examined and those of the inflation rates examined so that the probabilities of individual outcomes may be determined. At this stage, it may be necessary to specify whether the outcomes in the real domain and those in the inflation rate domain are independent or related. Figure 10–3 shows contour lines of the hypothetical joint probability distributions in the independent case and the dependent case, respectively.

Figure 10–3
Probability contours of joint probability distribution of real outcomes and price changes

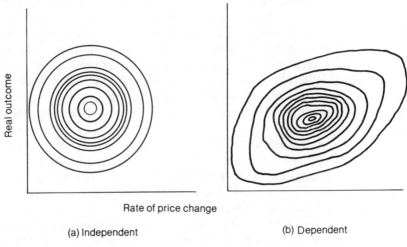

Real outcome

Rate of price change

(a) Independent   (b) Dependent

The determination of whether or not real outcomes are inflation-rate-dependent has obvious implications in terms of the need to produce accurate inflation rate projections, and perhaps for whether the analysis should be undertaken in real dollar-real discount rate or nominal dollar-nominal discount rate terms. While either may be done correctly, an additional element of risk is created by dependence and must be taken into account in the analysis. Of course, if the relationship is positive, as sketched in Figure 10–3(b), the project provides a potential inflation hedge and may be more acceptable in an inflationary environment than it would be if prices are expected to be stable. A negative relationship has, of course, contrary implications. An alternative approach to this problem which incorporates the inflation (risk) adjustment into the required rate of return will be examined in Section 11.7.

10.9   Some strategic considerations

An argument that is frequently raised in inflationary periods is that "We should build our plant this year because it will cost more next year." The potential fallacy implicit in such an assessment should be obvious by now. The new plant will cost more in nominal dollars, but the dollars themselves will cost less in real terms. This type of thinking is one of the more unfortunate by-products of accounting systems based on nominal-dollar, historical costs. Other things being equal, the reported profit generated by the plant this year will be larger than that on the plant built next year, because the nominal dollar depreciation charge will be smaller. Real dollar cash flows, at least before tax, should be equivalent. But income taxes, based on nominal dollar profits, will be larger on the plant built this year than on next year's plant. Building next year will leave a larger fraction of the before-tax income in the company's hands and could well be the decisive factor in opting for delay. This is particularly true if the inflation rate is expected to moderate, because the incentive to delay thus created will be reduced in future periods.

Any decision to delay, of course, must take into account the extent to which the investment is to be financed with funds already in the company's treasury or with funds to be raised at the time the construction takes place. The dollars already raised are expensive dollars and holding them for a year simply permits them to shrink in real value. Unless the prospective tax saving from postponement is impressive indeed, it will ordinarily be better to get on with it and to complete the construction now if the funds are already at hand. But if the funds are not at hand and inflation rates are expected to moderate, the case for delay becomes more compelling. Nominal costs of capital, as we have seen, increase during inflation and are particularly affected by near-term prospects. If costs of capital drop, bonds may be refunded, but there are apt to be penalty clauses in the trust indenture which impose extra costs in so doing, and common stock equity cannot be refunded in any event. A further factor to be taken into account if the funds are in hand and if future inflation rates are expected to moderate is that temporarily high interest rates may permit handsome returns on cash invested in long-term bonds during the period of postponement. The possibility that the real costs of capital raised during a sharply inflationary period may turn out to be excessive in comparison with that of funds raised after the rate of inflation has dropped must be added to the potential tax savings and evaluated as a factor favoring postponement.

Much will depend on the prospective price increase of the capital asset to be acquired. If its total cost is likely to rise at a rate lower than the price level as a whole, postponement becomes attractive. However, construction costs in general and land costs in particular have more typically increased faster than the general price level in sharply inflationary periods, although they have shown correspondingly rather more downward flexibility as inflationary pressures ease. If inflation is expected to persist for several years, there may well be a case for pushing construction now, rather than delaying. But if inflation rates are likely to drop in the foreseeable future, the case for delay may well be persuasive. Where major projects are under consideration, a careful analysis of construction union contract dates, sensitive capital goods prices, and land costs, as well as internal cash flows and the timing of external funds requirements and the opportunities for temporary investment should be undertaken before making a commitment to proceed or delay.

Under inflationary conditions, with some prospect of moderation in inflation rates, firms may be tempted because of the potential cost of capital savings to spend first by depleting working capital and to plan on undertaking permanent financing later. That such a decision involves the acceptance of sharply increased financial risk should be self-evident. The increase in insolvency rates that usually accompanies the later stages of inflationary periods suggests that this risk is one many companies have been prepared to take. Utility companies, in particular, have been prone to take this course as they are more or less obligated by franchise conditions to provide capacity to serve growing markets and may have little room for postponement in programmed capital expenditures. It is tempting particularly when earnings have been depressed and interest coverage weakened due to regulatory lags to lean on or squeeze working capital accounts to find the funds and hope to finance on more favorable terms later. But this is a temptation which should be curbed, if not avoided entirely.

A somewhat more complex problem is posed for the company with an aging (if not obsolescent) plant, competing in a market dominated by competitors with more modern facilities and where the company is faced with a decision to replace (or not) at nominal plant costs some two to four times those of the existing competitor's plants. This is a situation in which a number of petroleum refiners and steel producers found themselves in the mid-1970s. In most instances, markets were weak and provided book rates of return on competitors' historical costs that are no more than remunerative in relation to the costs of capital. At existing prices, rates of return on new investment appeared hopelessly inadequate. In such circumstances, should the plant be replaced, abandoned, or simply nursed along and kept going with some upgrading?

Presumably prices have failed to increase sufficiently to provide an attractive rate of return on new plants because there is excess capacity, at least in the short run, in the industry within the relevant market area. The company has inadvertently or otherwise found itself in the position of being a marginal supplier in a market with excess capacity; the inadequate prices are a signal that no additional capacity is needed at this time. The market is trying to eliminate the excess capacity and has, perhaps, selected the company as a candidate for elimination. The product market is, however, relatively myopic and is unable to distinguish between a temporary glut and a long term supply-demand imbalance. If the former, prices will eventually have to rise to a level where replacement of existing plants can be justified. If the latter, there is no reason to suppose that prices will rise until some capacity has been eliminated. Replacement can be justified in the latter case only if there are other candidates for elimination, and if the company has sufficient financial staying power to stick it out until the others have been eliminated. This is unlikely to be a highly profitable exercise, and any analysis which suggest that it will be should be critically scrutinized by somebody who has no vested interest in the decision.

Even if the glut appears temporary, and there appears to be some prospective advantage to being first on the scene, perhaps because construction costs are rising more quickly than price levels and product prices will ultimately have to reflect other peoples' replacement costs, there is little need for hurry. Early replacement may freeze technology into a less sophisticated or more expensive mold than that available to latecomers. Even if there are no such complications and profits will be higher than those of competitors who replace later because of disparate rates of price change, profits will be delayed longer and possibly worth less in present value terms. In the meantime, the additional financial obligations incurred to finance the replacement may make the company more, rather than less, vulnerable to the existing market weakness.

In summary, high inflation rates create additional uncertainties to add to those already inherent in the capital-expenditure decision process and thus imply a need for utmost caution. Rising nominal prices tend to distract attention from the behavior of relative prices which are the critical determinants of resource allocation in the economy. As we have seen, the effects of inflation as expressed in nominal prices may be to make bad decisions look good initially, but it will make them look worse later on.

Notes

[1] This modern-day manifestation of the never-resolved medieval debate over universals has appropriately in the light of the spirit of the age been translated from the theologi-

cal realm into the monetary, but the terminology still contains semantic traps for the unwary. It is, naturally, the nominal dollar which is real and can be felt in your pocket, while the real dollar has no physical manifestation.

2 With some exceptions. Civil service pensions in Canada and the United Kingdom are fully indexed and thus represent real dollar claims. They are not transferable, however. Index-linked bonds have emerged in many of the countries where high rates of inflation have been endemic. These, at least approximately, represent marketable claims in real rather than nominal currency units. See M. Sarnat, "Purchasing Power Risk, Portfolio Analysis and the Case for Index-Linked Bonds," *Journal of Money, Credit and Banking* 5 (August 1973), pp. 836–45.

3 For an examination of some of the problems associated with price indexes, see K. J. Arrow, "The Measurement of Price Changes," in U.S. Joint Economic Committee. *The Relationship of Price to Economic Stability and Growth,* 85th Congress, 2d Session (1958), pp. 77–88; and H. E. Riley, "The Price Indexes of the Bureau of Labor Statistics," *Relationship of Price,* pp. 107–16.

4 Canadian Institute of Chartered Accountants Accounting Research Committee, *Current Cost Accounting: Exposure Draft* (Toronto: CICA, December 1979); Financial Accounting Standards Board, *Financial Reporting and Changing Prices,* Statement Number 33, (Stamford, Conn.: FASB, 1979); "Inflation Accounting," Report of the Inflation Accounting Committee (Sandilands Report), HMSO (Cmnd 6225) 1975.

5 I. Fisher, *The Theory of Interest* (1930). Reprint. (New York: A. M. Kelley, 1970), chaps. 2 and 9.

6 J. M. Keynes, *The General Theory of Employment, Interest, and Money* (London: Macmillan & Co., 1936), chap. 19.

7 For a complete analysis of the term *structure problem,* see R. Kessel, *The Cyclical Behavior of the Term Structure of Interest Rates* (New York: National Bureau of Economic Research, 1965); and B. G. Malkiel, *The Term Structure of Interest Rates* (Princeton: Princeton University Press, 1966).

8 A. B. Laffer and R. Zecker, "Some Evidence on the Formation, Efficiency and Accuracy of Anticipations of Nominal Yields," *Journal of Monetary Economics* 1 (July 1975), pp. 327–42.

9 E. F. Fama, "Forward Rates as Predictors of Future Spot Rates," *Journal of Financial Economics* 3 (October 1976), pp. 361–77.

10 See also, for example, G. P. Jenkins, *Inflation: Its Financial Impact on Business in Canada* (Ottawa: Economic Council of Canada, 1977).

11 The interested reader may wish to examine the behavior of stock prices during 1967–68 and 1974–75.

12 G. E. P. Box and G. M. Jenkins, *Time Series Analysis Forecasting and Control,* 2d ed. (San Francisco: Holden-Day, 1976), is perhaps the definitive treatment.

13 E. F. Fama, "Short-Term Interest Rates as Predictors of Inflation," *American Economic Review* 65 (June 1975), pp. 269–82.

14 D. N. Dreman, *Psychology and the Stock Market* (New York: AMACOM, 1977) and; C. MacKay, *Selections from Extraordinary Popular Delusions and the Madness of Crowds* (London: Unwin Books, 1973).

15 M. J. Gordon and P. J. Halpern, "Bond Share Yield Spreads under Uncertain Inflation," *American Economic Review* 66 (September 1976), pp. 559–65.

16 For an examination of monetary events and the influence of policy during the period, see J. K. Galbraith, *The Great Crash* (Harmondsworth, Essex: Penguin, 1961) esp. chaps. 7–9; J. K. Galbraith, *Money* (New York: Bantam, 1976), esp. chaps. 10–15; M. Friedman and A. J. Schwartz, *A Monetary History of the United States 1867–1960* (Princeton: Princeton University Press, 1963), chap. 6–9.

17 J. M. Keynes, *General Theory,* ch. 19.

[18] M. H. Spencer, C. G. Clark, and P. W. Hoguet, *Business and Economic Forecasting: An Econometric Approach* (Homewood: Richard D. Irwin, 1961) is a partial exception.

[19] Any good industrial organization text will provide a starting point. The authors have found J. A. Shubin, *Managerial and Industrial Economics* (New York: Ronald Press, 1961) particularly useful for the type of study required.

[20] W. Leontief, *The Structure of The American Economy 1919–29* (Cambridge: Harvard University Press, 1941).

Problems

1. *a.* Prepare the analog of Table 10.1 for a different country or a different set of commodities.

   b. Using wage rate data, exchange rate data, and/or input-output data, account as far as is possible for the differences in price behavior of the different commodities in your table.

2. Which of (*a*) general price-level-adjusted financial statements, (*b*) current-cost-adjusted financial statements, or (*c*) unadjusted financial statements provides, in your judgment, a better measure of the performance of management during an inflationary period from the stockholders' point of view?

3. Two public utilities in different jurisdictions are subject to cost-of-service regulation. A has a rate base which is based on original cost less depreciation and gets a rate of return equal to its cost of capital as measured in the marketplace. B has a replacement cost less depreciation rate base and receives a rate of return equal to the risk-free, real rate of interest plus a risk premium which, for the sake of the problem, may be assumed to equal the risk premium component of A's rate of return.

   a. To what extent are the stockholders of A and B exposed to or protected from the risks of (*i*) anticipated, (*ii*) unanticipated inflation?

   b. Who bears the remaining inflation risk in the two cases?

Explicit recognition of risk and uncertainty

11.1 Nature of the problem

Risk exists because we are unable to make perfect forecasts. If we could, as the certainty assumption implies, we would never make unprofitable decisions, could plan to meet all commitments with precision, and life would be dull indeed. While handling risk in the decision process poses both conceptual and practical problems, it is here that the decision maker plays a vital role in society. In a static society, there is no risk; bearing the risk associated with economic change is the basic social function of the entrepreneur, and in the view of a number of economists,[1] profit is the reward for providing this service.

Some economic theorists have tried to distinguish between risk and uncertainty. The usual basis for such a distinction is whether the probability distribution of outcomes is known or unknown.[2] Such a distinction rests on an objectivist, frequency concept of probability which has been subject to serious challenge.[3] Even when the frequency concept of probability is inadmissible due to lack of direct evidence, we usually have developed from experience or can develop by simulation studies[4] useful ideas about the probability distributions of possible outcomes. It makes sense to use such information to the fullest extent possible in making decisions.

A possible exception arises where outcomes depend on the consciously chosen strategies of competitors or suppliers, where the number of participants in the market is small, and where the opponents' strategies will be chosen to maximize their expected utilities. A more elaborate theory of behavior is needed for such situations and is provided by the theory of games.[5] Application of this theory to the capital-expenditure decision process will be examined in Chapter 13. We prefer to reserve the term *uncertainty* for this type of conflict situation and to speak of *risk* in the simpler situations where some kind of probability distribution, whether objective or subjective, can be generated.

Risk, as we have defined it, can be classified in a number of ways depending, for example, on whether it is the result of vagaries in the

345

marketplace or of intrinsic stochastic properties of the production function. We need not go into details here, although we shall retain the distinction between *operating* (*business*) *risk* (fluctuations in operating earnings before interest and taxes) and *financial risk* (additional fluctuations in earnings per share induced by the use of leverage in the capital structure). In particular, we shall be concerned with how the former concept of risk is affected by the choice of projects and how its level may be controlled.

To the firm, risk is the possibility of unforeseen fluctuations in its cash flow—of deviations of cash flow from its most probable or expected value. All risk arises from such deviations; more specialized ideas of risk which we may use are derivative from risk defined in this manner. For example, the risk of insolvency arises because of the possibility that a succession of unplanned cash deficits will exhaust liquid assets and leave the firm unable to meet commitments as they fall due.

Risk implies that cash flows are not known with certainty as we had earlier assumed, but they must be regarded as random variables. In place of a series of cash flows C_t, we must define the joint probability distribution of cash flows for the corresponding periods. Distributions of cash flows in successive periods may be independent of one another, but we should not assume a priori that they are. By discounting, we were able to compress the time series of certain cash flows into a single measure of merit. In the risk case, we may use discounting as well, but we are faced with a strategic choice of how we will use the procedure and what result we would prefer to obtain from it. Suppose we sample by randomly selecting a value from the unconditional marginal distribution of the cash flow for each period over our planning horizon which has been incorporated in the joint probability distribution described above. We may then calculate an internal rate of return for each possible series of cash flows so derived. The results may then be collected and shown in a graph (see Figure 11–1).

Alternatively, we may calculate the benefit-cost ratio or net present value for each possible stream and construct the probability distribution of benefit-cost ratios, for example, as in Figure 11–2. However, we prefer to use the familiar concept of net present value, derived in a way which acknowledges the existence of risk and incorporates risk into the evaluation of the cash flows used to reach an accept-reject decision. While the notion of distribution sampling is a useful one and provides the basis for risk-analysis studies,[6] it is much more efficient to use, whenever possible, the ideas which are derived from the contemporary theory of finance.

An alternative representation of the risk associated with a particular

Figure 11–1
Probability distribution of rates of return

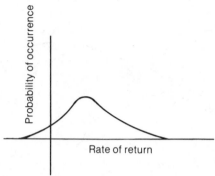

project is possible if the number of possible outcomes is finite (or if a finite number of alternatives affords an adequate representation in the case where the outcomes are characterized by a continuous distribution). This representation uses a tree diagram as shown in Figure 11–3 in which outcomes appear as nodes along the branches. The values of the outcomes may be expressed as present values or shown as undiscounted; probabilities of their occurrence are also specified. In Figure 11–3, R_{ti} identifies the ith outcome in period t and will occur with probability P_{ti}. The probabilities of the states that can be reached from a given node sum to the probability of reaching the node in question. In Figure 11–3 we have, for example:

$$P_{21} + P_{22} = P_{11}$$

and

$$P_{31} + P_{32} + P_{33} + P_{34} = P_{11}$$

Figure 11–2
Probability distribution of benefit-cost ratios

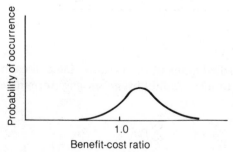

Figure 11–3
Tree diagram

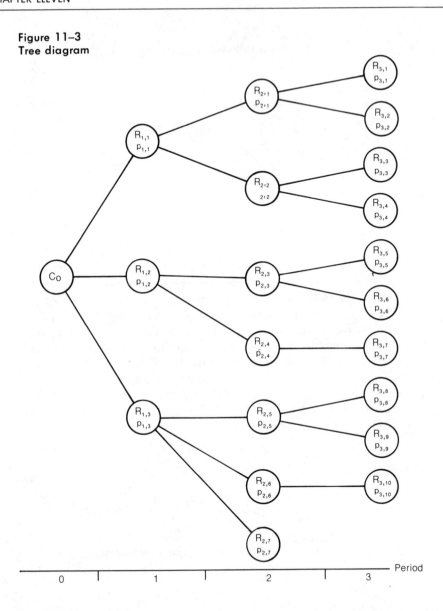

The sum of probabilities of the various states in each period do not necessarily add to one; certain branches may terminate in earlier periods. Thus:

$$\sum_i p_{3i} = 1 - p_{27}$$

since R_{27} is the last outcome along its particular branch. Conditional probabilities are defined in the usual way, for example:

$$p(R_{33}|R_{22}) = p_{33}/p_{22}$$

The tree diagram provides a useful framework for examining problems involving risk. Not only does it permit all the usual measures of risk to be computed, but it also permits computation of the rate of uncertainty resolution which can be measured as the extent to which the average coefficient of variation of outcomes flowing from the nodes in each period is reduced from one period to the next. This has been proposed as a significant dimension of the risk associated with a particular project,[7] although its precise implications have not been determined. Rapid resolution of uncertainty implies that the greatest risks associated with a project are faced in the early years; once these have passed, remaining outcomes are more certain. Russian roulette with five chambers loaded provides more rapid uncertainty resolution than Grand Prix auto racing, although the risks to the participants may be similar. As the example implies, rapid uncertainty resolution may not be unambiguously preferred to slow uncertainty resolution.

11.2 Measuring risk

How can we measure risk? Or can we? In principle, we can; at least where we can derive a probability distribution of outcomes, we can use a measure of its dispersion as an ad hoc measure of risk. In practice, measurement may prove quite difficult, and many practical businessmen as well as economic theorists have argued against it.[8] The principal allegations against it seem to be that so many factors must be considered in attempting to evaluate risk that it is either impossible, too time consuming, or too expensive to do so with enough accuracy to be of any use. A second problem is that it is alleged that even if we had accurate measurements, the state of theoretical development is such that we could not use them operationally. It is our view that neither of these arguments remains valid. In the first place, developments in the theory of finance show us how we should, in principle, measure the relevant dimensions of risk and how such measures may be used in decision making. Second, arguments based on computational difficulties are no longer valid given the decreasing cost and increasing availability of sophisticated calculators and computers.

We must attempt to measure risk for risk is a fact of business life, and some provision must be made for it if only to ensure the firm's survival. Could we not, however, take sufficient account of it by utilizing the expected values of the probability distributions we have been examining and trusting these to work as actuarial equivalents to the rate of return or benefit-cost ratio in the certainty case?

Our answer must, in general, be no. First of all, an attempt to maximize expected income under conditions of risk has long been recognized as capable of leading to ridiculous decisions, such as paying an infinite sum to play the notorious St. Petersburg game.[9]

Second, it is contrary to observed behavior in that most firms hedge certain risks and insure against others at a cost which is in excess of the expected value of receipts from the contract. Finally, although limited liability relieves the stockholder of the threat of losses in excess of the amount invested, lesser losses are transmitted to him either as reduced dividends or capital losses in the value of his stock.

Starting from the observation that insurance is a frequently bought commodity, we are led to the premise that most people have an aversion to risk (that is, the risk of large, catastrophic losses) and are willing to pay small, certain amounts to avoid it. On the other hand, it is also observed that people will buy lottery tickets of various sorts and that such purchases imply a preference for, rather than an aversion to risk.[10] This seeming paradox can be resolved by assuming that people distinguish between different risks and have different aversions or affinities to them. For now, however, we will proceed on the assumption that business risks are sufficiently homogeneous to be valued in a consistent manner, and that people have an aversion to such business risks and are willing to forego income in order to avoid them. We then need to ask what trade-off function links the two, and how we may determine how much income individuals are willing to forego to reduce risk by any given amount?

The explanation of the individual's response to risk requires an excursion into utility theory. From this, we will then consider how individuals' preferences combine in the market for firms' securities and then the criteria according to which the firms' capital-expenditure decisions ought to be made.[11]

The notion of measurable utility is a theoretical artifact which tends to make most businessmen and many economists uncomfortable. Nevertheless, it is useful to assume its existence in order to solve the problem we have set for ourselves. While some of the decision rules which have been prepared make explicit use of the utility concept, we shall show that the problem can be resolved without using it directly. We prefer to do so.

Utility in classical economic theory is a measure of the satisfaction derived from the ownership or use of some commodity. For our purposes, we need only be concerned with the utility of money (wealth).

This utility can be measured by any index which is unique up to a linear transformation, that is, the units of measurement may be multiplied or divided by any arbitrary constant and the zero point arbitrarily fixed.[12]

We can derive such a measure by taking two arbitrary sums, say $1 and $1 million, and assigning to these the respective utilities of 0 and 1. To derive the utility of any sum between these amounts we need, in principle, merely to ascertain the probability U_i at which the individual is indifferent between having the sum S_i with certainty and a lottery ticket offering: (a) $1 million with probability U_i or (b) $1 with probability $(1 - U_i)$. It can be shown that U_i may be interpreted as a measure of the utility of the sum S_i which meets our requirements.[13] The sum S_i is the certainty equivalent of the underlying lottery. For an individual who is risk averse, S_i will be less than the sum $1,000,000 \, U_i + 1(1 - U_i)$. A more intuitive way to characterize a risk averter is to say that a given risk of loss has a stronger impact than a potential gain of the same amount. If we define a symmetrical wager whose payoffs are equal in absolute magnitude, although one is negative while the other is positive and both are equally likely to occur, the expected value of the wager is zero, but the risk averter's certainty equivalent is negative. This implies the risk averter would prefer to pay a certain amount to avoid the wager. The maximum amount that would be given up by such an individual is called a risk premium and is the difference between the utility of the expected value and the expected value of the utility.

In the example we have just considered, both the return on and the risk inherent in the wager can be summarized by the expected return and standard deviation of return, respectively. If the standard deviation increases while the expected value remains constant, the certainty equivalent value will decrease for any risk averter. For these special wagers, expected utility decreases as standard deviation increases (holding expected value constant), while expected utility increases as expected value increases (holding standard deviation constant). Furthermore, in these special cases, we may use standard deviation as a measure of risk. We will later discuss other circumstances in which it may similarly be used.

In what follows, we will be concerned not with the absolute amounts of wealth committed to various wagers, but rather with the proportions of initial wealth invested in different risky assets. Thus, we will find it more convenient to develop our analysis in terms of rates of return. Suppose we are considering two risky assets to purchase and place in a portfolio. Suppose further we know the expected values and standard deviations of the returns of the two assets individually, as well as the covariance of their returns. Then, if we invest in the proportions x_1 and x_2, such that $x_1 + x_2 = 1$, by elementary probability theory we may write the expected value and variance of the return on the portfolio so formed as:

$$E(\tilde{r}_p) = x_1 E(\tilde{r}_1) + x_2 E(\tilde{r}_2) \qquad (11.2.1)$$

and

$$\sigma^2(\tilde{r}_p) = x_1{}^2\sigma^2(\tilde{r}_1) + x_2{}^2\sigma^2(\tilde{r}_2) + 2x_1 x_2 \ \text{cov}(\tilde{r}_1, \tilde{r}_2) \qquad (11.2.2)$$

where the tilde ($\tilde{\ }$) on a variable indicates it is random. $E(\tilde{r}_p)$ is the expected return on the portfolio, $\sigma^2(\tilde{r}_p)$ is the variance of portfolio return, and $\text{cov}(\tilde{r}_1, \tilde{r}_2)$ is the covariance between the returns on the individual securities. The two measures $E(\tilde{r}_p)$ and $\sigma^2(\tilde{r}_p)$ can be used to characterize the utility of the portfolio in three cases: (a) for symmetrical two-point wagers as in example 11.2.2; (b) when return distributions are multivariate normal; or (c) when the utility function may be assumed quadratic over some relevant range of wealth. In any of these circumstances, the individual indifference curves may be represented as shown in Figure 11–4.

Figure 11–4
Investor's preferences for standard deviation of return and expected value of return

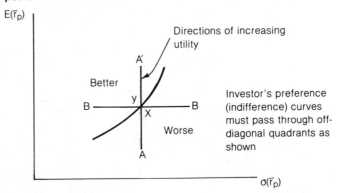

11.3   Portfolio theory: selection and diversification

We wish to demonstrate briefly how a suitably diversified selection of risky assets may provide efficient portfolios, that is, portfolios whose anticipated standard deviation of return is minimized for a given level of return, or conversely, whose return is maximized for a given level of risk (standard deviation). We will then use this information as a basis for arguing how the returns of risky portfolios are determined in equilibrium in the capital markets.

Consider first a portfolio consisting of two risky assets. We already know how to calculate the expected return and standard deviation of return on such a portfolio from equations 11.2.1 and 11.2.2. Recalling also from elementary probability theory that $\text{cov}(\tilde{r}_1,\tilde{r}_2) = \rho_{12}\sigma(\tilde{r}_1)\,\sigma(\tilde{r}_2)$, where ρ_{12} is the correlation coefficient between the assets' returns, we may imagine three possible relationships between them: (a) perfect positive correlation ($\rho_{12} = +1$); (b) perfect negative correlation ($\rho_{12} = -1$); and (c) imperfect correlation ($-1 < \rho_{12} < +1$), all illustrated in Figure 11-5.

Figure 11-5
Risk-return combinations for portfolios composed of two risky assets

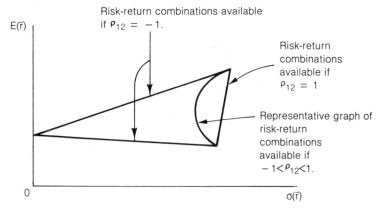

Risk-return combinations available if $\rho_{12} = -1$.

Risk-return combinations available if $\rho_{12} = 1$

Representative graph of risk-return combinations available if $-1 < \rho_{12} < 1$.

In the case of perfect negative correlation, it is possible to select the two risky assets in such proportions that the resulting portfolio is, in fact, riskless.[14] In general, however, we are more concerned with the case of imperfect correlation, where the available risk-return combinations must lie within the triangular area of Figure 11-5 along a line such as the typical curved line shown. This curved line must bend to the left as shown and cannot bend to the right at any point (otherwise more efficient portfolios can be made up of the same underlying securities).

The most significant feature of the risk-return relationship between imperfectly correlated assets is that it permits us to predict that most investors will tend to hold diversified portfolios: it is not likely that many investors would put all available wealth into holding a single asset. As Figure 11-6 reminds us, the indifference curves in risk-return space show that utility increases with expected return and decreases with risk. This implies that no investor would ever choose a portfolio on the line segment OA, but rather will choose some point along the (positively sloping) line segment OB. An investor facing the choice of combinations of assets A and B will normally hold some of both, that is, a diversified portfolio, which places the portfolio risk-return combination somewhere along OB. This result may not be true for all investors as some may choose to hold only B, but it will normally be true for most. It is significant that not all combinations of A and B are efficient. All portfolios along the segment OA are dominated by portfolios along OB of equal risk, but higher return. Thus, the segment OB is an efficient frontier because all investors will attempt to increase expected return while minimizing standard deviation and so will prefer portfolios lying on the positively sloped segment OB. It is a frontier because portfolios with risk-return combinations above and/or to the left of OB are unattainable.

Figure 11–6
Diversified portfolios composed of risky assets

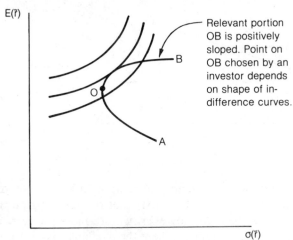

Relevant portion OB is positively sloped. Point on OB chosen by an investor depends on shape of indifference curves.

The analysis for two risky assets can be generalized to portfolios composed of any number of risky assets. To extend our results for two risky assets to many, we must simply recognize that both individual assets and portfolios may be represented as points in Figure 11–5. We observe that since a particular point represents a particular risk-return combination, two or more assets (or portfolios) may have the same combination and will, therefore, appear the same from the investor's viewpoint. Put differently, perfect substitutes will plot at the same point in Figure 11–5. The results of combining assets or portfolios into other portfolios may be derived by repeated application of the results for two assets. The risk-return representation of many risky assets will consist of a number of lines similar to *AOB*. The envelope of these lines lying furthest in the direction of increased utility (up and to the left) will form the efficient frontier in the case of many risky assets.[15]

We now consider the special case in which one of the many assets is riskless instead of risky. The risk-return combination for such an asset will plot as a point along the vertical axis as shown by r_f (the notation we will use to signify risk free) in Figure 11–7.[16] Where such an asset is

Figure 11–7
Portfolio choice when a risk-free asset is available

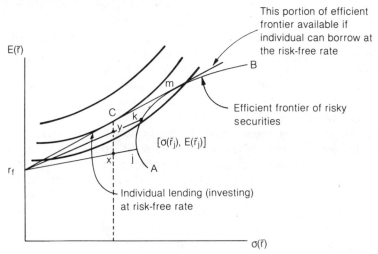

available and is combined with the risky assets in the investors portfolio, the risk-return of this combination will plot along a straight line like $r_f j$ in Figure 11–7 (where j is a risky portfolio of the efficient frontier) since $\sigma^2(r_f)$ and $\text{cov}(r_f, \tilde{r}_j)$ are both zero by definition, and the portfolio standard deviation reduces to:

$$\sigma(\tilde{r}_p) = x_j \sigma(\tilde{r}_j)$$

where x_j is the proportion of the investor's wealth in the portfolio j of risky assets and $x_f + x_j = 1$.

Suppose now that the investor had chosen the combination represented by the point x along $r_f j$ as having the maximum risk (standard deviation) he was willing to accept in his overall portfolio. If, however, he selected the risky portfolio k (also on the efficient frontier) to combine with the riskless asset, then he could have the portfolio y with the same risk as x, but a greater expected return. By repeated application of the same reasoning, the investor will finally select the risky portfolio m located at the point where the straight line through r_f (representing possible risk-return combinations) is just tangent to the efficient frontier. The greatest available return for the specified risk is then found in the portfolio C. We note also that it would not pay the investor to consider points farther along the efficient frontier AB to the right of m as the slope of the straight line would again decrease.

As a matter of common usage, the risk-free asset is usually taken to be a government security, treasury bill, or similar short-term free of default risk. When the investor purchases some of this riskless asset for his portfolio, we refer to him as lending at the riskless rate. Lending takes place in any portfolio (point) from r_f up to, but not including, the point m. We can extend the straight line beyond the point m, indicating that an investor may wish to invest more than his initial wealth to achieve even higher risk-return combinations. This can be accomplished by borrowing at the riskless rate and levering the portfolio by placing all his wealth plus the amount borrowed in the risky portfolio m. One of the assumptions of the perfect capital-market model is that investors are able to borrow at the riskless rate.

One important intermediate result may be noted. Given our assumptions that the individual investor can borrow or lend at the same (riskless) rate and that he has determined the efficient frontier for the available risky assets, then we may infer that the individual's choice of the portfolio of risky assets to hold is independent of (separate from) his attitudes toward risk as expressed in his risk preference (risk-return utility) function. Provided the standard deviation and expected return are the only characteristics of interest to the individual, then the optimal portfolio of risky assets for that individual does not depend on his attitudes toward risk. This is referred to as the separation theorem.

If any risky assets are held, they will be the whole of portfolio m. How portfolio m is combined with the riskless asset does depend on risk-return preferences, but not the composition of m. Since this separation theorem applies to all market participants, we have a very important result which allows us to abstract from individuals' attitudes toward risk when attempting to determine equilibrium positions in the market for risky assets.

To this point, we have been discussing the behavior of a single individual investor and his choice of risk-return combinations. We note that the efficient frontier of Figure 11–7 is expressed in terms of *expected* risk and return, that is, it represents the (subjective) evaluation of the individual based on combination of his expectations of the risk and return of the available risky assets. If we assume further that information is freely available to all participants, since all market participants may be assumed rational, they will all evaluate this information in the same way. That is, we may assume that all investors will hold the same (homogeneous) expectations with regard to the joint distribution of returns on risky assets.[17] Thus the efficient frontier as shown for an individual investor in Figure 11-7 will be the same for every market participant at the particular point in time. But since all market participants will not necessarily hold the same initial portfolios, we can imagine a considerable amount of (costless) transacting taking place in the market so that asset prices adjust to achieve the appropriate required (expected) return commensurate with their perceived risk (and the supply of the asset available to the market). Finally, in equilibrium, each investor who holds risky assets will hold some portion of the risky portfolio m in combination with the riskless asset. Since all investors will hold some of portfolio m (or else hold only the risk-free asset), and since this is the only portfolio of risky assets held by anyone, then the portfolio m must consist of all risky assets in the market, since all assets must be held by someone in equilibrium. Not surprisingly then, the portfolio m is referred to as the market portfolio, consisting of all risky assets.

Since all investors holding risky assets will hold portfolio m, all available (efficient) risk-return combinations must lie along the straight line $r_f m$ and its extension. This line is referred to as the capital market line (*CML*), (see Figure 11-8). It describes the equilibrium relationship

Figure 11-8
The capital market line

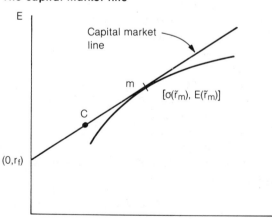

between risk and return. The slope of the *CML* is known as the (per unit) market price of risk and may be written as:

$$\frac{E(\tilde{r}_m) - r_f}{\sigma(\tilde{r}_m)} \qquad (11.3.1)$$

where $\sigma(\tilde{r}_m)$ and $E(\tilde{r}_m)$ are the (expected, equilibrium) risk and return of the market portfolio. Using the *CML* we may write an expression for the expected return for any portfolio as a function of its risk and in particular for portfolio *C:*

$$E(\tilde{r}_C) = r_f + \left[\frac{E(\tilde{r}_m) - r_f}{\sigma(\tilde{r}_m)} \right] \sigma(\tilde{r}_C) \qquad (11.3.2)$$

11.4   Systematic versus unsystematic risk

A major implication of the portfolio theory is that unless we hold only the riskless asset any portfolio containing risky assets, however well (efficiently) diversified, will still have some level of risk that cannot be diversified away. This latter is inescapable, that is, undiversifiable. At the level of individual assets, not all of the risk associated with the return on a risky asset is of concern to the risk-averse investor, only the part which cannot be diversified away.[18] Thus we may partition the risk of an asset into two parts: undiversifiable (systematic,) risk and diversifiable (unsystematic,) risk, or:

Total risk = Systematic risk + Unsystematic risk

where total risk for an individual asset has been characterized by the standard deviation of its return (or its variance in some instances).

The systematic risk of an asset is determined to be that portion of total risk (associated with the return) which is correlated with overall economic movements in general and movements in the market in which the asset is traded in particular. For instance, securities of firms having little unique business risk characteristics will have relatively large systematic risk factors. Conversely, firms whose operating characteristics are uncommon may have relatively small systematic risk. The securities of such firms will be highly sought after for what should be obvious reasons. Unfortunately, nearly all assets (securities) have some systematic risk.

We now consider the widely used, empirical market model, expressed by the regression equation:[19]

$$\tilde{r}_{jt} = \alpha_j + \beta_j \tilde{r}_{Mt} + \tilde{\epsilon}_{jt} \qquad (11.4.1)$$

where *t* is a time period subscript. This model says that the return on security *j* is linearly related to the return on some market index M[20] (not the same thing as the market portfolio m) plus some random error term. Assuming normal distribution theory applies to the coefficients of 11.4.1, we have:

$$\hat{\beta}_j = \frac{\text{cov}(\tilde{r}_j, \tilde{r}_M)}{\sigma^2(\tilde{r}_M)} \qquad (11.4.2)$$

The notation $\hat{\beta}_j$ signifies that this risk measure is an estimate based on the market index and not on the market portfolio. We note also that since α_j is a constant, the variance of return on security j in 11.4.1 may be written as the sum:

$$\sigma^2(\tilde{r}_j) = \hat{\beta}_j^2 \sigma^2(\tilde{r}_M) + \sigma^2(\tilde{\epsilon}_j) \qquad (11.4.3)$$

where $\sigma^2(\tilde{r}_M)$ and $\sigma^2(\tilde{\epsilon}_j)$ are the variances of the market index and unsystematic components, respectively. The first term on the right-hand side of 11.4.3 is the systematic risk, and since $\sigma^2(\tilde{r}_M)$ is common to all assets, the significant measure is $\hat{\beta}_j$. The form of equation 11.4.3 may be compared with the verbal statement of the partitioning of total risk. It is some version of these $\hat{\beta}_j$'s which are measured, reported, discussed, and compared. Clearly, $\beta_M = 1$ (by definition), and this measure is frequently used as a benchmark for comparing the systematic risk measures of individual securities. Securities whose βs are greater than 1.0 are more risky than the market (average), and conversely securities whose βs are less than 1.0 are less risky than the market. The larger the β-value for a security, the greater is its systematic (undiversifiable) risk.

Since the unsystematic risk of a security can be diversified away in any portfolio containing an adequate number of securities, it can be eliminated without cost and does not command a risk premium. We may conclude that for purposes of constructing portfolios, the systematic risk is the relevant risk and may be measured by the β-coefficient. It is a further virtue of these coefficients (by their definition and the additivity property of covariances) that the corresponding measure for any portfolio is simply the weighted average of the βs for its individual component securities. Therefore:

$$\hat{\beta}_p = \sum_j x_j \hat{\beta}_j \qquad (11.4.4)$$

where x_j is the (market value) proportion of the portfolio invested in security j.

Again, to avoid any possible misunderstanding, we repeat that systematic risk is not a measure of total risk, and that total risk is not the important value-determining measure. Two securities with the same systematic risk could well have widely differing total risks, depending on their relative unsystematic risk characteristics.

We mentioned earlier that operating characteristics of a firm may influence its systematic risk. It is constructive to consider some evidence regarding what those operating characteristics might be and their effects. A series of empirical studies has been reported which suggests important correlations between such measures as earnings variability or covariability, and operating and financial leverage and empirical, market-determined measures of systematic risk for individual firms.[21] The interesting question is whether we may find satisfactory explanations for these observed correlations. Lev[22] has hypothesized that the firm's operating leverage (the ratio of fixed to variable operating costs) is a determinant of systematic risk. Operating leverage affects contribution margin and thus earnings variability. In general, the higher the operating leverage (that is, capital intensity), the greater the potential earnings volatility. A statistically significant association was found. Hamada[23] has linked the Modigliani-Miller capital-structure hypothesis to the contemporary theory, investigating particularly the relationship between a firm's financial risk, as measured by financial leverage (capital structure), and systematic risk. Such a relationship is implied by the Modigliani-Miller hypothesis; systematic risk of levered firms in a given (total) risk class should vary with leverage, and the empirical results tend to confirm this. Lev and Kunitzky[24] investigated other organizational factors based on proposals of organization theorists. The hypothesis is mainly that firms attempt to avoid environmental uncertainty by smoothing their operations (flows of inputs and outputs).[25] Smoothing may be achieved by maintaining inventories, training a labor force, integrating vertically, and adopting peak-load pricing policies. If the hypothesis is valid, then stability of such factors should affect risk and measures of the two should show association, that is, the greater the stability, the smaller the risk. Empirical results were consistent with this hypothesis.

To summarize these studies, there appears to be some evidence that operating leverage, financial leverage, and the stability of the firm's operations all are determinants of the firm's systematic risk. Operating leverage and stability of the firm's operations may be characteristics of the undertaking and thus affect business risk. Leverage, of course, will affect financial risk.

11.5 Relationship between risk and return for individual assets: the security market line

We have established earlier that given a choice between two assets with the same expected rate of return, the risk-averse investor will choose the less risky of the two assets. But, two assets which differ in risk could not continue to offer the same expected rate of return for exactly that reason. While they do, the situation is unstable, or in disequilibrium, and the actions of investors seeking to rebalance their portfolios will be such as to increase the price of the lower-risk asset and/or decrease the price of the higher-risk asset so that the expected return of the lower-risk asset decreases relative to that of the higher-risk asset. That is, the market required return for the higher-risk asset must be higher in order that the market in which the assets are traded may reach equilibrium. A major contribution of contemporary financial theory is to specify the relationship between required return and risk and consequently how individual assets will be priced in equilibrium. We here present an intuitive approach to these important results of the theory. Their derivation is examined in Appendix II.A at the end of this chapter. The importance of this theory is that it provides us with a consistent method of finding required rates of return for risky assets.

It is useful to pause briefly to distinguish between the notions of the expected and required rate of return. The expected rate of return is the rate of return investors expect an asset to earn during some specified future period. Except for the riskless asset (a special case), the expected rate of return may be viewed as the expected value of some (subjective) probability distribution of future returns. Under uncertainty, after the fact, the actual realized rate of return will likely differ from the expectation. The required rate of return is the minimum expected return that will induce investors to buy a particular risky asset.

In Section 11.3, we introduced the notion of a *riskless asset*. We now define the difference between the return on the riskless asset and the required return on any risky asset to be a *risk premium*. While we used the *CML* to find the expected return for any portfolio as a function of portfolio risk, we will use contemporary financial theory to provide models which attempt to explain the magnitudes of risk premia, and which we may use to evaluate risky investments (within the limitations of our data and some additional caveats we discuss in Chapter 12).

The equilibrium required rate of return on any risky asset is equal to the riskless rate of return plus its own particular risk premium. Thus:

$$E(\tilde{r}_j) = r_f + \text{risk premium}_j \qquad (11.5.1)$$

Since, as we have seen, only systematic risk commands a risk premium, we may expect to find the risk premium related to our measure of systematic risk, β_j. Indeed it is, and we find that:

$$E(\tilde{r}_j) = r_f + \beta_j[E(\tilde{r}_m) - r_f] \qquad (11.5.2)$$

this equation is sometimes called the *security market line* (*SML*) and is shown in Figure 11–9.

Figure 11–9
The security market line

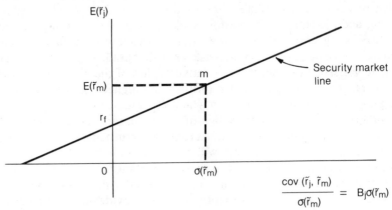

The important implication of this result is that it shows how we may write an expression for the equilibrium required rate of return, which we may then use subsequently as a risk-adjusted discount rate for capital-budgeting decisions. That is:

$$k = r_f + \beta_j [E(\tilde{r}_m) - r_f] \qquad (11.5.3)$$

We note that except for the fact that the β_j in equation 11.5.2 is defined in terms of the market portfolio, it is of the same form as the empirically derived, statistically based $\hat{\beta}_j$ of equation 11.4.2 defined in terms of some market index. This has lead some observers to suggest that the empirical measures be substituted for the theoretical measures for practical purposes. Before we hasten to endorse this view, we note that the relevant βs for capital-expenditure decisions will be those associated with projects and not necessarily with the existing firm, otherwise there would be no need to concern ourselves with measurement as we could use the required return for the existing firm (as measured, for instance, by the weighted average cost of capital). Thus we recommend caution before seizing on the apparent similarity and defer further discussion of this issue until Chapter 12.

11.6 The capital asset pricing model and required rates of return

We established in Chapter 1 that in a world of certainty and perfect capital markets a manager can act in the best interests of stockholders without specific knowledge of their preferences because the only constraint on the stockholders' consumption decisions is the present value of their individual wealth. Under uncertainty, but again with perfect capital markets, a manager need not know the details of the stockholders' risk-return preferences either: the same market-value criterion applies.[26] Accordingly, the best action that the manager can take on behalf of the firm's owners is to maximize the present (market) value of their investment. Even if more than one type of security is issued by the firm, the same market-value criterion applies, although some qualifications may be required.[27]

The managers of a firm may implement the market-value criterion if it can be related to the firm's expected earnings (cash flows) and their particular risk characteristics. We recall the security market line relationship developed in Section 11.5 which related the required return on the securities of firm j to its risk according to:

$$E(\tilde{r}_j) = r_f + \beta_j[E(\tilde{r}_m) - r_f] \tag{11.6.1}$$

We now wish to use this relationship to find an expression for the present (market) value of a risky project in terms of its uncertain future earnings. For this purpose, we now assume that the firm will operate for one period only, earning an income (in cash), and then liquidate by selling all assets for cash. Let us define the total cash flow, earnings plus liquidating value, as $\tilde{X}_j$, and the current value as V_{0j}. Then we may write:

$$\tilde{r}_j = \frac{\tilde{X}_j - V_{0j}}{V_{0j}} = \frac{\tilde{X}_j}{V_{0j}} - 1$$

Substituting and solving for V_{0j} as we do in Appendix 11.A to define the capital asset pricing model (CAPM), we find:

$$V_{0j} = \frac{E(\tilde{X}_j)}{1 + r_f + \beta_j[E(\tilde{r}_m) - r_f]} \tag{11.6.2}$$

where

$$\beta_j = \frac{\text{cov}(\tilde{X}_j|\tilde{X}_j, \tilde{r}_m)}{\sigma^2(\tilde{r}_m)}$$

Equation 11.6.2 tells us that we may interpret the value of $E(\tilde{r}_j)$ derived from the SML (which as we have seen in the CAPM in another form) as the required return for the project to be applied to the expected value of the cash flow for discounting purposes. We draw attention to the fact that the definition of β_j in equation 11.6.2 requires that to calculate correctly the covariance of the cash flow with the market return, the cash flow must be scaled or normalized by dividing by its expected value so that it will be in units corresponding to rates of return. In

Chapter 12, we present an example which illustrates the effect of this adjustment on making the necessary numerical computations.

By analogy with the earlier discussion of net present value as a criterion in Chapter 3, we may wish to compare V_{0j} with the initial outlay to determine whether or not the project should be accepted or rejected, and this is correct as far as the present example is concerned. Before we become too enthusiastic about this result, we warn the reader that its apparent elegant simplicity is somewhat misleading as the underlying theory is based on the concept of a single period as is our example, and it does not generalize so easily to many periods as we might wish. Under the earlier assumption of certainty, this distinction was irrelevant since all discounting was done (in principle) at what we now call the riskless rate. As we will discuss in Chapter 12, in a multi-period context estimation of the appropriate risk-adjusted discount rate is not always quite so straightforward as our example suggests.

11.7 Effects of uncertain inflation on required returns

As we established in Chapter 1, interest, or the required rate of return, is rent on borrowed money or the price of money. Thus, r_f is the price of money to a riskless borrower for a particular period of time. As we also discussed in Chapter 10, in the presence of inflation the riskless rate is a *nominal* rate, consisting of a *real* (inflation-free) rate of return, plus an *inflation premium* equal to the anticipated rate of inflation. We now inquire what the effect of inflation will be on the required rate of return of a risky asset in the context of the contemporary theory we have been considering. We will consider the question in two parts: (1) the effect on the riskless return and (2) the effect on the risk premium. This is equivalent to asking about the effects on the intercept and slope of the *SML,* respectively.

The effect on the riskless rate is as we have already specified. The *nominal* riskless rate increases by the amount of the (increase in) anticipated inflation. In Figure 11–10, the intercept of the SML shifts upward by this amount.

The more interesting question is what happens to the risk premium for the asset as captured in the expression for the SML? This question has been addressed by Chen and Boness,[28] who have developed a variation on the SML for the expected rate of return for a stock when there is uncertain inflation. In particular, they show that the covariance used to estimate the relevant systematic risk of the asset must be adjusted to

Figure 11–10
Effect of anticipated inflation on nominal risk-free rate

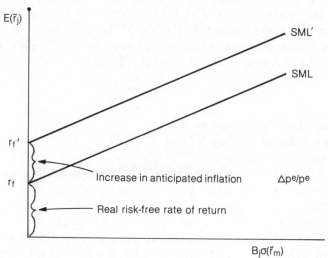

allow for the relationship between the asset's return and the rate of inflation. That is:

$$E(\tilde{r}_j) = r_f + \left[\frac{E(\tilde{r}_m) - r_f}{\sigma(\tilde{r}_m)}\right]\left[\frac{S \, \text{cov}(\tilde{r}_j,\tilde{r}_m) - W \, \text{cov}(\tilde{r}_j,\tilde{r}_a)}{\sigma(\tilde{r}_m)}\right] \quad (11.7.1)$$

where the returns are now nominal magnitudes, $\tilde{r}_a$ is the uncertain rate of inflation, S is the (nominal) aggregate market value of all stocks, and W is the (nominal) aggregate investible wealth of all investors.

From 11.7.1, we may redefine:

$$\beta_j = \frac{S \, \text{cov}(\tilde{r}_j,\tilde{r}_m) - W \, \text{cov}(\tilde{r}_j,\tilde{r}_a)}{\sigma^2(\tilde{r}_m)}$$

Under uncertain inflation, the systematic risk consists of two components: the covariance between the stock's rate of return and that of the market portfolio as before and the covariance between the stock's rate of return and the inflation rate. If the latter covariance is positive, the stock will show a higher nominal return the higher the inflation rate. This is desirable because part or all of the loss in real return will be offset thereby. Thus, stocks with positive return-inflation covariances will require lower returns in the market than would otherwise be the case without inflation because of their inherent inflation-hedging property. The converse will also be true of stocks with negative return-inflation covariances.

The underlying assumption here is that the market-equilibrating process takes place in terms of real rather than nominal returns, even though the market price of risk is expressed in nominal returns. This latter tends to imply that the slope of the SML would probably increase with increasing inflation (depending on the relative changes in magnitudes of $E(\tilde{r}_m)$, r_f, and $\sigma^2 - (\tilde{r}_m)$ with inflation).

11.A Appendix: Derivation of the Capital Asset Pricing Model (CAPM)

The contemporary financial theory which describes equilibrium conditions in capital markets under uncertainty is based on a particular set of assumptions regarding the individual investors who participate in the market and about the structure of the market itself. The following assumptions, which we summarize here, are more restrictive than necessary to yield the desired result, however, the ones we give are useful for expository purposes as they permit the least complicated discussion.

1.   Individual investors seek to maximize expected utility from their portfolios of assets. The only portfolio characteristics of concern are the expected return and standard deviation (or variance). Investors prefer greater expected return, thus for any given standard deviation of return, the portfolio offering the greatest expected return will be preferred. Investors are averse to risk, thus for any given expected return, the portfolio offering the least standard deviation of return will be preferred.

2.   The capital market is perfect in the sense that there are no taxes and no transactions costs, information is available without cost, assets are completely divisible, and the market is perfectly competitive.

3.   Since there are no personal taxes on income or wealth, investors are indifferent between dividends or capital gains on their assets. They can always achieve the same cash position by costlessly selling some of their assets to realize the capital gain and thereby convert some portion of their wealth to cash for consumption purposes.

4.   All investors have a single-period planning horizon and forecast the joint distribution of returns on all assets for the period ahead. The horizon period is timeless in the clock sense, being a market period, and is the same for all investors.

5.   Since all investors in the market have access to the same information at no cost, and all evaluate this information in the same way to arrive at the same joint distribution of returns on assets, the market participants share homogeneous expectations.

6. Every investor in the market has the same opportunities to invest, although the amounts invested will differ because of different initial wealth positions.

7. Investors may borrow and lend without limit at the risk-free rate of interest.

8. The stock (supply) of risky assets in the capital market is given. All securities (claims against assets) have been issued for the coming period, and all firms' operating and financing decisions have been made.

The function of the market is to price correctly all the assets and securities. The purpose of the theory is to provide a consistent explanation of how this process is accomplished even though some of the assumptions may not appear to have much empirical validity.

We next present a brief development of several results from contemporary financial theory, based on these assumptions, which were presented earlier in only a brief overview in the body of the chapter. Suppose we may assume a perfectly competitive capital market where all investors currently have the same (homogeneous) expectations with regard to the joint distribution of returns on risky assets to be obtained one period into the future. We continue to assume the existence of a risk-free asset so that the efficient frontier faced by all investors will consist of combinations of the risk-free asset and the risky market portfolio m.

Since all investors' choices always involve purchasing either the risk-free asset or a combination of the risk-free asset and portfolio m, then the combined actions of all investors imply that the returns on both m and the risk-free asset will be determined by investors' aggregate demand for risky investments. The total demand by all investors for the risky portfolio m determines the total demand for each asset in that portfolio. Further, every risky asset in the market must be contained in m, and each must ultimately be priced in equilibrium so that the proportions held in each individual portfolio will just exactly sum to the supply of that asset in the market at that point in time. Similarly, the total demand for the risk-free asset is the sum of each individual's demand for it. These choices must establish a particular required rate of return for each and every asset. This implies a particular, market-determined *price* for each asset.

Since each investor chooses the preferred combination of risk and return by choosing the proportions of portfolio m and the risk-free asset to be held, the risk of all portfolios will increase linearly as the proportion of the risk-free asset decreases. The expected return and standard deviation of each investor's portfolio are represented by:

$$E(\tilde{r}_p) = xr_f + (1 - x)(E(\tilde{r}_m) \qquad (11.A.1)$$

and

$$\sigma(\tilde{r}_p) = (1 - x)\sigma(\tilde{r}_m) \qquad (11.A.2)$$

respectively, where x is the proportion of the risk-free asset held. An investor who chooses only to hold the market portfolio m attains exactly the risk and return for that portfolio, as shown in Figure 11–A.1.

Figure 11–A.1
The capital market line

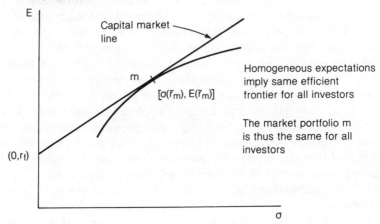

Notes: 1. Line has slope = $(E(\tilde{r}_m) - r_f)/\sigma(\tilde{r}_m)$, known as the market price (per unit) of risk.
2. Line represents locus of equilibrium portfolio choices

$$E(\tilde{r}_p) = r_f + \left[\frac{E(\tilde{r}_m) - r_f}{\sigma(\tilde{r}_m)}\right] \sigma(\tilde{r}_p)$$

and gives the trade-off between risk and return for any efficient portfolio.

The line which represents the portfolio combinations that may be chosen by investors is called the capital market line. It describes the equilibrium relationship between risk and return. The slope of this line is known as the market price (per unit) of risk and may be written as:

$$\frac{E(\tilde{r}_m) - r_f}{\sigma(\tilde{r}_m)} \qquad (11.A.3)$$

Using the capital market line, the relationship between return and risk any individual portfolio may be written as:

$$E(\tilde{r}_p) = r_f + \left[\frac{E(\tilde{r}_m) - r_f}{\sigma(\tilde{r}_m)}\right] \sigma(\tilde{r}_p) \qquad (11.A.4)$$

We now use the ideas we have just developed to find an equilibrium risk-return relationship for any particular risky asset in m. In this way, we can learn how the assets (and securities) of a particular firm are valued and ultimately how the firm's capital-expenditure decisions can be expected to affect value. We here find that the risk of a particular asset must be measured according to how it contributes to the risk of the market portfolio m, that is, how the systematic risk of the asset is defined in the theory. The standard deviation of any one particular asset's return is not the appropriate measure of its risk. To get our desired result, we will present a somewhat intuitive development of the security market line.[29] For this purpose, consider ownership of all assets to be represented by securities.

We now examine how the inclusion of any particular security j affects the risk of the market portfolio m. To do this, we will conduct an imaginary experiment, varying the proportion of j in combination with m (which already contains j in equilibrium), to study how the slope of the expected value-standard deviation curve for a portfolio consisting of m and j will change as the proportion of j changes. Figure 11–A.2

Figure 11–A.2
Derivation of the security market line

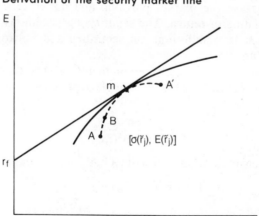

shows the capital market line, the efficient frontier of risky securities, and the locus of expected value-standard deviation combinations for the portfolio having extra proportions of j. Let x be the proportion of security j in combination with m, so that when $x = 0$ we have portfolio m alone. When $x = 1$ we have security j alone, and for $0 < x < 1$ we have combinations of j and m. When $x < 0$, we have m with some of the original j removed. We now wish to find an expression for the change in expected return per unit of risk as we vary x, evaluated particularly at the point $x = 0$.[30] This expression is:

$$\frac{\sigma(\tilde{r}_m)[E(\tilde{r}_j) - E(\tilde{r}_m)]}{[\text{cov}(\tilde{r}_j,\tilde{r}_m) - \sigma^2(\tilde{r}_m)]}$$

But, when $x = 0$ we have the point of tangency with the capital market line, so this expression must also equal the slope of that line. Thus we may equate:

$$\frac{E(\tilde{r}_m) - r_f}{\sigma(\tilde{r}_m)} = \frac{\sigma(\tilde{r}_m)[E(\tilde{r}_j) - E(\tilde{r}_m)]}{[\text{cov}(\tilde{r}_j,\tilde{r}_m) - \sigma^2(\tilde{r}_m)]}$$

or,

$$E(\tilde{r}_j) = r_f + \left[\frac{E(\tilde{r}_m) - r_f}{\sigma(\tilde{r}_m)}\right]\left[\frac{\text{cov}(\tilde{r}_j,\tilde{r}_m)}{\sigma(\tilde{r}_m)}\right] \tag{11.A.5}$$

Equation 11.A.5 is the security market line, which expresses the equilibrium market required rate of return for security j in terms of the return on the risk-free asset and a premium for risk. This risk premium is the product of the market price of risk and the risk measure for the particular security j. The latter is expressed in terms of the contribution of j to the risk of the market portfolio and not in terms of its own standard deviation of return. The security market line is illustrated in Figure 11–A.3. In equilibrium, all securities and portfolios must lie along the security market line.

We show also another measure commonly used to describe the risk of a particular security, that is, its β-coefficient. This measure is defined as:

$$\beta_j = \frac{\text{cov}(\tilde{r}_j,\tilde{r}_m)}{\sigma^2(\tilde{r}_m)} \tag{11.A.6}$$

Using this measure, we may rewrite 11.A.5 more compactly as:

$$E(\tilde{r}_j) = r_f + \beta_j[E(\tilde{r}_m) - r_f] \tag{11.A.7}$$

Thus β_j measures the responsiveness of a particular security's expected return to the risk premium on the market portfolio m.

While the security market line shows the equilibrium relationship between a security's risk and its market-required rate of return, we may also find it convenient to express this relationship in terms of the current market price of the firm's securities. To this end, we define the (uncertain) market price of the security one period hence as $\tilde{P}_j$, and its current price as P_{0j}. Thus:

$$\tilde{r}_j = \frac{\tilde{P}_j - P_{0j}}{P_{0j}} = \frac{\tilde{P}_j}{P_{0j}} - 1 \tag{11.A.8}$$

Figure 11–A.3
The security market line

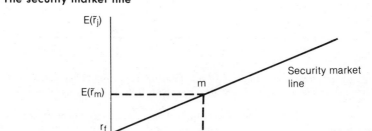

But we already know the security market line representation of the firm's expected return, so we may substitute the definition of equation 11.A.8 and solve for P_{0j}. From elementary probability theory, we also know that constants may be factored out of covariance terms, so we find:

$$\frac{E(\tilde{P}_j)}{P_{0j}} - 1 = r_f + \left(\frac{1}{P_{0j}}\right)\left[\frac{E(\tilde{r}_m) - r_f}{\sigma(\tilde{r}_m)}\right]\left[\frac{\text{cov}(\tilde{P}_j, \tilde{r}_m)}{\sigma(\tilde{r}_m)}\right]$$

Solving for P_{0j}, we get:

$$P_{0j} = \frac{E(\tilde{P}_j) - \left[\dfrac{E(\tilde{r}_m) - r_f}{\sigma(\tilde{r}_m)}\right]\left[\dfrac{\text{cov}(\tilde{P}_j, \tilde{r}_m)}{\sigma(\tilde{r}_m)}\right]}{1 + r_f} \qquad (11.A.9)$$

Equation 11.A.9 is known as the capital asset pricing model and is a general expression for the value of any risky asset in equilibrium. The numerator is the certainty equivalent of the uncertain future price $\tilde{P}_j$. This amount may then be discounted at the risk-free rate to find the current market value.

We may also find a risk-adjusted discount rate version of this model as well. This may be written as:

$$P_{0j} = \frac{E(\tilde{P}_j)}{1 + r_f + \left[\dfrac{E(\tilde{r}_m) - r_f}{\sigma(\tilde{r}_m)}\right]\left[\dfrac{\text{cov}(\tilde{P}_j|\tilde{P}_j, \tilde{r}_m)}{\sigma(\tilde{r}_m)}\right]} \qquad (11.A.10)$$

Note particularly that the covariance term is not the same in the two variations of the model since the certainty-equivalent risk adjustment factor must be scaled to the same dimensions as price, whereas in the risk-adjusted discount rate version, the adjustment has the dimensions of a rate of return.

Notes

1 F. H. Knight, *Risk, Uncertainty and Profit* (Boston: Houghton Mifflin, 1923), and J. A. Schumpeter, *The Theory of Economic Development* (Cambridge: Harvard University Press, 1934).

2 Knight, *Risk, Uncertainty and Profit*. Alternatively, uncertainty can be regarded as the case where compounding of probabilities, that is, the consideration of probability distributions of probability distributions is necessary. See A. G. Hart, "Risk, Uncertainty, and the Unprofitability of Compounding Probabilities," in *Studies in Mathematical Economics and Econometrics* (Chicago: University of Chicago Press, 1942), pp. 110–18.

3 F. P. Ramsay, *The Foundations of Mathematics* (London: Macmillan & Co., 1931), and L. J. Savage, *The Foundation of Statistics* (New York: Wiley, 1954).

4 H. A. Meyers, ed., *Symposium on Monte Carlo Methods* (New York: Wiley, 1956).

5 J. Von Neumann and O. Morgenstern, *The Theory of Games and Economic Behavior*, 3d ed. (Princeton: Princeton University Press, 1953).

6 D. B. Hertz, "Risk Analysis in Capital Investment," *Harvard Business Review*. (January–February 1964), pp. 95–106.

7 A. A. Robichek and S. C. Myers, "Valuation of the Firm: Effects of Uncertainty in a Market Context," *Journal of Finance* 21 (1966), pp. 215–27.

8 See also, Hart, "Risk, Uncertainty, and the Unprofitability."

9 D. Bernoulli, "Exposition of a New Theory on the Measurement of Risk," (1730), reprinted in *Econometrica* (1954), pp. 23–36.

10 M. Friedman and L. J. Savage, "The Utility Analysis of Choices Involving Risk," *Journal of Political Economy* 56 (August 1948), pp. 279–304.

11 A detailed development may be found in E. H. Neave and J. C. Wiginton, *Financial Management: Theory and Strategy* (Englewood Cliffs, N.J.: Prentice-Hall, 1980), chap. 5.

12 This is the kind of index of temperature which was used prior to the discovery of absolute zero and which is still used in the Fahrenheit and Celsius scales.

13 Von Neumann and Morgenstern, *Theory of Games*, pp. 617–33.

14 Certain types of hedges may be set up to approximate this situation. For further discussion and examples, see Neave and Wiginton, *Financial Management*, chap. 6.

15 It is possible to write general expressions corresponding to equations 11.2.1 and 11.2.2, but since we will not make use of them directly, we do not include them here. The interested reader may consult W. F. Sharpe, *Portfolio Theory and Capital Markets* (New York: McGraw-Hill, 1970), chap. 4.

16 Alternatively, if we do not want to imagine a riskless asset, we could always select a subset of the risky assets which are sufficiently negatively correlated to yield a portfolio whose risk-return value will plot on the vertical axis, as we have just seen. For reasons which will become clear later, this is called a *zero-β* portfolio. The possibility of being able to construct such a portfolio in principle is important in that it assures us that the theory on which we will be basing our recommendations could be developed even if there did not actually exist a riskless asset of the kind we are assuming.

17 A summary of the assumptions which characterize a perfect capital market under conditions of uncertainty is provided for the reader's convenience in Appendix 11-A.

18 The extent of the reduction of risk by diversification has been studied empirically by J. L. Evans and S. H. Archer, "Diversification and the Reduction of Dispersion: An

Empirical Analysis," *Journal of Finance* (December 1968), pp. 761–69; and by W. H. Wagner and S. C. Lau, "The Effect of Diversification on Risk," *Financial Analysts' Journal* (November–December 1971), pp. 48–53.

[19] W. F. Sharpe, "Capital Asset Prices: A Theory of Market Equilibrium under Conditions of Risk," *Journal of Finance* (September 1964), pp. 425–42.

[20] Indexes such as the New York Stock Exchange Index, the Standard and Poor 500, or the Toronto Stock Exchange 300 are representative.

[21] R. Ball and P. Brown, "Portfolio Theory and Accounting," *Journal of Accounting Research* 7 (Autumn 1969), pp. 300–323, W. H. Beaver, P. Kettler, and M. Scholes, "The Association between Market Determined and Accounting Determined Risk Measures," *The Accounting Review* 45 (October 1970), pp. 654–82; N. J. Gonedes, "Evidence on the Information Content of Accounting Numbers: Accounting-Based and Market-Based Estimates of Systematic Risk," *Journal of Financial and Quantitative Analysis* 8 (June 1973), pp. 407–43; and W. J. Breen and E. M. Lerner, "Corporate Financial Strategies and Market Measures of Risk and Return," *Journal of Finance* 28 (May 1973), pp. 339–51.

[22] B. Lev, "On the Association between Operating Leverage and Risk," *Journal of Financial and Quantitative Analysis* 9 (September 1974), pp. 627–41.

[23] R. S. Hamada, "The Effect of the Firm's Capital Structure on the Systematic Risk of Common Stocks," *Journal of Finance* 27 (May 1972), 435–52.

[24] B. Lev and S. Kunitzky, "On the Association between Smoothing Measures and the Risks of Common Stocks," *The Accounting Review* 49 (April 1974), pp. 259–70.

[25] R. M. Cyert and J. G. March, *A Behavioral Theory of the Firm* (Englewood Cliffs, N.J.: Prentice-Hall, 1963).

[26] This results from a second portfolio separation theorem, outside our present scope, whereby choice of risky assets (that is, portfolio selection) is shown to be independent of consumption decisions, which again depend only on wealth. See Neave and Wiginton, *Financial Management,* chap. 7, for further discussion.

[27] Even with more than one security, the market value criterion works in the interest of all investors unless risky debt is issued and side payments between stockholders and bondholders are not permitted. See E. F. Fama and M. H. Miller, *The Theory of Finance* (New York: Holt, Rinehart & Winston, 1972), pp. 179–81, for this result in a perfect capital market.

[28] A. H. Chen and A. J. Boness, "Effects of Uncertain Inflation on the Investment and Financing Decisions of a Firm," *Journal of Finance* 30 (May 1975), pp. 469–84.

[29] A detailed derivation, with examples, may be found in Neave and Wiginton, *Financial Management,* chap. 7.

[30] Actual derivation requires the use of calculus techniques beyond the scope of this book, so we state the results without proof. Proof may be found in Neave and Wiginton, *Financial Management.*

Problems

1. Suppose that a firm expects its future market value one period hence will be $1 million and notes that its current market value (number of shares outstanding times the market price per share) is $900,000. The expected return on the market portfolio is assumed to be 20 percent and the risk-free rate 10 percent. Suppose further that the firm has available a new investment project, which may only be accepted or rejected in its entirety, which is economically independent of the existing firm or any other contemplated

opportunities. The project requires an initial outlay of $50,000 and is expected to generate a cash flow $(\tilde{X})$ one period hence of $125,000. Further, we are told that cov $(\tilde{X}, \tilde{r}_m)/\sigma^2(\tilde{r}_m)$ is 150,000.

a. Should the new project be accepted or rejected? (Hint: First calculate the covariance of the existing firm with the market divided by the variance of the market return and then find the current market value of the existing firm plus the new project. The difference between this and the current value of the existing firm alone may then be compared with the required outlay.)

b. Find the expected internal rate of return for the project and compare it with the market required rate of return.

c. Calculate the β coefficient for the existing firm, the new project, and the combination of the two. What are the old and new required rates of return for the firm?

2. If the expected rate of return on the market portfolio is 15 percent and the risk-free rate is 5 percent, what is the β for a project which has a required return of 10 percent? What assumptions concerning this project and/or market conditions do you need to make to calculate this β?

3. You believe that the shares of FBN Company will be worth $100 each one year from now. If the β for FBN is 2.0, the risk-free rate is 8 percent and the expected return on the market is 18 percent, how much would you be willing to pay for one share of FBN today?

Project selection under risk

12.1 When should risk be considered explicitly?

In our analysis preceding Chapter 11, where risk was not explicitly considered, the condition for the acceptability of a project was the net present value condition that:

$$V_j - C_j \geq 0 \qquad (12.1.1)$$

where V_j is the present value of expected cash inflows (benefits) from project j, and C_j is the present value of costs associated with project j. Adding the net present (market) value of existing operations V_0 to both sides, we have:

$$V_0 + V_j - C_j \geq V_0 \qquad (12.1.2)$$

that is, the project must increase, or at least not decrease, the net present value of the firm. Explicit consideration of risk introduces the possibility that the required rate of return (cost of capital) may change, because project j may be perceived by the market as altering the operating risk of the firm. The basic (market-value rule) criterion is unchanged, but now the consequences of a change in the required rate of return must be taken into account. As a first approximation, the effect of changing the cost of capital from k_0 to k_0' can be incorporated by computing an implicit perpetuity at the former rate, recapitalized at the latter. This yields:

$$(k_0/k_0')(V_0 + V_j - C_j) \geq V_0 \qquad (12.1.3)$$

Unless the ratio k_0/k_0' differs significantly from 1, equation 12.1.3 reduces to 12.1.2. Market institutions provide threshold values of k_0/k_0' and define the amount of change in risk which requires consideration. Stock prices are quoted in eighths, implicitly these are rounded and a change of at least one sixteenth of a point is the minimum which will produce a revised valuation. For a stock trading in the $100 range, the values of k_0/k_0' adjacent to 1 are 1.000625 and 0.999375. This is equivalent to a change of .625 basis points in a required yield of 10 percent or one of 0.5 basis points in a required yield of 8 percent.

Unless the change in required rate of return is at least of this magnitude, no explicit consideration of risk is necessary.

Another way of approaching this problem is to compare the systematic risk of the firm presently with that of the firm with the new project included. If the systematic risk presently can be designated as β_0, then by equation 11.4.4 with the new project added, the systematic risk will be:

$$\beta_0' = x_0\beta_0 + x_j\beta_j \tag{12.1.4}$$

where x_0 is the proportion of the firm's investment represented by present operations, $x_0 = V_0/(V_0 + C_j)$, and x_j is the proportion of the firm's investment represented by project j, $x_j = C_j/(V_0 + C_j)$. We may compute the relative change in systematic risk by the ratio β_0'/β_0.

We recall that equation 11.5.3b gave an expression for the required rate of return which we reproduce here:

$$k = r_f + \beta_j[E(\tilde{r}_m) - r_f] \tag{12.1.5}$$

This applies equally to a firm. The risk premium could be written as:

$$\beta_j[E(\tilde{r}_m) - r_f] = k - r_f \tag{12.1.6}$$

Now, if we add a project to the existing firm, the new required rate of return for the firm may be written as:

$$k_0' = r_f + \frac{\beta_0'}{\beta_0}\, \beta_0[E(\tilde{r}_m) - r_f] \tag{12.1.7}$$

If we had been able to estimate the required rate of return (cost of capital) of the original firm, k_0, as discussed in Chapter 5, and if we can obtain an estimate of the riskless rate, r_f, by combining 12.1.6 and 12.1.7, we may write:

$$k_0' = r_f + \frac{\beta_0'}{\beta_0}\, (k_0 - r_f) \tag{12.1.8}$$

to determine the new overall required rate of return and the ratio k_0/k_0'.

We consider again our earlier example where the addition of a new project increased the systematic risk enough that we found the minimum detectable change in k_0/k_0' from 1 to 0.999375 because of an implied increase in the overall required rate of return from 10 to 10.00625. We now assume further that r_f is 4 percent and β_0 is 1, which latter implies it is reasonable to assume that $E(\tilde{r}_m)$ is also 10 percent. Using equation 12.1.5 to represent k_0, and 12.1.8 for k_0', we may form their ratio, substitute for the assumed values, and calculate the ratio β_0'/β_0 to be 1.00104. Since β_0 was assumed to be 1, this implies β_0' is 1.00104.

Referring back to equation 12.1.4, we may ask in what proportions the new project may be included, and what maximum β_j it would have, to give the minimally detectable change in required yield? The following shows the answer for a selected range of proportions.

x_j	β_j
0.01	1.1042
0.05	1.0208
0.10	1.0104
0.20	1.0052
0.50	1.0021
0.80	1.0013

Note that β_j approaches 1.00104 as x_j approaches 1.0, as it must in this example.

Thus the effect of the new project on the systematic risk of the firm can be defined as a function of the size of the new investment relative to existing operations and its systematic risk characteristics. It is clear that small projects may have systematic risk many times greater than that of the firm as a whole without increasing the latter's systematic risk to the point where the required return and market price are affected significantly.

It is, of course, necessary to have some idea of the project's systematic risk before applying this test. This does not, however, require a detailed analysis of risk, but rather some notion of comovement of project return with the market return to estimate covariance and thus systematic risk. We provide an example in the next section illustrating how such estimates may be calculated. If these estimates suggest that the project may alter the firm's systematic risk significantly, a more carefully detailed analysis of project risk would be warranted. If not, the project may be accepted if its expected net present value is positive.

This latter statement follows from our conclusion in Chapter 3 that economically independent projects may be evaluated independently. In our example of this section, we have been considering the effect of adding only one project to the existing firm. But, projects are included in the capital budget for the period, and so the relevant reference set for comparative purposes is not the existing firm, but rather the existing firm plus any projects already adopted and included in the current capital budget. However, unless we are prepared to make a detailed analysis of risk for each project, which we are attempting to avoid insofar as possible, we seem to be faced with a paradox!

The basic capital-budgeting procedure must select the set of projects which maximizes the current market value of the firm, now with due consideration for changes in valuation induced by changes in systematic risk. This sounds somewhat similar to the selection problem we treated in Chapter 7 by mathematical programming techniques, and no doubt it could be formulated in a similar way.[1] We do not believe, however, that such an approach would prove to be very practical. Instead, we choose to approach this problem using a systematic search procedure. The rationale behind this procedure is that as the effective discount rate is decreased, more projects become acceptable, and that any project accepted at a given required rate will remain acceptable at a lower required (ignoring possible multiple-rate projects). The search procedure begins by finding the project having the greatest increment to risk, yet remains acceptable, then considers other projects in turn until the list of acceptable projects is completed. Since risk-increasing projects may be unacceptable when their addition to current operations is considered but become acceptable as the dilution effect of a larger operating base becomes effective, it is necessary to iterate through the list until no further projects can be added.

The search procedure is as follows:

1. Each project is considered as a potential addition to the firm's existing operations.[2] To determine its impact, values of β_0' are computed for each project combined with current operations according to equation 12.1.4. Revised overall required rates of return (k_0') are then computed using equation 12.1.5.

2. Prospective additions are ranked in descending order of k_0'.

3. The new market value of the firm which would result from adoption of the project at the head of the list is computed using:

$$(k_0/k_0')V_0 + V_j' - C_j' \qquad (12.1.9)$$

where V_j' and C_j' are computed at k_0', and the first term reflects the revaluation of the existing firm that results from the change in the overall required rate of return.

4. Test whether the new market value of the firm calculated in number 3 exceeds the current market value V_0. If not, the project does not pass the test (for the present) and is transferred to a list of provisionally rejected projects. Repeat number 3 for the next project on the list of projects not yet considered.

5. If the new market value of the firm including the project exceeds the current market value, the project is accepted. Current operations are redefined to incorporate the new project, so that V_0 becomes the result of calculating equation 12.1.9, while β_0 becomes β_0' and k_0 becomes k_0'. The provisionally rejected projects of number 4 are restored

to the list of projects under consideration, and the analysis is repeated starting at 1.

6. When the bottom of the list of projects under consideration is reached, and the last remaining project is rejected, the procedure is ended. All of the projects on the provisionally rejected list at this point have been considered as additions to the last accepted budget and were rejected. As there has been no further change in the composition of the accepted set to warrant their inclusion, they become the rejected set.[3]

12.2 Estimating risk-adjusted discount rates for cash flows

For practical application of contemporary theory to the analysis of capital-expenditure decisions, it is necessary to estimate both the expected cash flows that a project will generate and the risk-adjusted discount rate to apply to those cash flows. Unless we have data from previous experience with similar projects, we must estimate cash flows and required returns jointly. This is best seen in the following example.[4]

Example 12.2.1: Suppose we undertake to estimate jointly, one period into the future, the return on the market portfolio and cash flows for a project we wish to examine for its acceptability. We imagine three possible economic or market conditions as states of the world: poor, normal and good, with subjective probabilities 0.2, 0.4, and 0.4, respectively. We assume the risk-free rate is 4 percent. The return on the market portfolio and the project cash flows are estimated for each state of the world as follows:

State of the world	Subjective probability (P_i)	Market portfolio return ($\tilde{r}_m$)	Project cash flow ($\tilde{X}_{jk}$)
Poor	0.2	−0.10	$ 50,000
Normal	0.4	0.10	100,000
Good...................	0.4	0.30	200,000

We indicated earlier that we preferred to work with risk-adjusted discount rates, and for the purpose of finding such a rate for this example, we will use the results of equation 11.6.2. We recall that we found that if we normalize the probability distribution of the cash flows by dividing each element by the expected value of the distribution, the resulting random variable has the same dimensions as a rate of return, and its distribution necessarily has an expected value of 1. Here, $E(\tilde{X}_{jk}) = \$130,000$.

With this result, we may recast our example data:

State of the world	Subjective probability (P_i)	Market portfolio return ($\tilde{r}_m$)	Normalized project cash flow ($\tilde{X}/\bar{X}$)
Poor	0.2	−0.10	0.385
Normal	0.4	0.10	0.769
Good	0.4	0.30	1.538

From these data we calculate $E(\tilde{r}_m) = 0.14$, $\sigma(\tilde{r}_m) = 0.15$, $E(\tilde{X}/\bar{X}) = 1$, $\sigma(\tilde{X}/\bar{X}) = 0.46$, and $\text{cov}(\tilde{X}/\bar{X},\tilde{r}_m) = 0.07$. We may then calculate $\beta_j = (0.07)/(0.15)^2 = 3.11$, and from equation 11.6.1, $E(\tilde{r}_j) = 0.04 + 3.11(0.14 - 0.04) = 0.351$, or 35.1 percent. We will take this to be the appropriate risk-adjusted discount rate for the period for which the cash flow data were derived, and denote it as k_X (referring to the fact that it was derived from cash flow data).

We may apply this procedure to the market portfolio return and cash flow distributions for as many future periods as we believe they may be different and obtain a specific risk-adjusted discount rate for those periods which reflect our beliefs as impounded into the underlying model. How we may actually use these rates in making capital-expenditure decisions is not quite so straightforward as we might hope and requires additional considerations which we next discuss. Before doing that, however, we note two important qualifications regarding the risk-adjusted discount rate we have calculated: (a) it is only as accurate (in the sense of correct, after the fact) as our forecasts of market portfolio return and cash flow distributions turn out to have been; (b) it is only as valid as the capital-market theory on which it is based.[5]

12.3 Certainty equivalents versus risk-adjusted discount rates: Problems of multi-period valuation

Here we consider again a problem first mentioned in Section 7.2 which arises if we naively apply risk-adjusted discount rates to expected cash flows in straightforward analogy with the procedures we used in Chapter 3 under certainty.[6] Let us suppose that we apply the risk-adjusted discount rate just calculated to the expected value of the distribution of cash flows to be received t periods into the future. The present value then will be:

$$V_{Xt} = \frac{\bar{X}_t}{(1 + k_X)^t} \qquad (12.3.1)$$

Let us now write the numerator of the certainty equivalent form of the CAPM of equation 11.A.9 as $\sigma_t \bar{X}_t$, so that we have also:

$$V_{Xt} = \frac{\alpha_t \bar{X}_t}{(1 + r_f)^t} \qquad (12.3.2)$$

Since we presume that the two estimates of V_{Xt} should be the same, we equate:

$$\frac{\alpha_t \bar{X}_t}{(1 + r_f)^t} = \frac{\bar{X}_t}{(1 + k_X)^t}$$

or:

$$\alpha_t = \frac{(1 + r_f)^t}{(1 + k_X)^t} \qquad (12.3.3)$$

Since $k_X > r_f$, the certainty equivalent adjustment factor must be an exponentially decreasing function of t, which in turn implies an exponentially increasing risk pattern over time. While this result may reflect our current beliefs regarding some projects, it is much too restrictive to be generally valid. Furthermore, for some projects, such as mines and oil wells, our uncertainty will be sharply reduced once the investment has been made and we can better estimate the cash flows.

The difficulty lies in equating the two values to find α_t in equation 12.3.3. The certainty equivalent and risk-adjusted discount rate representations give the same result *only* in the single-period case for which the underlying theory was derived. To deal with multi-period problems in a formally correct manner, we need a theoretically based model which is itself multi-period.[7] If we can assume a perfect market for real capital goods, then the multi-period problem may be shown to reduce to a series of independent one-period problems.[8] Even if we cannot assume that the assets can be sold in a perfect market, it may be sufficient to assume that the firm itself may be sold by virtue of selling all the claims against it, that is, all its securities in a perfect capital market. Obviously, where a project is only one part of a large operation, selling claims solely against that project may not always be feasible.

This multi-period problem has been studied to some extent.[9] While detailed examination of the findings is beyond the scope of this book, some observations may be offered. If we insist that we must explicitly solve the multi-period problem without the assumption that claims may be traded in a perfect market, we are faced with the need to solve a particularly intractable stochastic, dynamic programming problem.[10] While the effort might yield some useful information, the implied computational burden is really too imposing in any realistic case. One important implication of the theoretical investigations is that if investors are not to hedge against future changes in portfolio opportunities, the portfolio opportunity set made up of the market portfolio and the riskless asset must be nonstochastic. This means that the risk-free interest rate and the market price of risk must be known, that is, nonstochastic, which further implies the return on the market portfolio must also be known. The only admissible uncertainty then is in the expected cash flows as assessed when the decision is to be made. If we wish to apply the current theory, we must assume that the market parameters do not vary stochastically through time, although we are not necessarily required to assume they are constant.[11] Since we have ruled out uncertainty about the market parameters, the only remaining source of uncertainty about the incremental (present) value of a project to the firm must be isolated in the expected value of the cash flows and their systematic risk at each point in time.

If the distribution of cash flows is known, and the returns on the market also, then the expected value and risk-adjusted discount rate can be calculated as our example of Section 12.2 showed. Under these assumptions, the value of the project cash flow occurring in period t may be expressed as:

$$V_{OX} = \prod_{k=1}^{t-1} \frac{1}{(1 + r_f(k))} \frac{\bar{X}(t)}{1 + k_X{}^{(t)}} \qquad (12.3.4)$$

where the subscript (t) indicates the values in time t. Note particularly that the risk-adjusted discount rate is relevant only at t when cash flow $X(t)$ is to be realized. For the intermediate periods between now and t, the risk-free rate must be applied. This appears contrary to the intuitive and widely used method of applying a risk-adjusted discount rate during all time periods.

For other cash flows occurring in each period from now to the relevant planning horizon, we may apply equation 12.3.4 period by period to find the total increment to value arising from a project. This result will generally be larger in magnitude than the result of applying the risk-adjusted rate period by period, so it might be argued that the latter is more conservative. But since it may also imply the rejection of many projects which in fact are value enhancing, this approach does not satisfy the wealth-maximizing criterion.

Since the market parameters have been assumed known in each period, if the cash flows are the same in any periods, the risk-adjusted discount rates may also be the same for those periods when the market parameters are the same. This will afford some economies in estimation.

12.4 Empirical validity of the capital asset pricing model

Our interest in the contemporary theory of finance is primarily, if not entirely, normative; that is, we wish to use it to aid capital-expenditure decision making to whatever extent may be practical. However, a considerable body of literature has been devoted to the positive aspects of the theory; that is, whether it explains or predicts observed phenomena. The importance of this research to us is that if the theory is empirically valid, then we may have more confidence that its normative application will lead us to make correct decisions in the sense that the capital market will perceive and evaluate our actions more or less in the manner we had intended.

A large number of studies has been conducted, and there is nothing to be gained by attempting to list them all here. We will only summarize briefly the main findings.[12] Various investigators have worked with different data. Sets of cross-sectional and time-series returns data have been examined as have returns data on both individual securities and portfolios. Regardless of which data were used, the essential intent was to test three main implications of the theory: (a) the risk-return relationship should be linear; (b) no measure of risk in addition to β should be related systematically to expected returns; (c) expected return should increase as a security's risk increases.

The major results of the various studies may be summarized as follows.

1. The evidence tends to show a significant positive linear relationship between (ex post) realized returns and measures of systematic risk. However, the magnitude of the relationship (slope of the line) has usually been found to be less than that predicted by the theory, which suggests that some other factors not included in the current theory may be important.

2. The risk-return relationship does appear to be essentially linear, as the studies do not show consistently any evidence of nonlinearity.

3. Tests that have attempted to discriminate between the effects of systematic and unsystematic risk have not yielded definitive results, as both kinds of risk appear to be positively related to security returns. There is, however, some evidence in these studies that suggests the

relationship between unsystematic risk and return may derive partly from measurement error. The other possibility is that unsystematic risk incorporates effects of other factors, as yet unidentified.

It seems clear that we cannot claim that the current theory has been wholly validated on the basis of this empirical evidence. In fact, serious problems are inherent in all the studies. Nevertheless, the empirical results do tend to support the view that, for the present at least, β is a useful measure of risk for our purposes since (empirically observed) "high-β" assets do tend to be priced to yield correspondingly high returns.

The studies on which we have based our conclusions have been criticized on the grounds that the market portfolio has not been identified, but rather only surrogate (index) measures have been used instead: hence, the tests have not been properly constructed. Roll[13] has argued that while the theory is testable in principle, no suitable tests have yet been effected. He contends that no correct and unambiguous test has appeared in the literature and that there is practically no possibility that such a test can be accomplished in the future. The main difficulty lies in the problem of identifying the market portfolio. For the theory states that the market portfolio contains *all* assets, marketable and otherwise: therefore, it is not directly observable. But the implications of the theory are not testable unless the exact composition of the true market portfolio is known and used in the tests. Any portfolio which is used as a surrogate and which is ex post efficient (properly valued) *must*, of necessity, plot as a point along the security market line. However, all other security's returns must also plot along the security market line in equilibrium and so will be related to (correlated with) the market surrogate return by definition. Thus, all the reported tests can be viewed as merely confirming the truth of this tautology.

For those concerned with positive theory, the evidence suggests we may have to look for some description of the risky asset pricing process which is richer and more general than the current theory. In fact, at the time of this writing, an alternative attracting considerable attention is the so-called arbitrage pricing theory.[14] It will, however, be some time before the implications of this theory for capital-expenditure decision making are fully understood. For the present, we are satisfied that when the analysis suggested in Section 12.1 indicates that if considering some risk-adjusted discount rate different from the firm's current required rate of return is desirable to properly evaluate a project, the β-based measures provide a *consistent* method of risk adjustment whose validity may well be within the practical accuracy limitations of the data we are able to derive from operating records and/or engineering studies. And even at that, for the reasons we have discussed, the decision maker will still need to exercise caution and judgment in applying these measures.

12.5 Handling risk by rules of thumb

The question of how to manage the level of risk by selecting projects which may substantially alter risk levels has already been addressed in Section 12.1.

We now consider two additional approaches that may also aid in evaluating capital-expenditure decisions under uncertainty; that is, computer simulation and payback as a supplementary criterion. We indicated in Section 12.3 that the theoretical representation of the multi-period valuation model is inherently a stochastic dynamic programming problem of a particularly intractible type. One way to deal with such problems practically is in the form of a decision tree, which may be described as contingency planning,[15] or through computer simulation models.[16] Instead of attempting to calculate probabilities directly using discrete probability distributions as in the decision tree approach, it is possible to use pseudo-random number generating algorithms on a computer to develop synthetic samples which give probabilities approximating continuous distributions. These distributions may be developed for operating incomes and net cash flows, then representative values may be strategically chosen for use in analyses such as we have shown by example. Clearly, considerable computing power is needed to support such efforts.

Many firms retain payback as a supplementary criterion because their managers apparently feel that since forecasting for periods beyond the payback period is very difficult, payback will tend to protect them from excessive exposure to risk.[17] Many firms, which have abandoned payback as a measure of desirability, retain it as a constraint in the hope of controlling risk and also maintaining desired liquidity levels. Among budgeting systems that attempt to make explicit provision for risk, this is one widely used provision. It is, therefore, pertinent to consider what kinds of risk payback protects against and how.

In the type of single-valued estimate usually considered, payback is simply a comparison of expected after-tax cash flows for the first few years with initial outlays. It does not protect against unforeseen poor outcomes in these initial years, which are admittedly the easiest to forecast but are also the most crucial from the point of view of solvency. It protects against bad results subsequent to the payback period by ignoring them entirely. Thus it may lead to acceptance of highly risky, but short-lived, projects and rejection of long-lived projects which are virtually risk free since it is not a measure of risk but an (inadequate) one of profitability. It has been claimed that it is a protection against obsolescence, but a leading critic has rightly pointed out that keeping existing equipment around until proposed replacements offer quick payback is a virtual guarantee of obsolescence.[18] In this respect, its operation is likely to be perverse. It is difficult to imagine situations in which its use as a supplementary criterion could afford systematic protection against risk. In those situations in which it would be operative, it merely imposes constraints on the time shape of the expected stream of cash flows, but none whatever on their variability. As such, it is a protection only against the long-term environmental risk resulting from a rate of economic growth and growth in markets below that forecast and not a particularly useful one.

12.6 Owners versus managers

Our discussion of systematic versus unsystematic risk suggests a source of potentially serious conflict between owners and managers which may materially affect the capital-expenditure decisions made by managers so that they will not necessarily be in the best interests of the owners or stockholders. We established earlier that it is the systematic risk which is of concern to stockholders since that is what determines the value of common stock in the capital market. Unsystematic risk will be diversified away in the stockholders' portfolios.

The reader may recall also from our discussion of bankruptcy risk in Section 6.7 that costs of bankruptcy may not be significant to the stockholder, but the penalties may well accrue to the managers of the firm in bankruptcy. From our present viewpoint, we can now recognize that bankruptcy risk depends on total risk, and as we observed earlier, the more different the operating characteristics of any particular firm from others, the greater will be the divergence between systematic risk and total risk. Stockholders will be concerned with the former, but managers will be more attuned to the latter.

Since it is not easy for stockholders to monitor the activities of managers, not only because they are disinclined to do so but because information about managers' performance is difficult to obtain, managers must be motivated to act in the best interests of stockholders. Various incentive schemes can be used to effect this motivation by rewarding the manager for following stockholders' preferences. For example, a stock option plan for managers is intended to give them a greater incentive to maximize share price than does a fixed salary arrangement. On the other hand, bonus payments based on current profit performance may lead to myopic, short-run optimizing behavior that ultimately causes stock prices to fall.

Unfortunately, such schemes resolve the motivation problem only partially, since under these arrangements the managers' compensation may be tied entirely to the fortunes of his firm. Managers may be less able to diversify their personal investments in that their stock option plan in the firm they manage may be their only major investment. Again, this would tend to cause them to be more concerned with total risk than with systematic risk.

This problem has been studied using the economic theory of agency.[19] In this theory, the stockholders' (principal's) problem is to design a compensation scheme that will cause an expected-utility maximizing manager (agent) to act so as to maximize the principal's utility as well. The theoretical argument is too detailed to present here, but it does suggest that the owners' problem of contracting for the services of a manager may be studied as a problem in buying information. In this case, the information purchased is the manager's opinion regarding possible excess returns from operation, and its price is the manager's fee.[20] The fee actually paid will depend also on whether the owner can evaluate the excess returns correctly. If so, the fee will be lower than otherwise, as the owner and manager will engage in a form of bargaining known as bilateral monopoly with indeterminate outcome a priori.

Analysis of this problem shows that if the manager is allowed to invest in the firm (through stock options), he will value the option less as the standard deviation (total risk) of the firm's return increases, requiring a larger fixed fee in compensation. The protection afforded the owner lies in keeping the fixed fee small enough so that the manager will accept the contract only if he believes the excess return is large enough to protect the owner. Such a participatory contract between an owner and a manager will require a higher rate of return from investment decisions than otherwise to compensate the owner for the costs of obtaining the information needed to design the contract.

Firms in uncommon lines of business will tend toward relatively smaller systematic risks and will also require special forms of compensation for managers as their corresponding expected returns will be small. An uncommon manager will be needed to recognize the potential of and correctly manage an uncommon firm.

A somewhat different aspect of the problem of correct objectives for the firm and the related criteria to provide to managers has been debated recently in the literature.[21] We have assumed in accordance with received theory that wealth maximization (the market-value rule) on behalf of the firm's stockholders was a sufficient condition. However, the papers cited have concluded that wealth (value) maximization may be neither a clearly defined firm objective nor even one preferred by a majority (or indeed any) of the firm's stockholders. These studies have shown that stockholders might, however, be unanimous regarding preferences over marginal changes in the firm's production plans (and capital budgets by implication) so long as the scope of these changes is limited in a particular way. Specifically, the admissible set can consist only of plans currently implemented by existing firms in the market. This is a highly restrictive condition on the proper development of capital market equilibrium theory because of its impact on generality. From a practical viewpoint, however, it may be less seriously damaging than might be first suspected since, many (most) capital-expenditure decisions involve technologies and, therefore, production plans which are well known and meet the restrictive condition for all practical purposes. The reader may recall the distinction we made between routine and strategic capital-expenditure decisions in Chapter 2. The more strategic the decision, the more the decision maker may be in trouble with this theoretical restriction, not to mention the real stockholders. It is perhaps speculation to suggest that this may explain why major technological innovations are usually brought about by zealous individual entrepreneurs, as well why the notion of an entrepreneurial firm may be a logical contradiction.

Notes

[1] See, for example, J. Cord, "A Method for Allocating Funds to Investment Projects when Returns are Subject to Uncertainty," *Management Science* 11 (1964), pp. 335–41.

[2] Spin-offs or disinvestment can be handled within the framework of the model as projects for which C_j and V_j are given negative signs.

[3] Minor projects, accepted without detailed risk analysis for the reasons already noted, are assumed to be incorporated into the existing firm before the procedure of selecting risky projects is started.

[4] This example was inspired, in part, by J. F. Weston, "Investment Decisions Using the Capital Asset Pricing Model," *Financial Management* (Spring 1973), pp. 25–33.

[5] Evidence regarding the validity of the theory and its implications for capital-expenditure decision making is discussed briefly in Section 12.4.

[6] The problem we now consider appears first to have been discussed by A. A. Robichek and S. C. Myers, "Conceptual Problems in the Use of Risk-Adjusted Discount Rates," *Journal of Finance* (December 1966), pp. 727–30.

[7] E. F. Fama and M. H. Miller, *The Theory of Finance* (New York: Holt, Rinehart & Winston, 1972), chap. 8.

[8] Ibid., p. 123.

[9] M. C. Bogue and R. Roll, "Capital Budgeting of Risky Projects with 'Imperfect' Markets for Physical Capital," *Journal of Finance* (May 1974), pp. 601–13; E. F. Fama, "Risk-Adjusted Discount Rates and Capital Budgeting under Uncertainty," *Journal of*

Financial Economics (August 1977), pp. 3–24; and S. C. Myers and S. M. Turnbull, "Capital Budgeting and the Capital Asset Pricing Model: Good News and Bad News," *Journal of Finance* 32 (May 1977), pp. 321–32. A detailed discussion of these papers may be found in E. H. Neave and J. C. Wiginton, *Financial Management: Theory and Strategy* (Englewood Cliffs, N.J.: Prentice-Hall, 1980), chap. 10.

[10] Bogue and Roll, "Capital Budgeting."

[11] The reader may recall our earlier discussion regarding inflation effects in Chapter 10.

[12] A more detailed discussion of important contributions may be found in Neave and Wiginton, *Financial Management,* chap. 8.

[13] R. Roll, "A Critique of the Asset Pricing Theory's Tests," *Journal of Financial Economics* 4 (March 1977), pp. 129–76.

[14] S. A. Ross, "The Arbitrage Theory of Capital Asset Pricing," *Journal of Economic Theory* 13 (December 1976), pp. 341–60, "The Current Status of the Capital Asset Pricing Model (CAPM)," *Journal of Finance* 33 (1978), pp. 885–901.

[15] Neave and Wiginton, *Financial Management,* chap. 15.

[16] D. B. Hertz, "Risk Analysis in Capital Investment," *Harvard Business Review* (January–February 1964), pp. 95–106, is frequently cited.

[17] H. M. Weingartner, "Some New Views on the Payback Period and Capital Budgeting Decisions," *Management Science* 15 (August 1969), pp. 594–607.

[18] G. Terborgh, *Business Investment Policy* (Washington, D.C.: Machinery and Allied Products Institute, 1958), p. 32.

[19] D. G. Heckerman, "Motivating Managers to Make Investment Decisions," *Journal of Financial Economics* 2 (1975), pp. 273–92.

[20] Excess returns are defined here as returns above those determined by the security market line. See *Fortune* (April 23, 1979), pp. 111–14, for discussion of the ability of some managers to perceive ways of generating excess returns.

[21] The point was originally raised in M. Jensen and J. Long, "Corporate Investment under Uncertainty and Pareto Optimality in the Capital Markets," *Bell Journal of Economics* 3 (Spring 1972), pp. 151–74. Citation of other contributions and some additional results may be found in S. Benninga and E. Muller, "Majority Choice and the Objective Function of the Firm under Uncertainty," *Bell Journal of Economics* 10 (Autumn 1979), pp. 670–82.

Problems

1. The management of the Foreseeable Future Company, in consultation with their investment bankers, have determined that there are four states of the world which are of concern to them one period hence and have estimated the subjective probability of each state's occurrence, along with the return on a representative market index and the firm as follows:

State	Probability	Market return	Firm return
1	0.1	−0.20	−0.35
2	0.3	0.05	0.00
3	0.4	0.20	0.25
4	0.2	0.25	0.50

The risk-free rate is expected to be 6 percent. Calculate the following:

a. The expected "market" return, and variance of return,

b. The expected return for Foreseeable Future, and the covariance of return with the market return,

c. The required return for Foreseeable. How does this compare with its expected return? What would you expect will happen to the market value of Foreseeable?

2. The following time series data have been determined for returns on a representative market index and for the Historical Heritage Company.

Year	Market return	Company return
1980	0.32	0.30
1979	0.17	0.10
1978	−0.08	−0.10
1977	0.17	0.20
1976	−0.08	−0.15
1975	0.32	0.35

The yield to maturity on Treasury Bills is 8 percent and is expected to remain at approximately that level. Calculate the following:

a. The expected market return and variance of return.

b. The expected return for Historical Heritage and the covariance of return with the market return,

c. The required return for Historical Heritage. How does this compare with its expected return? What do you expect will happen to the market value of Historical Heritage?

3. The Conserver Company has a capital structure which consists of equal proportions of debt and equity. The current weighted average cost of capital is 9 percent and the company's marginal tax rate is 50 percent. The current market value of Conserver is $1 million. A new project costing $500,000 has been proposed. It is claimed to have the same risk as the existing firm, and is expected to return 8.5 percent. This new project can be financed entirely with debt having a before-tax marginal cost of 5 percent. The operations manager claims that the project is acceptable because it returns more than the cost of its financing. As financial manager, how will you answer the operations manager? Will you recommend acceptance of the project? Explain.

4. The Venture Corporation is considering a new investment project with an expected return of 17 percent. This project is considered to be one third more risky than the average of the firm's existing operations. Presently, the

required return on the firm's equity shares is 18 percent and the current market value of the outstanding equity is $800,000, while the required rate of return on its debt is 9 percent and its current market value is $400,000. The risk-free rate of interest is 5 percent, and the variance of the market return is 0.08. Assuming there are no corporate income taxes, is the project acceptable? Explain.

Risk, conflict situations, and classical uncertainty

13.1 Introduction

To this point we have been discussing risky investment situations in which we have been able to define probability distributions of outcomes. Whatever their source, such distributions are treated the same way in the decision-making process. In chapter 11, we noted Knight's distinction between situations involving risk and those involving uncertainty.[1] This distinction hinged on whether or not the probability distribution of outcomes was or was not known. With the rise of subjective concepts of probability, the development of simulation techniques, and the availability of virtually unlimited computing power, the set of situations in which probabilities are unavailable is much narrower than it was in Knight's day. It is, however, not empty and remains in a set of situations usually defined in the price theory literature as oligopolistic interdependence.[2] Here, outcomes are dependent on the consciously taken decisions of rivals in the marketplace and will differ according to which decisions are taken. They are not random, although they may have random components, that is, the magnitude of the shared market. Because of the conscious response of opponents, it is not possible to express outcome in terms of a simple probability distribution, and the appropriate tool for analyses is no longer the calculus of probabilities but the theory of games.[3] The market structure involved may be characterized as oligopoly, bilateral monopoly, or oligopsony. Purely price-theoretic implications have been examined in a number of works,[4] the capital-investment implications have received rather less attention.

The following suggestions do not constitute a rigorous application of game theory to the problem since such an application is well beyond the scope of this book. First of all, the basic data of an oligopolistic market, such as the demand for its product, are random variables to which the theory of probability applies. Changing fortunes of firms in such a market are the result of risk factors and strategy choices, but there is no evidence that the capital market makes any distinction between the two. It is apt to regard all variability as due to risk, as we have defined that term, and to capitalize unstable income streams ac-cordingly. Nor is there any evidence that it should do otherwise, except that in doing so it may underestimate risk. Variance due to parameter shifts may be measurable, and that due to changes in strategy may be infinite. A sample variance can be computed for any sample of data, but it is not a reliable estimator of the population variance which re-mains infinite.[5]

A second fundamental problem is that most capital-budgeting prob-lems turn out not to be games of the simple two-person zero sum variety for which all solutions are known but to be non-zero sum games often for *n* persons. Here, not all solutions (in the von Neumann-Morgenstern sense) are known, and the very concept of solution be-comes ambiguous, with a number of solution concepts within the set of von Neumann-Morgenstern solutions having been advanced as more plausible than others.[6]

Finally, the concept of a mixed strategy, which plays a fundamental role in finding solutions to the two-person zero-sum games into which all larger games must be resolved, is unappealing at least intuitively in the capital-budgeting situation. It is quite feasible to quote prices day by day which vary in accordance with some predetermined probability distribution. It is not possible to vary the number of one's plants or service stations in the same fashion, since construction takes time, cannot be kept secret, and is irreversible in the short run.

Because of these problems, game theoretic models do not give us completely satisfactory decision models for use in making capital-expenditure decisions. While the practical man may choose in the end to assume a probability distribution over competitor behavior, forcing the problem within the known-distribution risk model described in Chapters 11 and 12, we believe game theory offers certain insights that carry us beyond that model and which may improve decisions.

The failure to conform to the convenient zero-sum game model is an analytical disaster but a social triumph, for zero-sum games involve inherently loser-take-all situations where one party's gain is another party's loss. As such they are pure conflict situations with few mitigat-ing features. Non-zero sum games, on the other hand, offer prospects of mutual gain through cooperative behaviour.

13.2 Non-zero sum games—interdependence recognized

Consider the following example. In a moderately sized town there are two banks, the First National and the State. Both have, at the moment, single offices in the downtown shopping area. The First National has adopted its capital budget and has considered all projects except the addition of two new branches. Estimated cost of capital is 5.5 percent, and the following estimates are based on present values calculated at that rate. Present value of the stockholder's interest in First National after certain additions is estimated at $3 million. Suppose each new branch costs $1 million. If the State Bank does not build any new branches, the value of the First National will be increased as follows, after deducting all costs:

	Value	Added benefits	Added costs	Net gain
No new branch	$3,000	—	—	—
New branch location A	3,900	$1,900	$1,000	$ 900
New branch location B	3,400	1,400	1,000	400
Both new branches	4,000	3,000	2,000	1,000

On this basis, the First National should build both branches.

However, there are a couple of other locations in town where new bank branches might be located and on which the State Bank is known to be considering building. Should State build these branches, values of First National will be as shown in its payoff matrix which gives its net present value under all strategy pairs which might be chosen by the two competitors (see Table 13–1).

Table 13–1
Payoff matrix: First National Bank

First National's strategy	State Bank's strategy			
	No new branch	New branch C	New branch D	Both new branches
No new branch	$3,000	$2,500	$2,600	$2,400
New branch A	3,900	3,300	3,100	2,700
New branch B	3,400	2,850	2,900	2,800
Both new branches	4,000	3,100	3,400	2,600

To take account of the possible effects of retaliation, we must examine the minimum entry in each row, to see in effect what would happen if the competition did its worst. The worst that can happen in each case is that State Bank builds two branches, in which case the values in the fourth column apply. Selecting that row which has the greatest *mini-*

mum entry gives us the optimum pure strategy for the First National Bank. This is to build branch B. We must carry our analysis further, however, and consider the State Bank's payoff matrix. Fortunately, First National has also evaluated the sites and can calculate the values for its competitor quite accurately. These appear in Table 13–2. State

Table 13–2
Payoff matrix: State Bank

First National's strategy	State Bank's strategy			
	No new branch	New branch C	New branch D	Both new branches
No new branch	$2,000	$2,900	$3,200	$2,600
New branch A	1,600	2,300	3,000	2,200
New branch B	1,800	2,200	2,800	2,400
Both new branches	1,400	1,900	1,500	2,000

Bank's optimum countermove against First National's decision to build branch B is to build branch D. If it does so, First National will be worth $2.9 million. If, however, First National could be sure of State's choice of D beforehand, it would choose to build both branches since this is its optimum counter-strategy to D and makes its value $3.4 million.

But suppose, for some reason, First National can lure State into moving first. Overall, State's optimum strategy can be found by examining Table 13–2 to find which column has the largest minimum element. This is the fourth column, and State's optimum strategy is to build both branches. If it does so, First National would be better off to build branch B, and its value would be only $2.8 million. It is potentially worth a great deal to First National to get State to commit itself first and to C only rather than to both branches. It is only slightly inferior from State's point of view and much better from A's. As a minimum, it may choose to wait, hoping that State will not do both at once. As a maximum, there are opportunities for collusion or merger, providing legal hurdles can be cleared. Merger is probably out in this two-bank situation because of the Clayton Act, even if the Comptroller of the Currency should consent, but there are many strategies short of this that are not illegal. For example, First National might suddenly become a bit uncooperative in dealing with a large customer whose operations were near site C, in the hope that he will tip State's decision in favor of that location.

Clearly, the competitive situation depicted in Tables 13–1 and 13–2 is not a pure conflict solution of the zero-sum variety. This is seen by computing Table 13–3, which is a combined payoff matrix found by adding First National's payoffs to State's payoffs. The competitive situation described is non-zero-sum because the entries in the combined payoff matrix differ.[7]

Table 13–3 is a condensed version of the payoff matrix for a game played between the coalition of the two banks and a fictitious player

Table 13–3
Combined payoff matrix: both banks

First National's strategy	State Bank's strategy			
	No new branch	New branch C	New branch D	Both new branches
No new branch	$5,000	$5,400	$5,800	$5,000
New branch A	5,500	5,600	6,100	4,900
New branch B	5,200	5,000	5,700	5,200
Both new branches	5,400	5,000	4,900	4,600

nature, whose only function is to lose what the coalition gains. It does indicate something that was not apparent from our earlier discussion, namely that joint gains are maximized when the combination (A and D) is built. This combination is unlikely to result without collusion, for State's safest strategy is to build both C and D, while First National's is to build B. The von Neumann-Morgenstern model does not predict any definite outcome for a situation of this type; their solution indicates a range of possible outcomes which may be attained by the participants depending on their bargaining ability and the institutional constraints within which they find themselves. Ignoring the institutional constraints for the moment, the combined payoff may be $6.1 million; within this total, First National must get at least as much as it could get by noncooperation and acting alone, that is, the maximin solution of Table 13–1 or the $2.8 million it could get by building B. State needs to get at least the $2 million minimax solution of Table 13–2, which it can get by building both branches. But these total only $4.8 million, and the optimum joint strategy is worth $6.1 million. How the differences of $1.3 million is shared is moot within the von Neumann-Morgenstern model.[8] Indeed, we are not even certain if the full $6.1 million will be obtained. Part of it may be frittered away if full collaboration cannot be achieved, since First National must be induced to build A rather than

B, and State must be induced to build D and to refrain from building C. This degree of cooperation is dependent not only on an absence of legal constraints but on the possibility of an exchange of values from one party to another, termed a *side payment* in the literature of game theory. This need not take the form of a bribe, nor is it likely to in a situation of this kind, but it could take the form of a slightly more generous valuation for the assets of one party to a merger. In this case, if merger could be attained, the combined values would total $6.1 million. Of this amount, First National would have to get at least $2.8 million, the smallest amount it could get by nonparticipation, while State would have to get at least $2 million, the worst it could get on its own, but the way in which the remainder would be divided is indeterminate within the von Neumann-Morgenstern solution concept.

Two somewhat more narrow solution concepts appear to have some appeal. One is the so-called Nash-Zeuthen solution, which was discovered by John Nash as a solution to the so-called bargaining problem in 1950,[9] and later recognized to having been independently proposed by Zeuthen, who operated without the tools of game theory, as a solution in an oligopoly context in 1930.[10]

The Nash solution simply specifies that the gain will be divided in such a way that their product is maximized. In the present context, this means that the product of First National's gain over $2.8 million and of State's gain over $2 million must be maximized. This is achieved by splitting the potential gain of $1.3 million (over the minimum values the participants can obtain on their own) evenly, so that First National gets $3.45 million and State, $2.65 million. The A–D payoffs in the initial matrices are $3.1 million and $3 million respectively; side payment of $350,000 from State to First National is required if the joint maximum is to be obtained and shared in this manner.

The other solution concept which has gained prominence in recent work is that of the core, which can loosely be defined as the set of nondiscriminatory solutions or imputations within the von Neumann-Morgenstern solution set. The core can be shown to converge, for large numbers of players, to the classic perfectly competitive solution. How many players are required to force the solution into the core is not clear and depends very much on how much collusion is tolerated within the institutional context. If no collusion is tolerated, it has been rather persuasively argued that two competitors are enough to force the solution into the core.[11] In this case, the core solution in the pure strategy context involves independent competitive behavior in which First National builds B and State builds A and C. In this case, First National gets $2.8 million and State gets $2.4 million. Nature, or the customers in this context, get the rest, which involves more service (branches B,

C, and D instead of A and D) and some consumers' surplus ($0.9 million, the difference between the B-C-D and the A-D entries in Table 13–3).

We are (as ever) somewhat less sanguine than Fama and Laffer about the likelihood of the core solution emerging. In this case, if an appropriate side payment can be arranged, the cooperative Nash-Zeuthen solution which involves joint profit maximization will emerge. Even if merger, which simplifies the side payment arrangement is impossible, side payments may be effected through correspondent arrangements and real estate transactions.

13.3 Institutional limitations on coalitions and side payments

The cooperative Nash-Zeuthen solution to the problem posed in Section 13.2 involved the two banks ganging up on consumers to limit service and to capture some of the consumers' surplus that would have been available in a purely competitive or core solution. In a consumerist economy, such a solution, however appealing to the banks, may well be viewed as antisocial or contrary to the public interest.

Just such a judgment has been, at least in part, embodied in U.S. law since the passing of the Sherman Act in 1890; reinforced by the Clayton Act (1914), while the Cellar-Kefauver Amendments of 1950 plugged a loophole in the Clayton Act. While the United States is perhaps unique in the depth and breadth of its antitrust legislation, most Western countries have legislation with a similar thrust, aimed at the maintenance of competition as the friend of the consumer in the short run and of economic efficiency and growth potential in the long.

We noted earlier that several outcomes short of joint profit maximization were possible. We believe, following von Neumann-Morgenstern, Stigler, and Telser,[12] that collusive solutions offer prospective gains over noncollusive solutions and will be adopted unless the costs associated with collusion outweigh the benefits to its practitioners. These costs include the costs of obtaining the information needed to maximize joint profits and to detect and police violations of the cartel agreement. These costs are analyzed by Stigler and form the basis of his theory of oligopoly.[13]

Society and in particular the consumers who are the losers in monopoly situations has no interest in simplifying the life of would-be cartel operators and has generally gone out of its way to make difficulties for them. This possibility has already been noted and may take many forms, ranging from the classic common-law rule that contracts in restraint of trade are unenforceable to the much more complex apparatus embodied in U.S. antitrust laws and similar legislation elsewhere. While these are not always obeyed, such laws raise the costs of collusive behavior, relative to competitive behavior and work to encourage the latter.

While this is not a treatise on antitrust law, we note that basic offenses under the Sherman Act involve severe penalties and clearly outlaw overt collaborative anticompetitive behavior, although it still occurs from time to time. Indeed they have been interpreted as going beyond overt collusive behavior and have outlawed conscious parallelism in which decisions are taken in the anticipation of comparable competitor response.[14] The interpretation given in *American Tobacco* v. *the United States* is so broad that almost any consideration of probable competitor response in the decision-making process, may constitute an offense. As such consideration seems to us to be not only normal but required by directors' obligation to manage firms prudently in the interests of stockholders, at least in those cases where there are limited numbers of competitors. We also believe that aggressive application and widening of the conscious parallelism rule, at least in a criminal context, or where triple damages are levied in a civil proceeding, to embody rather more potential for harm than good. Preventing overt conspiracy is another matter; if done effectively it should lead to core equilibria rather than full-blown monopoly. Admittedly this may fall short of the full competitive ideal, but it seems, to us at least, that the remedy for inadequate numbers is to increase the numbers, not to punish the few that are already there. Fortunately, there are indications that the rule of reason has been extended to conscious parallelism cases.[15]

While outright collaboration between competitors is outlawed, it should be noted that the gains obtainable via collaboration between competitors can also be obtained by merging with the competitor; indeed merger provides not only low-cost policing but a convenient mechanism for sharing the proceeds of monopolistic behavior.

13.4 Mergers and takeovers to internalize coalition gains

Any desired split of prospective monopoly profits can be capitalized and effected by an appropriate choice of prices or share exchange ratios in a merger situation. Not all mergers involve monopoly profits, of course; some involve other forms of synergy, and others apparently involve a triumph of hope over experience.[16] While mergers to achieve monopoly positions were commonplace in the 19th century and for some time thereafter, an attempt was made to outlaw them in Section 7 of the Clayton Act,[17] passed in 1914. Because of loopholes in the drafting, the restriction only applied to acquisitions of companies, not to the purchase of their assets, and the legislation remained a virtual dead letter until the passage of the Cellar-Kefauver Amendments in 1950. These have effectively prevented mergers between firms which compete in product markets or which might do so[18] and vertical combinations which restrict competition among suppliers. They have been also applied to conglomerate mergers where no apparent competitive relationship was evident,[19] but where firms were large, often with ridiculous results.

Nonetheless, studies of conglomerate mergers have shown that the market value of the combined firms often exceeds the sum of the values of the separate entities. The source of the capitalized gain is not too clear; the amounts involved appear to us to contradict in many cases the efficient markets hypothesis. Predominantly, the bulk of the gain goes to the acquired,[20] and not to the acquiring firm. Given the relative sizes, this involves a split of the gains from trade apparently compatible with the Nash bargaining model.[21]

Not all countries have antitrust laws as effective as those of the United States. While Canadian legislation is similar, for example, the case law is not. Maladroit selections of merger cases for prosecution, and the commonsense of judges have combined to create precedents which on the surface appear to suggest that almost any merger is legal.[22] As a consequence, two of the largest newspaper chains in the country, which compete in major markets, recently merged without obstacle.[23]

13.5 Relevance for capital budgeting

Much of the antitrust literature and its theoretical counterpart, the monopoly/oligopoly literature talks about prices, and price fixing is clearly its immediate target. The corresponding literature, when it enters the longer-run world of capital-expenditure decisions, becomes transformed and talks about rationalization and the avoidance of competitive waste and duplication. Competition in the provision of capacity has an obvious link via the competitive process with ultimate price behavior. Except in the merger legislation and literature, there is little recognition of this relationship in the antitrust literature.

For the capital-expenditure analyst, it is important to recognize two things. The most basic of these is that market structures evolve and that price-prime cost relationships normally evolve with them. Failure to recognize the probable nature of such evolution, for example, in a new product investment decision, can lead to excessively optimistic appraisals and is a potential source of expensive error. The second is simply that antitrust legislation exists and that the motives for any decision to invest or refrain from investing may be subject to hostile scrutiny in a courtroom years later on the basis of documentary evidence fished from corporate files. As noted earlier, we see a potential conflict between realistic analyses of particular investment decisions in a small-number context, where an awareness of probable competitor response is a vital ingredient on investment appraisal, and the more extreme conscious parallelism decisions. While the analyst should, in our view, take competitor reaction into account, care should also be taken to leave a documentary record that does not suggest and cannot be interpreted as suggesting that anything more is involved.

Notes

[1] F. H. Knight, *Risk, Uncertainty and Profit* See Also A. G. Hart, *Anticipations, Uncertainty and Dynamic Planning* (Chicago: University of Chicago Press, 1942).

[2] Classical treatments include F. Zeuthen, *Problems of Monopoly and Economic Warfare* (London: Routledge, 1930); H. von Stackelberg, *Marktform und Gleichewicht* (Berlin, 1934); and W. A. Fellner, *Competition Among the Few* (New York: Knopf, 1949).

[3] As derived from J. von Neumann and O. Morgenstern, *Theory of Games and Economic Behaviour*, 3d ed. (Princeton: Princeton University Press, 1953). See also R. D. Luce and H. Raiffa, *Games and Decisions* (New York: Wiley, 1957).

[4] Notably, M. Shubik, *Strategy and Market Structure* (New York: Wiley, 1961); L. G. Telser, *Competition, Collusion and Game Theory* (Chicago, Aldine-Atherton, 1972); and L. G. Telser, *Economic Theory and the Core* (Chicago: University of Chicago Press, 1978).

[5] It is tempting to speculate that strategy variance is at the heart of the observed infinite-variance stable pareto distribution of capital market outcomes described by Mandelbrot and others. See B. Mandelbrot, "The Variation of Certain Speculative Prices," *Journal of Business* 36 (October 1963), pp. 394–419.

[6] For this ambiguity, see Luce and Raiffa, *Games and Decisions,* chap. 6.

[7] If they were identical, the game would be constant sum; equivalent to zero sum by a subtractive transformation.

[8] See von Neumann and Morgenstern, *Theory of Games,* pp. 282–90. See also G. D. Quirin, "Simple Market Games and Neoclassical Models," *Zeitschrift fur Nationalökonomie,* 21 (1961), pp. 177–86.

[9] J. F. Nash, "The Bargaining Problem," *Econometrica* 18 (1950), pp. 655–62. The Nash-Zeuthen (N-Z) equilibrium used here is that relating to the division of the proceeding point profit maximization in a cooperative context, an alternative N-Z equilibrium in a fully competitive environment involves more output and more consumers' surplus.

[10] Zeuthen, *Problems of Monopoly.*

[11] E. F. Fama and A. B. Laffer, "The Number of Firms and Competition," *American Economic Review* 62 (September 1972), pp. 670 ff.

[12] Neumann and Morgenstern, *Theory of Games;* G. J. Stigler, *The Organization of Industry* (Homewood, Ill.: Richard D. Irwin 1968), chap. 5; and Telser, *Competition,* p. 178.

[13] Stigler, *Organization of Industry.*

[14] *American Tobacco Co.* v. *the United States* 321 U.S. 781 at 810 (1946); and *Theatre Enterprises Inc.* v. *Paramount Film Distributing Corp.* 346 U.S. 537 at 541 (1954).

[15] *U.S.* v. *Chas Pfizer & Co. Inc.,* 97F Supp. 91 (S.D. N.Y., 1973).

[16] G. Meek, *Disappointing Marriage: A Study of the Gains from Mergers* (Cambridge, England: Cambridge University Press, 1977).

[17] See also, for example, Ida M. Tarbell, *Life of E. H. Gary* (New York: Appleton, 1925).

[18] *U.S.* v. *Penn-Olin Chemical Co.,* 378 U.S. 158 (1964); and *U.S.* v. *Falstaff Brewing Corp.* 410 U.S. 526 (1973).

[19] *F.T.C.* v. *Proctor & Gamble* 366 U.S. 568 (1967).

[20] J. H. Lorie and P. Halpern, "Conglomerates: The Rhetoric and the Evidence," *Journal of Law and Economics* 13 (1970), pp. 149–66.

[21] Nash, "Bargaining Problem."

[22] *R.* v. *Canadian Breweries Ltd.* [1960] O.R. 601, 126 C.C.C. 133; and *R.* v. *B.C. Sugar Refining Company Limited* et al. [1960] 32WWR (NS) 577.

[23] See also J. S. Prichard, W. T. Stanbury, and T. A. Wilson, eds., *Canadian Competition Policy* (Toronto: Butterworth, 1979).

Problems

1. The following are payoff matrices for alternative investment strategies for A Inc. and B Ltd.

A, INC.
Payoff Matrix

B's strategy

		1	2	3	4
	1	9000	4000	7000	2000
A's	2	5000	3000	8000	7000
strategy	3	7000	8000	5000	9000
	4	4000	9000	6000	5000

B, LTD.
Payoff Matrix

B's strategy

		1	2	3	4
	1	14000	5000	5000	8000
A's	2	9000	7000	9000	14000
strategy	3	4000	9000	12000	7000
	4	8000	13000	10000	6000

What are the optimum strategies for A and B
  a.   If collusion is effectively prohibited?
  b.   If collusion is possible, but no side payment can be arranged?
  c.   If collusion and side payments are possible?

2. The following are payoff matrices for alternative investment strategies for Cee Gmbh. and Dee S.A.

CEE GMBH.
Payoff Matrix

Dee's strategy

		1	*2*	*3*
	1	18000	8000	14000
Cee's	2	12000	6000	16000
strategy	3	14000	16000	10000

DEE S.A.
Payoff Matrix

Dee's strategy

		1	*2*	*3*
	1	9000	19000	13000
Cee's	2	15000	21000	11000
strategy	3	13000	11000	17000

  a.   What are Cee's and Dee's optimum strategies
       (1)   If collusion is effectively prohibited?
       (2)   If collusion is possible, but no side payment can be arranged?
       (3)   If collusion and side payments are possible?
  b.   What is the difference between the strategic situation in this problem and that of problem 1 above?

Expenditure decisions and the growth process

14.1 Introduction

In Chapter 1, we examined the importance of capital-expenditure decisions to the firm. Now we wish to examine their social importance which is at least as great as their importance to the firm. Their social importance is twofold, involving not only the cyclical role of aggregate investment as a contributor to demand or the utilization of capacity, but its longer-term strategic role in the process of economic growth.

Almost all theories of business fluctuations have focused on the instability in the aggregate level of investment as a critical factor in the genesis of fluctuations in the level of economic activity. Many stabilization proposals seek to stabilize the level of activity by stabilizing the rate of investment spending.

Important as capital expenditures are in this role, they are if anything even more important in determining how much capacity there will be to utilize and what standard of living a society can generate for its members if fully utilized. This contribution to economic growth comes about in several ways. First of all, the aggregate stock of capital is increased, making possible a larger output level. At least in the United States, its direct role in this respect is not too great. Denison credits increased capital inputs with 0.8 percent of the total U.S. growth rate of 3.3 percent in 1950–62. The balance of 1.4 percent is contributed by increased productivity, that is, by increased output per unit of input. Thus the sheer quantity of capital only accounted for 24 percent of observed growth. The comparable contribution in Canada was 25 percent and for northeast Europe only 19 percent.[1]

But this is not all. A major portion of the productivity gain is the consequence of technological change, of rearranged industrial structure, and the use of improved technologies. This reallocation and improvement is ultimately associated with the capital-expenditure process since new technology is frequently embodied in specific types of equipment and is, therefore, not available until new investments are made. These factors in the United States accounted for 1.1 percent or another third of the total output gain, raising the total contribution of capital expenditures to the growth rate to 57 percent. Growth in quality and quantity of labor accounted for another 33 percent, leaving some 10 percent to be accounted for by economies of scale.

Any concern over growth rates must reflect itself in a concern over the volume and effective utilization of capital expenditures in the economy, and policies intended to influence these variables have become major economic tools in the past generation.

We do not propose to enter the growth—no-growth debate here. However, even if continued population growth is regarded as undesirable, there is little evidence of satiation in any part of the world. There remains widespread poverty which would be but slightly mitigated even by the most draconian redistributive measures. At least within the context of per capita incomes, we believe a plausible case for growth can be made,[2] particularly if growth is measured giving appropriate recognition to negative externalities, as we suggested in Chapter 9.

There is a rather different argument to the effect that growth is not so much bad as likely to prove impossible, so that our survival may depend on being able to adapt ourselves to a no-growth situation.[3] This view can only be sustained by ignoring the role of the price system in rationing scarce resources and encouraging substitution.[4]

The issues involve not only ensuring an appropriate rate of growth in investment but in ensuring that investment is efficiently used. Given the magnitude of expenditures controlled by governments in the modern world, and the generally deficient expenditure decision systems in place in governments, it is no longer appropriate to suggest, with J. M. Keynes, that concern over whether resources are being used efficiently is misplaced.[5] The potential influence of misallocation on growth rates is perhaps best illustrated by considering that in a country such as Canada, where net investment is perhaps 15 percent of net national product and 40 percent of investment is accounted for by governments and housing, earning only 12 percent on the latter portion instead of 25 percent available in the remainder of the private sector will suffice to reduce the growth rate from 3.75 to 3 percent. Efficient utilization of savings flowing into investment is capable in our view of increasing growth rates in the indicated order of magnitude without any increase in the volume of net investment. Efficient utilization is largely a matter of applying the techniques we have discussed earlier (see Chapters 8 and 9).

This does not mean that budgeting techniques in the private sector are so perfect that allocation therein cannot be improved. Our analysis does, however, suggest that use of efficient decision-making rules within firms will result in allocation patterns that are at least as efficient as those generated within capital market institutions. Consequently, the

frequently expressed concern that retained earnings enable corporations to bypass the marketplace and avoid the latter's allocative processes is largely misplaced. Use of retained earnings saves financing
costs and at least in publicly held and traded companies leaves decisions as fully exposed to the review of the market-place as are decisions taken with newly raised money.

14.2 Approaches to influencing the rate of investment

Improvements in the allocation of investment, even if successful, take
time and are restricted in the amount of additional growth they contribute. They may, in a cyclical context, produce results usually deemed
perverse, that is, they may increase unemployment at a time when
unemployment is already high. Perhaps because cyclical concerns have
tended to dominate growth in the formulation of economic policy, the
latter has tended to focus on influencing the rate of investment.

In the cyclical context, given contemporary technology, attempts to
do very much with the investment rate are apt to be perverse. The
project conception-design-approval-construction sequence is simply
too long and uncertain in length, relative to the usual recession-
depression-revival-boom sequence. Even if policy makers knew where
they stood in respect of the latter, which is seldom the case, they could
have little confidence that investment programs initiated to repel a
recession would not inadvertently add to inflationary pressures during
the ensuing boom instead. Measures to stretch out or otherwise reduce
the investment rate during boom periods by interrupting or delaying
projects underway may be more effective if strong enough but such
imposed delays increase construction costs and interest-during-
construction and most firms will seek to finish what they start as close
to original schedules as possible. These factors mitigate against the use
of investment-rate-modifying policies in a cyclical context; most other
discretionary countercyclical policies have similar defects, however.[6]

If the conception-design-approval-construction sequence has length-
ened in such a way as to make it difficult to induce the insertion of
appropriate doses of investment at appropriate points in the cycle, it
has also worked to discourage the bunching up of investment that was
such a critical factor in earlier business cycles. In the postwar period,
the major volatile factor in cyclical fluctuations, at least in North America, has been inventory investment and liquidation. Fixed investment
has played, at most, a secondary role.

As we enter the 80s, the major macroeconomic problems seem to be
persistent inflation and the failure of economies subject to stagnation

and low growth to absorb available manpower. Both seem to be susceptible in some measure to manipulation on the supply side of the economy in a way that they are not susceptible to the manipulation of effective demand. Because of its role in expanding capacity, the management of capital investment will become an important factor in supply-side economic policy.

In theory, the rate of capital expenditures ought to be subject to influences on the supply side of the capital market as well as on the demand side. The former include factors affecting the cost and availability of funds; the latter factors affecting profitability. Since it is the gap between the cost of funds and the prospective rate of return on a project which determines whether its net present value is positive, the effect might be expected to be symmetrical. The available econometric evidence suggests that it is not, and that investment is not particularly responsive to capital market supply side variables, and particularly so to variations in the cost of funds.[7] While it is possible to quibble over some of these results, the overall impression remains; manipulating interest rates via monetary policy may not do much to alter investment rates. Part of the reason, we suspect, is that the observed range of variation in nominal interest rates conceals a much smaller variation in real interest rates. Low elasticities computed with respect to the former may well be quite respectably large with respect to the theoretically relevant real variable. Even if this is so, much larger changes in nominal rates than we have yet experienced will have to be produced if we are to influence investment rates via the cost of funds. After all 16 percent interest with 12 percent inflation represents a real rate of only 4 percent.

On the demand side, most econometric models have employed modified accelerator models and a few other variables. Again, speaking generally, the accelerator variables linking investment to the rate of change in consumption or aggregate demand have been the most important, while corporate profitability plays a small role. Again there are serious problems of interpretation. At the microeconomic level, we would expect the anticipated profitability of projects to be the most important variable. The accelerator variables may act as a surrogate for anticipated sales volumes and may be the best indicator of typical prospective profitability that is available to us. They may be far superior to present profitability, which is always lowest just before profits recover, and which may be more of a supply of funds variable than a demand variable. The issue of interpretation is important; too literal an interpretation of the accelerator variables may lead to the inference that it is not possible to influence private investment at all, except indirectly via enhanced effective demand. This in turn may lead to despair and the substitution of second-rate public investment or public consumption for the supposedly static private investment when it is the latter which it is desired to change.

14.3 Measures used to influence the rate of investment

Commonly used measures intended to alter private investment decisions by altering their profitability include a variety of tax incentives, of which accelerated depreciation and investment tax credits are the most common, and outright subsidization either of the investment itself or of some of the operating costs. The manipulation of prices, either directly, as in the European Economic Community's common agricultural policy, or indirectly, via tariff protection, is also commonly used, particularly where a selective stimulus is desired.

The basic mechanics of these devices runs from the simple to the complex. Their evaluation is perhaps most easily carried on using equivalent annual costs or capital recovery factors, described in Section 3.12, and defined as the annual income necessary to amortize an investment over its lifetime while providing a return at a specified level. For the following discussion, we assume that income payments are received monthly, although they are stated at an annual rate which is 12 times the monthly rate. A required rate of return of 15 percent after taxes is also assumed.

Consider, under these assumptions, an investment of $1,000 having an expected ten-year life and zero-salvage value. In the absence of taxes, such an investment would have to generate $193.60 ($16.13 monthly) to provide the required rate of return and permit recovery of the capital invested. However, because of income taxation, this amount must be increased. If there were no provisions for capital recovery through depreciation, and the tax rate was 50 percent, the required annual amount would be doubled, to $387.20. But most tax systems permit recovery through depreciation, depletion, or similar mechanisms of most types of initial investment. Recovery on a straight-line basis gives a depreciation charge of $100.00 per year, which results in an offset against taxes otherwise payable of $50.00 per year. So the net annual income per year which we must anticipate if the investment is to be just worthwhile is reduced by the latter amount to $337.20. This can be regarded as the basic annual cost under a standard tax system.

The mildest form of incentive is accelerated depreciation. In the United States, the use of declining balance (DDB) at double the appreciable straight-line rate, with a switch to straight line when the latter exceeds DDB, is one such option, the other is sum-of-the-years' digits (SYD). These improve profitability by enhancing the present value of the depreciation stream. In the present case, it is increased from its $516.32 present value under straight line to $626.59 using DDB. This results in an increase in the tax offset which reduces to an annual amount of $60.60, versus the $50.00 offset available under straight line. Thus, under DDB, the annual cost is only $326.60. This is 3.1 percent less than the $337.20 under straight line. The cost saving is enough to produce after taxes an increase of about 0.7 percent in the internal rate of return or the investment. Results under SYD are not too different. The impact varies, of course, with the life of the asset.

One extreme of accelerated depreciation is provided in those cases where a 100 percent write-off is permitted. Even this is not offset directly against the investment but against the ensuring years' income. Assuming mid-year receipt of a $1,000 write-off, the present value of the deduction is $932.49, that of the tax offset $466.24. Translated into equivalent annual cost terms, the annual saving is $90.26. This leads to annual costs of $296.94, almost 12 percent less than the $337.20 cost under straight line. This could produce after taxes, an increase of 2.6 percent in the internal rate of return on an otherwise marginal investment.

In some instances, write-offs at rates in excess of 100 percent may be permitted. This will, of course, improve profitability even more. Canadian tax law, for example, once provided a 100 percent write-off of certain exploration expenses and an additional 25 percent for qualifying investors as earned depletion for a total of 125 percent. In this context, 125 percent would reduce the equivalent annual cost to $274.37, appreciably less than in the standard case but still well in excess of that applying in the zero tax case. Even write-offs of 166.66 percent available for a time under other Canadian legislation for "frontier" oil exploration do not do that. This write-off is worth $150.44 and reduces annual cost to $236.76.

In general, however, and operating at depreciation rates below 100 percent, accelerated depreciation provides a modest incentive to invest. Rather more oomph can be provided by investment tax credits, which permit part or all of the investment to be offset against taxes payable in the current year, rather than being recovered via depreciation. The depreciation basis is, of course, reduced by the amount of the credit. A 10 percent credit on our $1,000 investment should produce a reduction of $100 in this year's taxes, permitting the remaining $900 to be recovered via DDB in the usual manner. The former is worth $93.25, the latter $54.54, for a total of $147.79, reducing annual cost to $239.41, significantly less than the cost even with 125 percent write-off and almost as low as that produced with a 166.66 percent write-off. The significantly more generous investment tax credit rate of 15 percent produces $139.88 worth of immediate tax savings and reduces the residual tax offset to $51.51, a total offset of $191.39, reducing equivalent annual cost to $195.81. This is a reduction of 42 percent in the cost of using the asset and can raise an ordinarily marginal asset's rate of return from 15 percent to a healthy 24.1 percent.

To the extent that capital subsidies do not have to be deducted from the asset's basis for depreciation purposes, they offer even more bang than investment tax credits, which are a specialized form of capital subsidy requiring such deduction. Protective tariffs and other price-raising schemes may also alter profitability dramatically. Note in particular that effective rates of protection are almost invariably higher than nominal rates, because the rate is applied to the entire price of the import but all of the benefit accrues to net value added by capital, except in cases where strong unions have been able to capture it for labor. (Steel in the United States may constitute such an example.) The acceleration is even greater where different rates apply at raw material and finished goods stages. Thus, an industry which has 30 percent raw material costs, 40 percent labor costs, and 30 percent capital costs, operating in an environment in which innocuous tariff rates of 5 percent apply to raw materials and 10 percent to finished commodities, enjoys an escalation of 28.3 percent in the margin available to capital, computed as follows:

World price	$100.00
Domestic price (world × 1.10)	110.00
Raw materials (world × 1.05)	31.50
Value added	$ 78.50
Labor	40.00
Available for capital	$ 38.50
As percentage of capital cost	128.33

This simplifies the problem to the extent that it assumes investment to be responsive to nothing but profitability. It does not consider the very real question of whether the elasticity of investment in respect of prospective profits may not differ from one industry to another, nor does it consider the differences in risk resultant from different incentive structures. For tax-based incentives, accounting opinion has closed around the concept of normalization, that is, the recording of tax savings in cases other than the base case as deferred taxes shown on the liability side of the balance sheet. In general, we are sympathetic with the accountants' view, to the extent that we would regard it as dangerous (if not illegal, in the light of accounting conventions) to use cash accruals from tax incentives to retire debt or pay dividends. They are thus frozen, possibly payable under certain scenarios, increase the extent to which the tax-deferring company trades on the equity and consequently increase its risk.

Nor have we considered the question of whether corporate taxes are shifted or not. We are mindful of the debate over short-run shifting, but regard it as quite beside the point. Long-run shifting would imply that prices ultimately change to reflect changes in long-run costs including costs of capital inputs. If there is no shifting, the cost reductions accruing on new investment stay with the company. If there is, the cost reductions are reflected in product prices and the costs of those companies which do not invest increase relative to those which do. In either case, the incentive effect is undiminished.

Notes

[1] D. Walters, *Canadian Growth Revisited,* (Ottawa: Economic Council of Canada, 1970); and E. F. Denison, *Why Growth Rates Differ* (Washington, D.C.: Brookings Institute, 1967).

[2] For an opposing view, see E. J. Mishan, *The Costs of Economic Growth* (Harmondsworth, Essex: Penguin, 1969).

[3] See also D. H. Meadows et al., *The Limits to Growth* (London: Earth Island, 1972).

[4] See also G. D. Quirin, S. P. Sethi, and J. D. Todd, "Market Feedbacks and Limits to Growth," *INFOR* 15 (February 1977), pp. 1–21.

[5] J. M. Keynes, *The General Theory of Employment, Interest and Money,* (London: Macmillan & Co. 1936), pp.

[6] M. Friedman, "The Effects of a Full Employment Policy on Economic Stability: A Formal Analysis" in *Essays in Positive Economics* (Chicago: Phoenix, 1966), pp. 117–32.

[7] See also R. Eisner, *Factors in Business Investment* (Cambridge: Ballinger, 1978); and J. F. Helliwell, ed., *Aggregate Investment* (Harmondsworth, Essex: Penguin, 1976).

Problems

1. What is the reduction in equivalent annual cost obtainable by adopting
   a. Sum-of-the-years digits (SYD),
   b. Double-declining balance (DDB)
   depreciation as opposed to straight line for assets having lives of 5, 10, and 40 years, respectively, if the after-tax cost of capital is 10 percent?

2. The most widely used form of value-added tax (VAT) permits tax credits on purchases to be offset immediately against tax payable on sales whether the purchases are on income or capital account. Laffland is considering abolishing its present 50 percent corporate income tax and replacing it with a 25 percent VAT. How will investment incentives under the latter compare with those under the present tax system which include the use of DDB depreciation and an 8 percent investment tax credit? Assume a 15 percent cost of capital.

3. *a.* Investment in crude oil production facilities in the United States is encouraged by tax provisions which permit 22 percent of gross income (not to exceed 25 percent of the net) to be deducted as depletion allowance in addition to the usual provisions for depreciation and the investment tax credit. How does the depletion allowance affect the annual income required to justify investment in an oil well if the cost of capital is 25 percent in oil production?

    b. How does the equivalent annual cost of a $10 million crude investment compare with that of a $10 million refining investment on which no depletion allowance is provided but for which the cost of capital is only 15 percent because of lower risk?

    c. It is sometimes argued that the corporate income tax discriminates inappropriately against high-risk investments and that the depletion allowance provides a desirable offset against this tendency. If one accepts this argument, what rate of depletion allowance is just sufficient, under the facts outlined above, to produce a situation in which the increase in equivalent annual costs, as compared with a no-tax situation, is the same for the crude investment as for the refinery investment?

4. It is sometimes suggested that accelerated depreciation provides a means whereby investment can be encouraged at zero or even negative social cost because the present value of the tax saving to the corporations at their cost of capital rate (assume 15 percent) is greater than the present value of the tax deferral at a social discount rate of 3 percent. Evaluate this argument critically.

Index